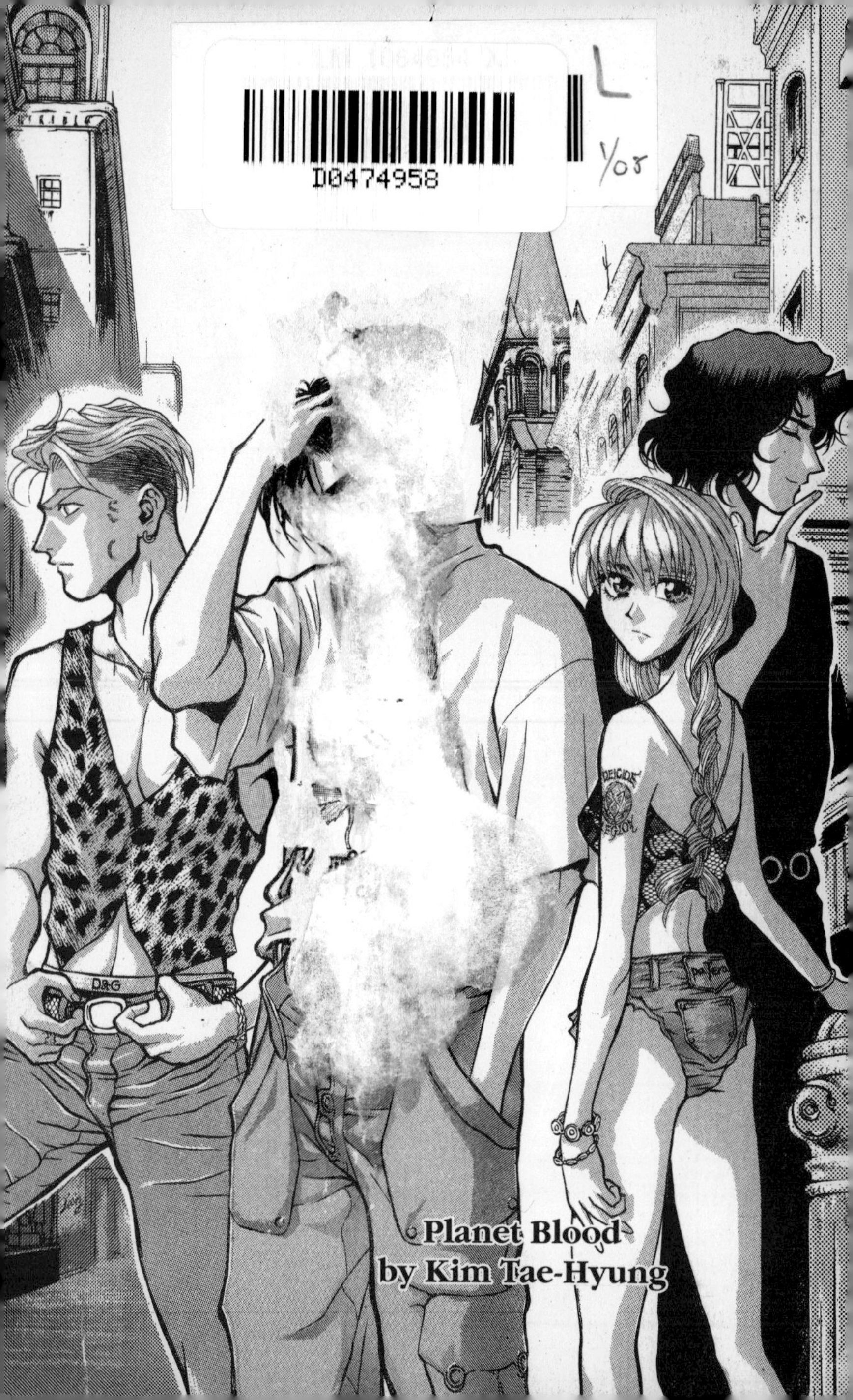
Planet Blood
by Kim Tae-Hyung

Planet Blood Vol. 2
created by Kim Tae-Hyung

Translation - Woo Sok Park
English Adaptation - Mike W. Barr
Associate Editor - Aaron Sparrow
Copy Editor - Brandon Montclare
Retouch and Lettering - Eva Han
Production Artist - Eric Pineda
Cover Layout - Raymond Makowski

Editor - Luis Reyes
Digital Imaging Manager - Chris Buford
Pre-Press Manager - Antonio DePietro
Production Managers - Jennifer Miller and Mutsumi Miyazaki
Art Director - Matt Alford
Managing Editor - Jill Freshney
VP of Production - Ron Klamert
Editor-in-Chief - Mike Kiley
President and C.O.O. - John Parker
Publisher and C.E.O. - Stuart Levy

A  Manga

TOKYOPOP Inc.
5900 Wilshire Blvd. Suite 2000
Los Angeles, CA 90036

E-mail: info@TOKYOPOP.com
Come visit us online at www.TOKYOPOP.com

ISBN: 1-59532-538-7

First TOKYOPOP printing: April 2005
10 9 8 7 6 5 4 3 2 1
Printed in the USA

Volume 2

Created by
Kim Tae-Hyung

HAMBURG // LONDON // LOS ANGELES // TOKYO

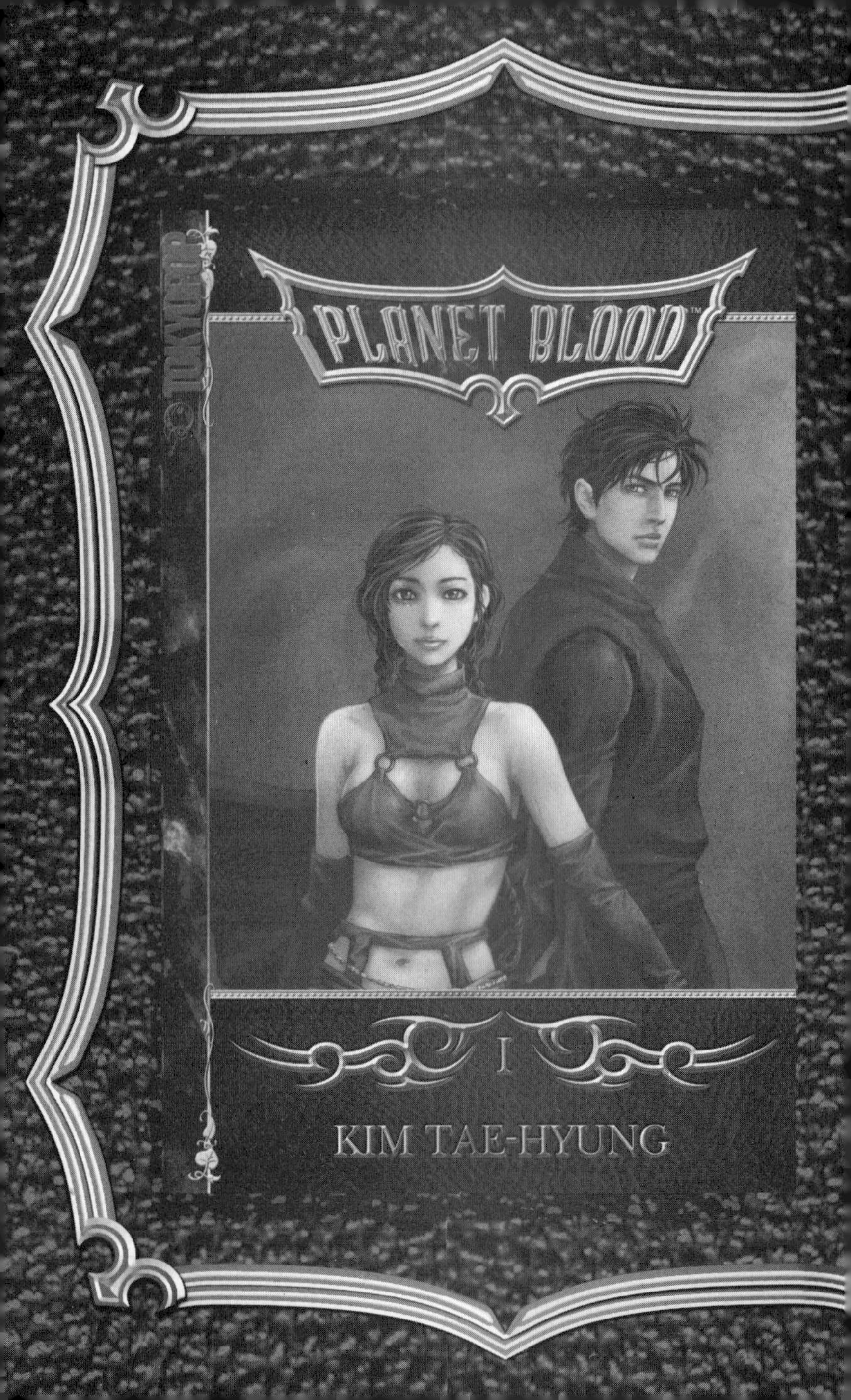
PLANET BLOOD™
I
KIM TAE-HYUNG

In the year Universal Century 0091, the Mars and Moon colonies are embroiled in a bloody war over repatriation rights for the newly restored Earth. The desperation of battle drives the Moon colony to use their deadliest weapon, attack satellite Dike. The subsequent blast opens up a rift in time and space, sending Mars Force mecha pilot Sinan into an entirely new world.

Horai is a land akin to Europe's Middle Ages; kings and princes mount large-scale military campaigns to acquire as much land as possible. Traces of magic exist in Horai, manifest in very few individuals and in the six legendary Neoptolemos, scrolls presumed to be able to unlock vast amounts of power, the kind of power that could tip the balance in Horai's incessant warning.

Still reeling from the implications of his strange surroundings, Sinan thwarts a group of thugs from attacking Princess Mayi. With no idea where he is and no place to go, Sinan joins a grateful Mayi and is introduced to Noodles, leader of a rebel group that is trying to restore him to his rightful place on Pratria's throne, the very throne on which sits his twin brother, Zetsos. To complicate matters further, Pratria has a third party vying for its crown—Pantera, illegitimate half-brother to Noodles and Zetsos.

Now Sinan finds himself in the company of Noodles' allies, in search for the six Neoptolemos, relics that could give Noodles the advantage over his brother's vast armies, enabling him to restore the countries of Horai to their rightful heirs...and forever alter the course of history for the world that has become known as Planet Blood.

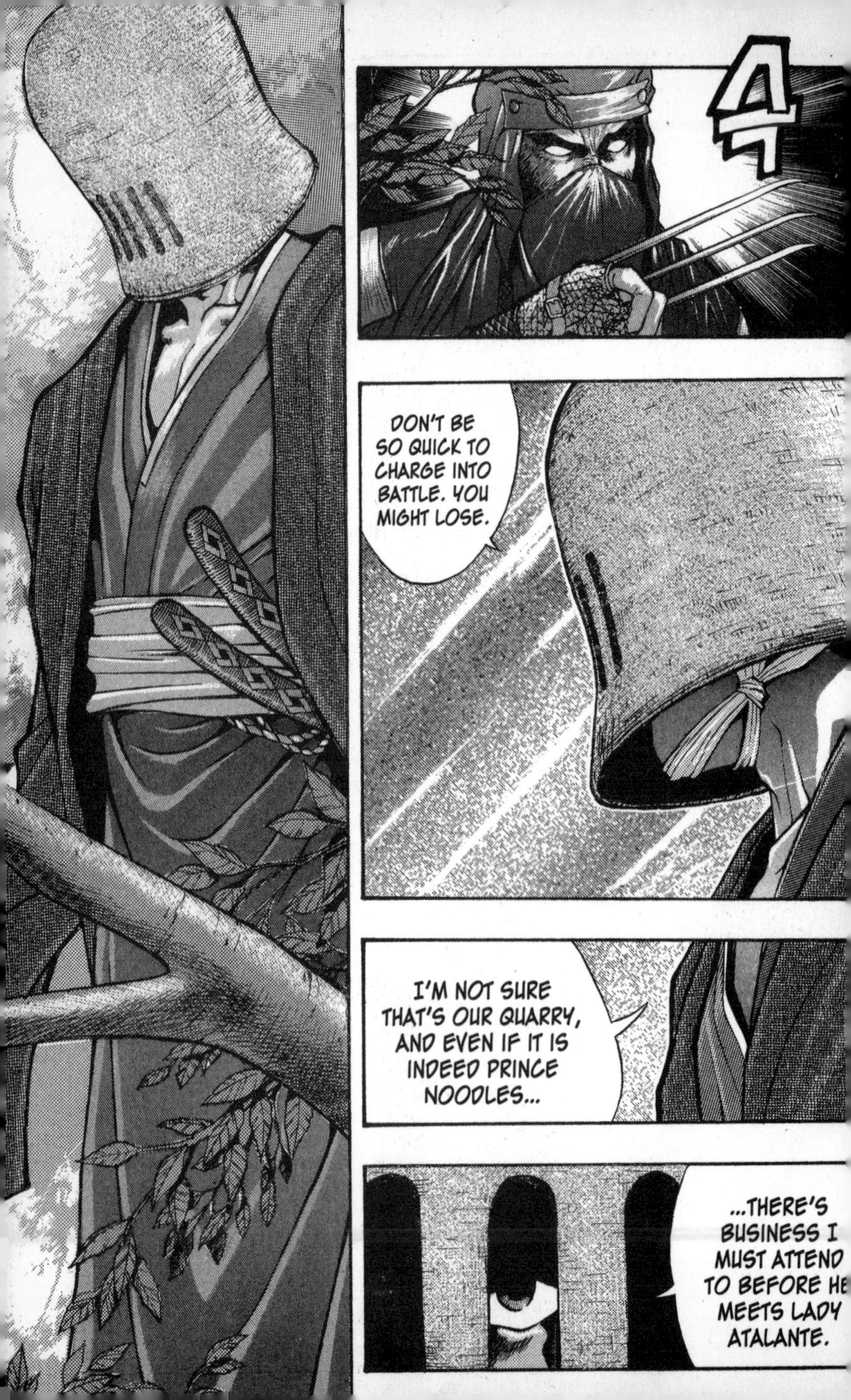

DON'T BE SO QUICK TO CHARGE INTO BATTLE. YOU MIGHT LOSE.
I'M NOT SURE THAT'S OUR QUARRY, AND EVEN IF IT IS INDEED PRINCE NOODLES...
...THERE'S BUSINESS I MUST ATTEND TO BEFORE HE MEETS LADY ATALANTE.

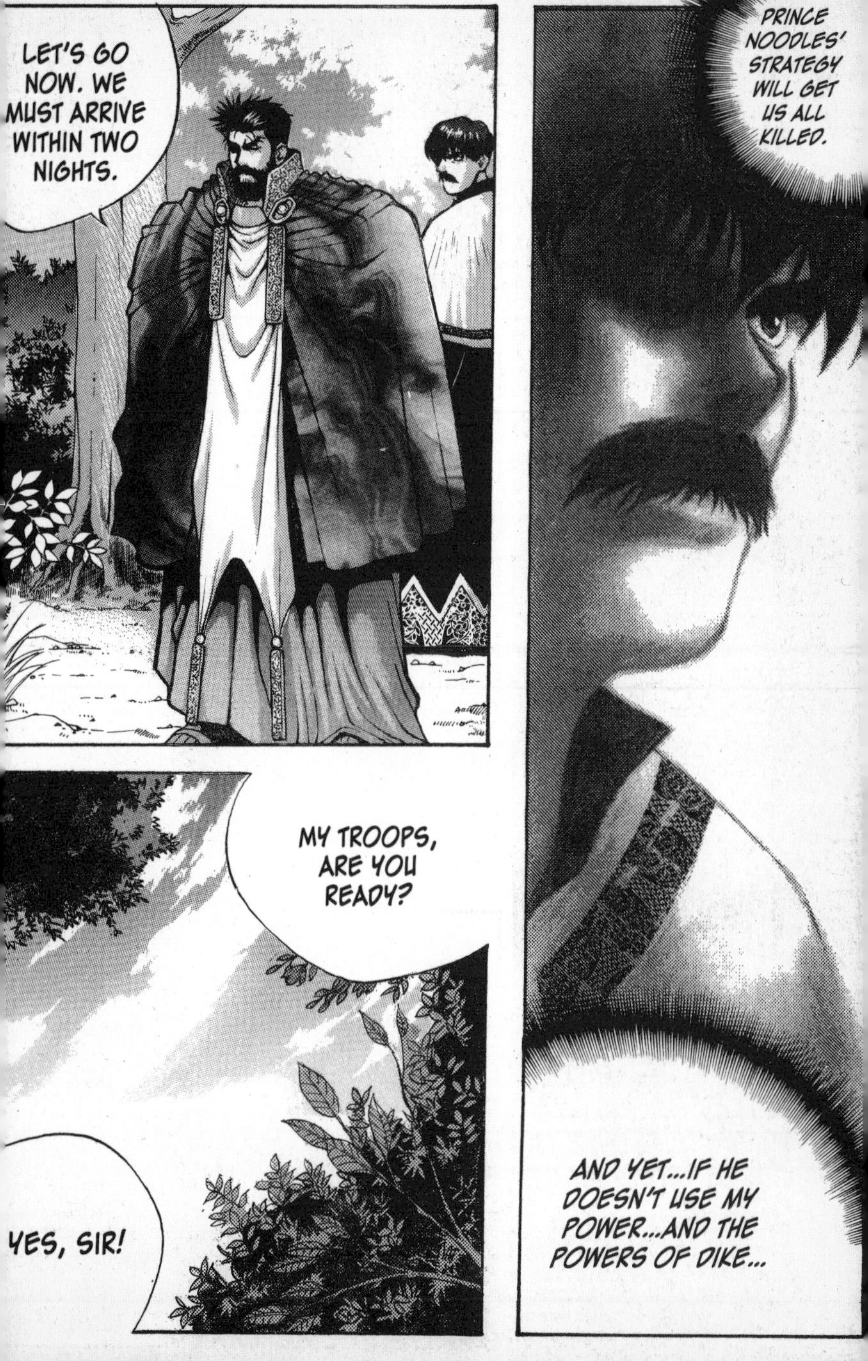
LET'S GO NOW. WE MUST ARRIVE WITHIN TWO NIGHTS.
MY TROOPS, ARE YOU READY?
YES, SIR!
PRINCE NOODLES' STRATEGY WILL GET US ALL KILLED.
AND YET...IF HE DOESN'T USE MY POWER...AND THE POWERS OF DIKE...

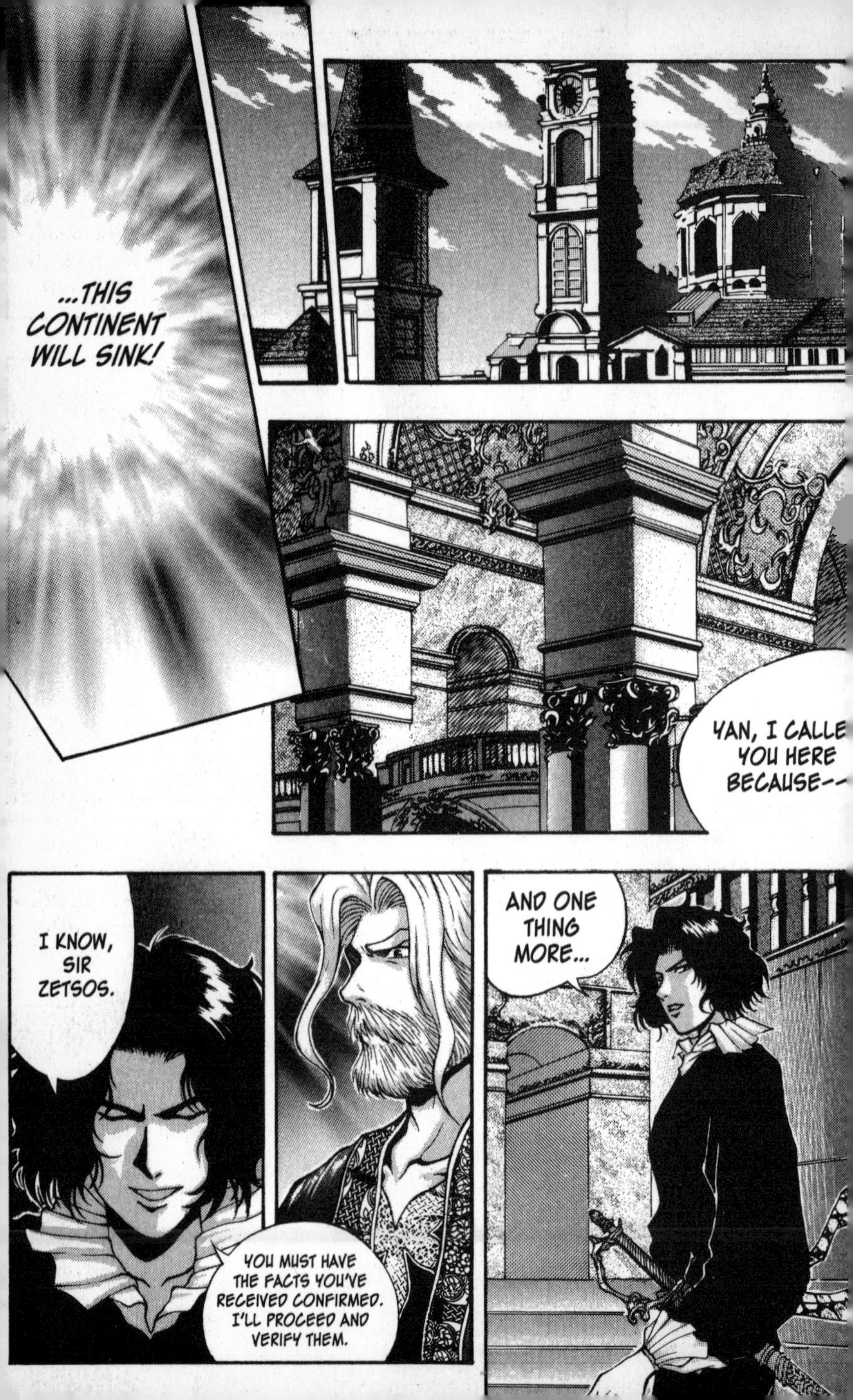
...THIS CONTINENT WILL SINK!
YAN, I CALLE YOU HERE BECAUSE--
I KNOW, SIR ZETSOS.
YOU MUST HAVE THE FACTS YOU'VE RECEIVED CONFIRMED. I'LL PROCEED AND VERIFY THEM.
AND ONE THING MORE...

IF THEIR LEADER IS INDEED NOODLES, I WILL SLAY HIM.

KILL HIM? I'D LIKE TO SEE THAT.

I DON'T BELIEVE THAT'S WITHIN YOUR POWERS.

THIS ENCOUNTER IS MOST OPPORTUNE. I WAS ALWAYS CURIOUS OF HIS ABILITIES.

NOODLES' DESTINY IS TO DIE BY MY SWORD.

YAN...YOU'VE BEEN AN ENIGMA EVER SINCE YOU APPEARED THREE YEARS AGO.

AND IF YOU FIGHT NOODLES, YOU WILL DIE.

IF YOU'RE CAPABLE OF TURNING AGAINST ME, I'D RATHER SEE YOU DEAD NOW.

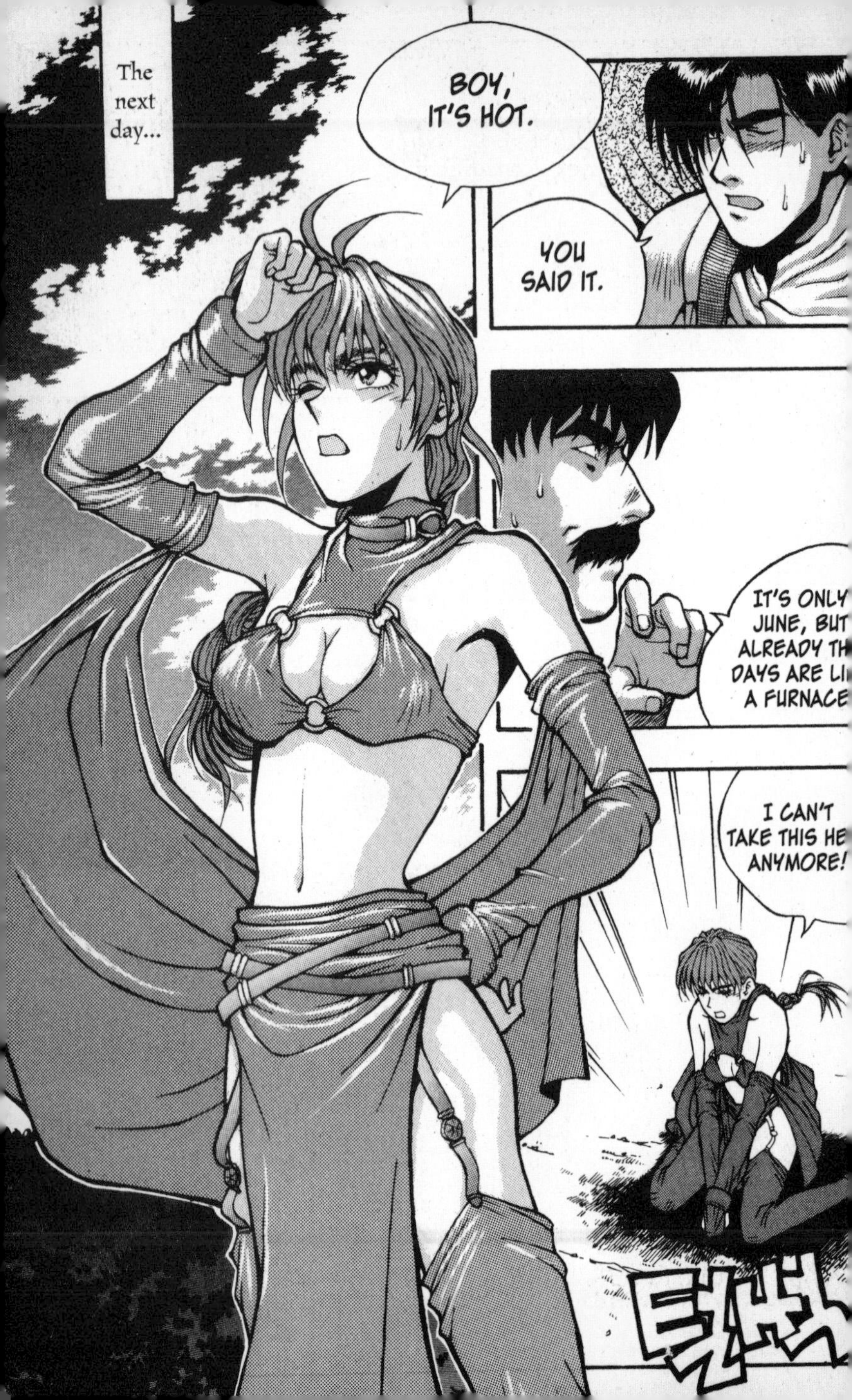
The next day...
BOY, IT'S HOT.
YOU SAID IT.
IT'S ONLY JUNE, BUT ALREADY TH DAYS ARE LI A FURNACE
I CAN'T TAKE THIS HE ANYMORE!

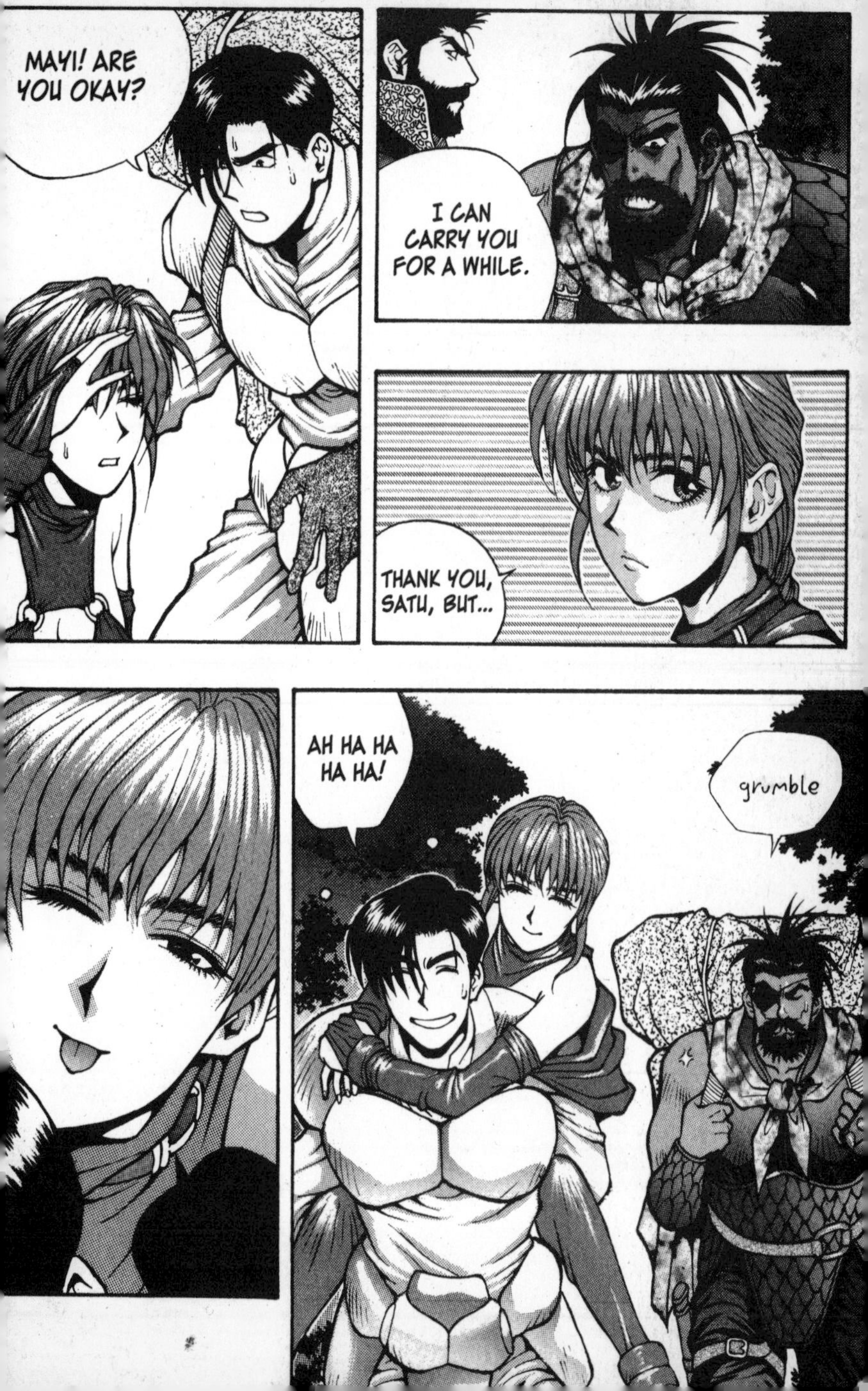
MAYI! ARE YOU OKAY?
I CAN CARRY YOU FOR A WHILE.
THANK YOU, SATU, BUT...
AH HA HA HA HA!
grumble

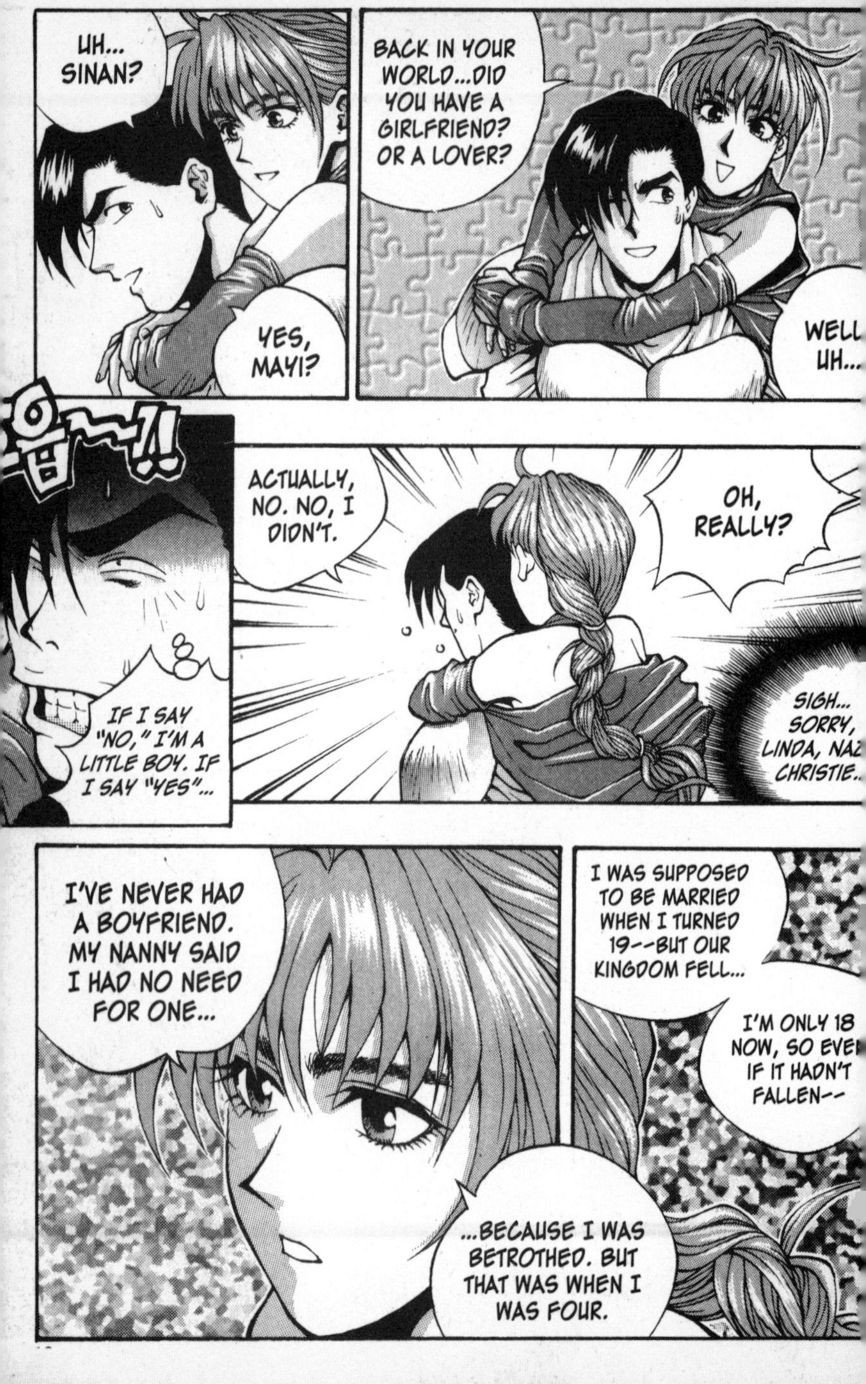
UH... SINAN?
YES, MAYI?
BACK IN YOUR WORLD...DID YOU HAVE A GIRLFRIEND? OR A LOVER?
WELL UH...
읍~!!
IF I SAY "NO," I'M A LITTLE BOY. IF I SAY "YES"...
ACTUALLY, NO. NO, I DIDN'T.
OH, REALLY?
SIGH... SORRY, LINDA, NAZ CHRISTIE...
I'VE NEVER HAD A BOYFRIEND. MY NANNY SAID I HAD NO NEED FOR ONE...
...BECAUSE I WAS BETROTHED. BUT THAT WAS WHEN I WAS FOUR.
I WAS SUPPOSED TO BE MARRIED WHEN I TURNED 19--BUT OUR KINGDOM FELL...
I'M ONLY 18 NOW, SO EVE IF IT HADN'T FALLEN--

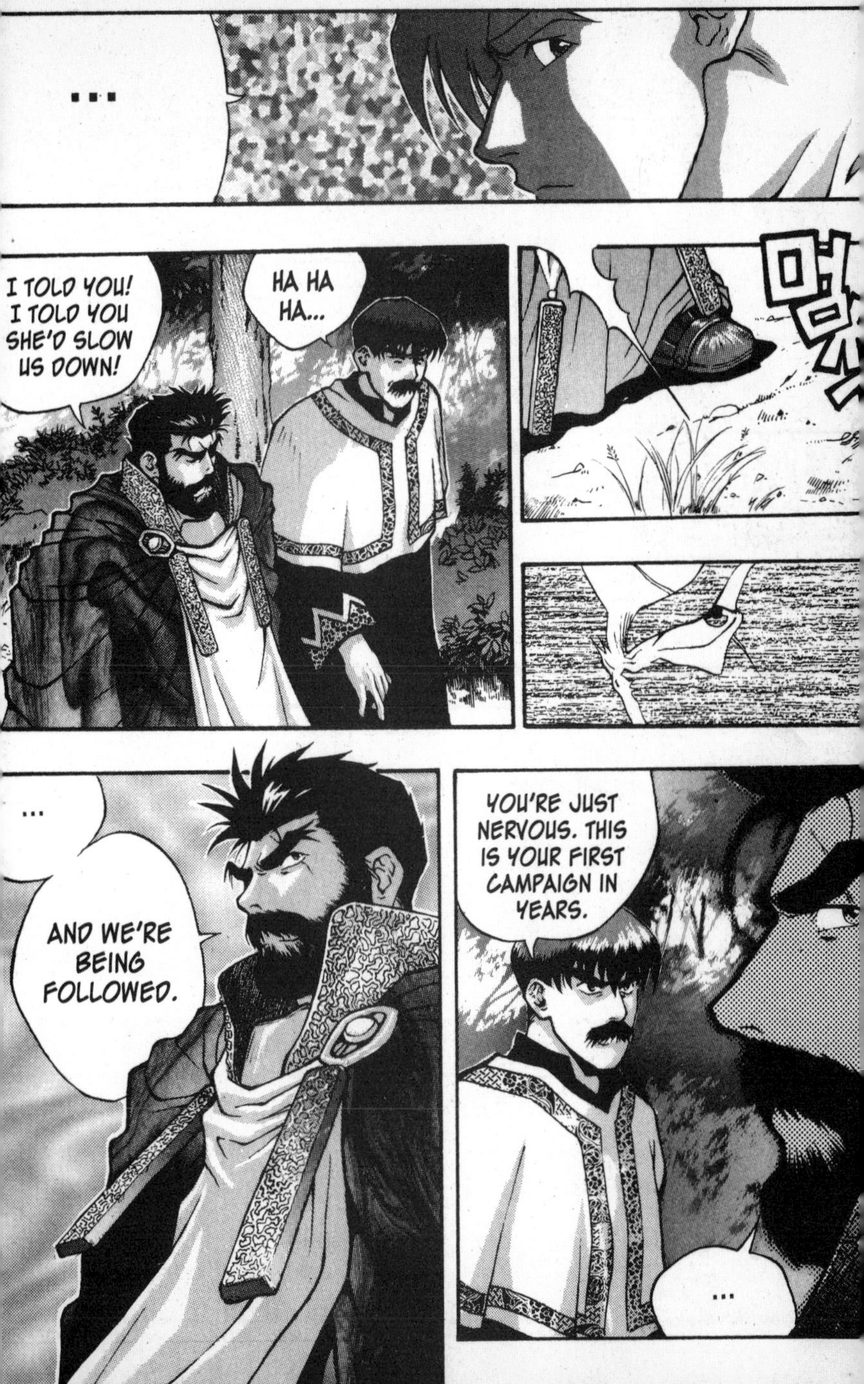
...
I TOLD YOU! I TOLD YOU SHE'D SLOW US DOWN!
HA HA HA...
멈
...
AND WE'RE BEING FOLLOWED.
YOU'RE JUST NERVOUS. THIS IS YOUR FIRST CAMPAIGN IN YEARS.
...

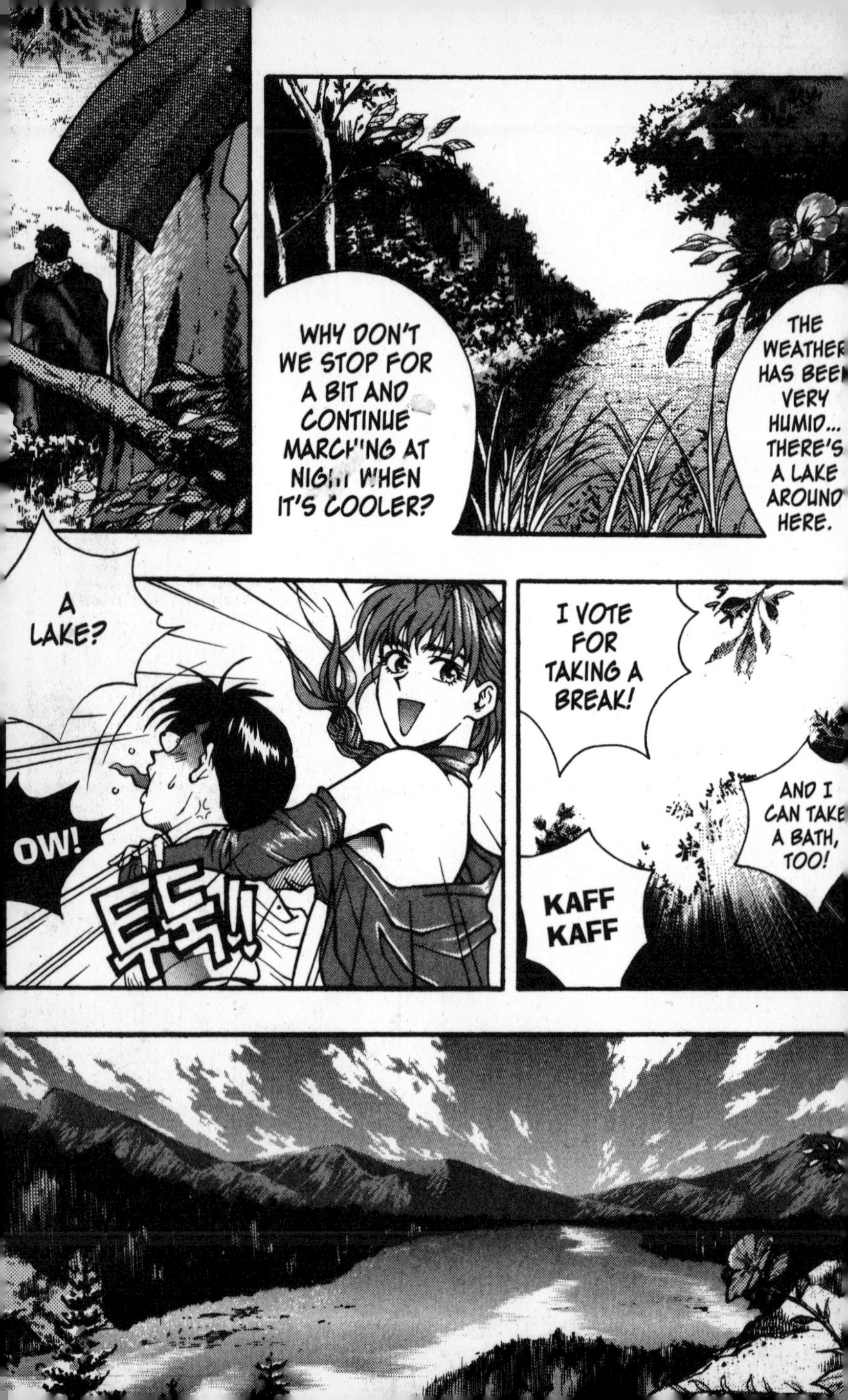

WHY DON'T WE STOP FOR A BIT AND CONTINUE MARCHING AT NIGHT WHEN IT'S COOLER?
THE WEATHER HAS BEEN VERY HUMID... THERE'S A LAKE AROUND HERE.
A LAKE?
OW!
투둑!!
I VOTE FOR TAKING A BREAK!
AND I CAN TAKE A BATH, TOO!
KAFF KAFF

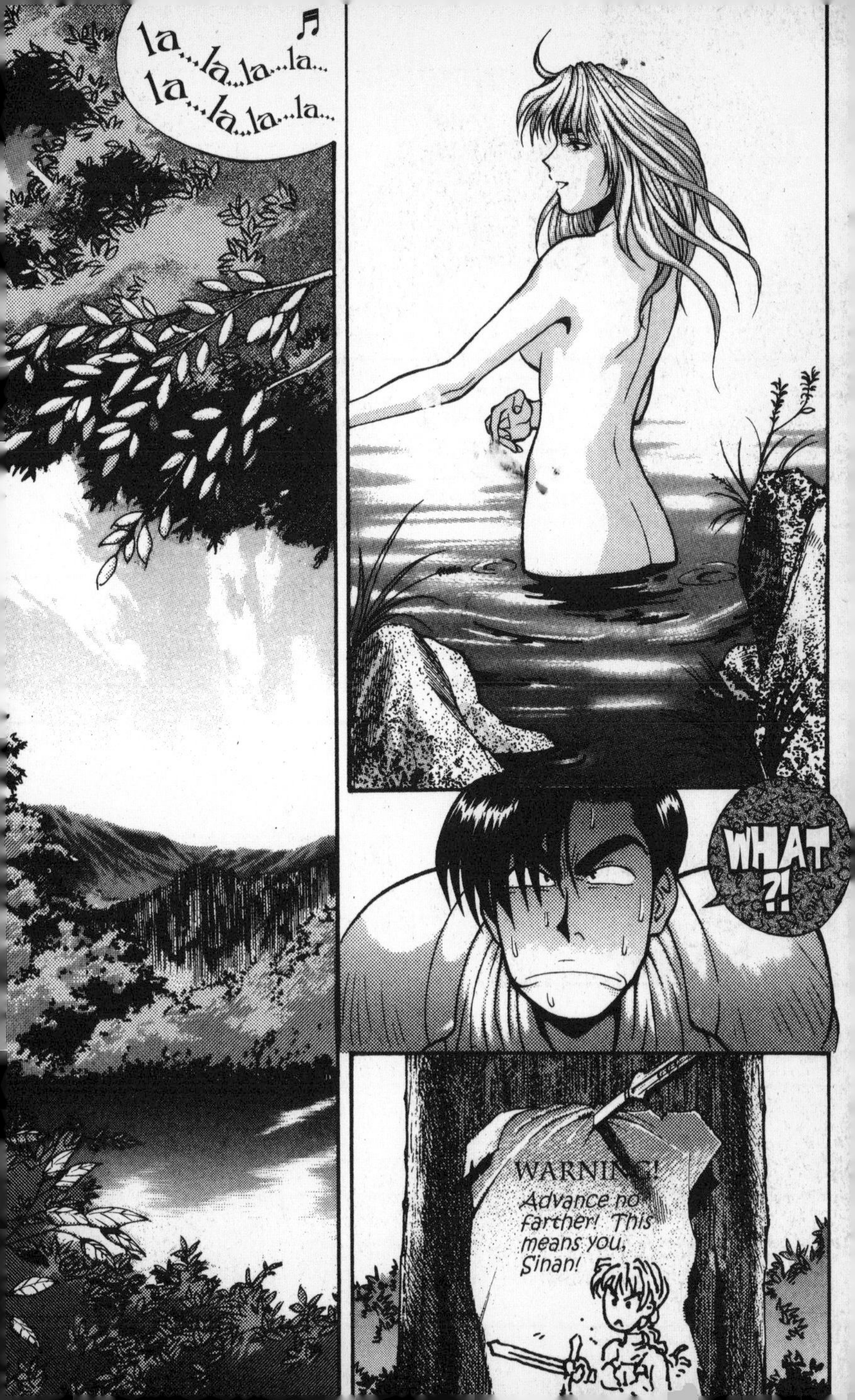la...la...la...la...
la...la...la...la...
WHAT?!
WARNING!
Advance no farther! This means you, Sinan!

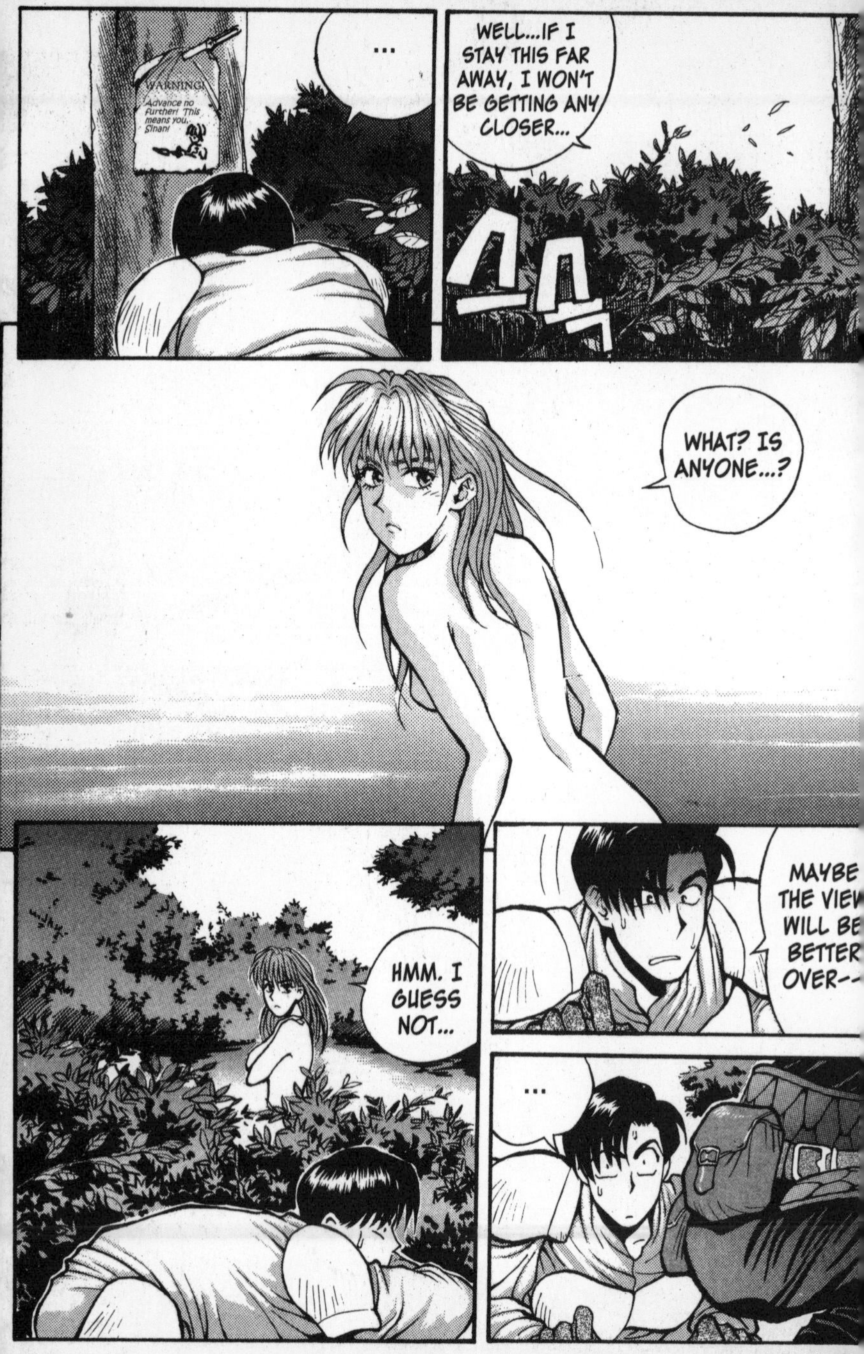
WARNING!
Advance no further! This means you, Sinan!
...
WELL...IF I STAY THIS FAR AWAY, I WON'T BE GETTING ANY CLOSER...
WHAT? IS ANYONE...?
HMM. I GUESS NOT...
MAYBE THE VIEW WILL BE BETTER OVER--
...

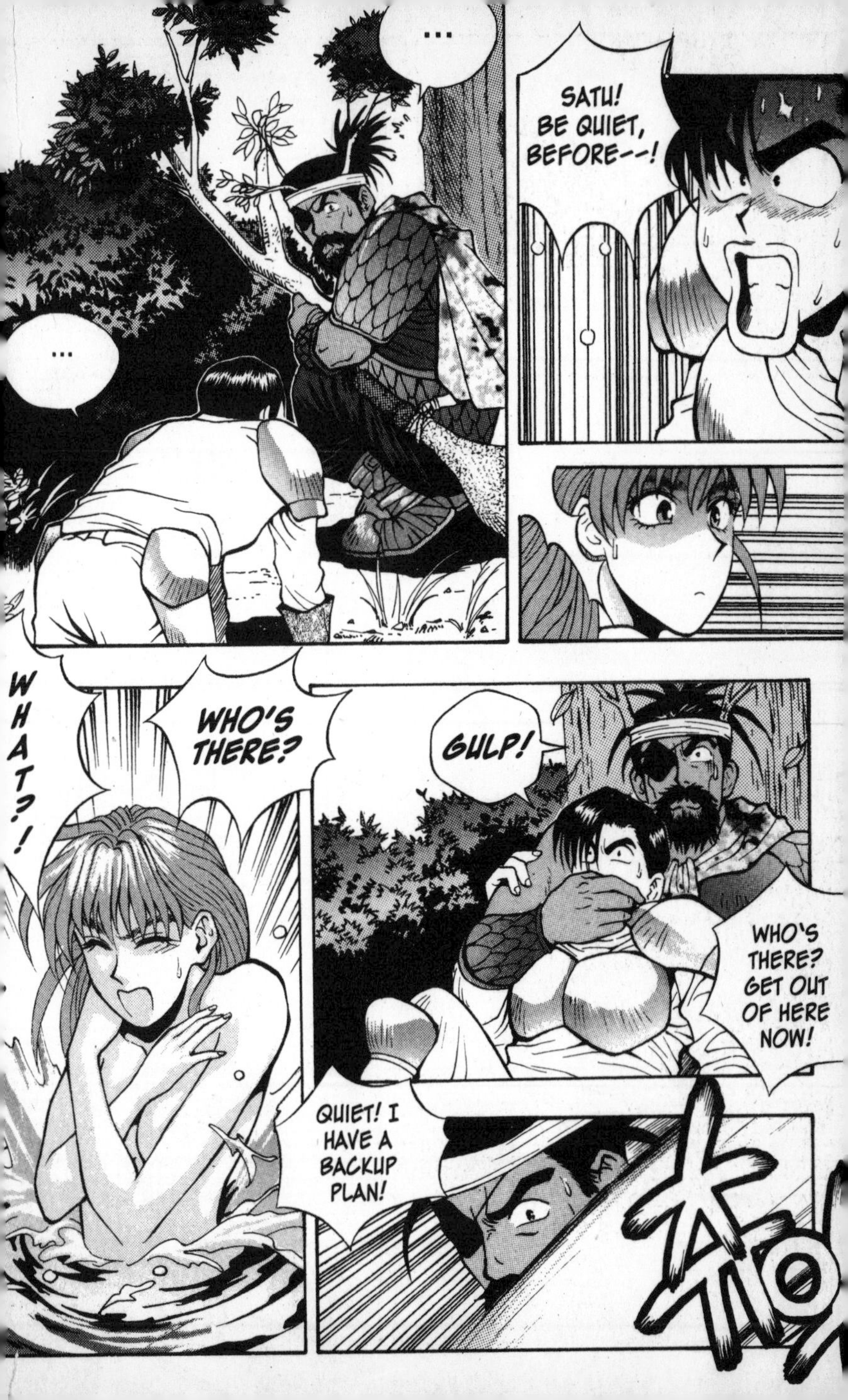
...
...
SATU! BE QUIET, BEFORE--!
WHAT?!
WHO'S THERE?
GULP!
WHO'S THERE? GET OUT OF HERE NOW!
QUIET! I HAVE A BACKUP PLAN!

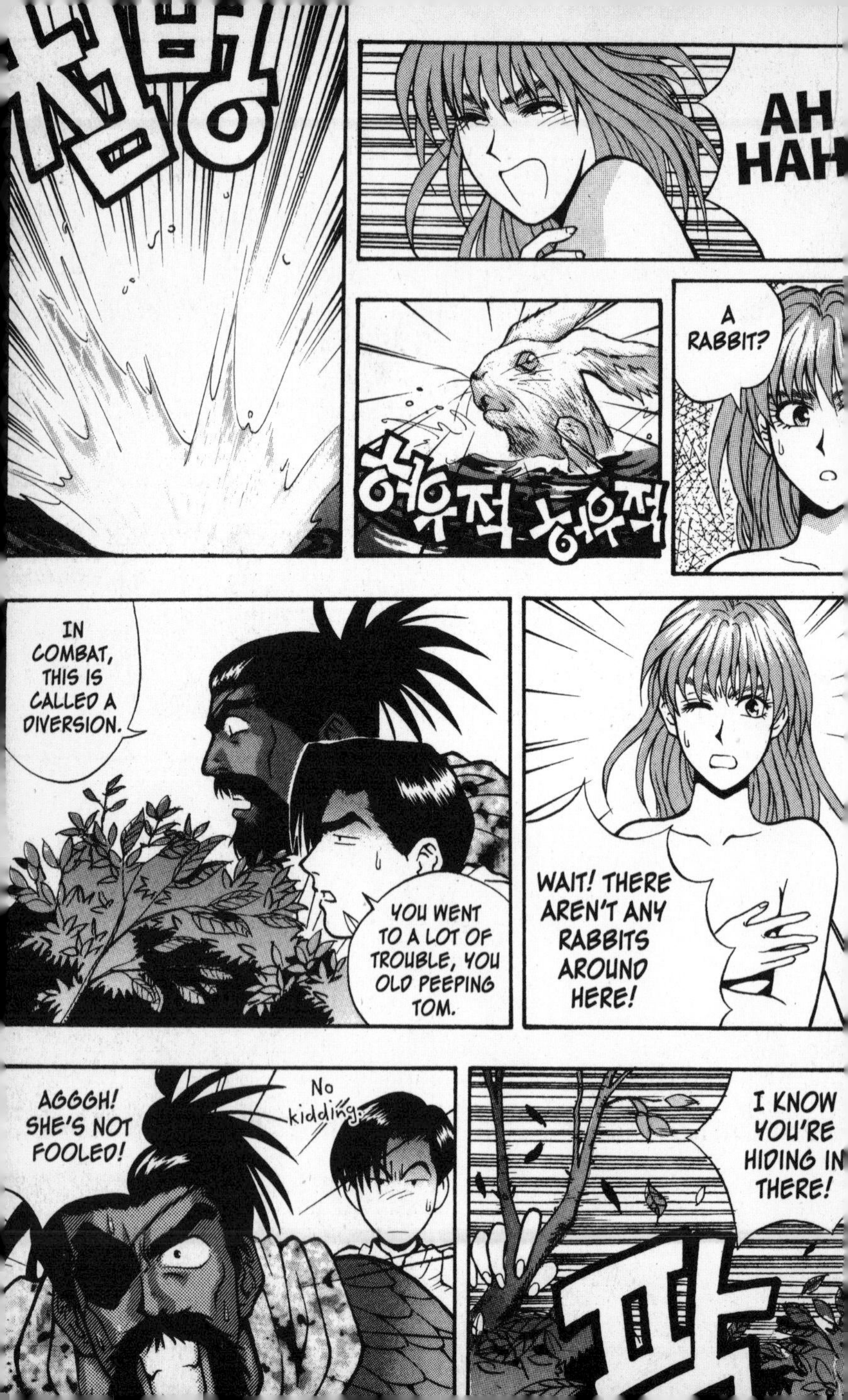

첨벙!
AH HAH
허우적 허우적
A RABBIT?
IN COMBAT, THIS IS CALLED A DIVERSION.
YOU WENT TO A LOT OF TROUBLE, YOU OLD PEEPING TOM.
WAIT! THERE AREN'T ANY RABBITS AROUND HERE!
AGGGH! SHE'S NOT FOOLED!
No kidding.
I KNOW YOU'RE HIDING IN THERE!
파

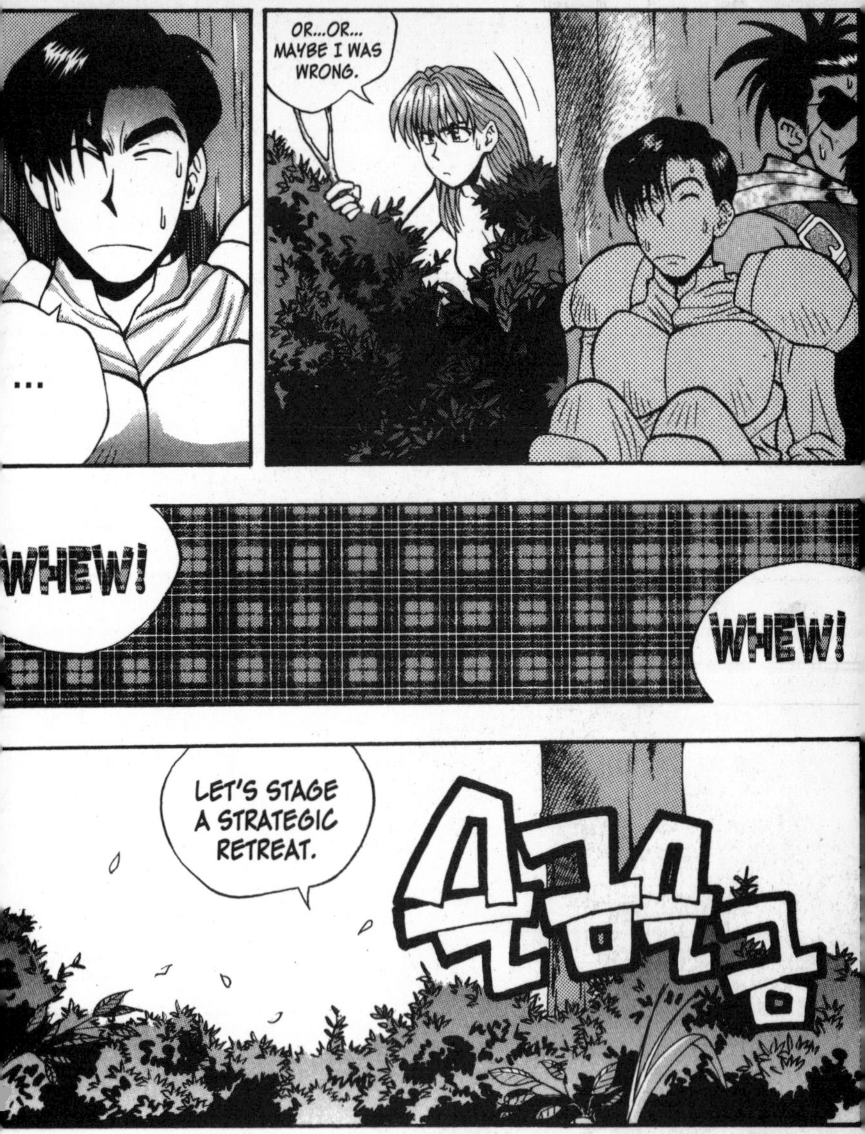
...
OR...OR... MAYBE I WAS WRONG.
WHEW!
WHEW!
LET'S STAGE A STRATEGIC RETREAT.

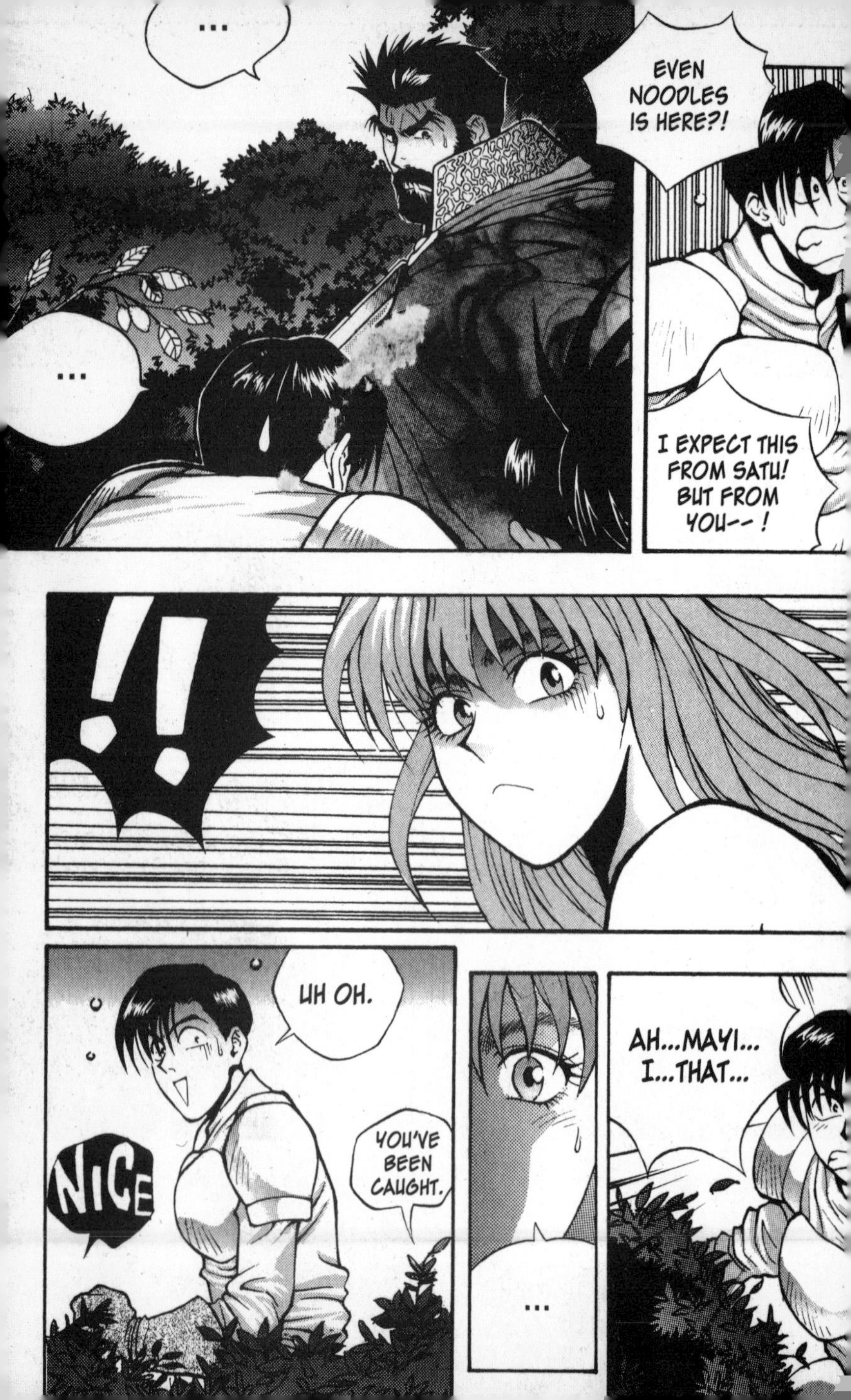
...
...
EVEN NOODLES IS HERE?!
I EXPECT THIS FROM SATU! BUT FROM YOU-- !
!!
UH OH.
NICE
YOU'VE BEEN CAUGHT.
...
AH...MAYI... I...THAT...

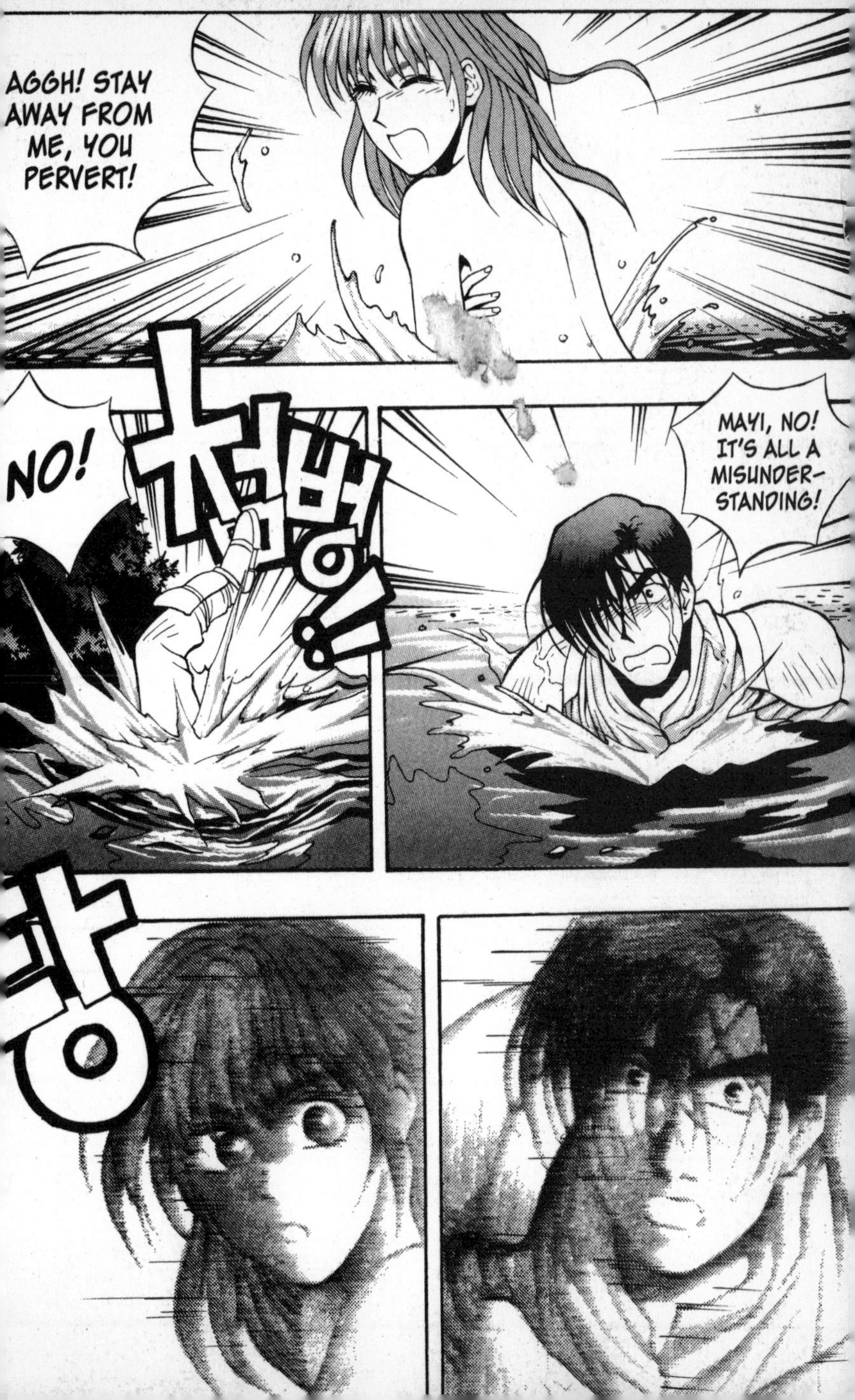
AGGH! STAY AWAY FROM ME, YOU PERVERT!
NO!
MAYI, NO! IT'S ALL A MISUNDER-STANDING!

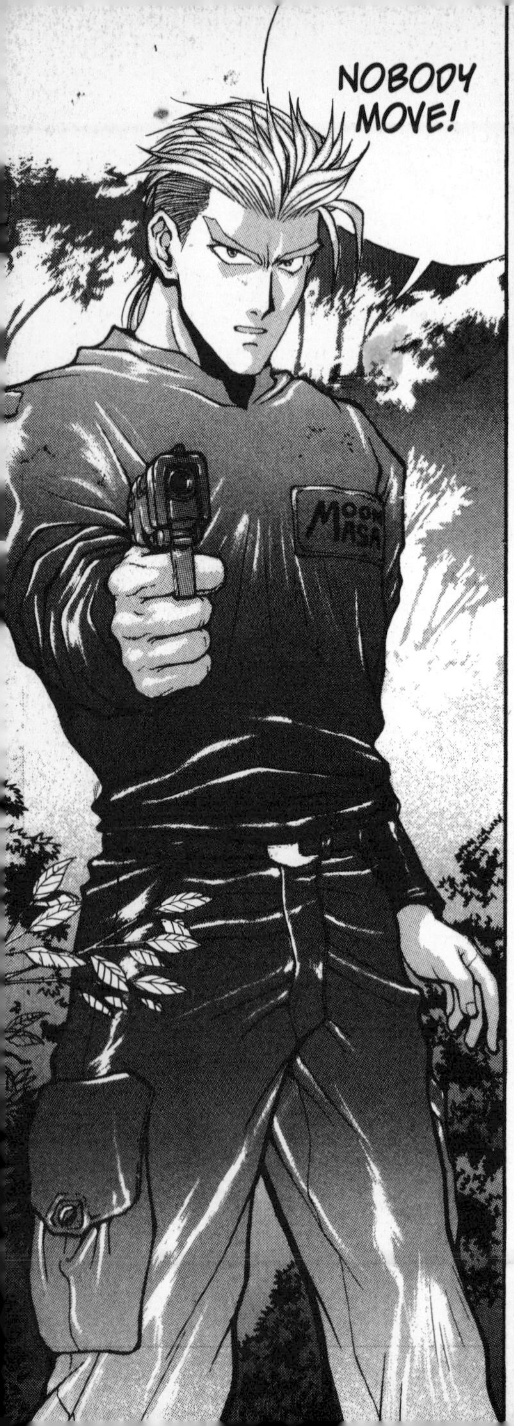
NOBODY MOVE!
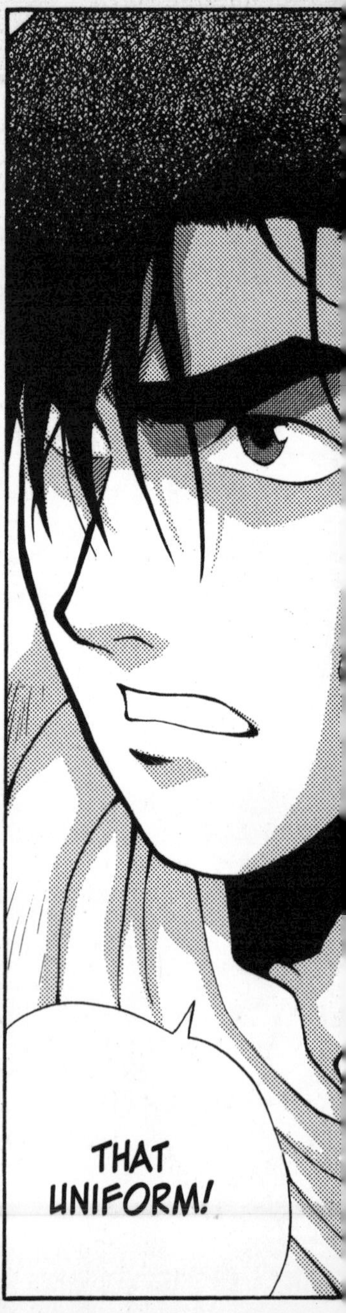
THAT UNIFORM!

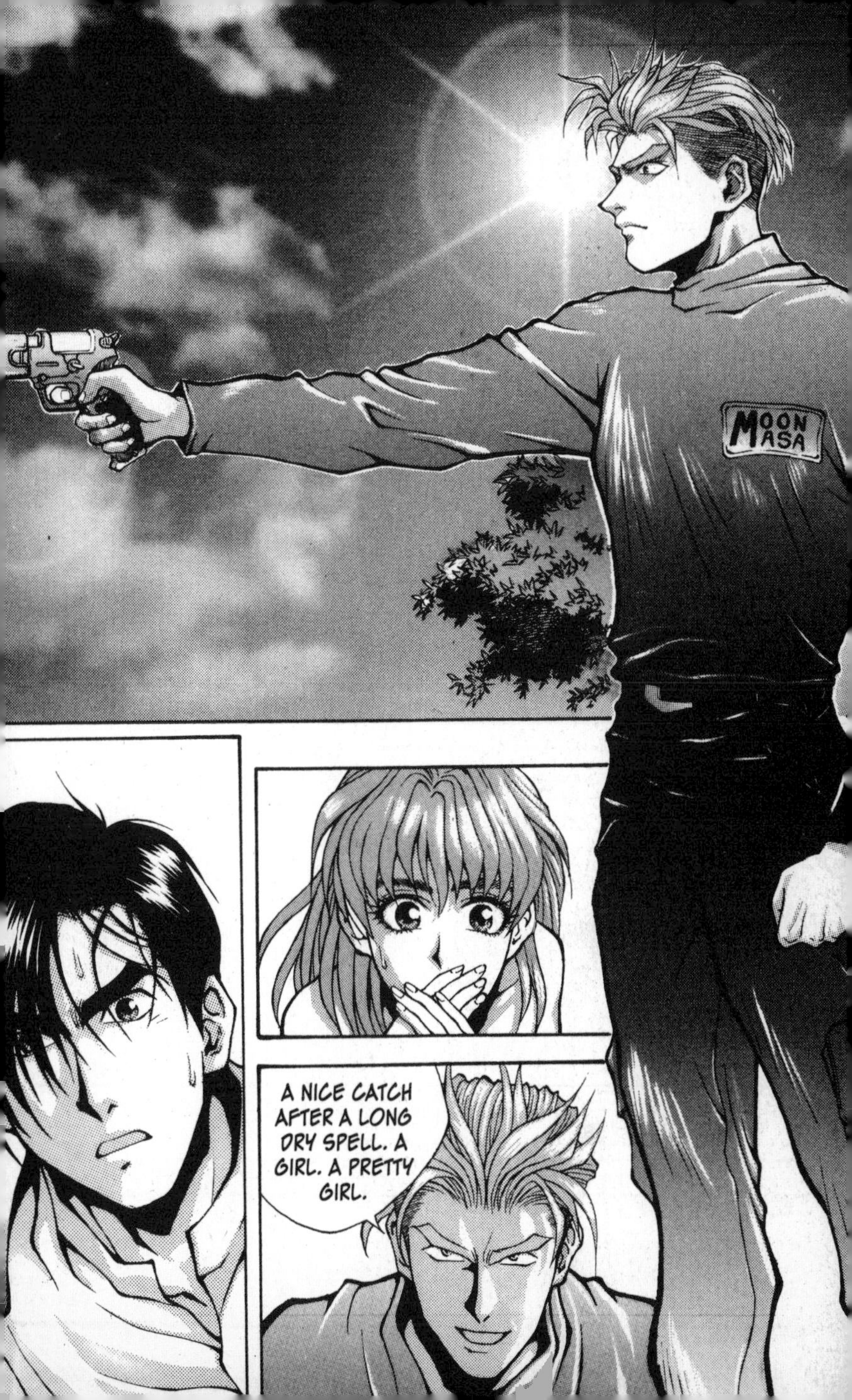
MOON MASA
A NICE CATCH AFTER A LONG DRY SPELL. A GIRL. A PRETTY GIRL.

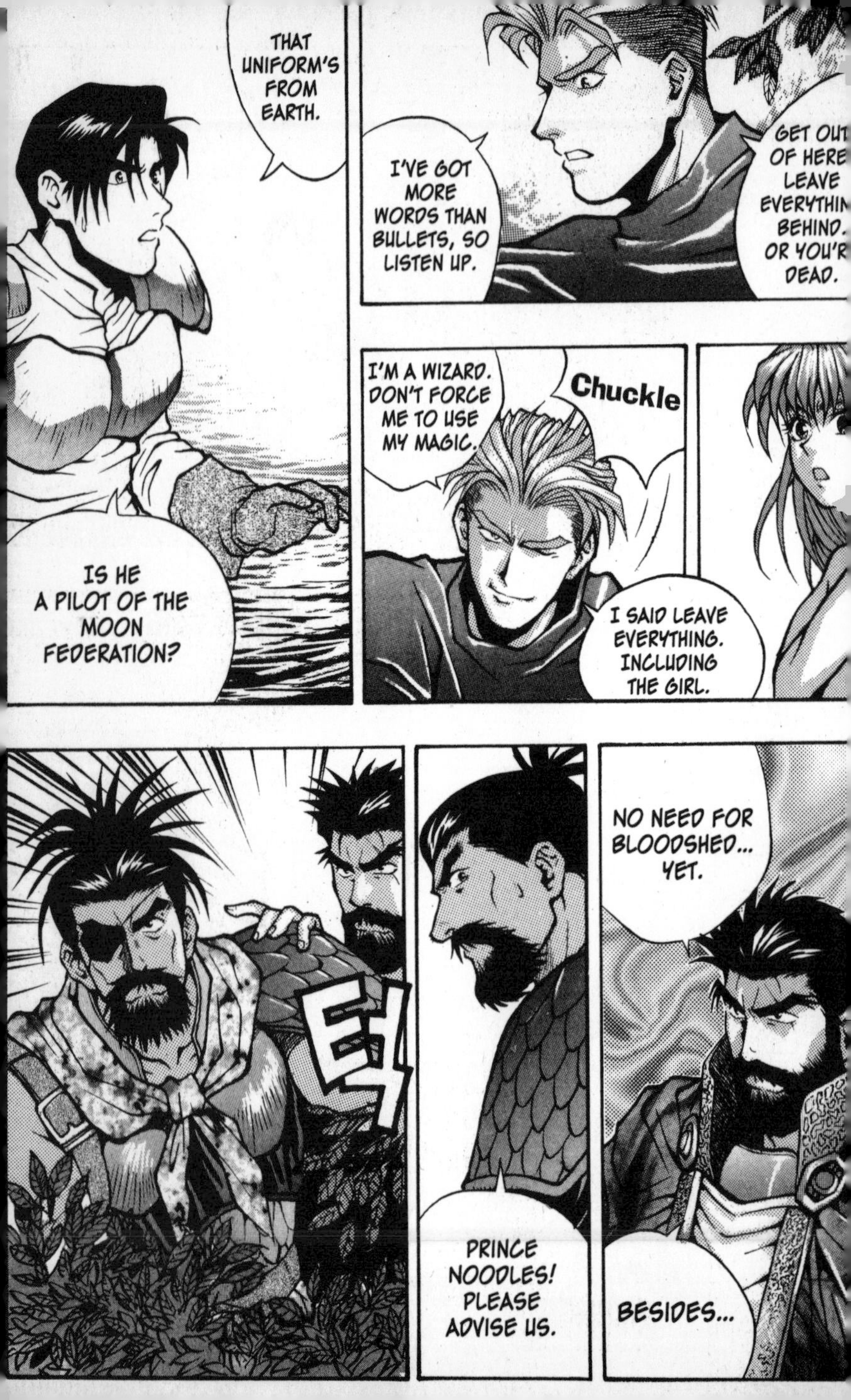
THAT UNIFORM'S FROM EARTH.
IS HE A PILOT OF THE MOON FEDERATION?
I'VE GOT MORE WORDS THAN BULLETS, SO LISTEN UP.
GET OUT OF HERE LEAVE EVERYTHING BEHIND. OR YOU'RE DEAD.
I'M A WIZARD. DON'T FORCE ME TO USE MY MAGIC.
Chuckle
I SAID LEAVE EVERYTHING. INCLUDING THE GIRL.
EH
PRINCE NOODLES! PLEASE ADVISE US.
NO NEED FOR BLOODSHED... YET.
BESIDES...

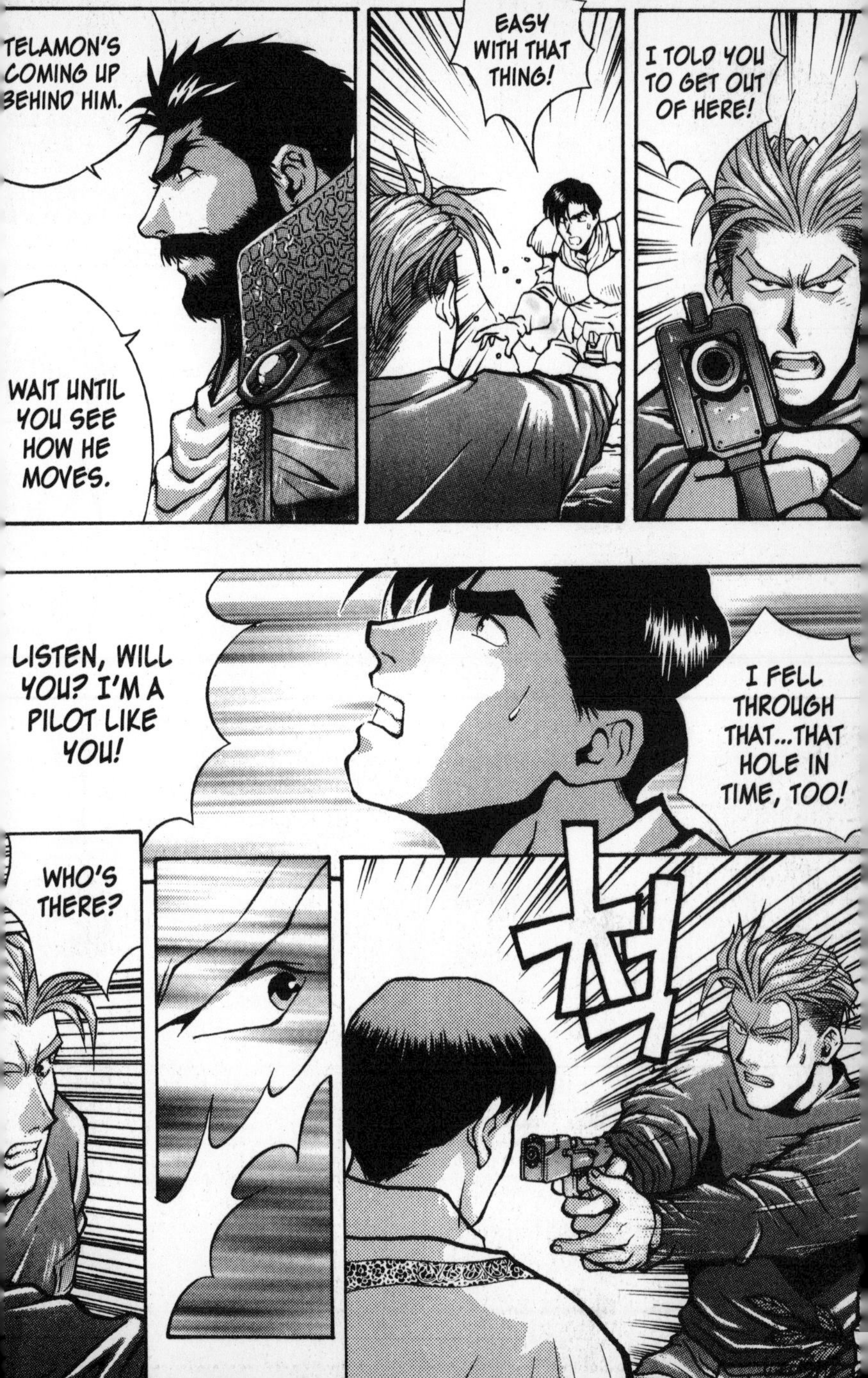
TELAMON'S COMING UP BEHIND HIM.
WAIT UNTIL YOU SEE HOW HE MOVES.
EASY WITH THAT THING!
I TOLD YOU TO GET OUT OF HERE!
LISTEN, WILL YOU? I'M A PILOT LIKE YOU!
I FELL THROUGH THAT...THAT HOLE IN TIME, TOO!
WHO'S THERE?

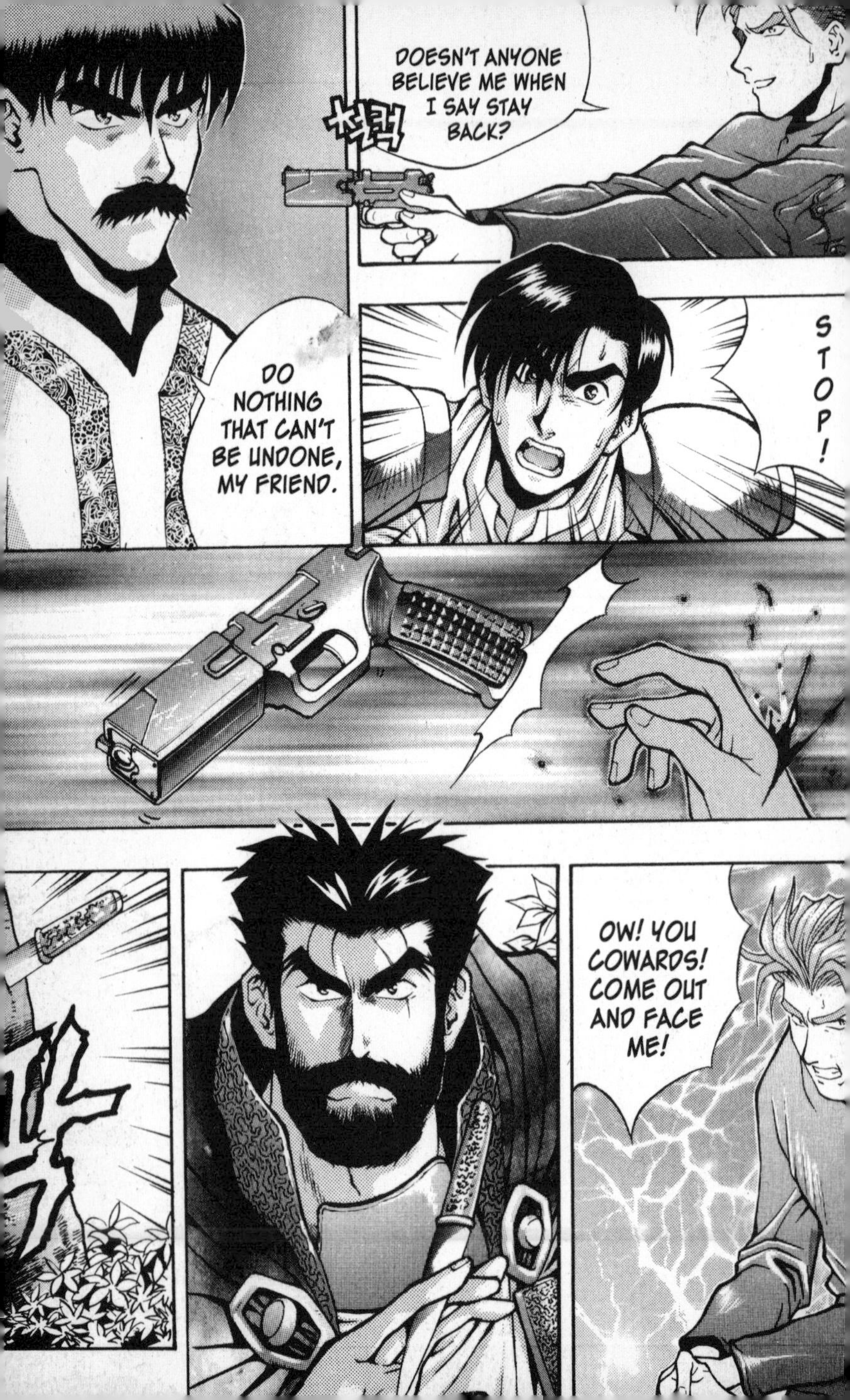
DO NOTHING THAT CAN'T BE UNDONE, MY FRIEND.
철컥
DOESN'T ANYONE BELIEVE ME WHEN I SAY STAY BACK?
STOP!
OW! YOU COWARDS! COME OUT AND FACE ME!

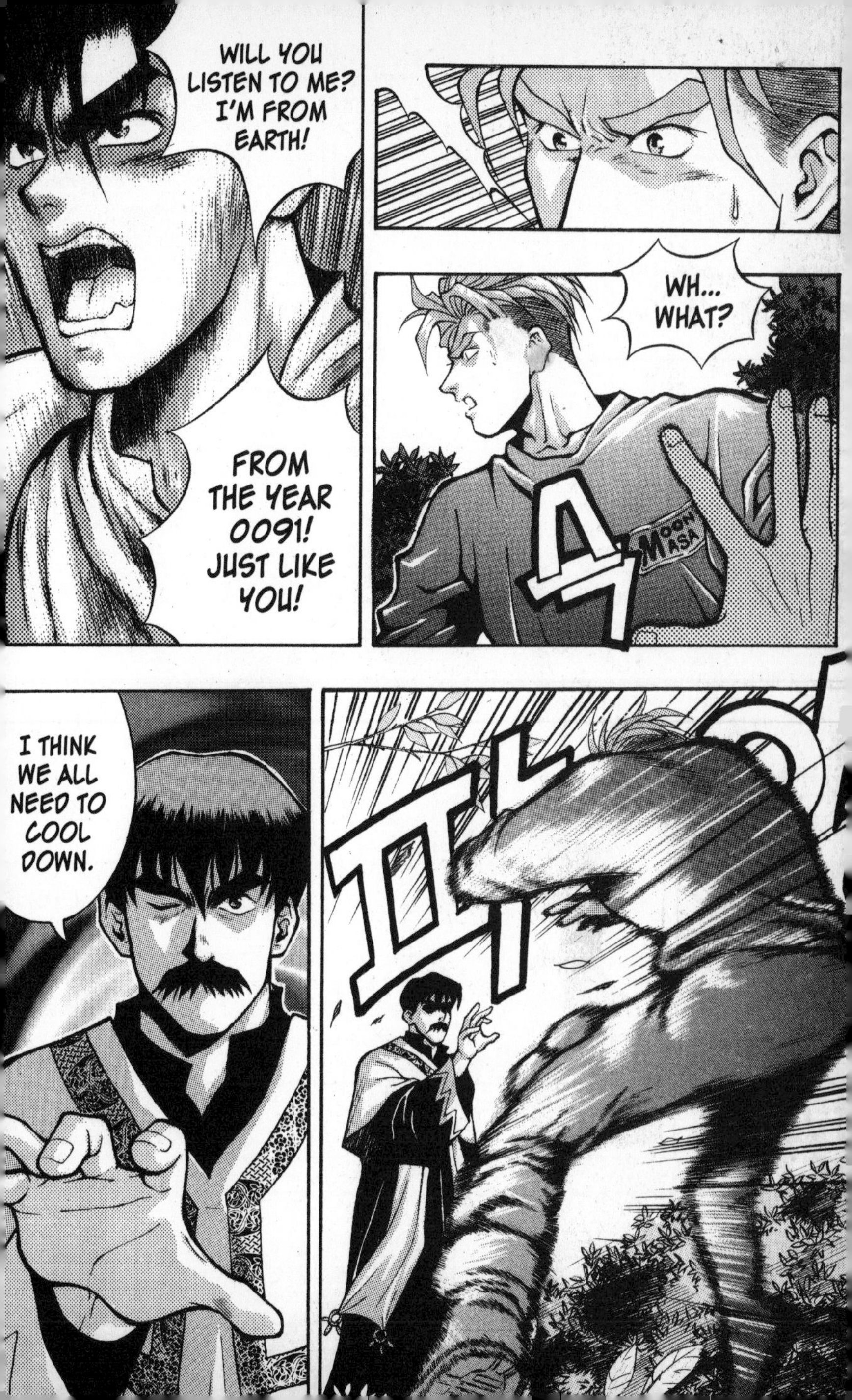
WILL YOU LISTEN TO ME? I'M FROM EARTH!
FROM THE YEAR 0091! JUST LIKE YOU!
WH... WHAT?
MOON MASA
I THINK WE ALL NEED TO COOL DOWN.

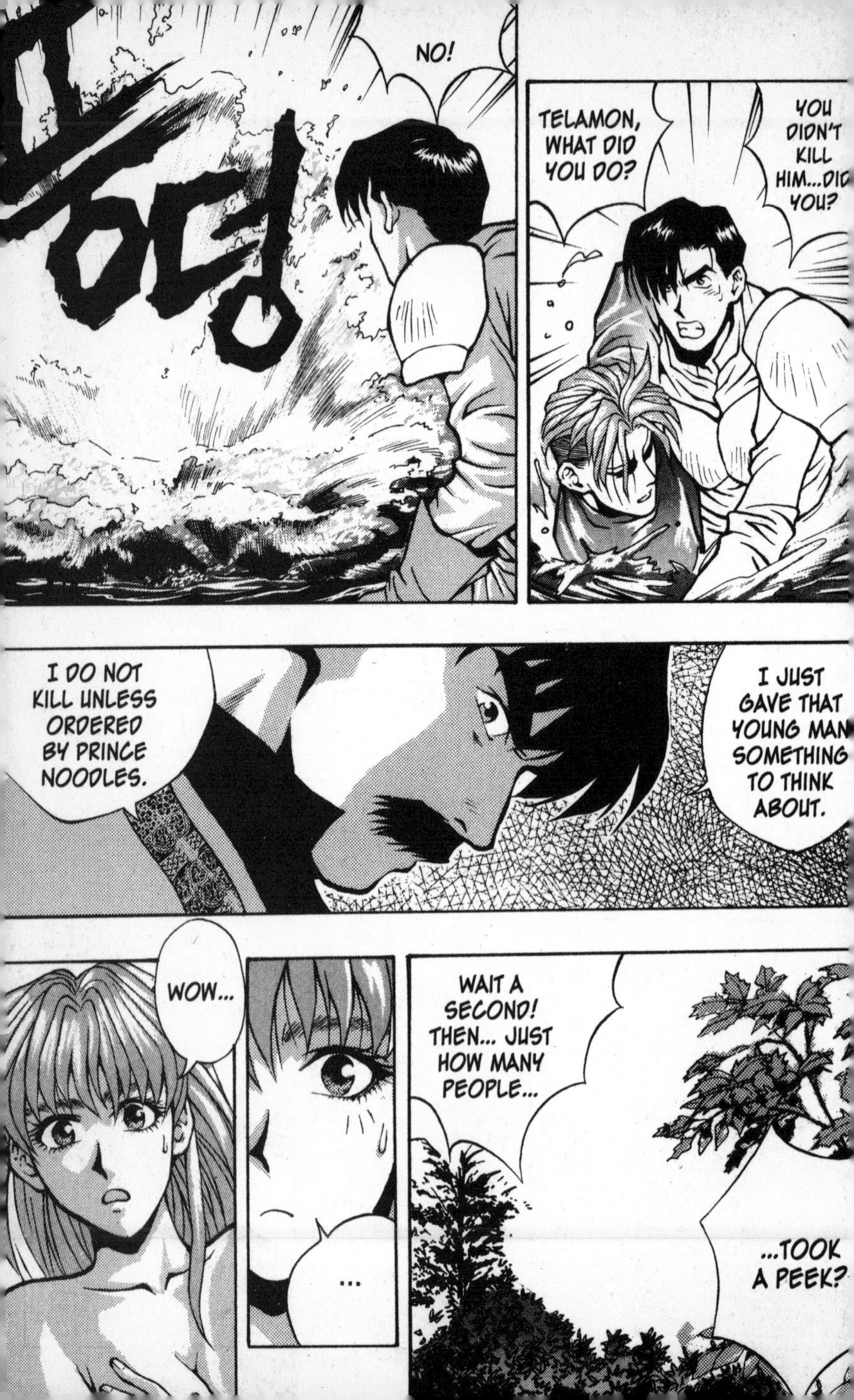
NO!
TELAMON, WHAT DID YOU DO?
YOU DIDN'T KILL HIM...DID YOU?
I DO NOT KILL UNLESS ORDERED BY PRINCE NOODLES.
I JUST GAVE THAT YOUNG MAN SOMETHING TO THINK ABOUT.
WOW...
...
WAIT A SECOND! THEN... JUST HOW MANY PEOPLE...
...TOOK A PEEK?

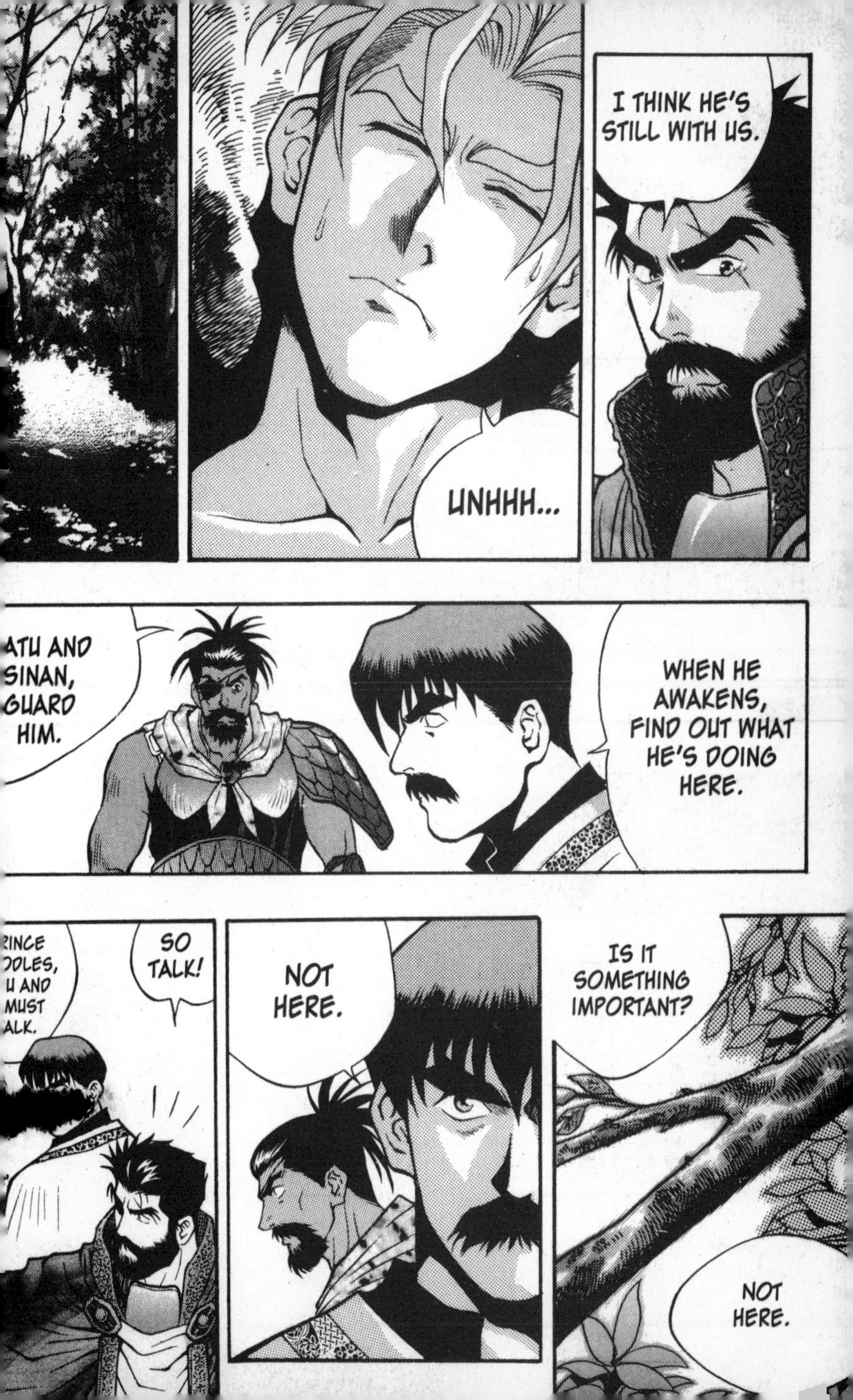
UNHHH...
I THINK HE'S STILL WITH US.
ATU AND SINAN, GUARD HIM.
WHEN HE AWAKENS, FIND OUT WHAT HE'S DOING HERE.
RINCE DLES, U AND MUST ALK.
SO TALK!
NOT HERE.
IS IT SOMETHING IMPORTANT?
NOT HERE.

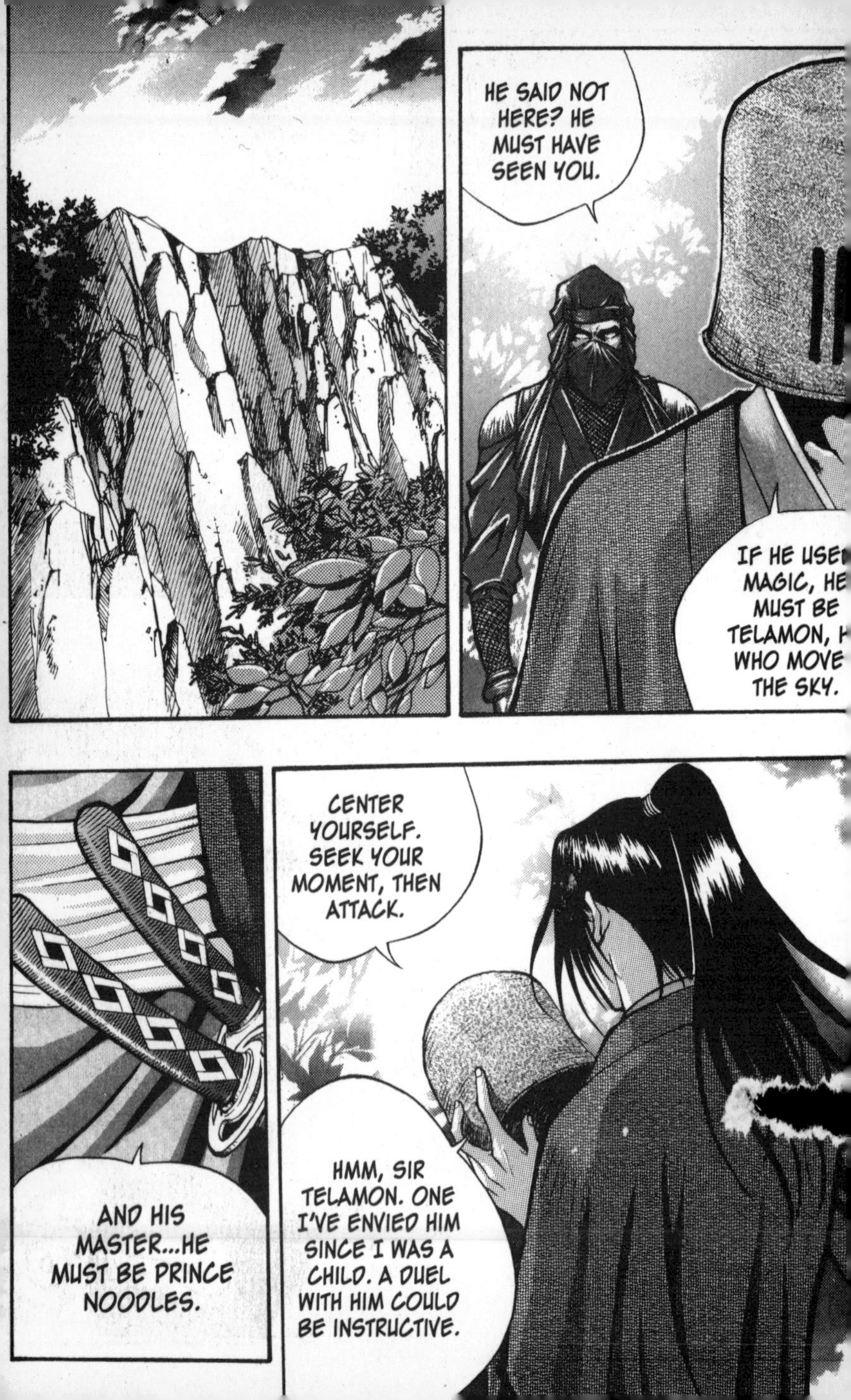
HE SAID NOT HERE? HE MUST HAVE SEEN YOU.
IF HE USE MAGIC, HE MUST BE TELAMON, H WHO MOVE THE SKY.
AND HIS MASTER...HE MUST BE PRINCE NOODLES.
CENTER YOURSELF. SEEK YOUR MOMENT, THEN ATTACK.
HMM, SIR TELAMON. ONE I'VE ENVIED HIM SINCE I WAS A CHILD. A DUEL WITH HIM COULD BE INSTRUCTIVE.

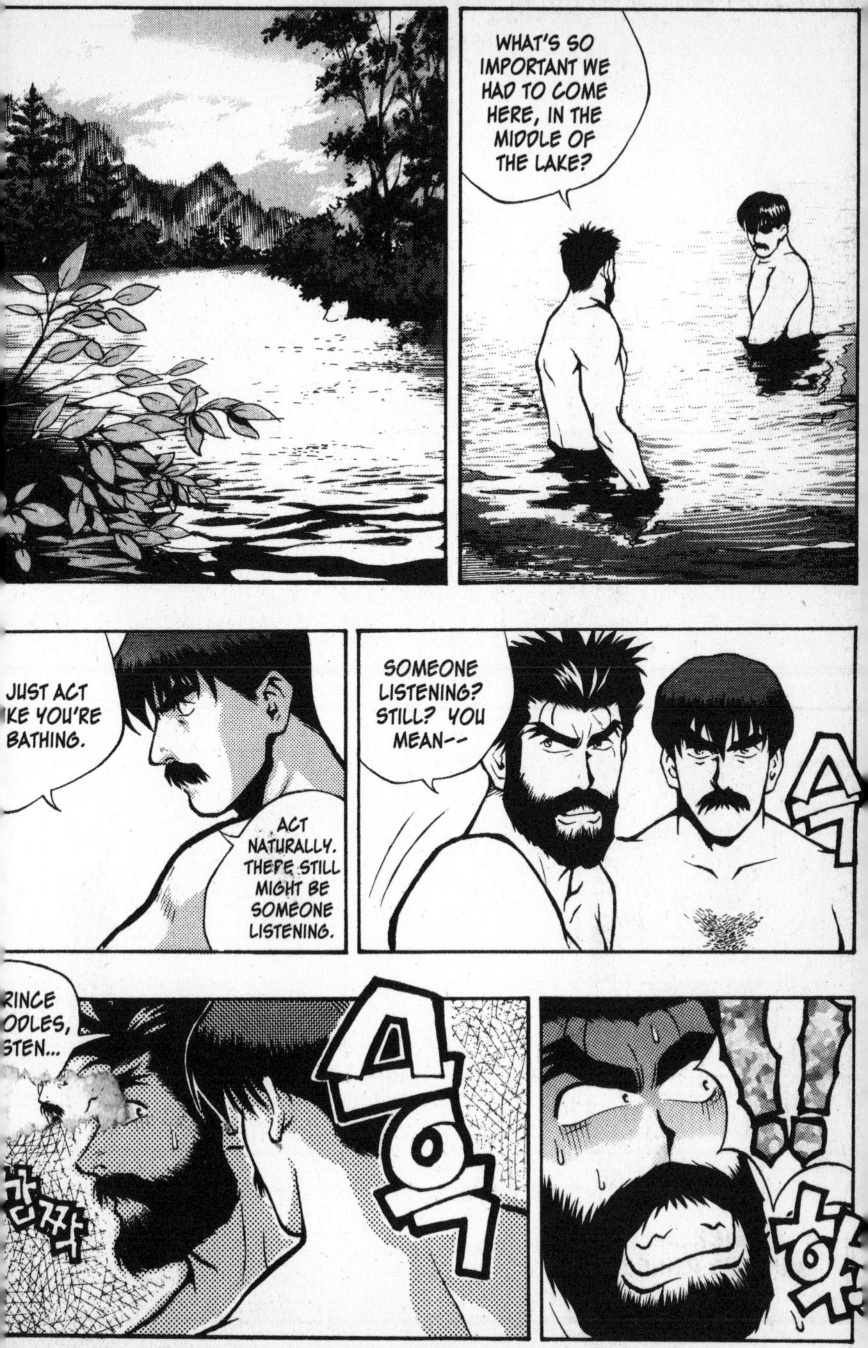
WHAT'S SO IMPORTANT WE HAD TO COME HERE, IN THE MIDDLE OF THE LAKE?
JUST ACT KE YOU'RE BATHING.
ACT NATURALLY. THERE STILL MIGHT BE SOMEONE LISTENING.
SOMEONE LISTENING? STILL? YOU MEAN--
RINCE ODLES, STEN...

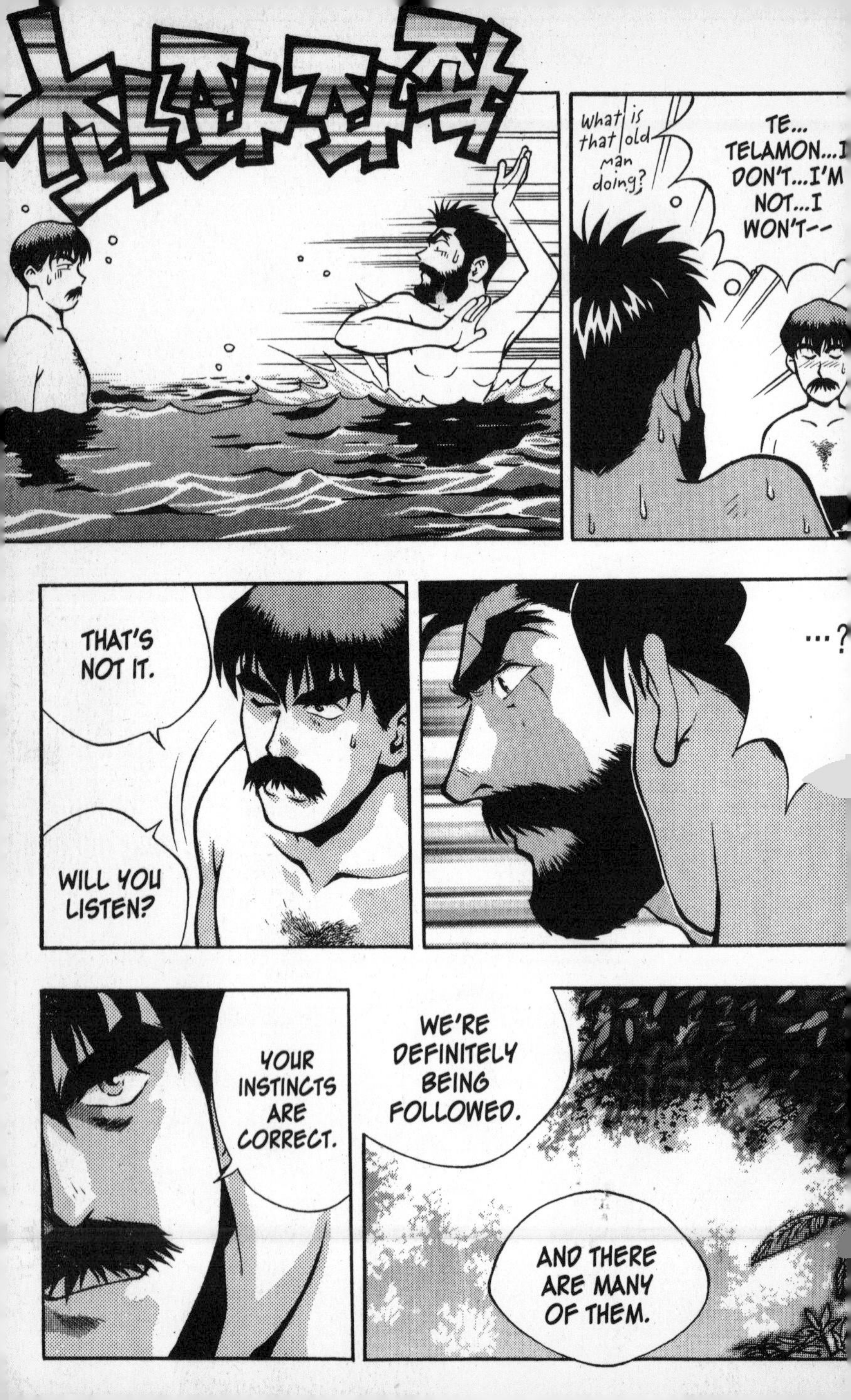
What is that old man doing?
TE... TELAMON...I DON'T...I'M NOT...I WON'T--
THAT'S NOT IT.
WILL YOU LISTEN?
...?
YOUR INSTINCTS ARE CORRECT.
WE'RE DEFINITELY BEING FOLLOWED.
AND THERE ARE MANY OF THEM.

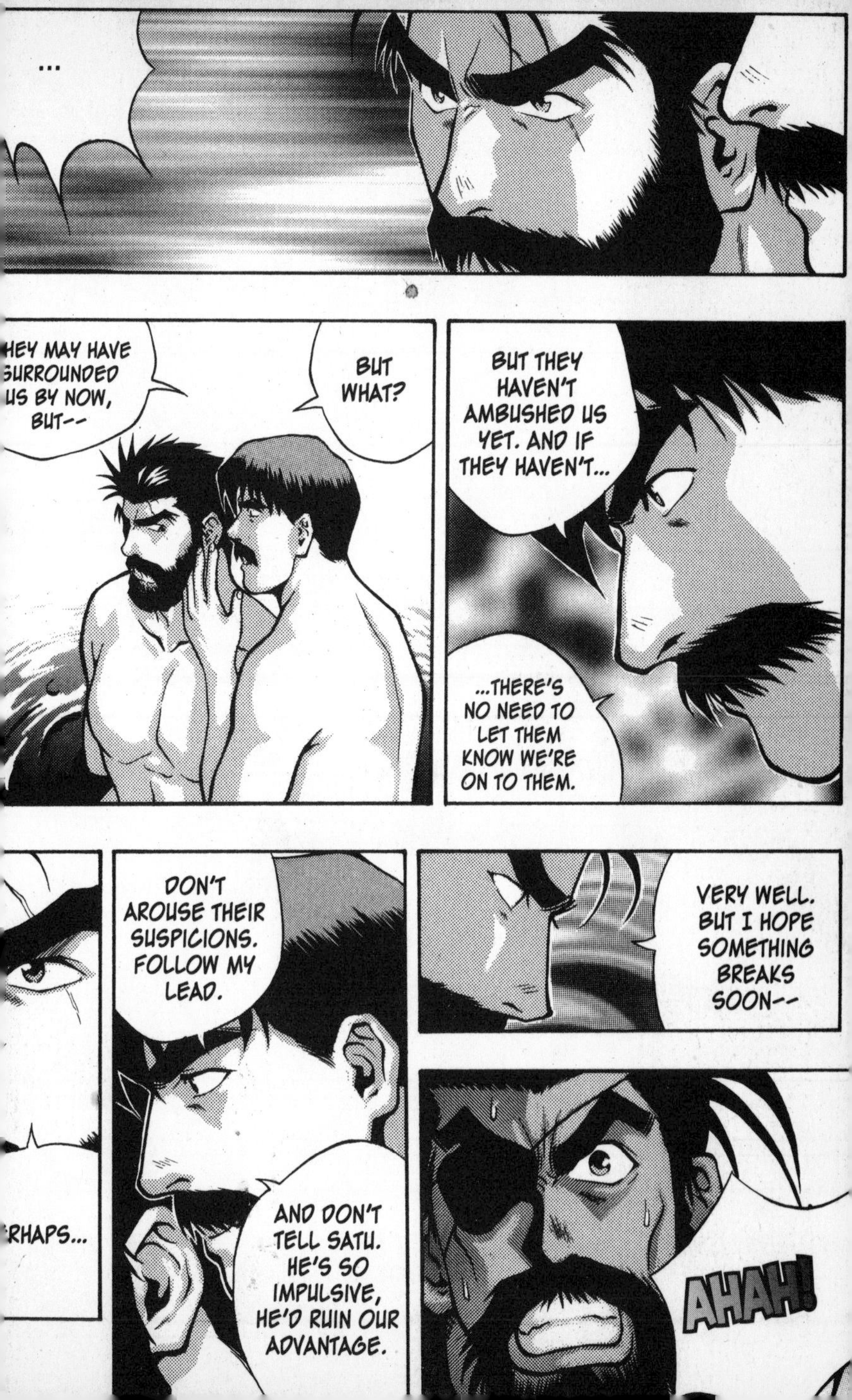
...
HEY MAY HAVE SURROUNDED US BY NOW, BUT--
BUT WHAT?
BUT THEY HAVEN'T AMBUSHED US YET. AND IF THEY HAVEN'T...
...THERE'S NO NEED TO LET THEM KNOW WE'RE ON TO THEM.
RHAPS...
DON'T AROUSE THEIR SUSPICIONS. FOLLOW MY LEAD.
AND DON'T TELL SATU. HE'S SO IMPULSIVE, HE'D RUIN OUR ADVANTAGE.
VERY WELL. BUT I HOPE SOMETHING BREAKS SOON--
AHAH!

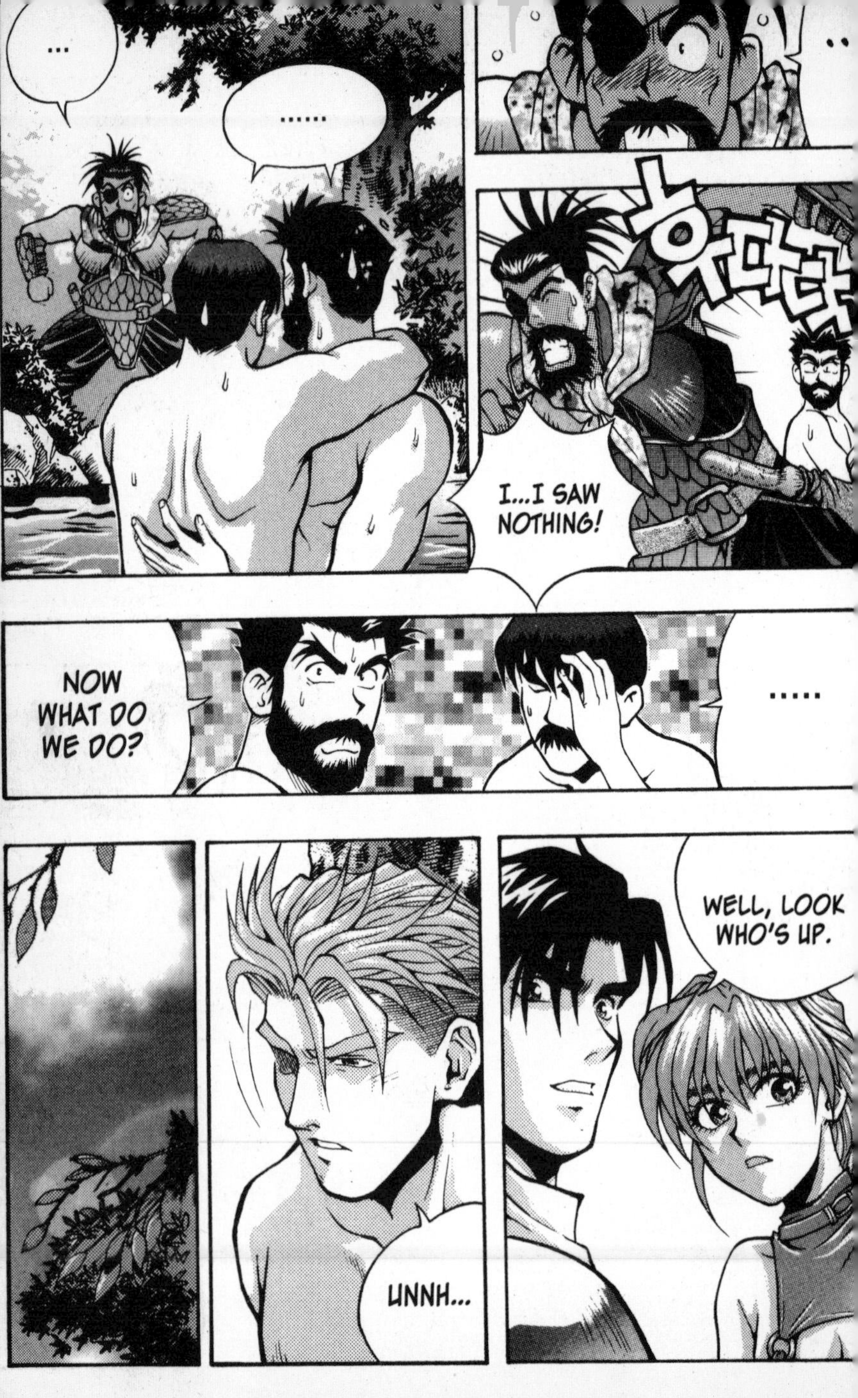
...
......
I...I SAW NOTHING!
NOW WHAT DO WE DO?
.....
UNNH...
WELL, LOOK WHO'S UP.

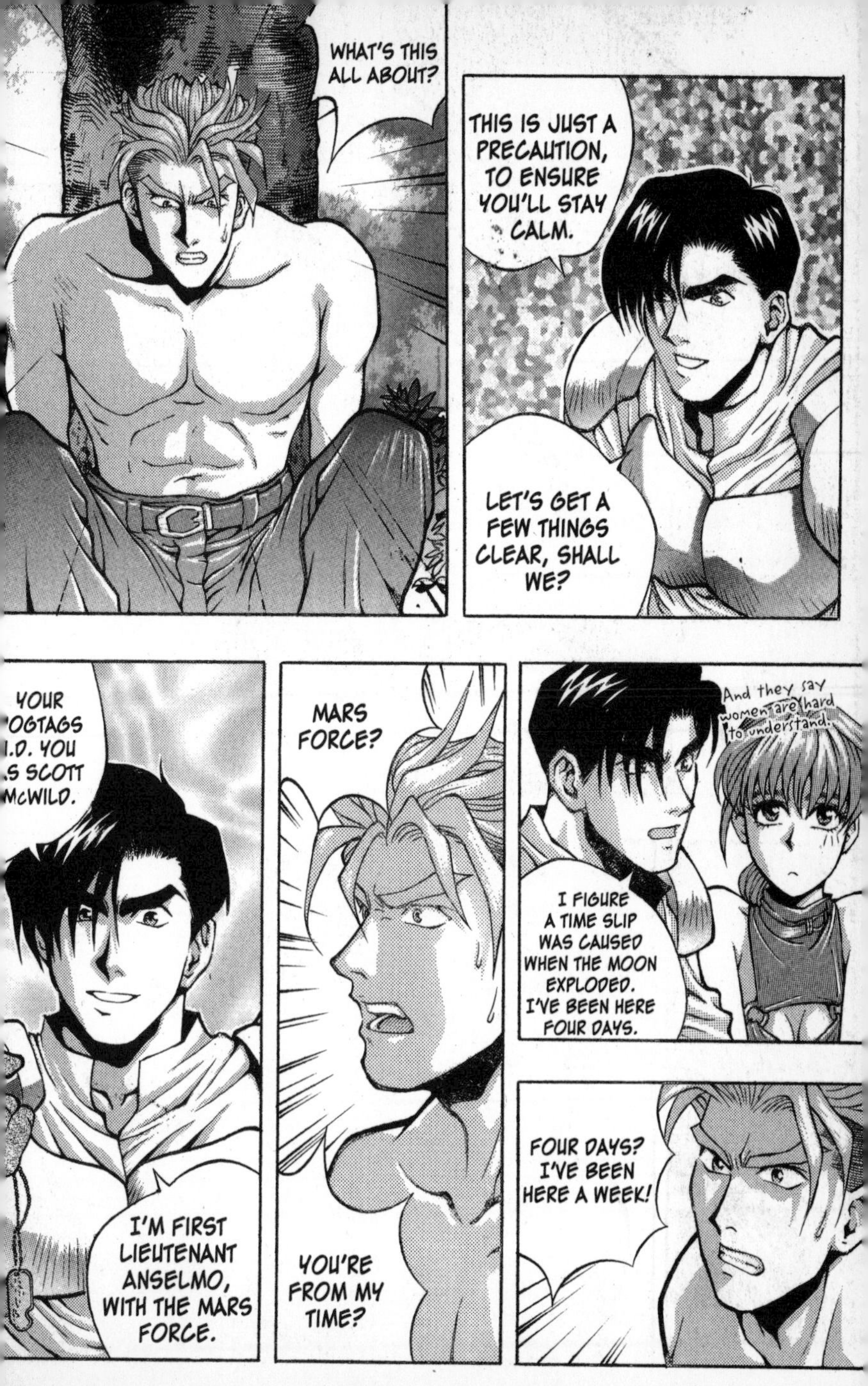
WHAT'S THIS ALL ABOUT?
THIS IS JUST A PRECAUTION, TO ENSURE YOU'LL STAY CALM.
LET'S GET A FEW THINGS CLEAR, SHALL WE?
YOUR OGTAGS .D. YOU S SCOTT McWILD.
I'M FIRST LIEUTENANT ANSELMO, WITH THE MARS FORCE.
MARS FORCE?
YOU'RE FROM MY TIME?
And they say women are hard to understand.
I FIGURE A TIME SLIP WAS CAUSED WHEN THE MOON EXPLODED. I'VE BEEN HERE FOUR DAYS.
FOUR DAYS? I'VE BEEN HERE A WEEK!

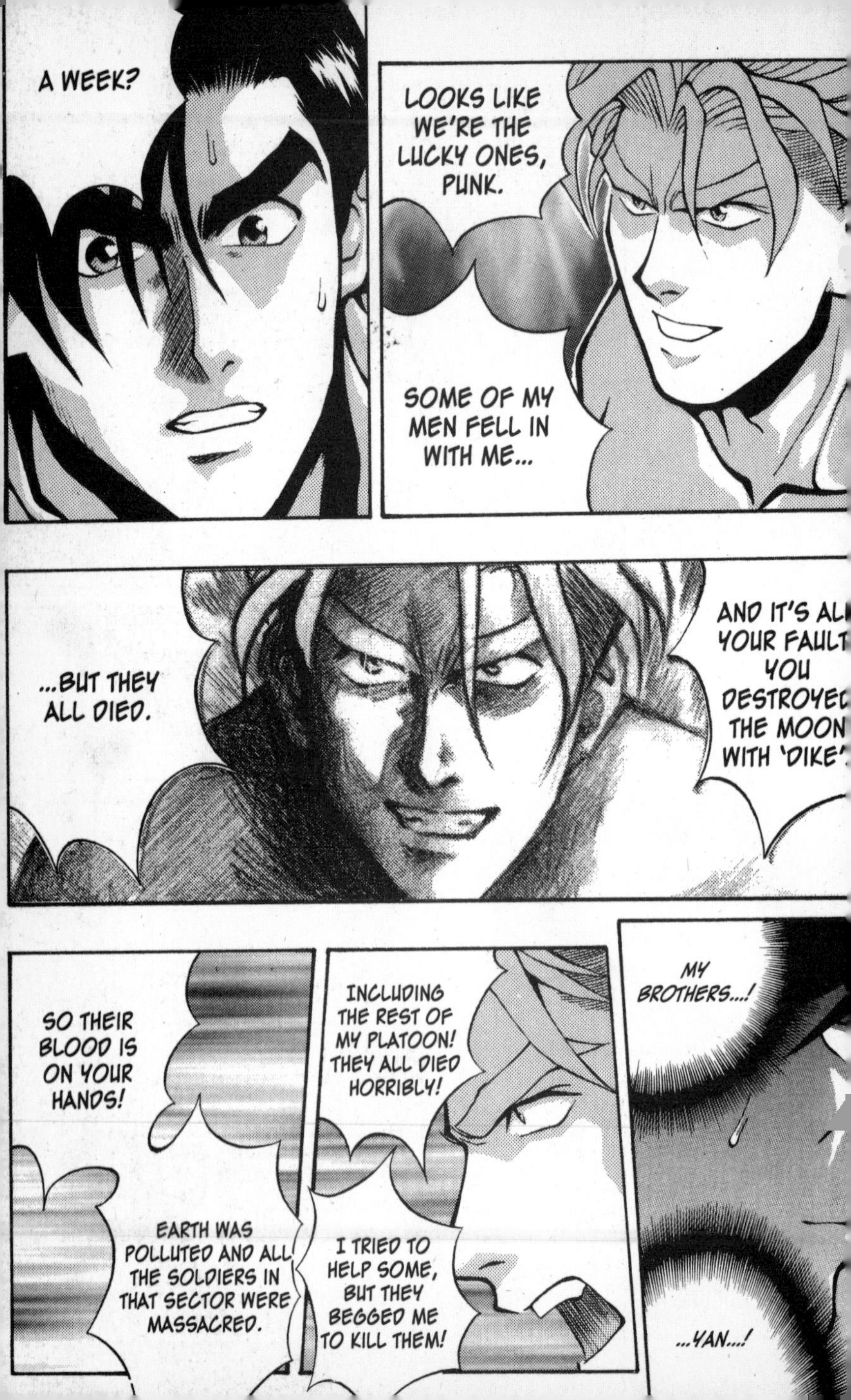
A WEEK?
LOOKS LIKE WE'RE THE LUCKY ONES, PUNK.
SOME OF MY MEN FELL IN WITH ME...
...BUT THEY ALL DIED.
AND IT'S ALL YOUR FAULT. YOU DESTROYED THE MOON WITH 'DIKE'.
SO THEIR BLOOD IS ON YOUR HANDS!
EARTH WAS POLLUTED AND ALL THE SOLDIERS IN THAT SECTOR WERE MASSACRED.
INCLUDING THE REST OF MY PLATOON! THEY ALL DIED HORRIBLY!
I TRIED TO HELP SOME, BUT THEY BEGGED ME TO KILL THEM!
MY BROTHERS...!
...YAN...!

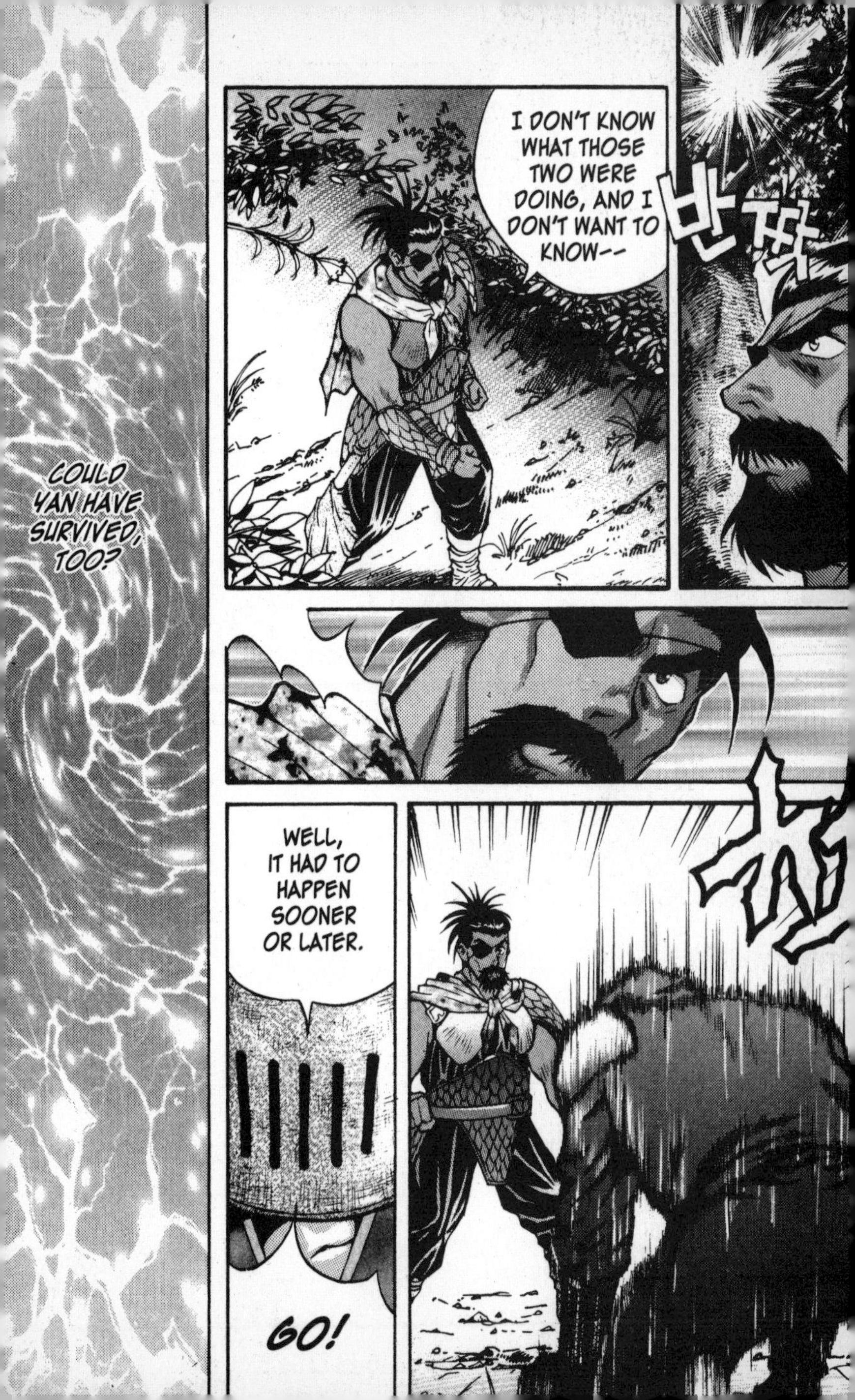
COULD YAN HAVE SURVIVED, TOO?
I DON'T KNOW WHAT THOSE TWO WERE DOING, AND I DON'T WANT TO KNOW--
WELL, IT HAD TO HAPPEN SOONER OR LATER.
GO!

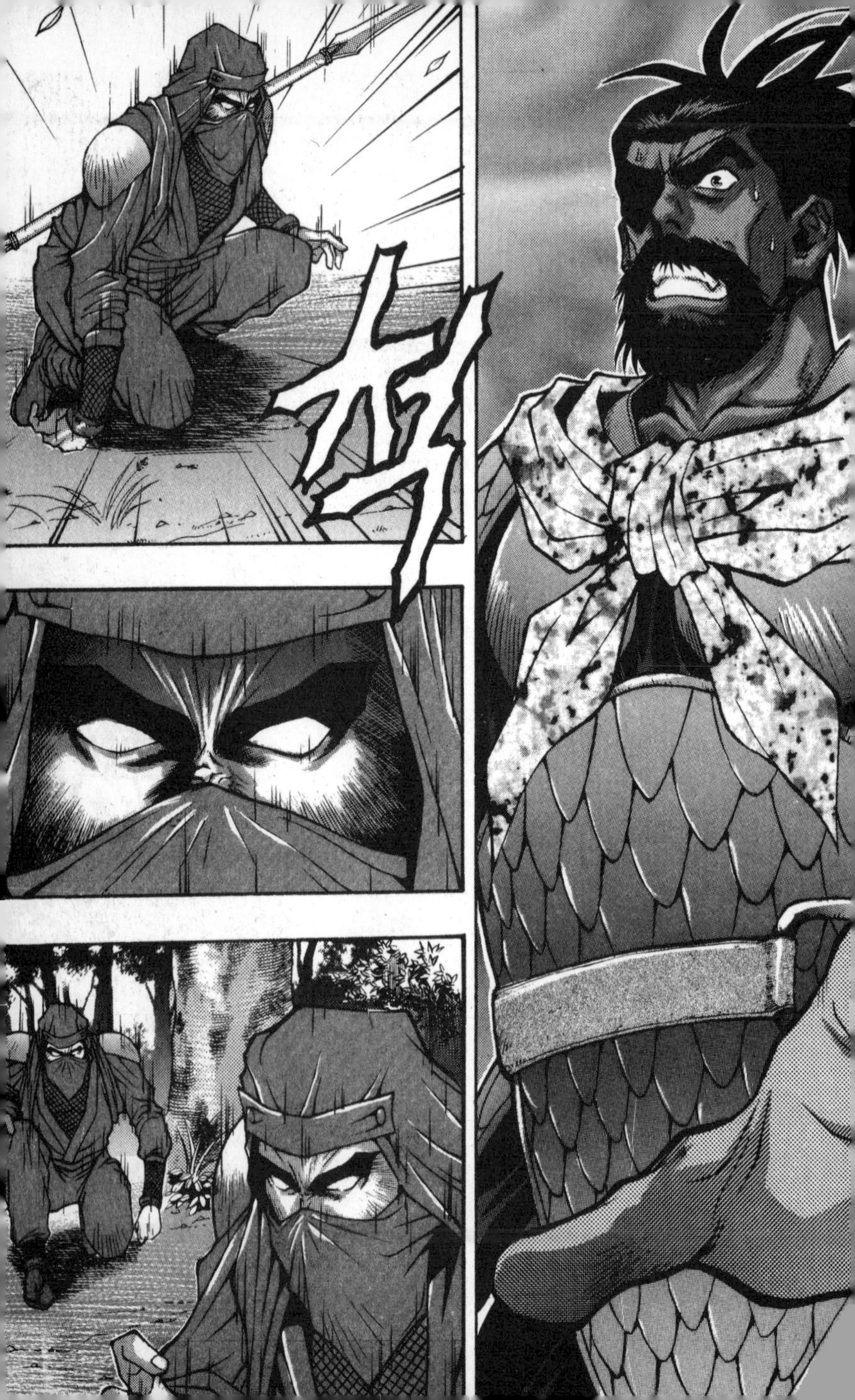

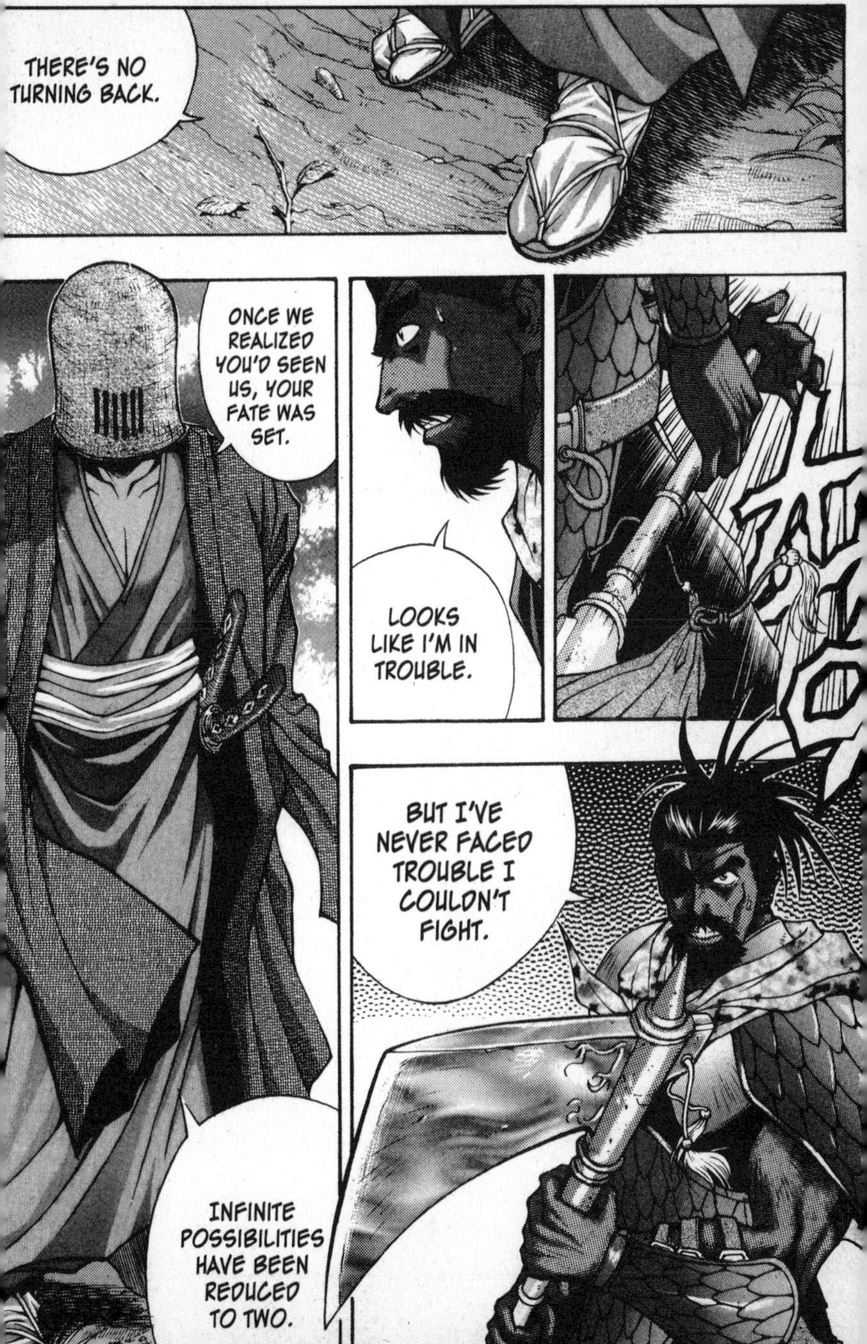
THERE'S NO TURNING BACK.
ONCE WE REALIZED YOU'D SEEN US, YOUR FATE WAS SET.
INFINITE POSSIBILITIES HAVE BEEN REDUCED TO TWO.
LOOKS LIKE I'M IN TROUBLE.
BUT I'VE NEVER FACED TROUBLE I COULDN'T FIGHT.

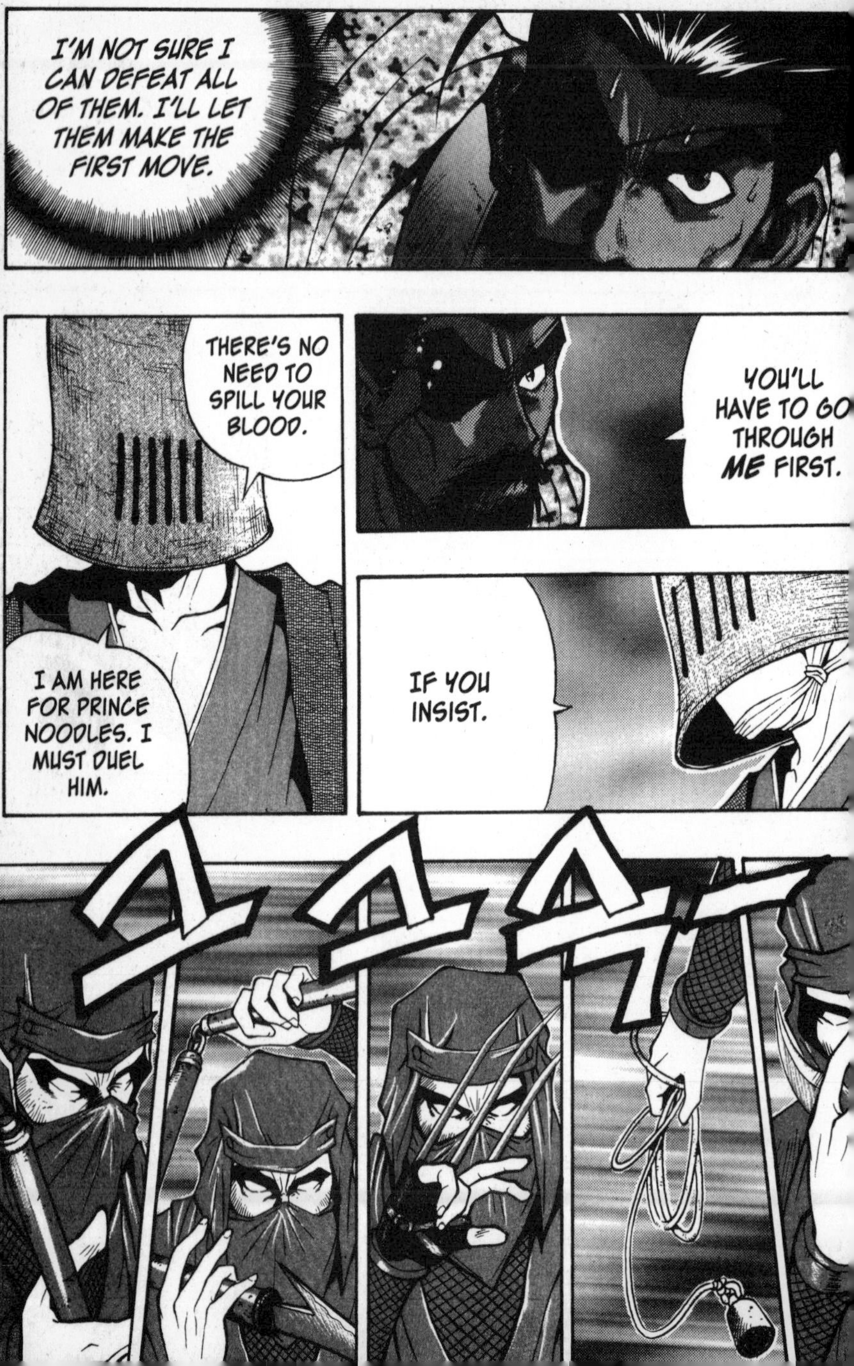
I'M NOT SURE I CAN DEFEAT ALL OF THEM. I'LL LET THEM MAKE THE FIRST MOVE.
THERE'S NO NEED TO SPILL YOUR BLOOD.
I AM HERE FOR PRINCE NOODLES. I MUST DUEL HIM.
YOU'LL HAVE TO GO THROUGH ME FIRST.
IF YOU INSIST.

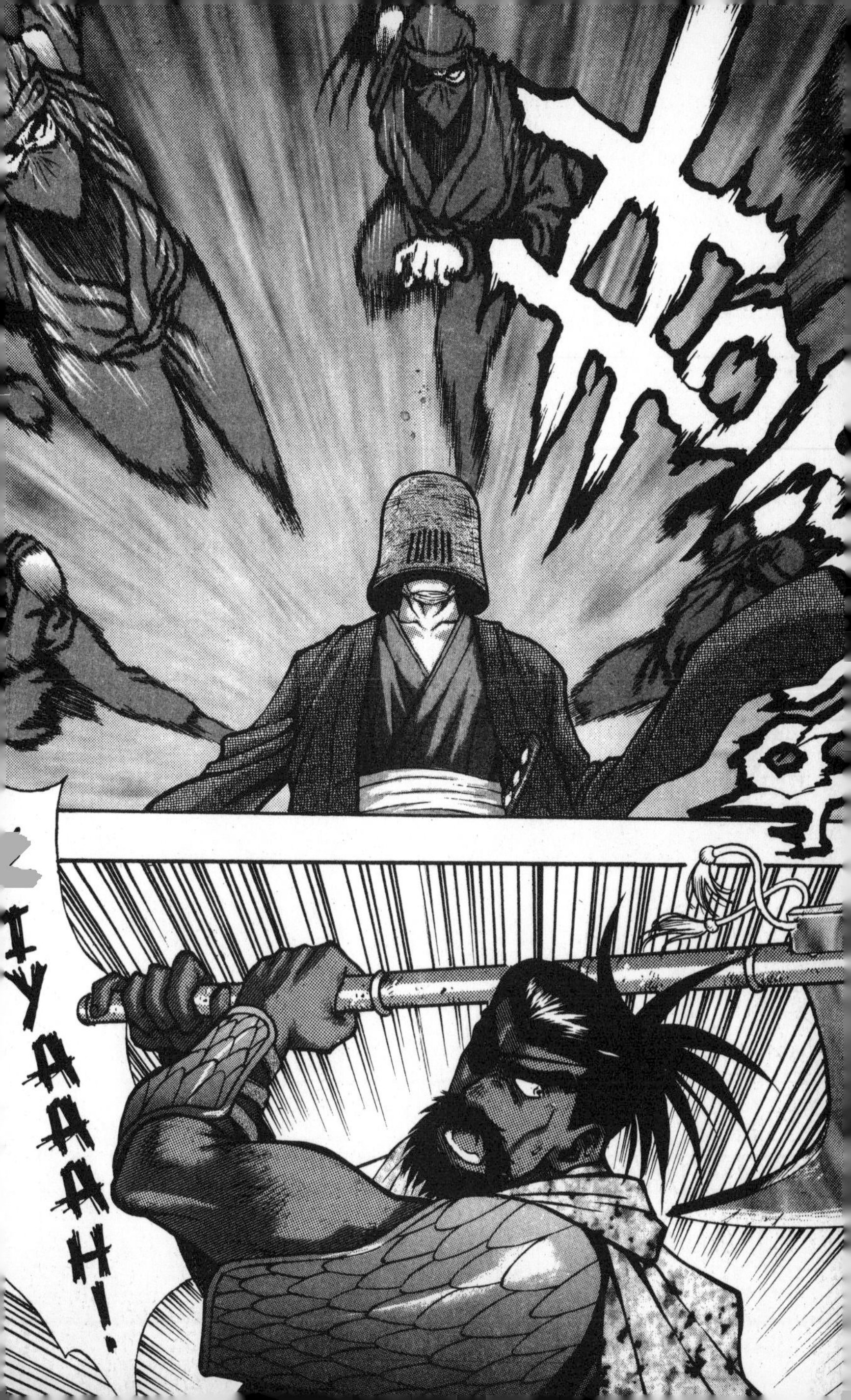
IYAAAH!

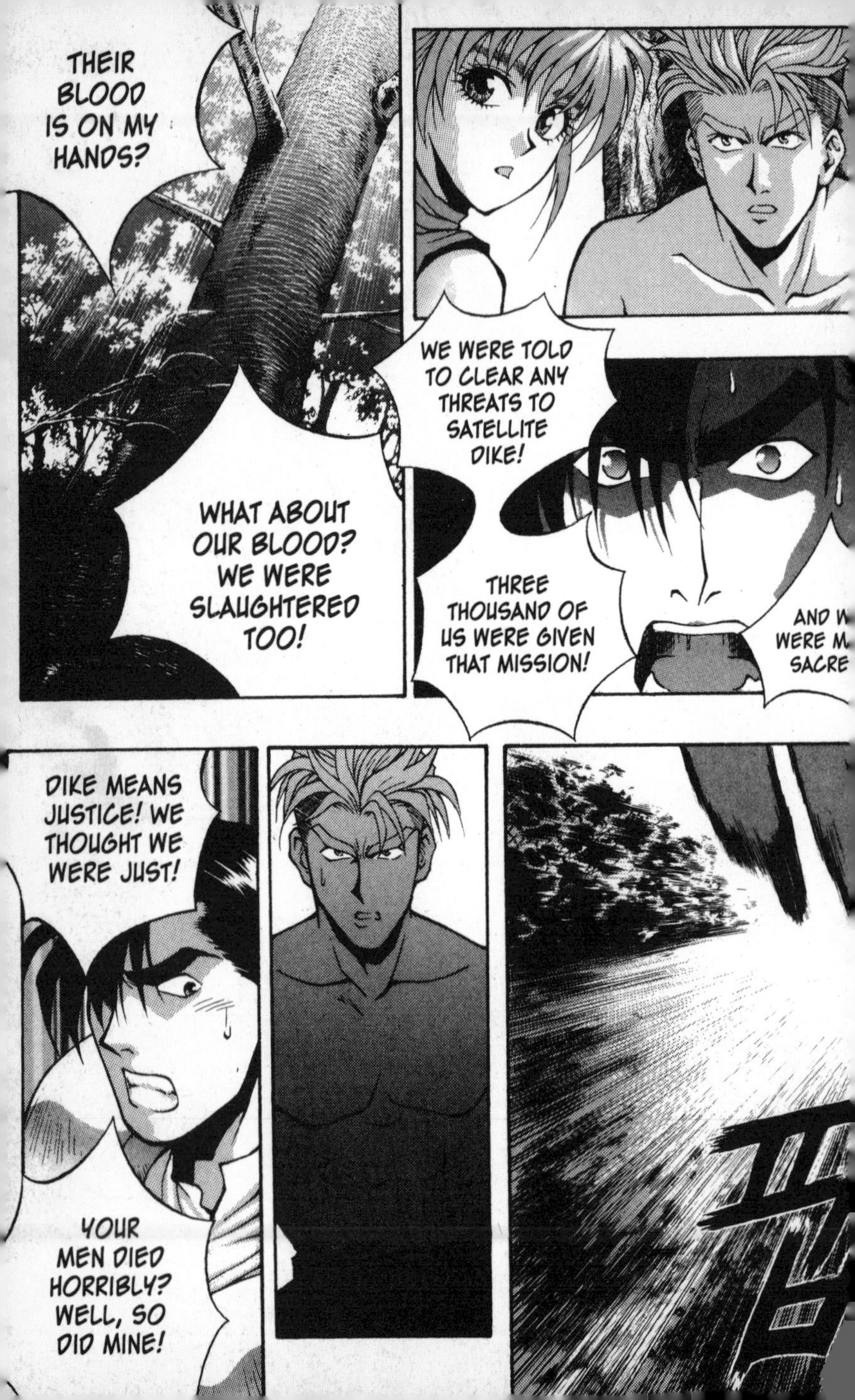
THEIR BLOOD IS ON MY HANDS?
WHAT ABOUT OUR BLOOD? WE WERE SLAUGHTERED TOO!
WE WERE TOLD TO CLEAR ANY THREATS TO SATELLITE DIKE!
THREE THOUSAND OF US WERE GIVEN THAT MISSION!
AND W WERE MA SACRE
DIKE MEANS JUSTICE! WE THOUGHT WE WERE JUST!
YOUR MEN DIED HORRIBLY? WELL, SO DID MINE!

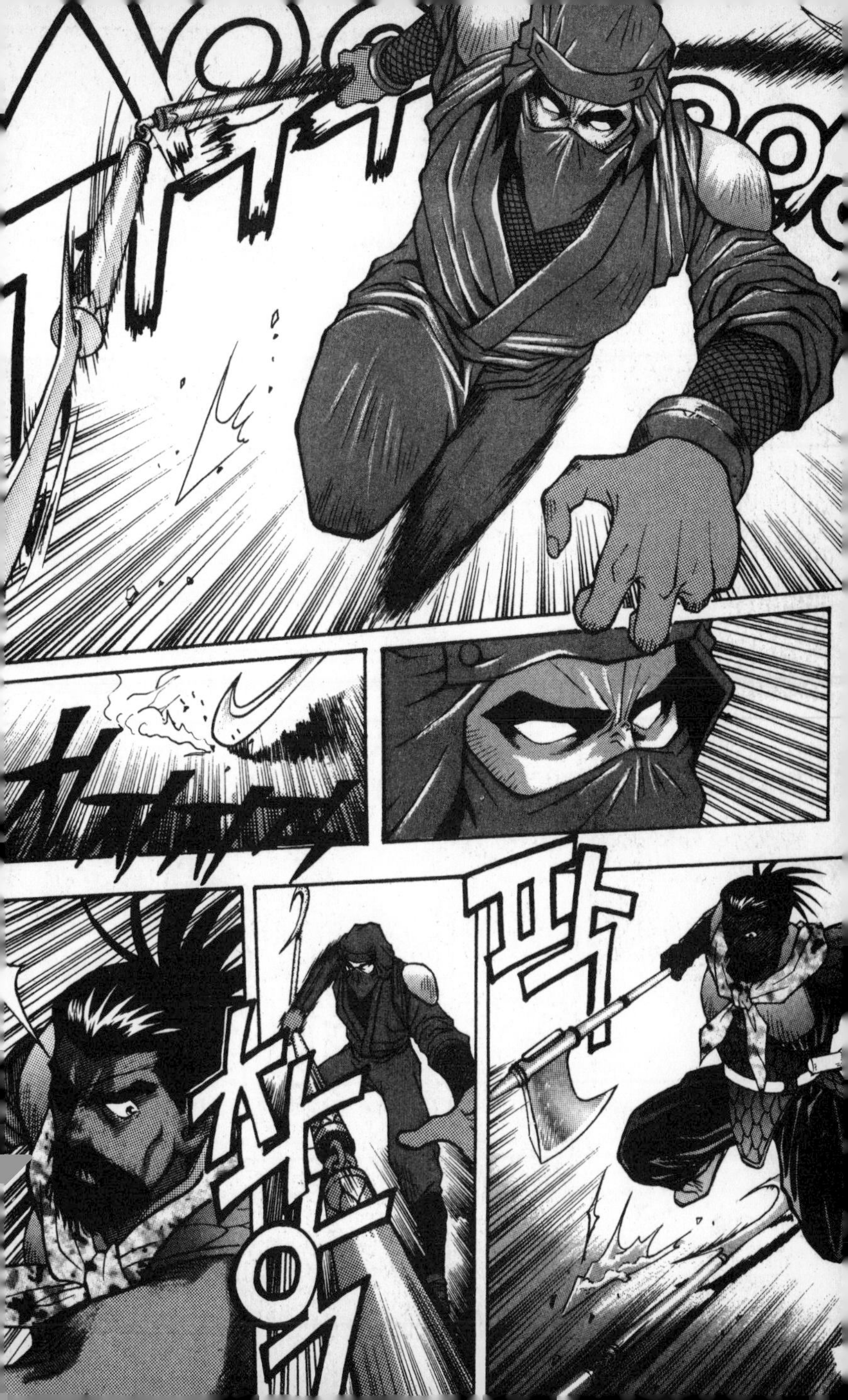

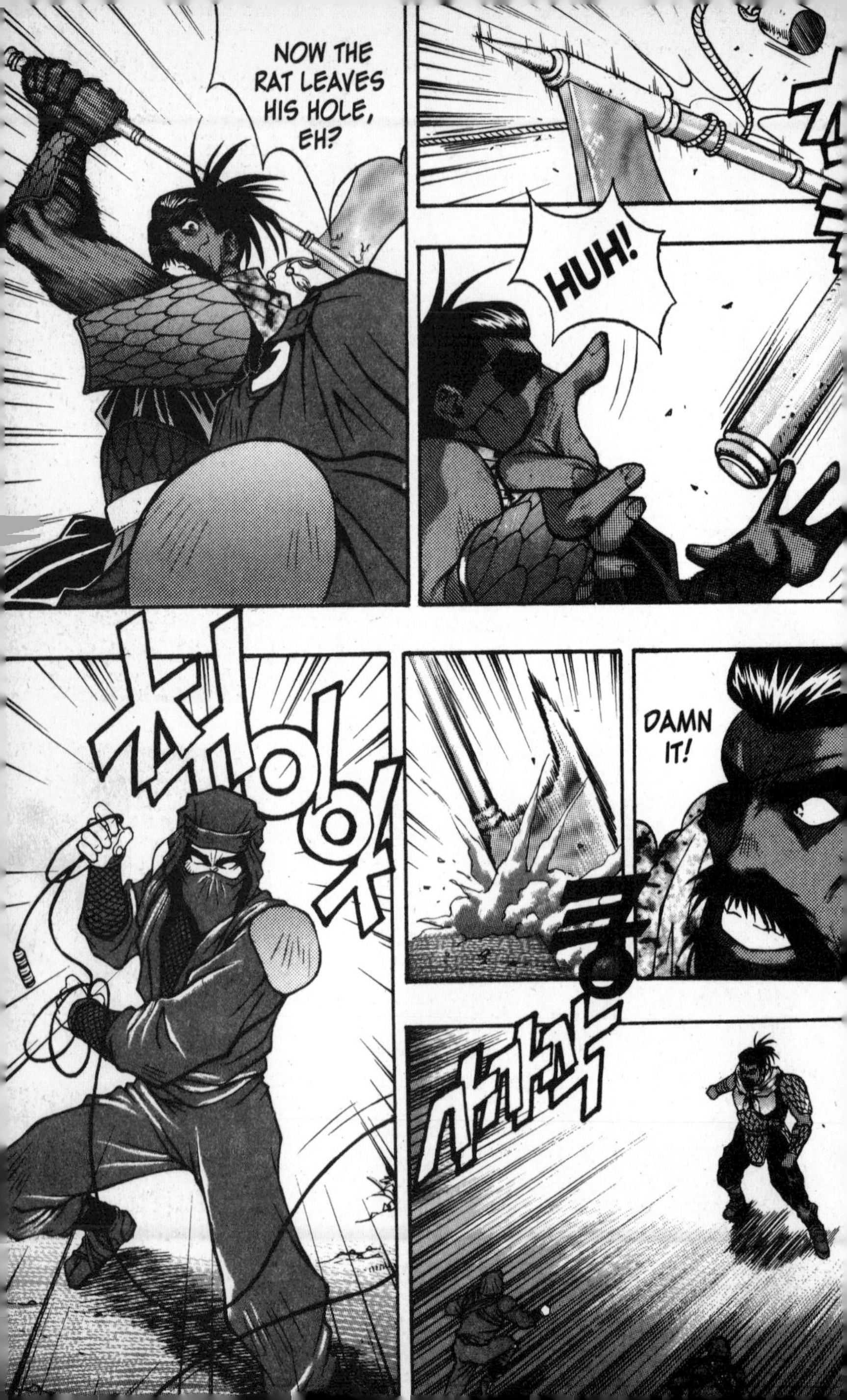
NOW THE RAT LEAVES HIS HOLE, EH?
HUH!
DAMN IT!

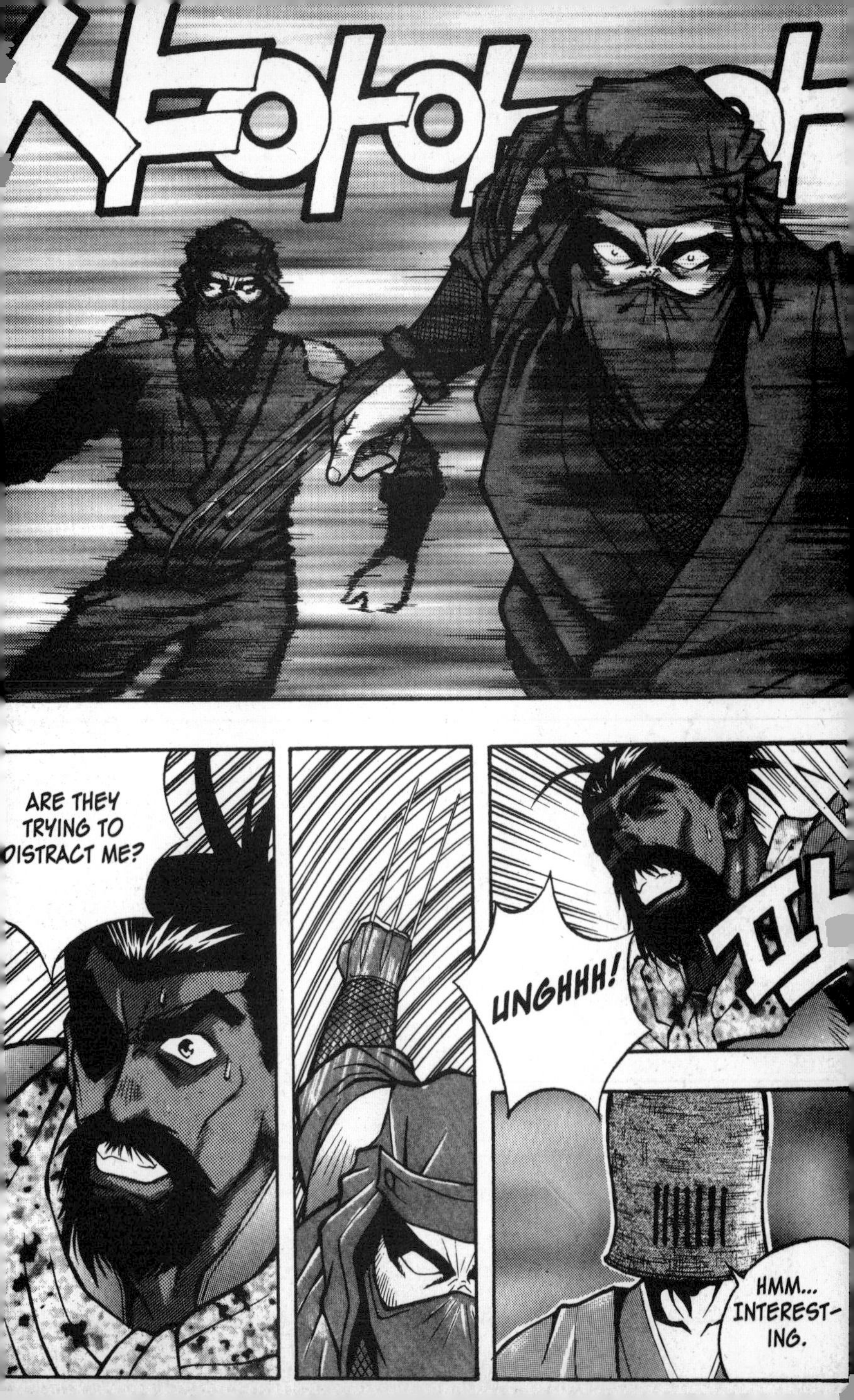
ARE THEY TRYING TO DISTRACT ME?
UNGHHH!
HMM... INTERESTING.

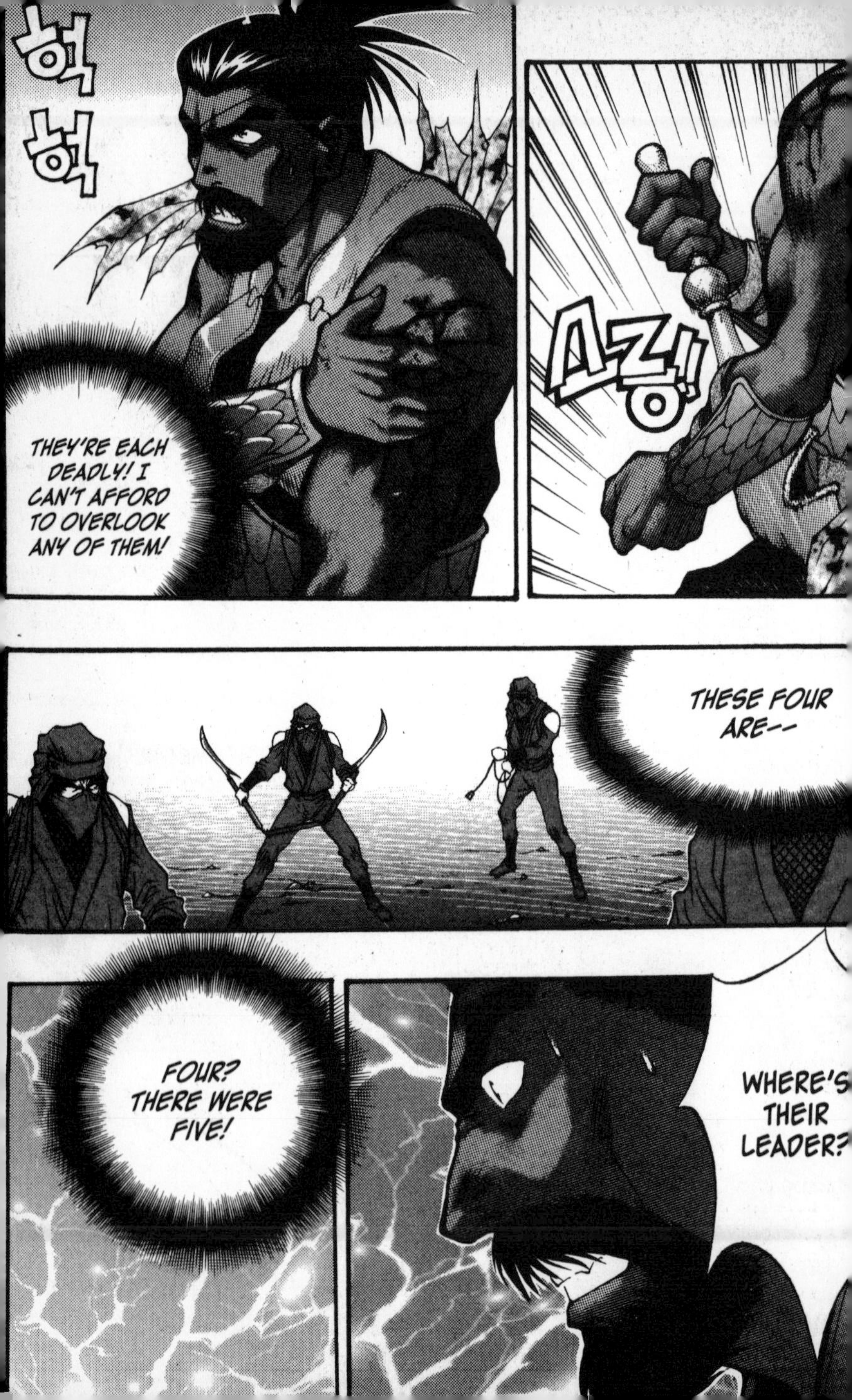
헉 헉
THEY'RE EACH DEADLY! I CAN'T AFFORD TO OVERLOOK ANY OF THEM!
THESE FOUR ARE--
FOUR? THERE WERE FIVE!
WHERE'S THEIR LEADER?

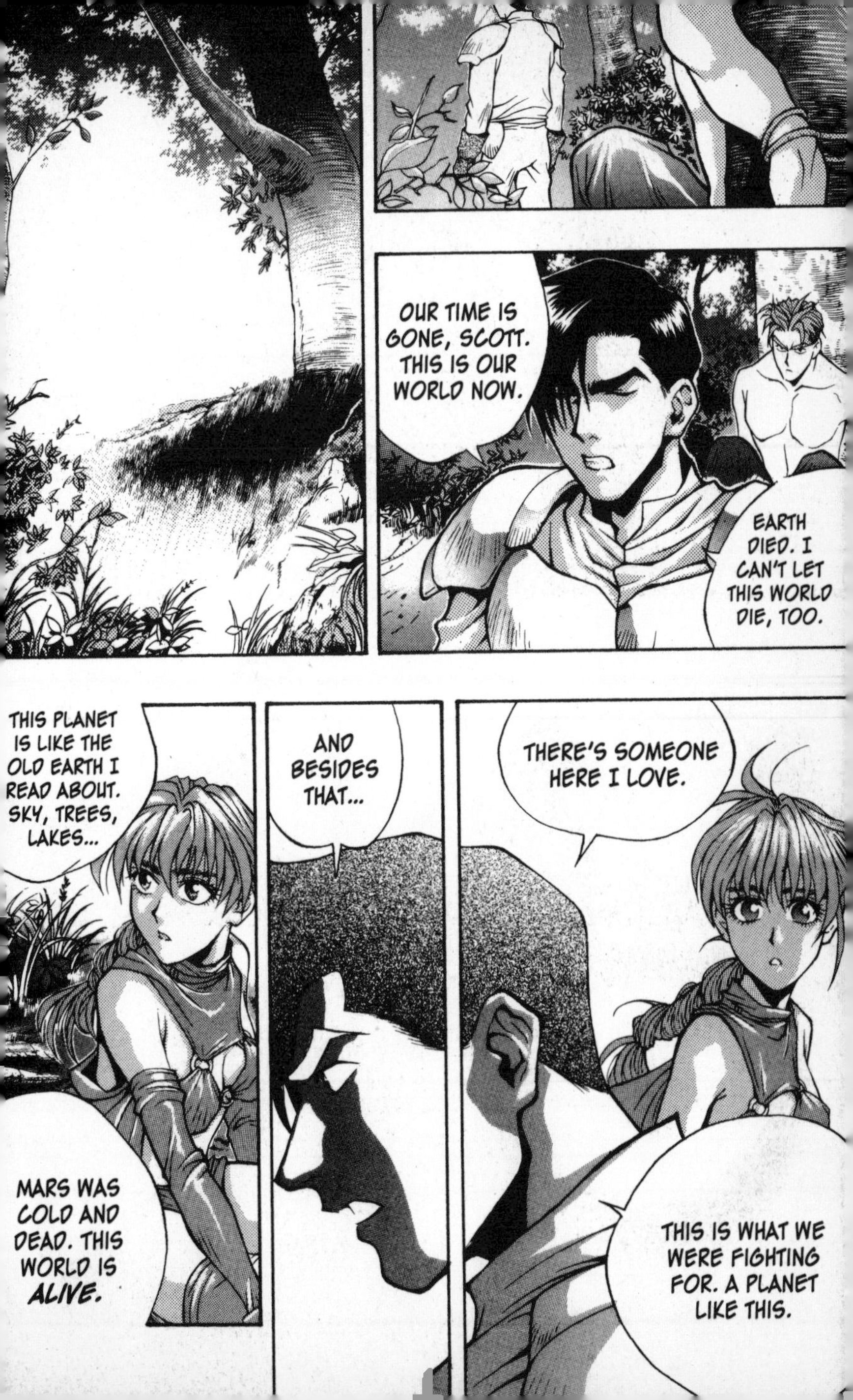
OUR TIME IS GONE, SCOTT. THIS IS OUR WORLD NOW.
EARTH DIED. I CAN'T LET THIS WORLD DIE, TOO.
THIS PLANET IS LIKE THE OLD EARTH I READ ABOUT. SKY, TREES, LAKES...
MARS WAS COLD AND DEAD. THIS WORLD IS *ALIVE*.
AND BESIDES THAT...
THERE'S SOMEONE HERE I LOVE.
THIS IS WHAT WE WERE FIGHTING FOR. A PLANET LIKE THIS.

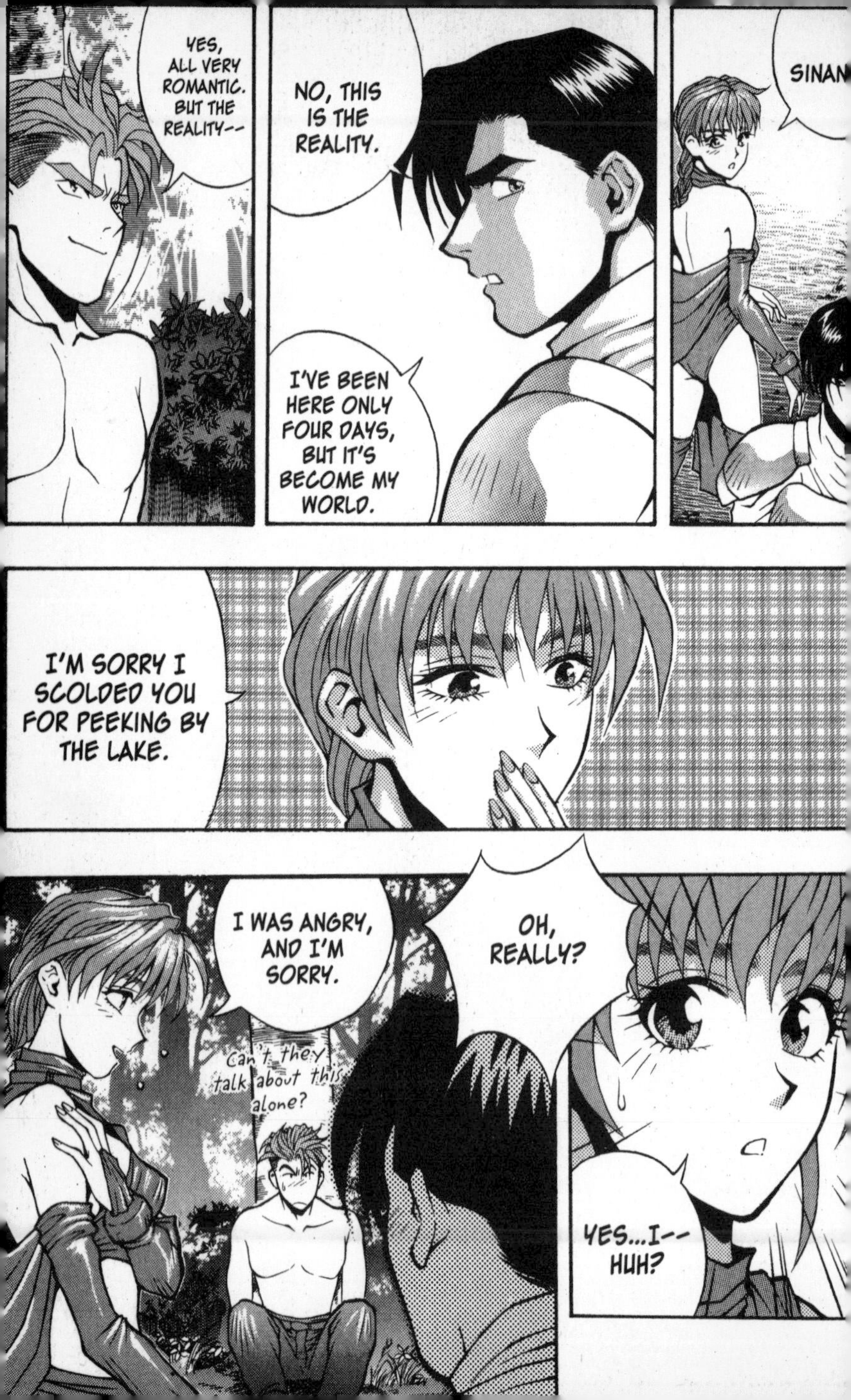
YES, ALL VERY ROMANTIC. BUT THE REALITY--
NO, THIS IS THE REALITY.
I'VE BEEN HERE ONLY FOUR DAYS, BUT IT'S BECOME MY WORLD.
SINAN
I'M SORRY I SCOLDED YOU FOR PEEKING BY THE LAKE.
I WAS ANGRY, AND I'M SORRY.
Can't they talk about this alone?
OH, REALLY?
YES...I-- HUH?

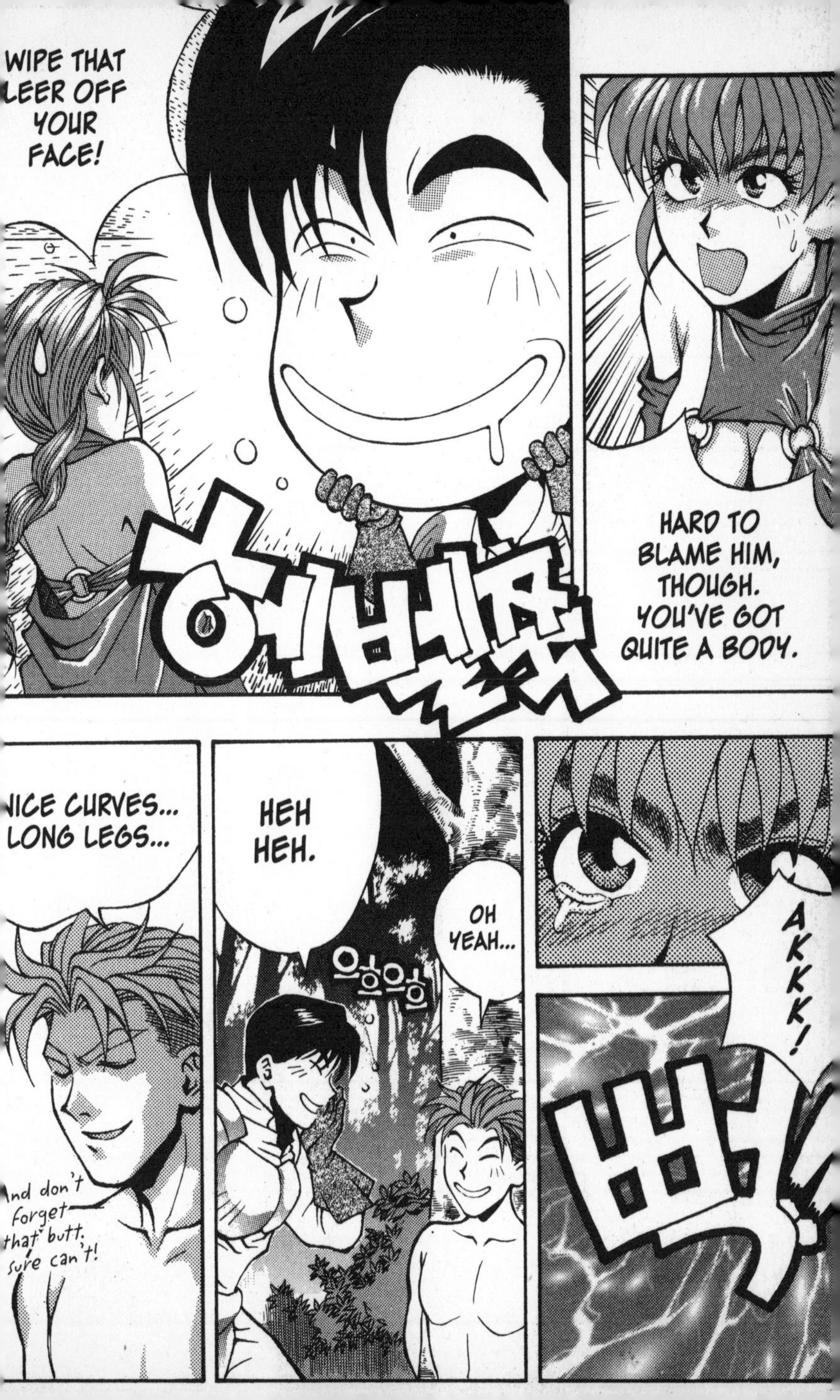
WIPE THAT LEER OFF YOUR FACE!
HARD TO BLAME HIM, THOUGH. YOU'VE GOT QUITE A BODY.
NICE CURVES... LONG LEGS...
And don't forget that butt, sure can't!
HEH HEH.
OH YEAH...
AKKK!

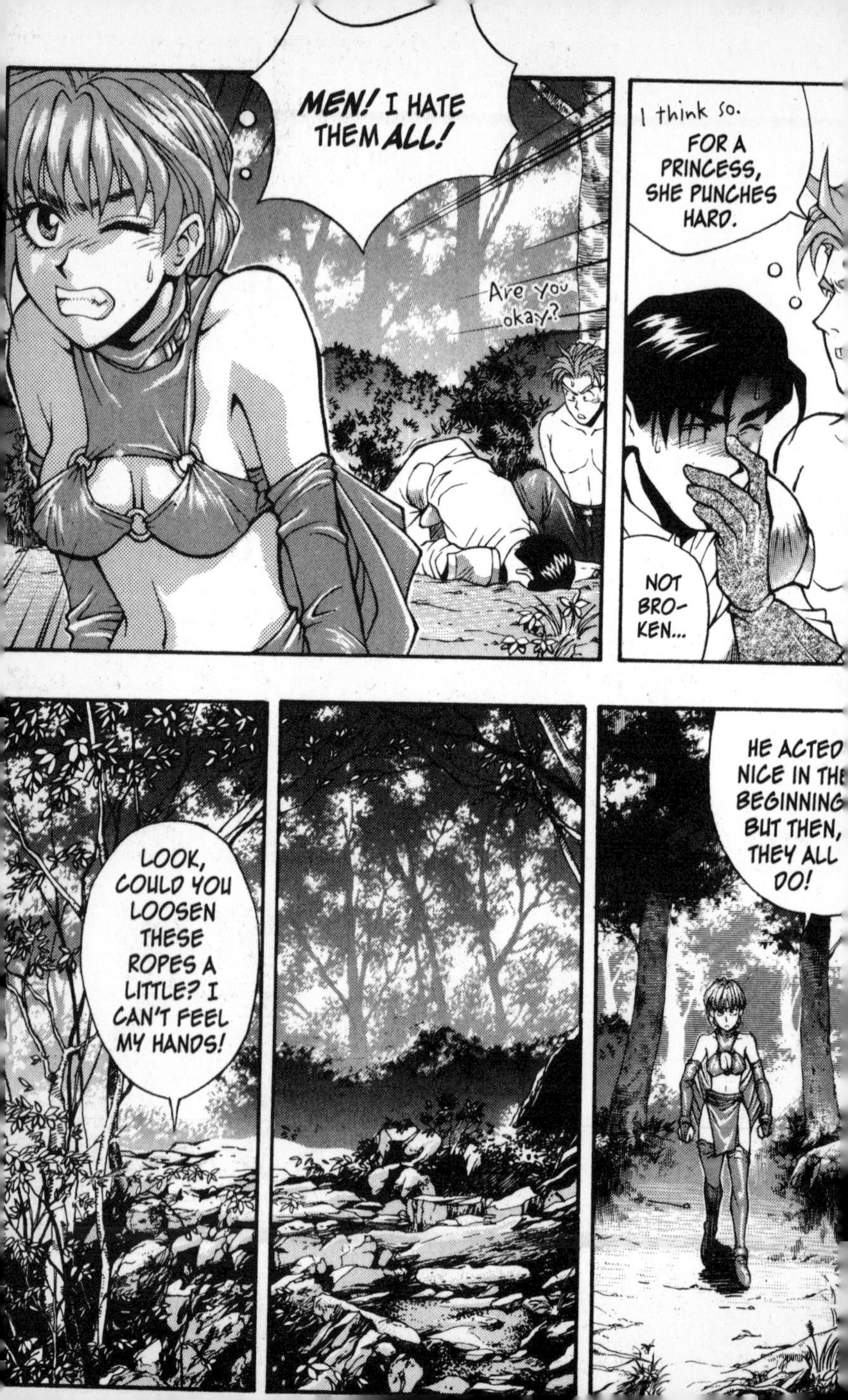
MEN! I HATE THEM ALL!
Are you okay?
I think so.
FOR A PRINCESS, SHE PUNCHES HARD.
NOT BRO- KEN...
LOOK, COULD YOU LOOSEN THESE ROPES A LITTLE? I CAN'T FEEL MY HANDS!
HE ACTED NICE IN THE BEGINNING BUT THEN, THEY ALL DO!

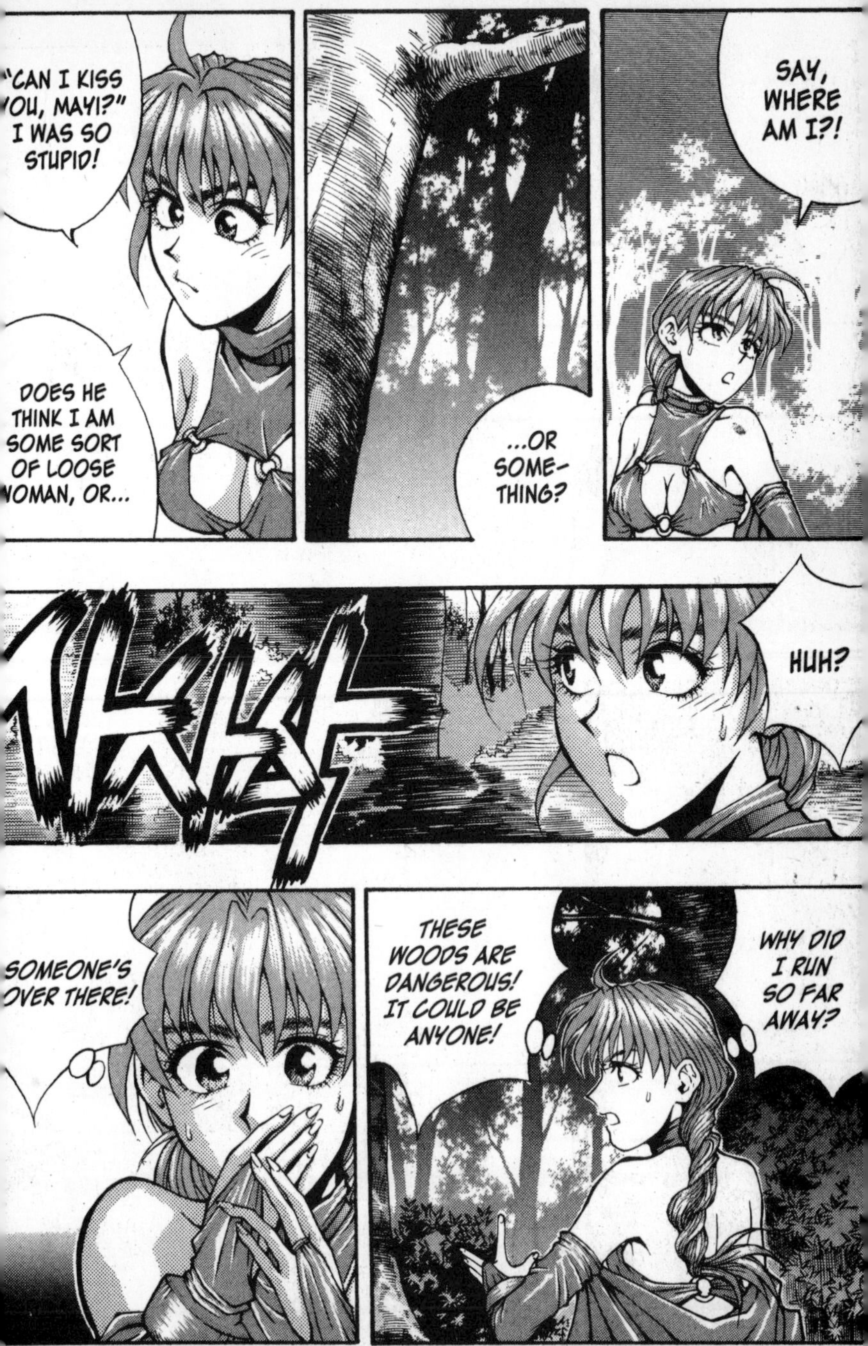
"CAN I KISS YOU, MAYI?" I WAS SO STUPID!
DOES HE THINK I AM SOME SORT OF LOOSE WOMAN, OR...
...OR SOME-THING?
SAY, WHERE AM I?!
HUH?
SOMEONE'S OVER THERE!
THESE WOODS ARE DANGEROUS! IT COULD BE ANYONE!
WHY DID I RUN SO FAR AWAY?

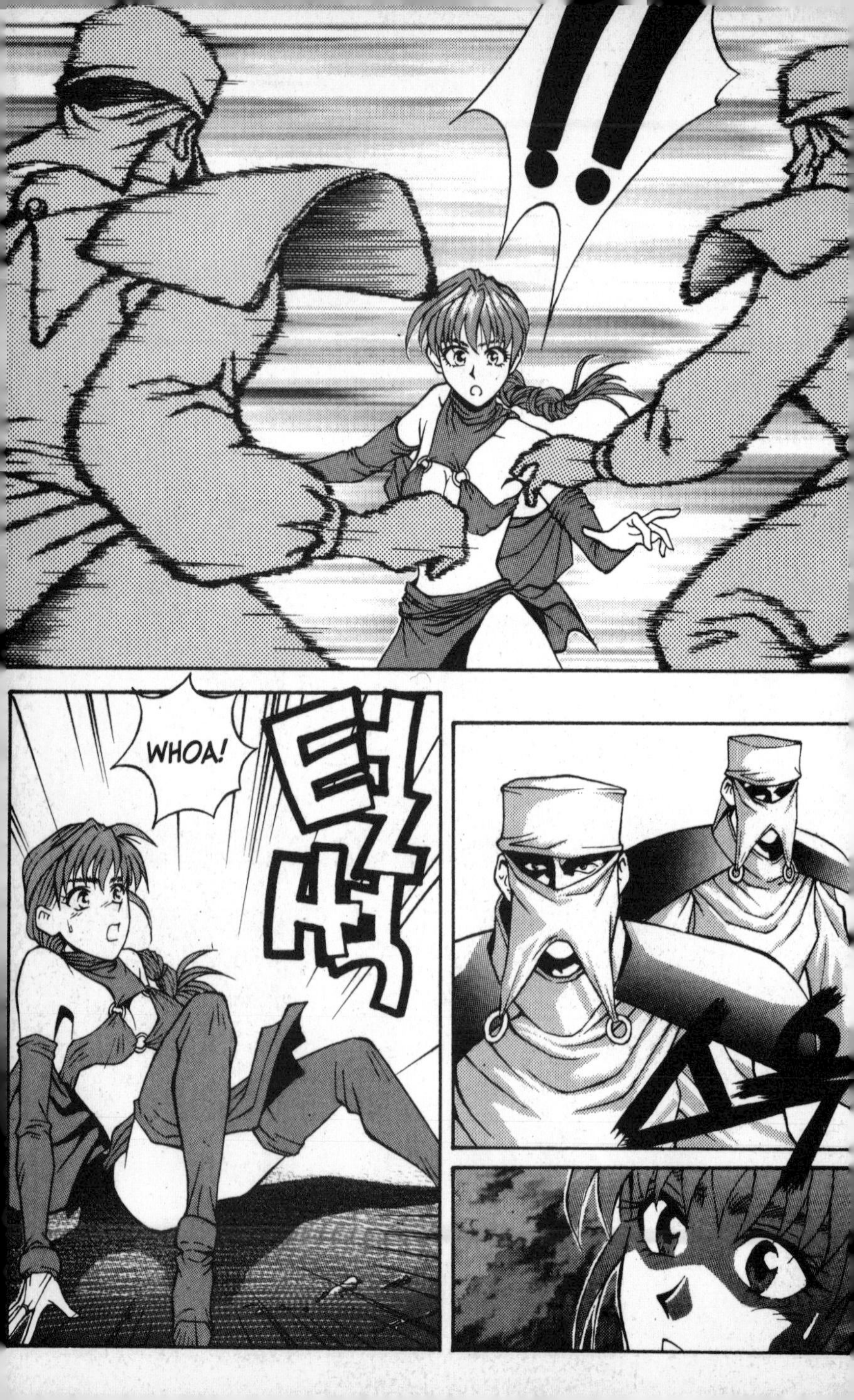
!!
WHOA!

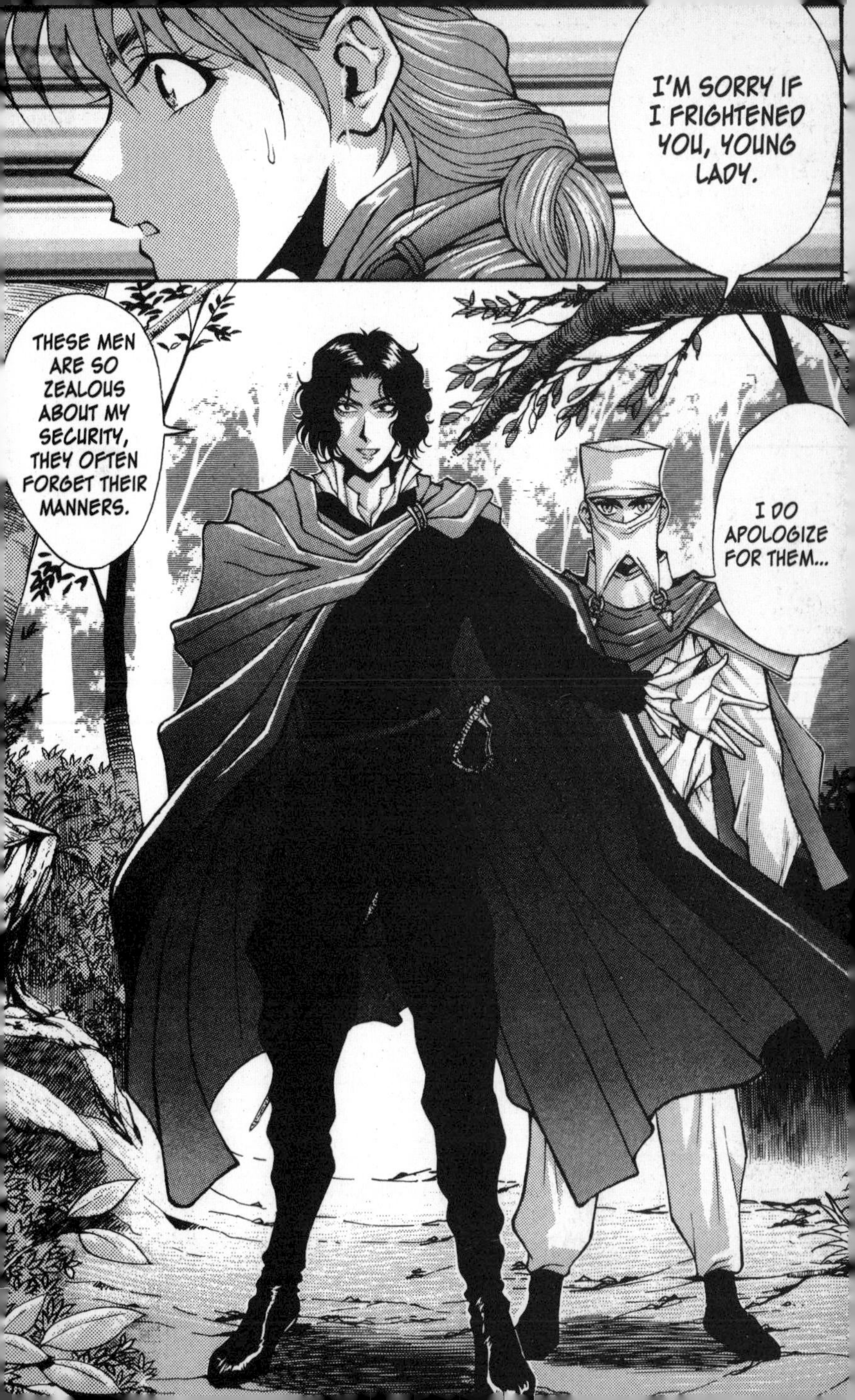
I'M SORRY IF I FRIGHTENED YOU, YOUNG LADY.
THESE MEN ARE SO ZEALOUS ABOUT MY SECURITY, THEY OFTEN FORGET THEIR MANNERS.
I DO APOLOGIZE FOR THEM...

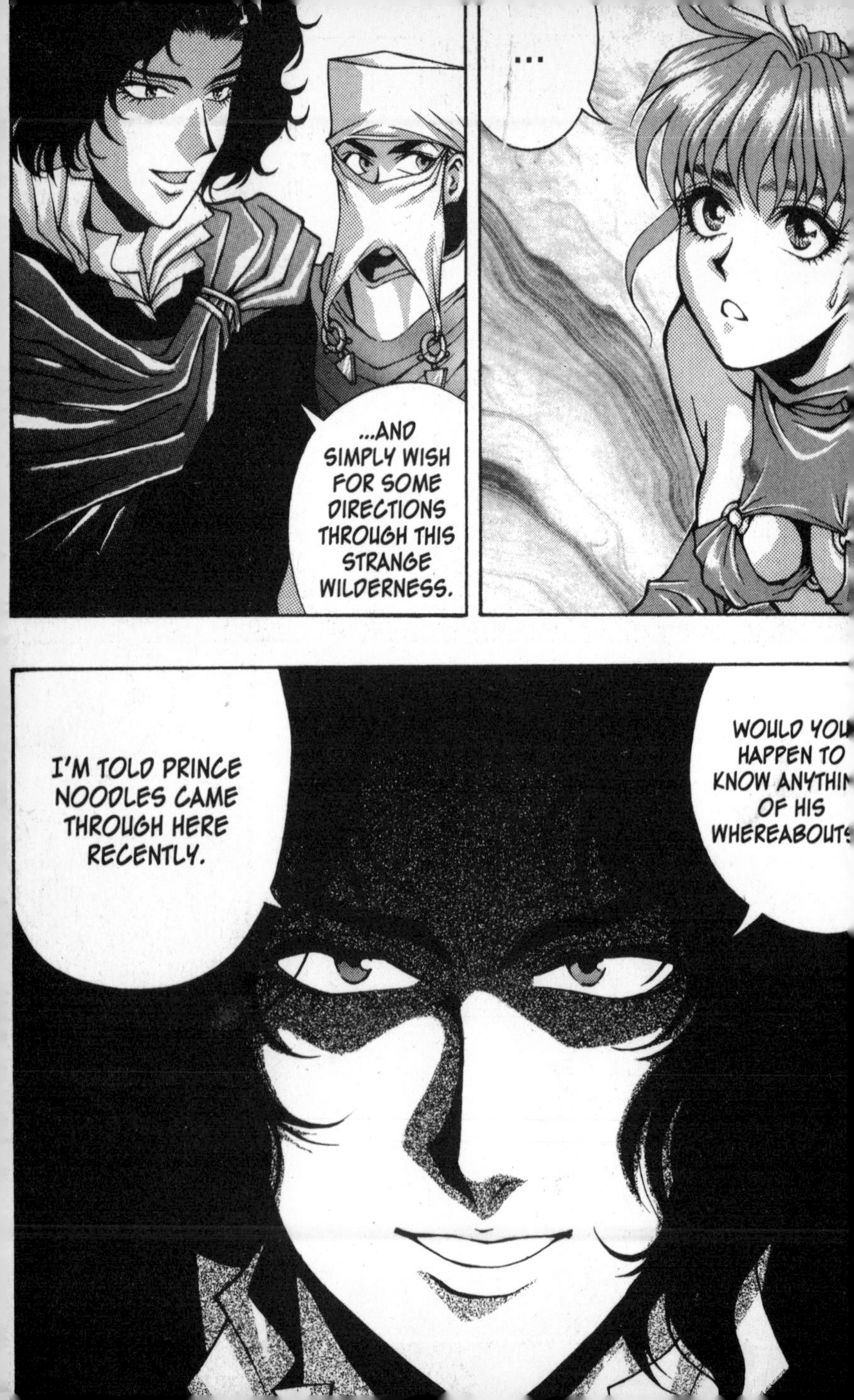
...
...AND SIMPLY WISH FOR SOME DIRECTIONS THROUGH THIS STRANGE WILDERNESS.
I'M TOLD PRINCE NOODLES CAME THROUGH HERE RECENTLY.
WOULD YOU HAPPEN TO KNOW ANYTHIN OF HIS WHEREABOUTS

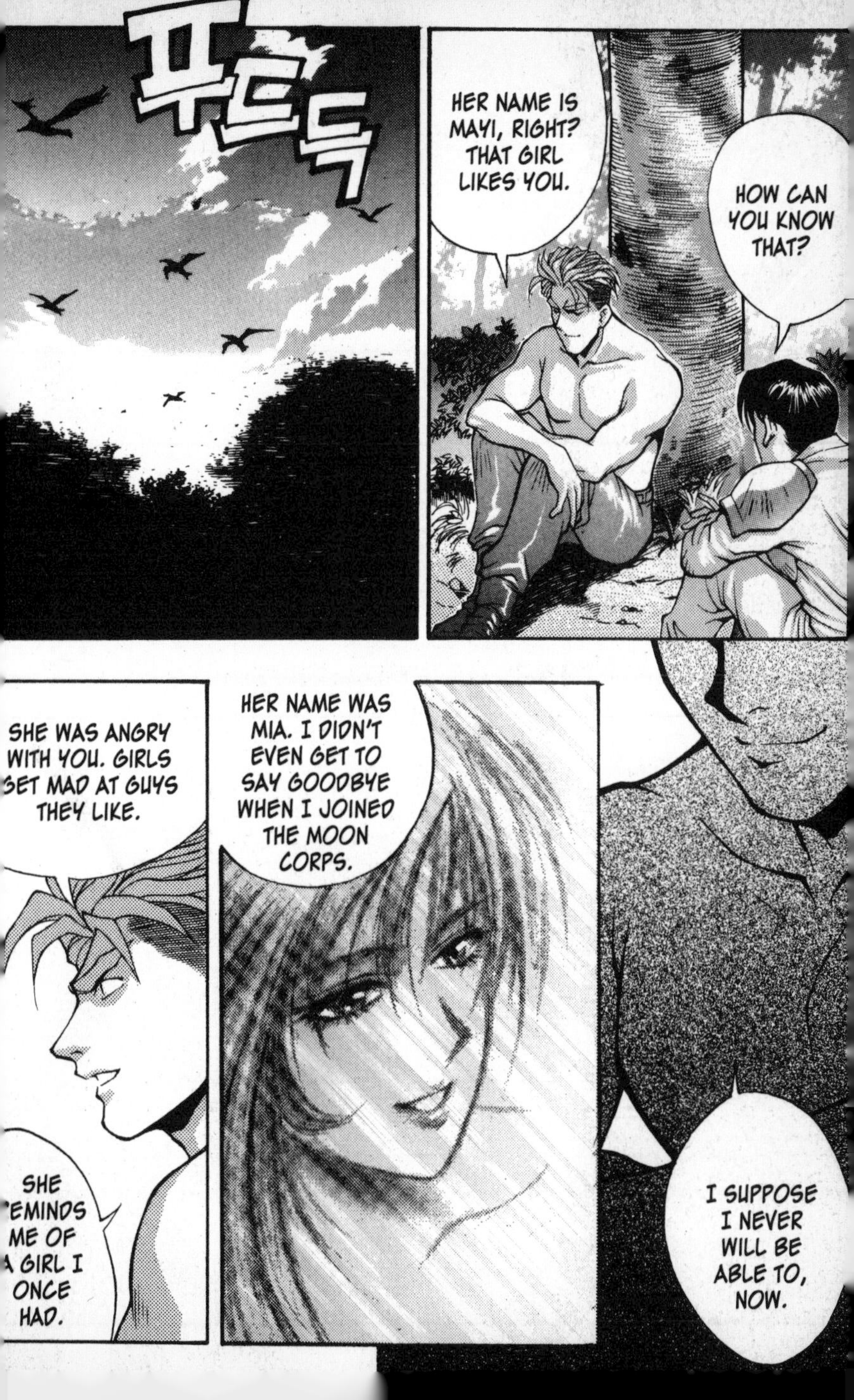

푸드득
HER NAME IS MAYI, RIGHT? THAT GIRL LIKES YOU.
HOW CAN YOU KNOW THAT?
SHE WAS ANGRY WITH YOU. GIRLS GET MAD AT GUYS THEY LIKE.
SHE REMINDS ME OF A GIRL I ONCE HAD.
HER NAME WAS MIA. I DIDN'T EVEN GET TO SAY GOODBYE WHEN I JOINED THE MOON CORPS.
I SUPPOSE I NEVER WILL BE ABLE TO, NOW.

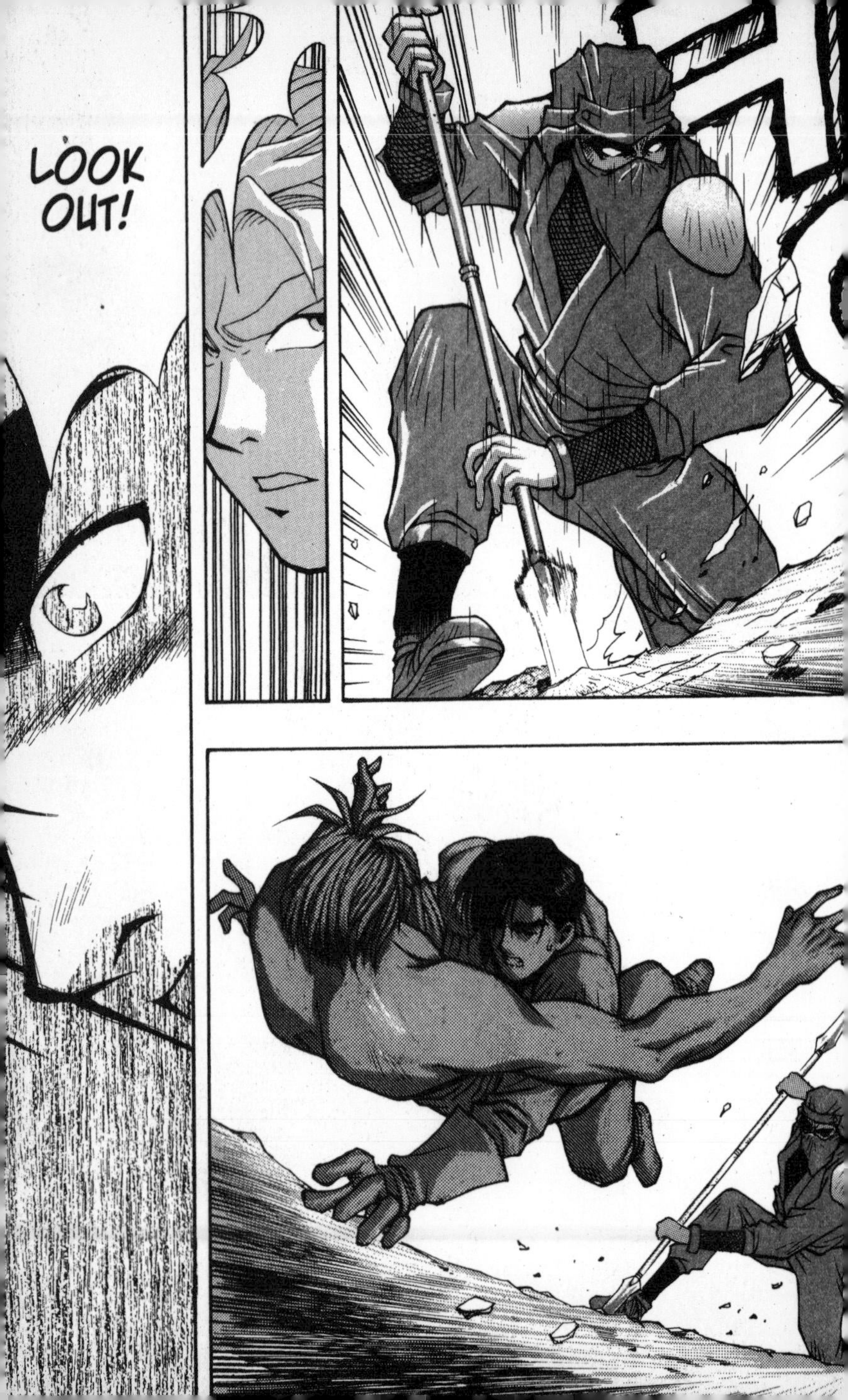
LOOK OUT!

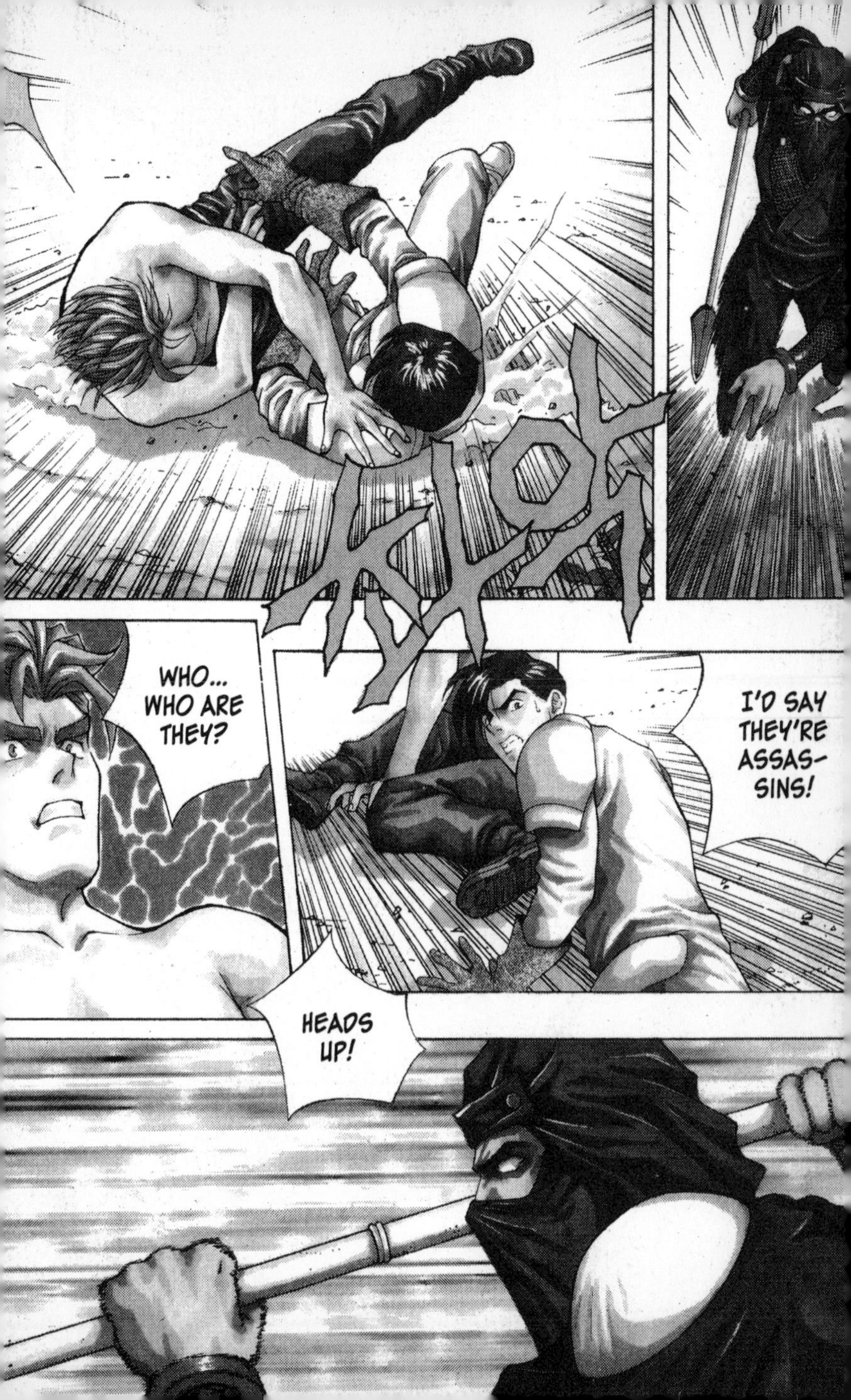
WHO... WHO ARE THEY?
I'D SAY THEY'RE ASSAS-SINS!
HEADS UP!

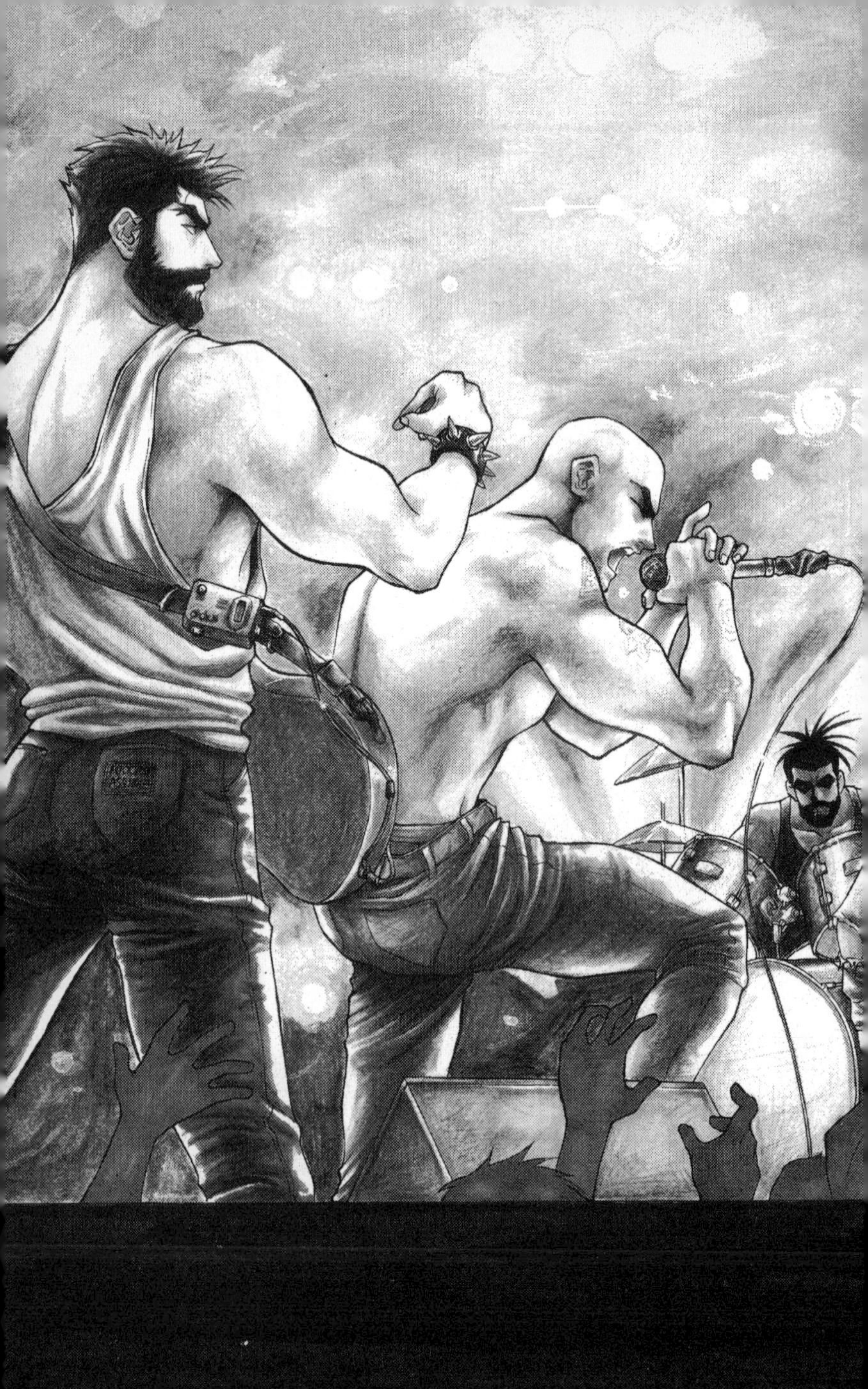

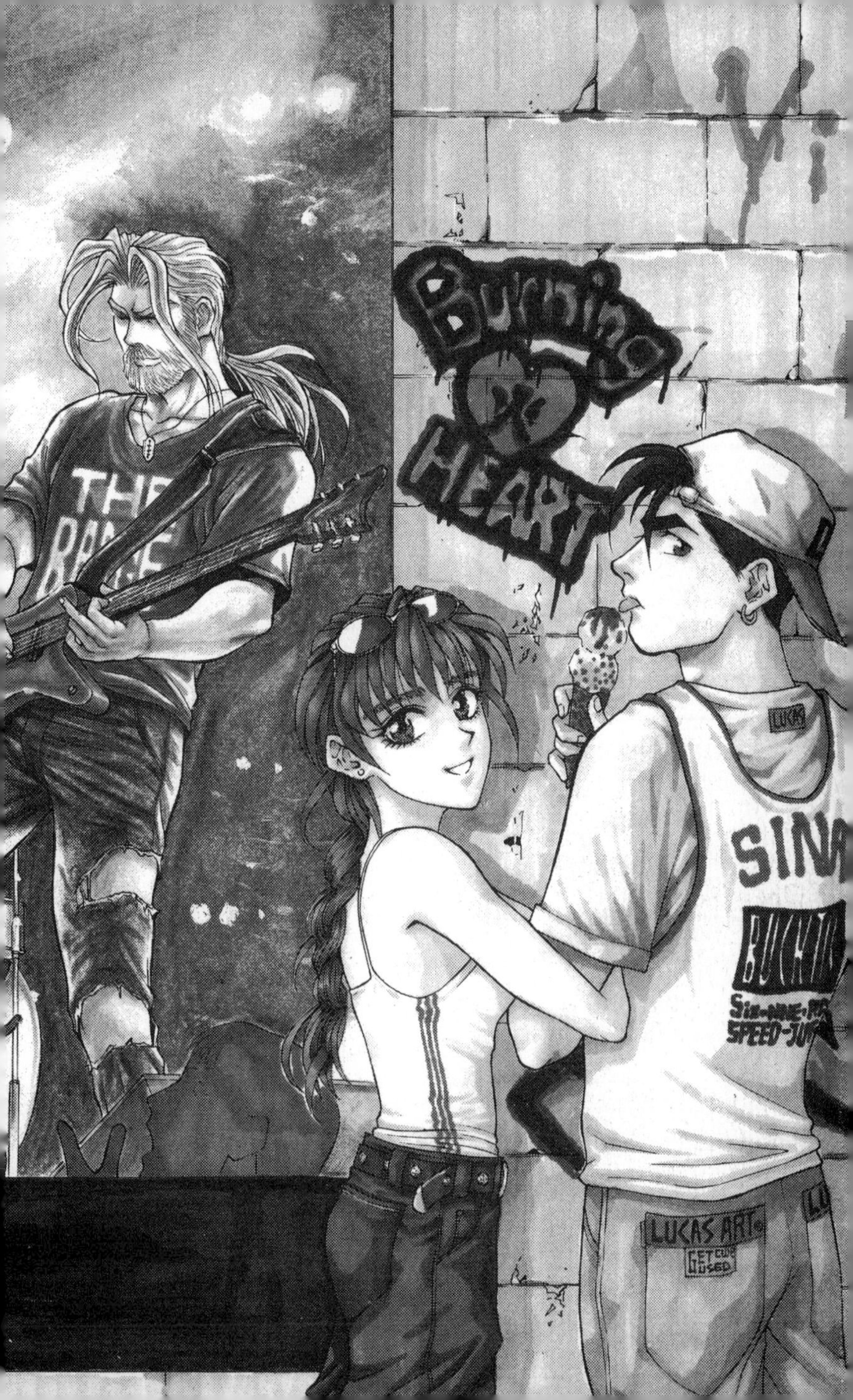
HEART
LUCAS
LUCAS ART

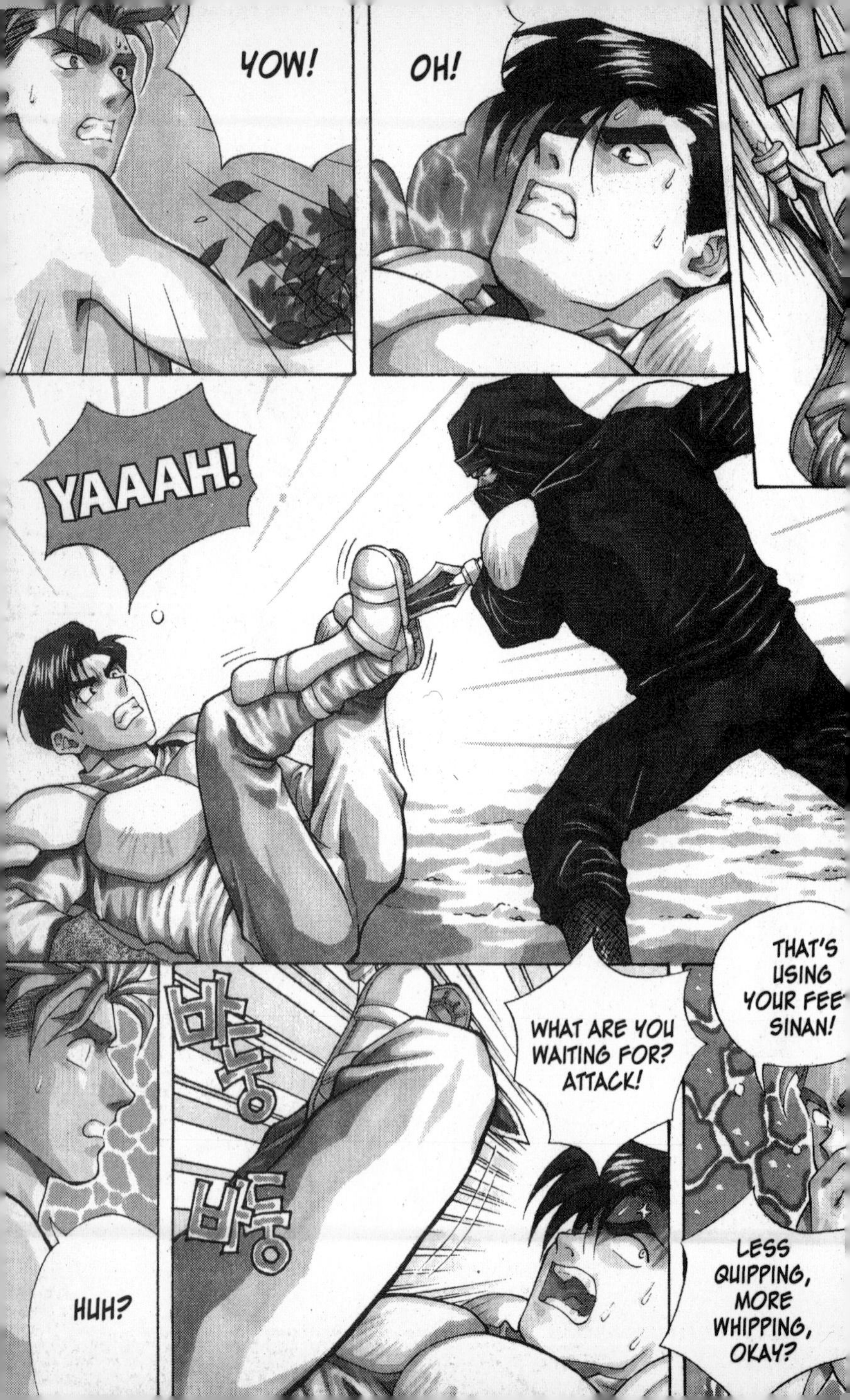
YOW!
OH!
YAAAH!
HUH?
바둥
바둥
WHAT ARE YOU WAITING FOR? ATTACK!
THAT'S USING YOUR FEE SINAN!
LESS QUIPPING, MORE WHIPPING, OKAY?

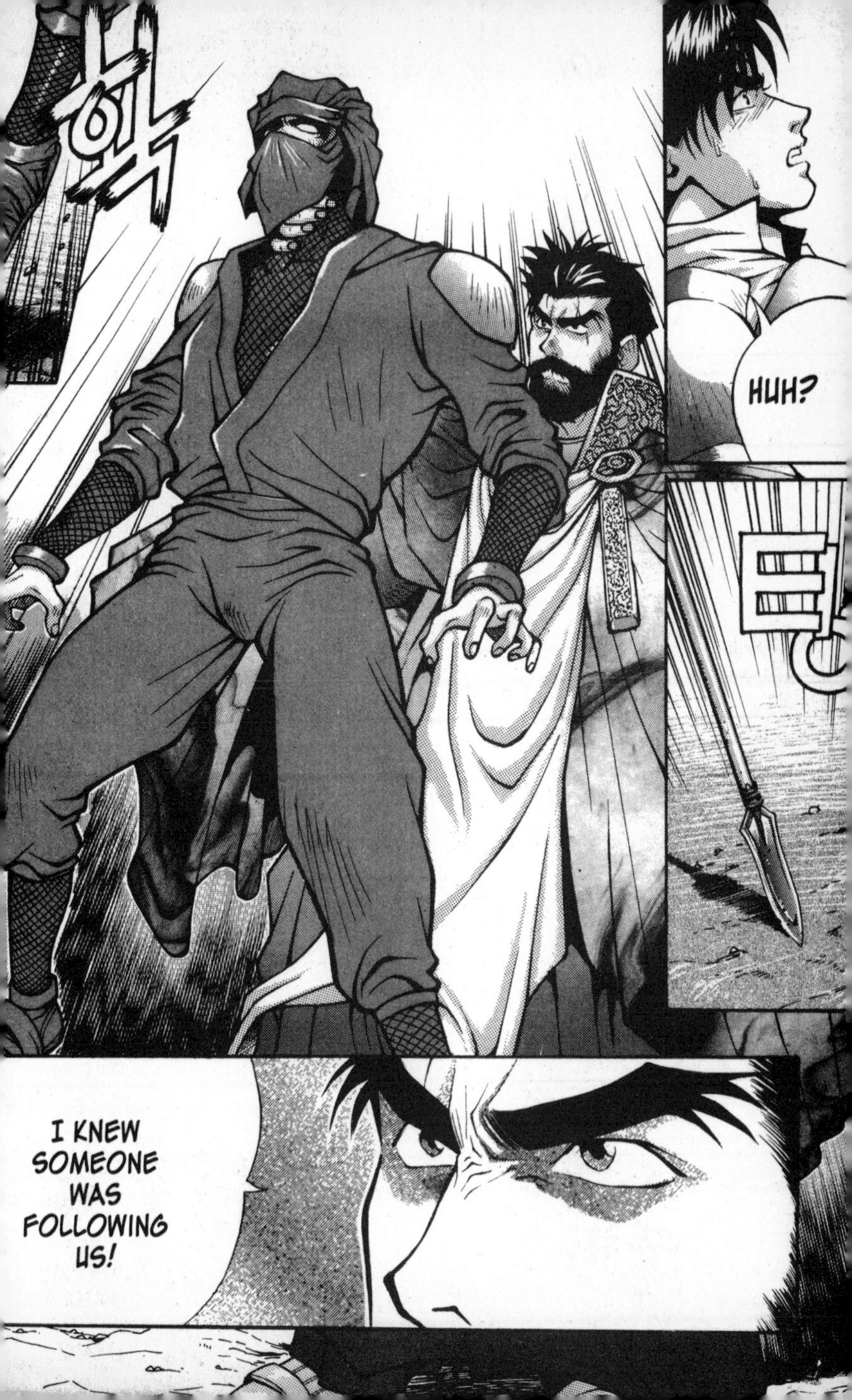
HUH?
I KNEW SOMEONE WAS FOLLOWING US!

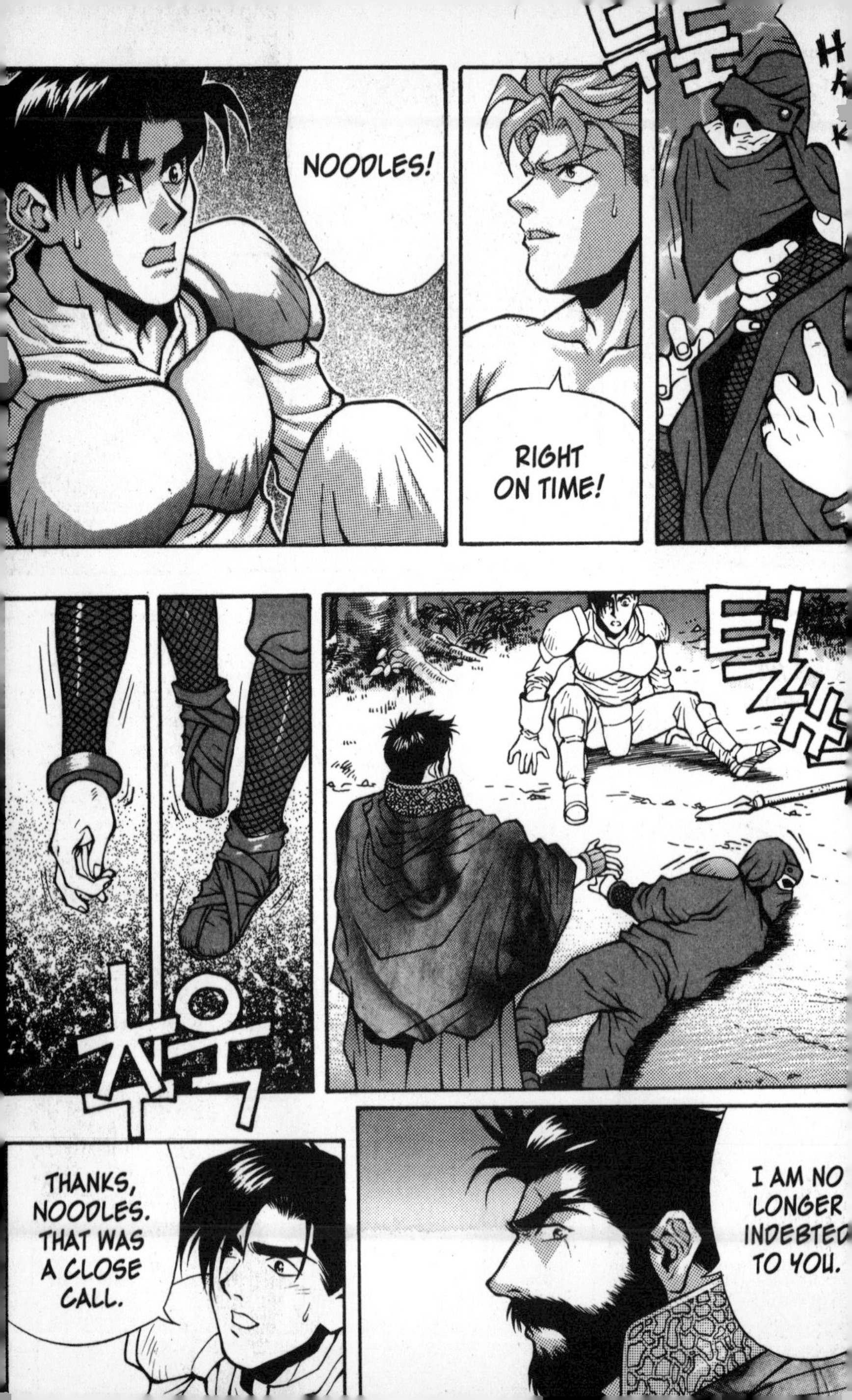
NOODLES!
RIGHT ON TIME!
HAKK
THANKS, NOODLES. THAT WAS A CLOSE CALL.
I AM NO LONGER INDEBTED TO YOU.

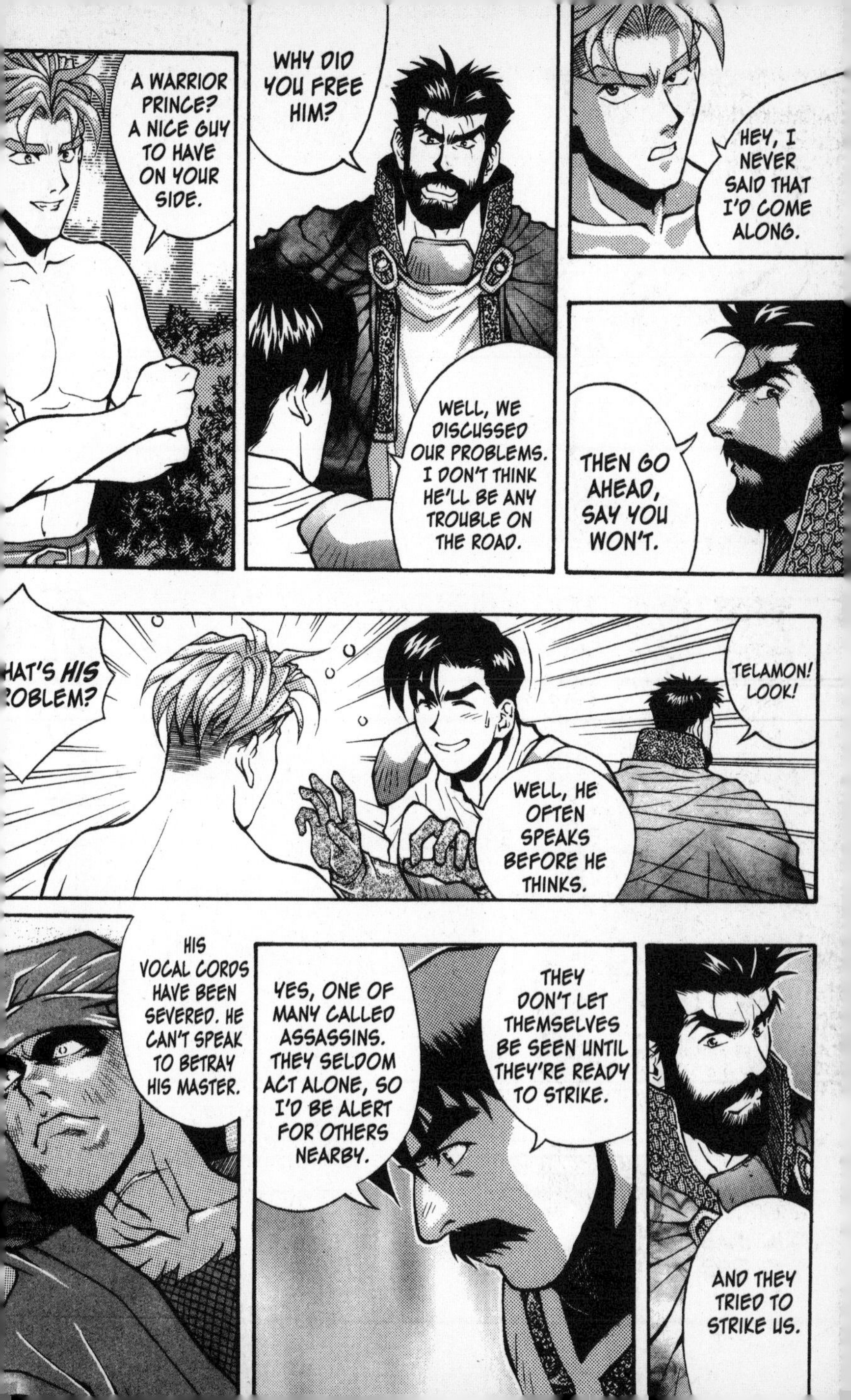

A WARRIOR PRINCE? A NICE GUY TO HAVE ON YOUR SIDE.
WHY DID YOU FREE HIM?
WELL, WE DISCUSSED OUR PROBLEMS. I DON'T THINK HE'LL BE ANY TROUBLE ON THE ROAD.
HEY, I NEVER SAID THAT I'D COME ALONG.
THEN GO AHEAD, SAY YOU WON'T.
HAT'S *HIS* ROBLEM?
WELL, HE OFTEN SPEAKS BEFORE HE THINKS.
TELAMON! LOOK!
HIS VOCAL CORDS HAVE BEEN SEVERED. HE CAN'T SPEAK TO BETRAY HIS MASTER.
YES, ONE OF MANY CALLED ASSASSINS. THEY SELDOM ACT ALONE, SO I'D BE ALERT FOR OTHERS NEARBY.
THEY DON'T LET THEMSELVES BE SEEN UNTIL THEY'RE READY TO STRIKE.
AND THEY TRIED TO STRIKE US.

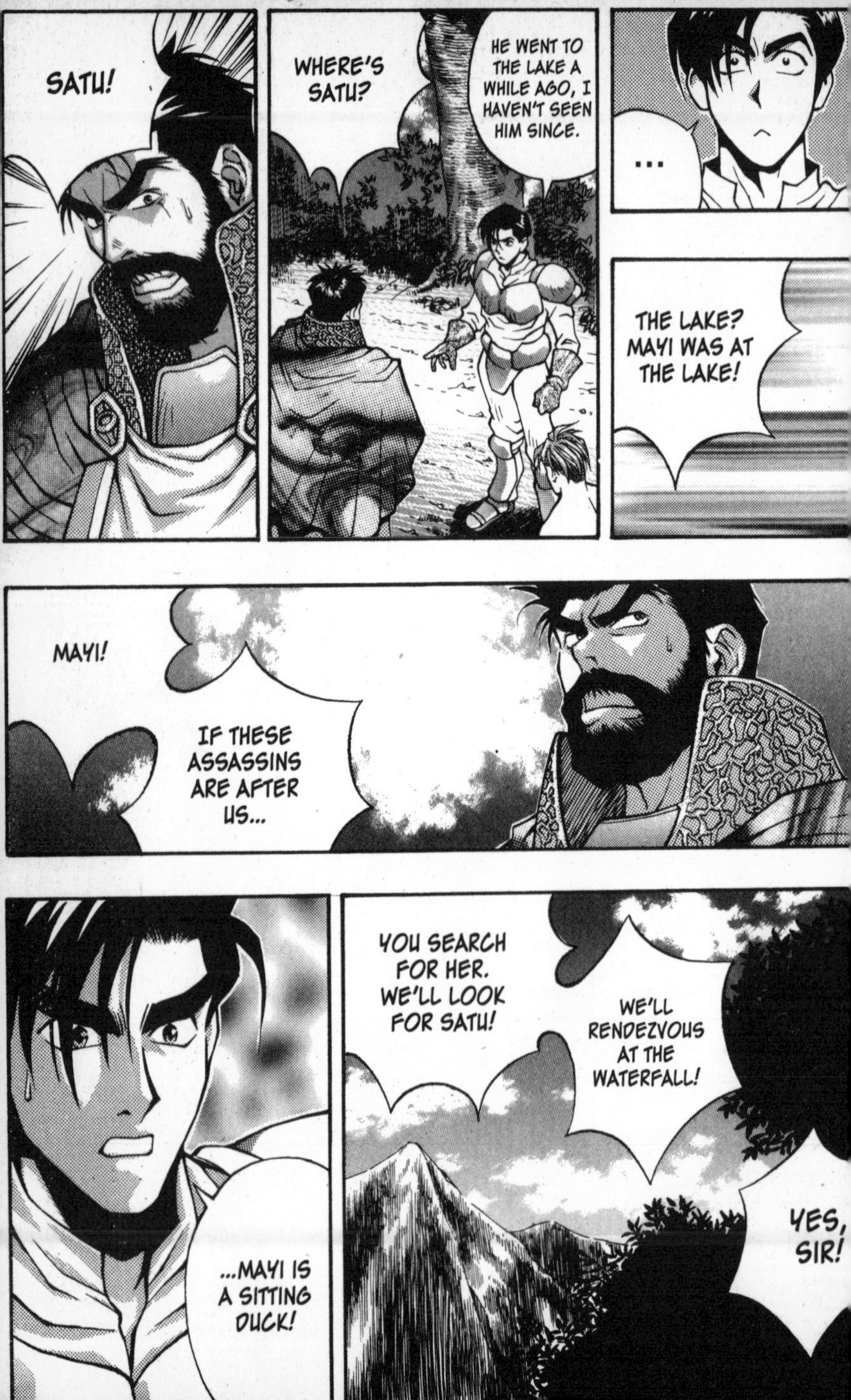
SATU!
WHERE'S SATU?
HE WENT TO THE LAKE A WHILE AGO, I HAVEN'T SEEN HIM SINCE.
...
THE LAKE? MAYI WAS AT THE LAKE!
MAYI!
IF THESE ASSASSINS ARE AFTER US...
...MAYI IS A SITTING DUCK!
YOU SEARCH FOR HER. WE'LL LOOK FOR SATU!
WE'LL RENDEZVOUS AT THE WATERFALL!
YES, SIR!

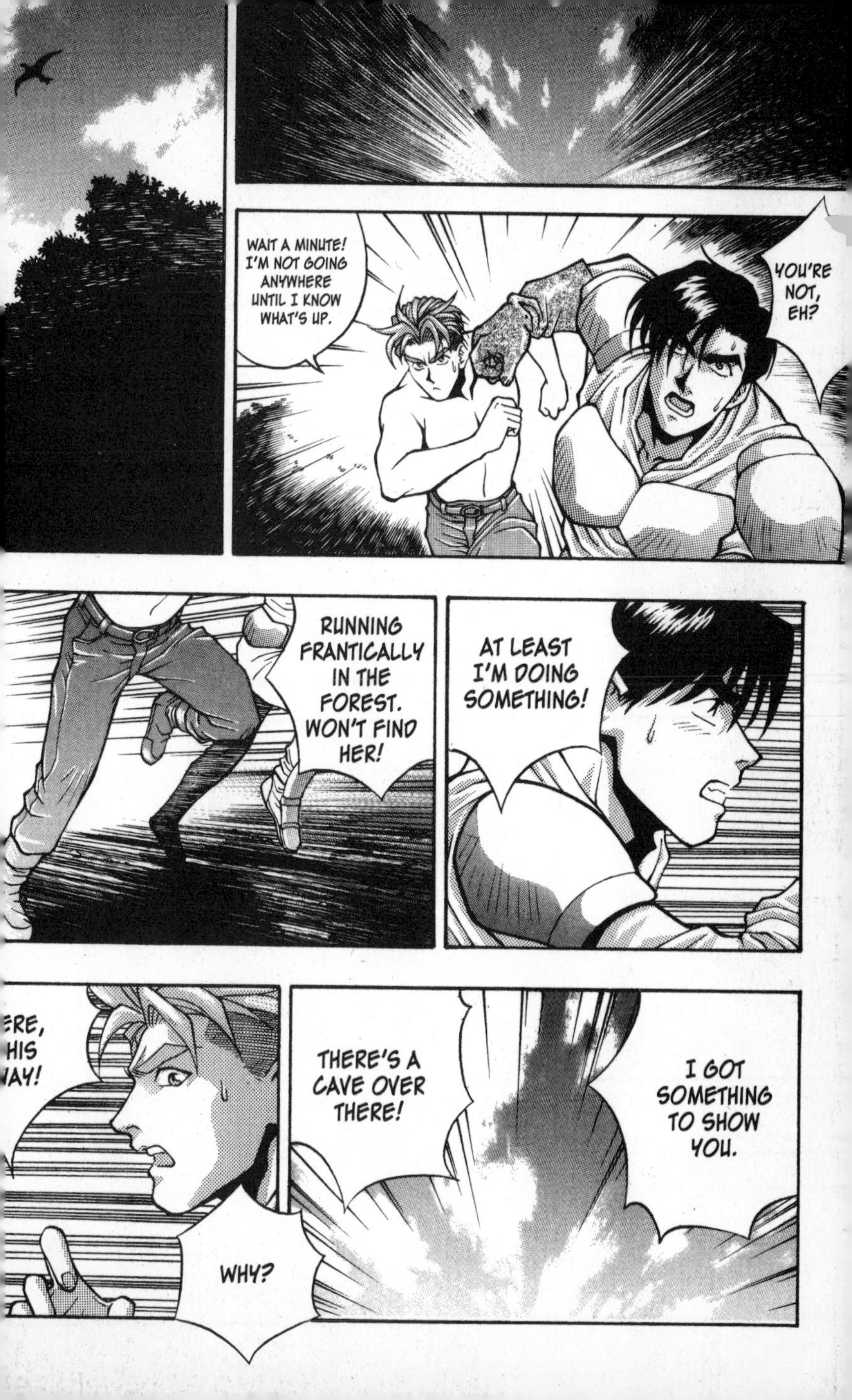
WAIT A MINUTE! I'M NOT GOING ANYWHERE UNTIL I KNOW WHAT'S UP.
YOU'RE NOT, EH?
RUNNING FRANTICALLY IN THE FOREST. WON'T FIND HER!
AT LEAST I'M DOING SOMETHING!
WHY?
THERE'S A CAVE OVER THERE!
I GOT SOMETHING TO SHOW YOU.

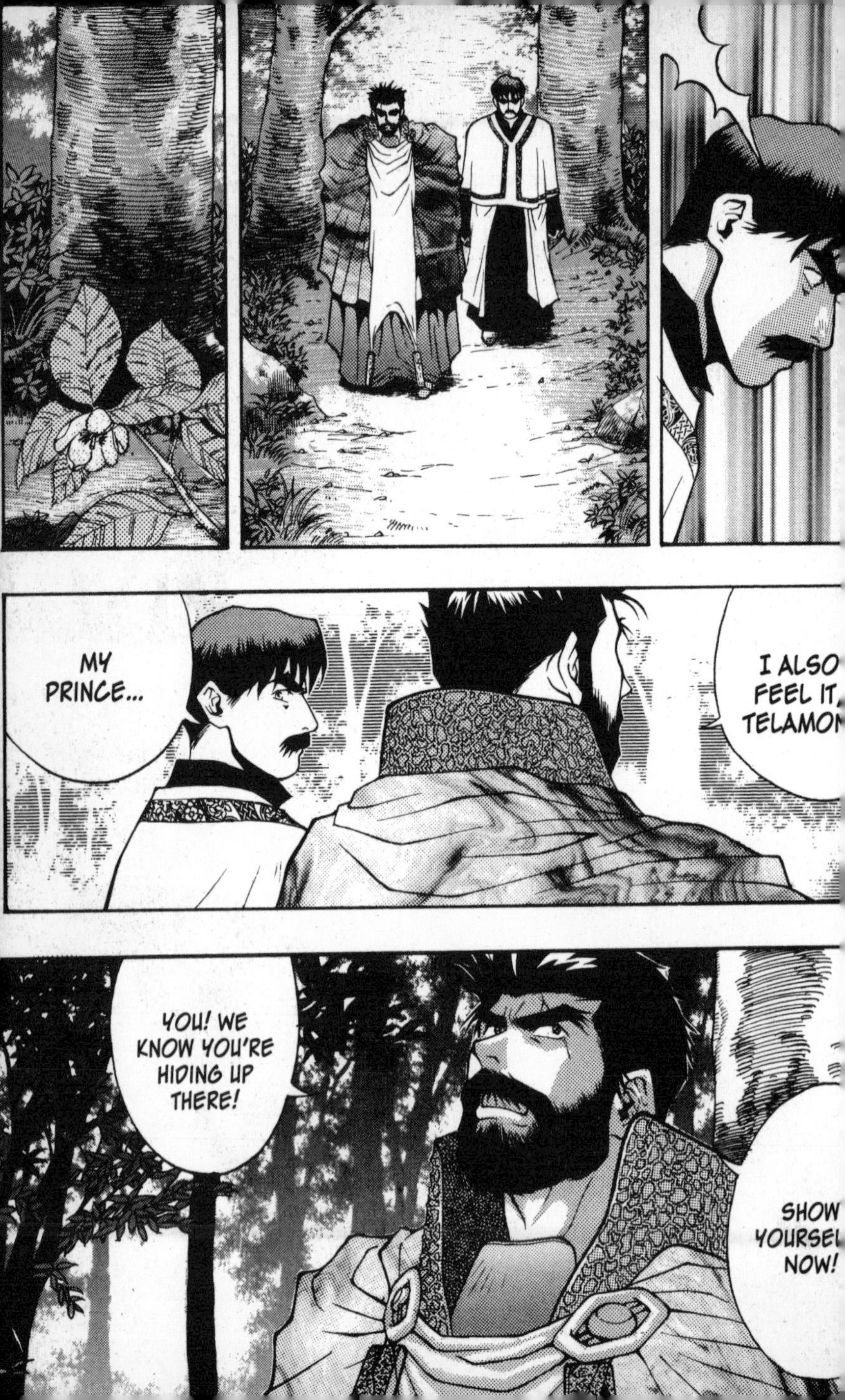
MY PRINCE...
I ALSO FEEL IT, TELAMON
YOU! WE KNOW YOU'RE HIDING UP THERE!
SHOW YOURSEL NOW!

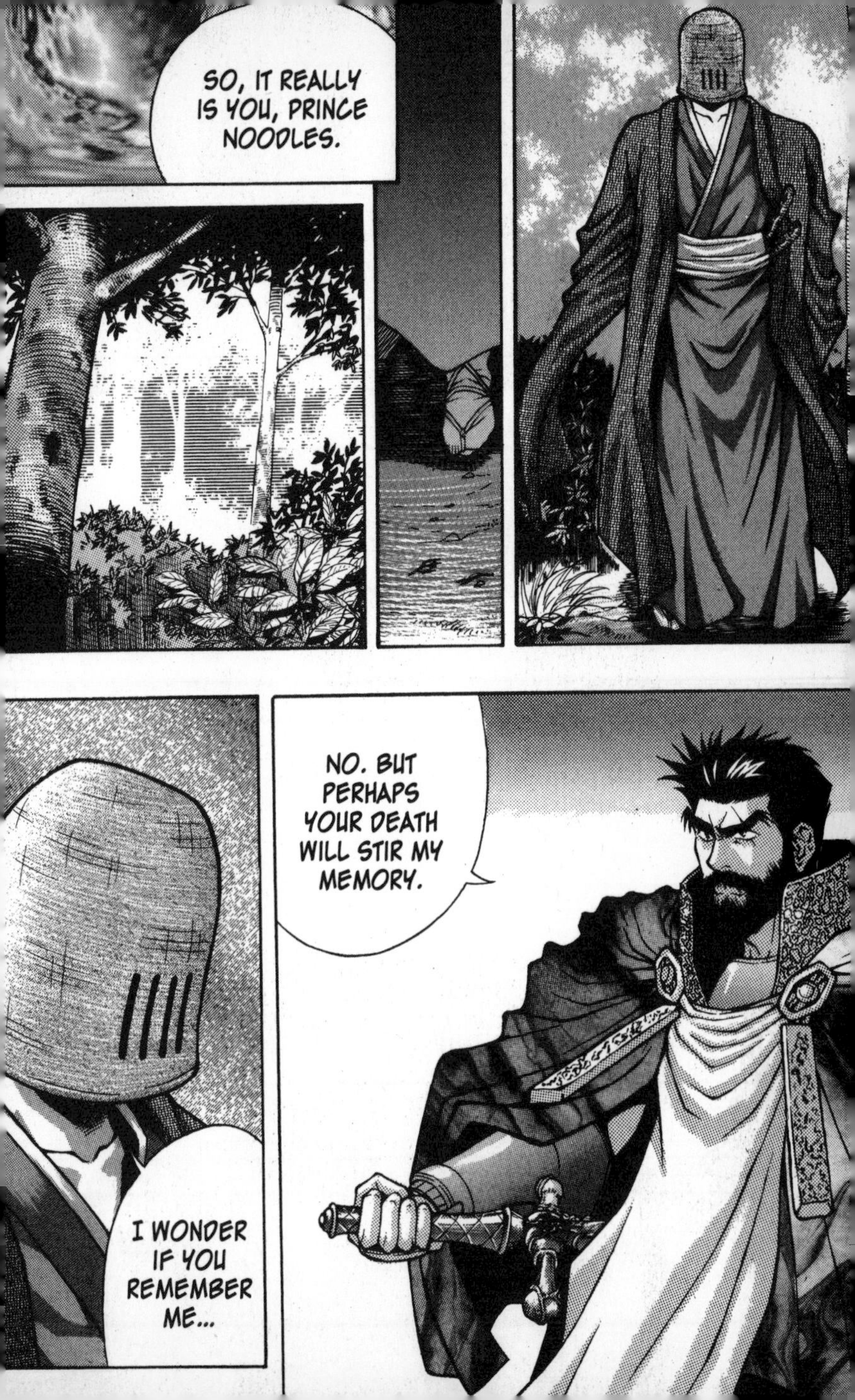
SO, IT REALLY IS YOU, PRINCE NOODLES.
I WONDER IF YOU REMEMBER ME...
NO. BUT PERHAPS YOUR DEATH WILL STIR MY MEMORY.

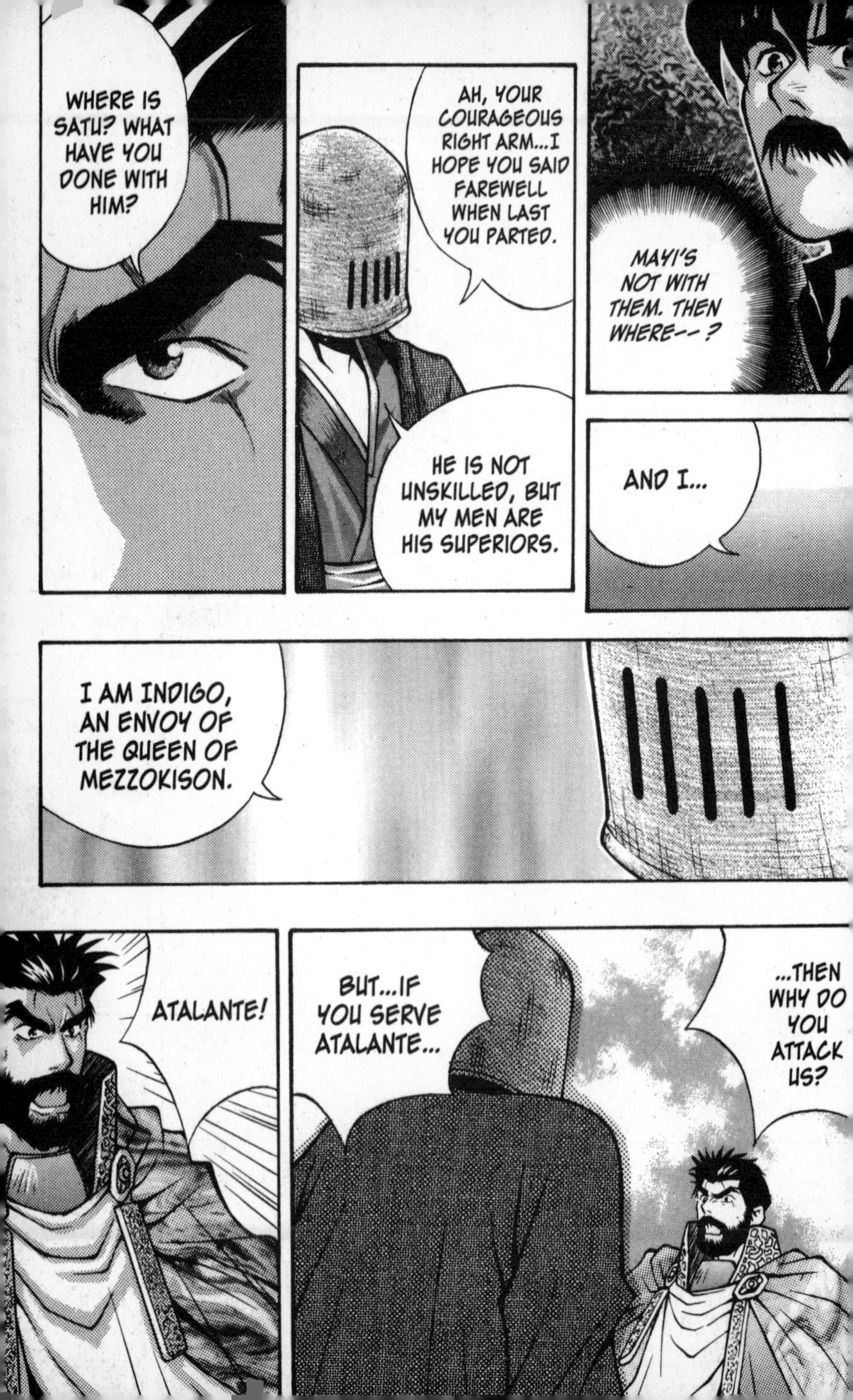
WHERE IS SATU? WHAT HAVE YOU DONE WITH HIM?
AH, YOUR COURAGEOUS RIGHT ARM...I HOPE YOU SAID FAREWELL WHEN LAST YOU PARTED.
HE IS NOT UNSKILLED, BUT MY MEN ARE HIS SUPERIORS.
MAYI'S NOT WITH THEM. THEN WHERE-- ?
AND I...
I AM INDIGO, AN ENVOY OF THE QUEEN OF MEZZOKISON.
ATALANTE!
BUT...IF YOU SERVE ATALANTE...
...THEN WHY DO YOU ATTACK US?

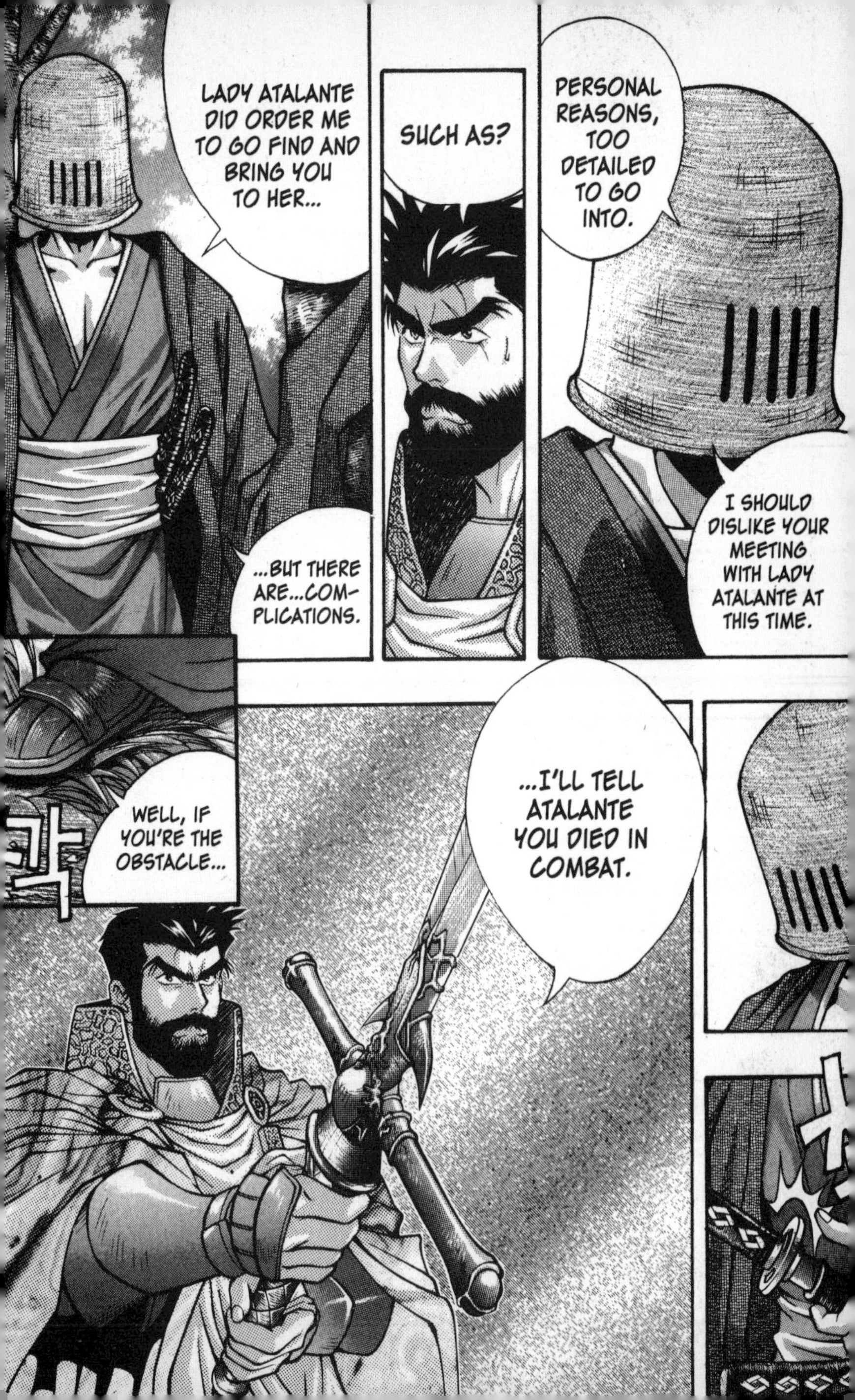
LADY ATALANTE DID ORDER ME TO GO FIND AND BRING YOU TO HER...
...BUT THERE ARE...COM-PLICATIONS.
SUCH AS?
PERSONAL REASONS, TOO DETAILED TO GO INTO.
I SHOULD DISLIKE YOUR MEETING WITH LADY ATALANTE AT THIS TIME.
WELL, IF YOU'RE THE OBSTACLE...
...I'LL TELL ATALANTE YOU DIED IN COMBAT.

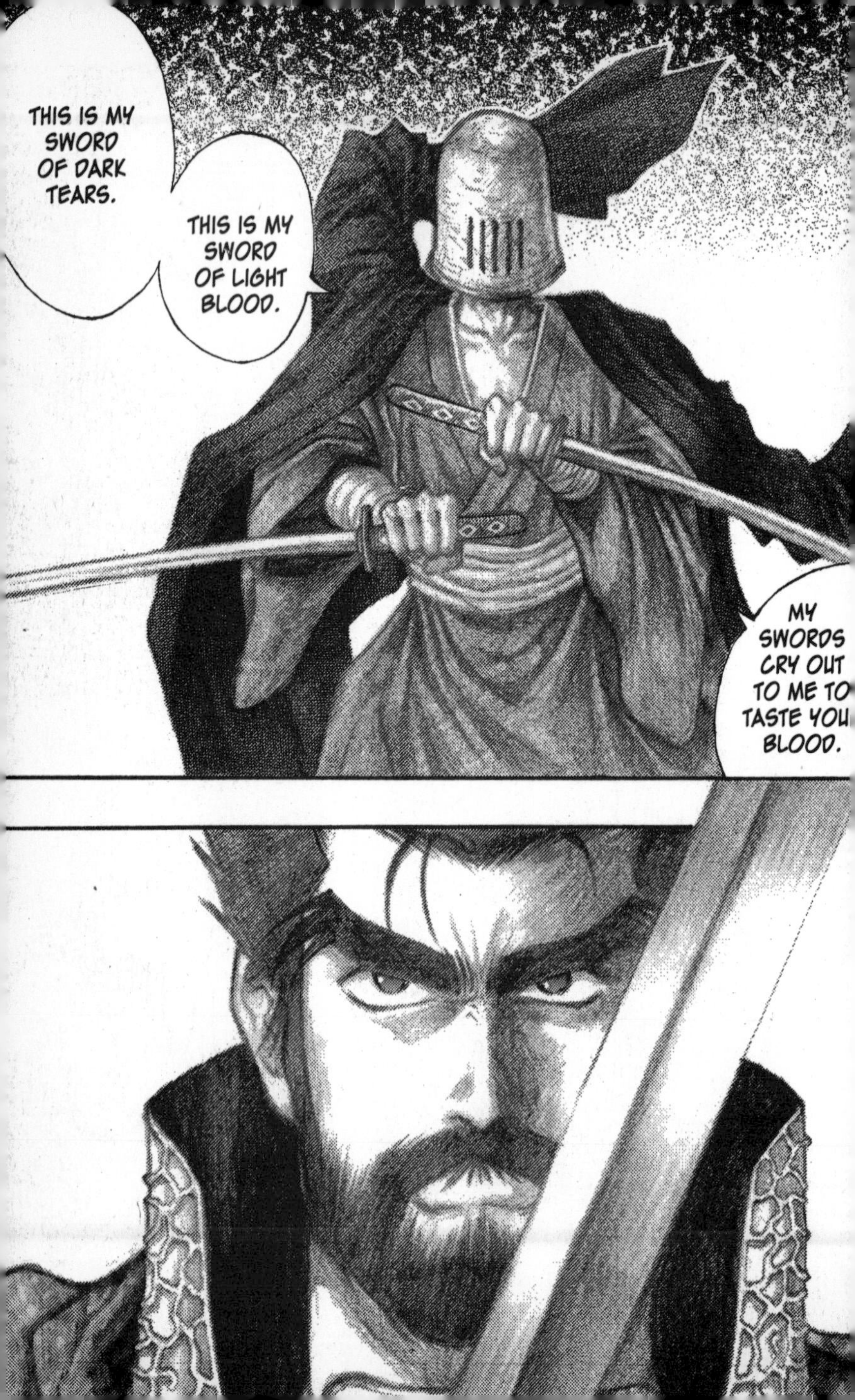
THIS IS MY SWORD OF DARK TEARS.
THIS IS MY SWORD OF LIGHT BLOOD.
MY SWORDS CRY OUT TO ME TO TASTE YOU BLOOD.

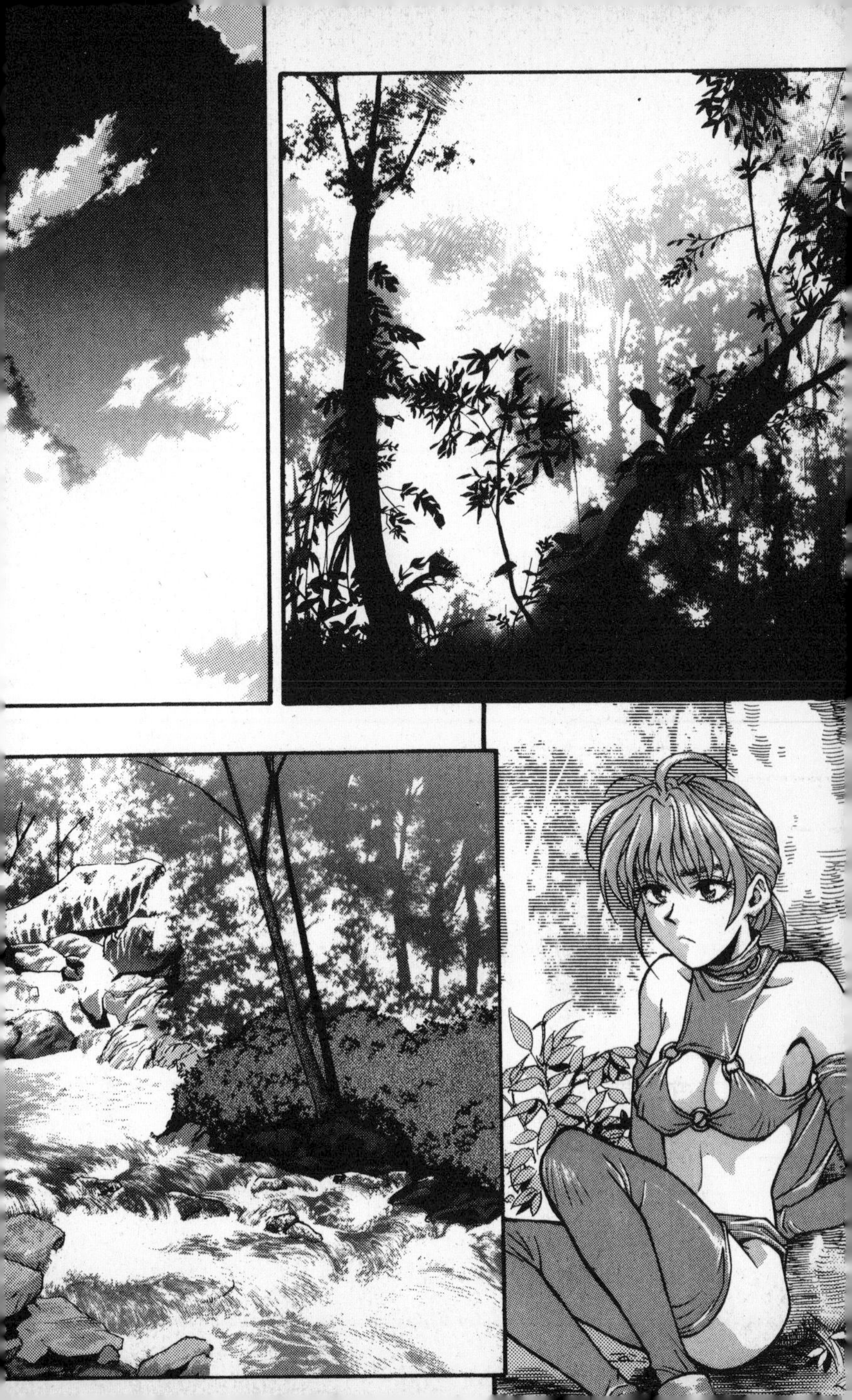

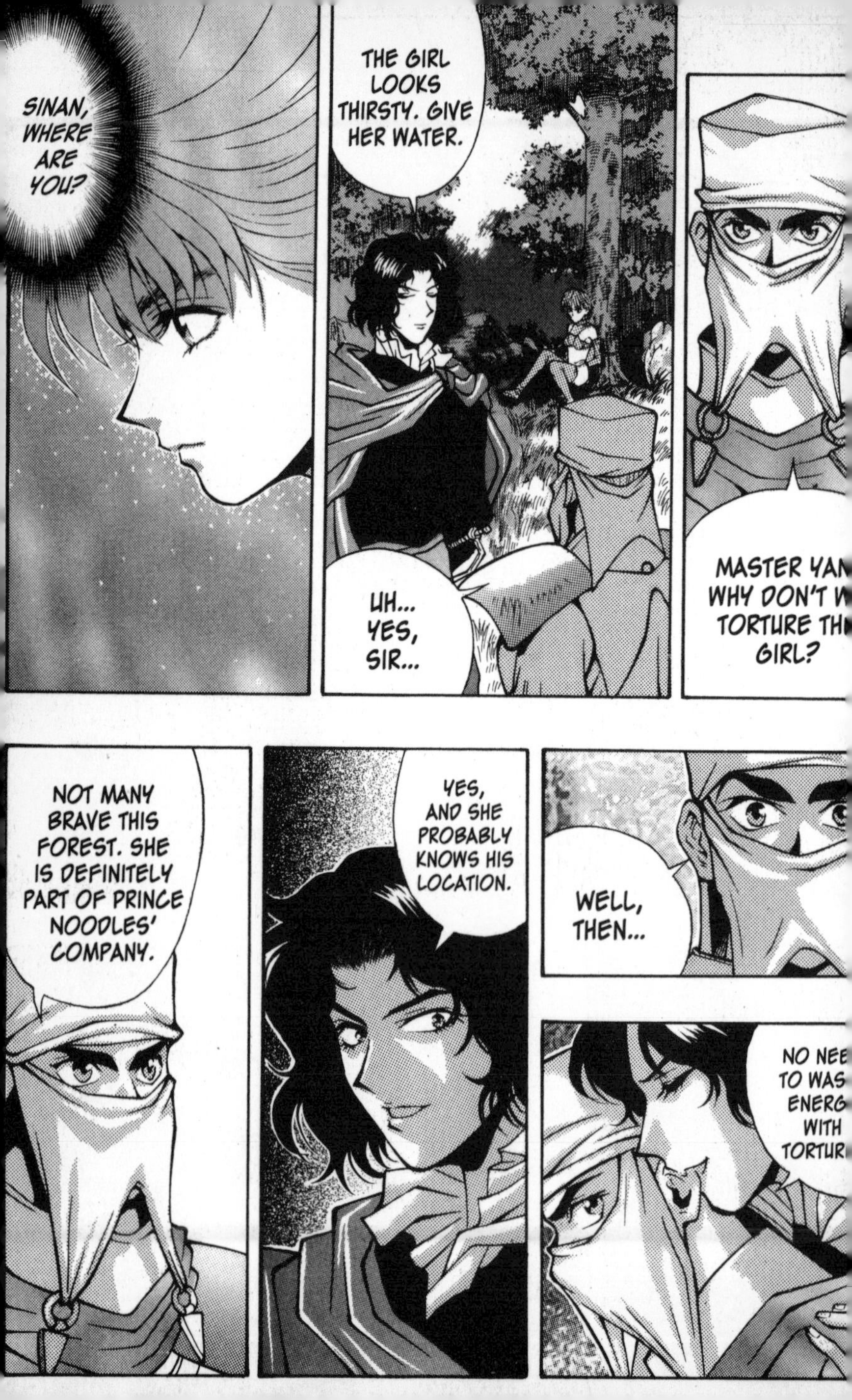
SINAN, WHERE ARE YOU?
THE GIRL LOOKS THIRSTY. GIVE HER WATER.
UH... YES, SIR...
MASTER YAN WHY DON'T W TORTURE TH GIRL?
NOT MANY BRAVE THIS FOREST. SHE IS DEFINITELY PART OF PRINCE NOODLES' COMPANY.
YES, AND SHE PROBABLY KNOWS HIS LOCATION.
WELL, THEN...
NO NEE TO WAS ENERG WITH TORTUR

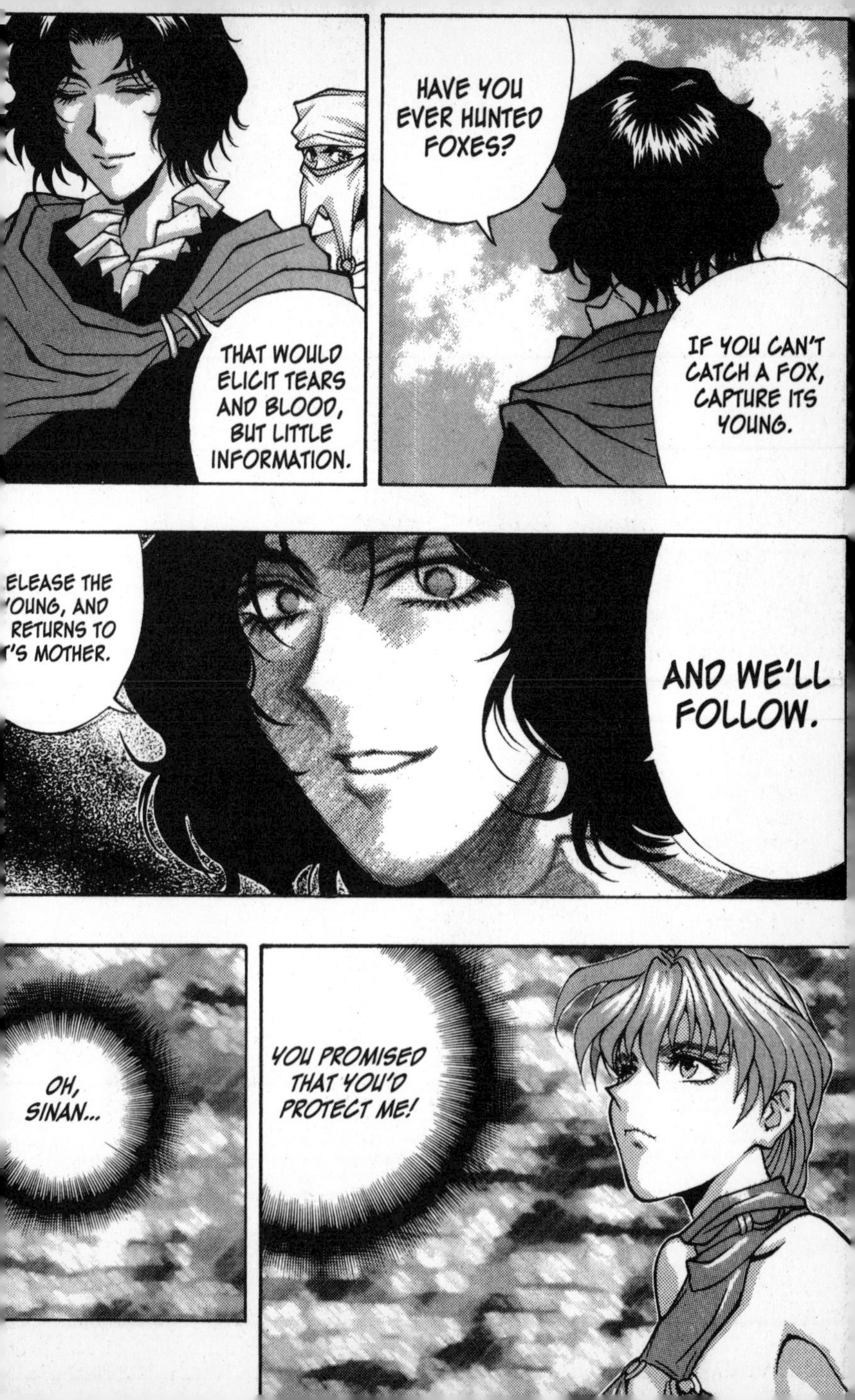
THAT WOULD ELICIT TEARS AND BLOOD, BUT LITTLE INFORMATION.
HAVE YOU EVER HUNTED FOXES?
IF YOU CAN'T CATCH A FOX, CAPTURE ITS YOUNG.
ELEASE THE 'OUNG, AND RETURNS TO 'S MOTHER.
AND WE'LL FOLLOW.
OH, SINAN...
YOU PROMISED THAT YOU'D PROTECT ME!

ALL RIGHT!
WE HAVE
IGNITION!

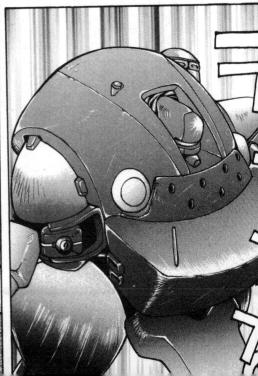

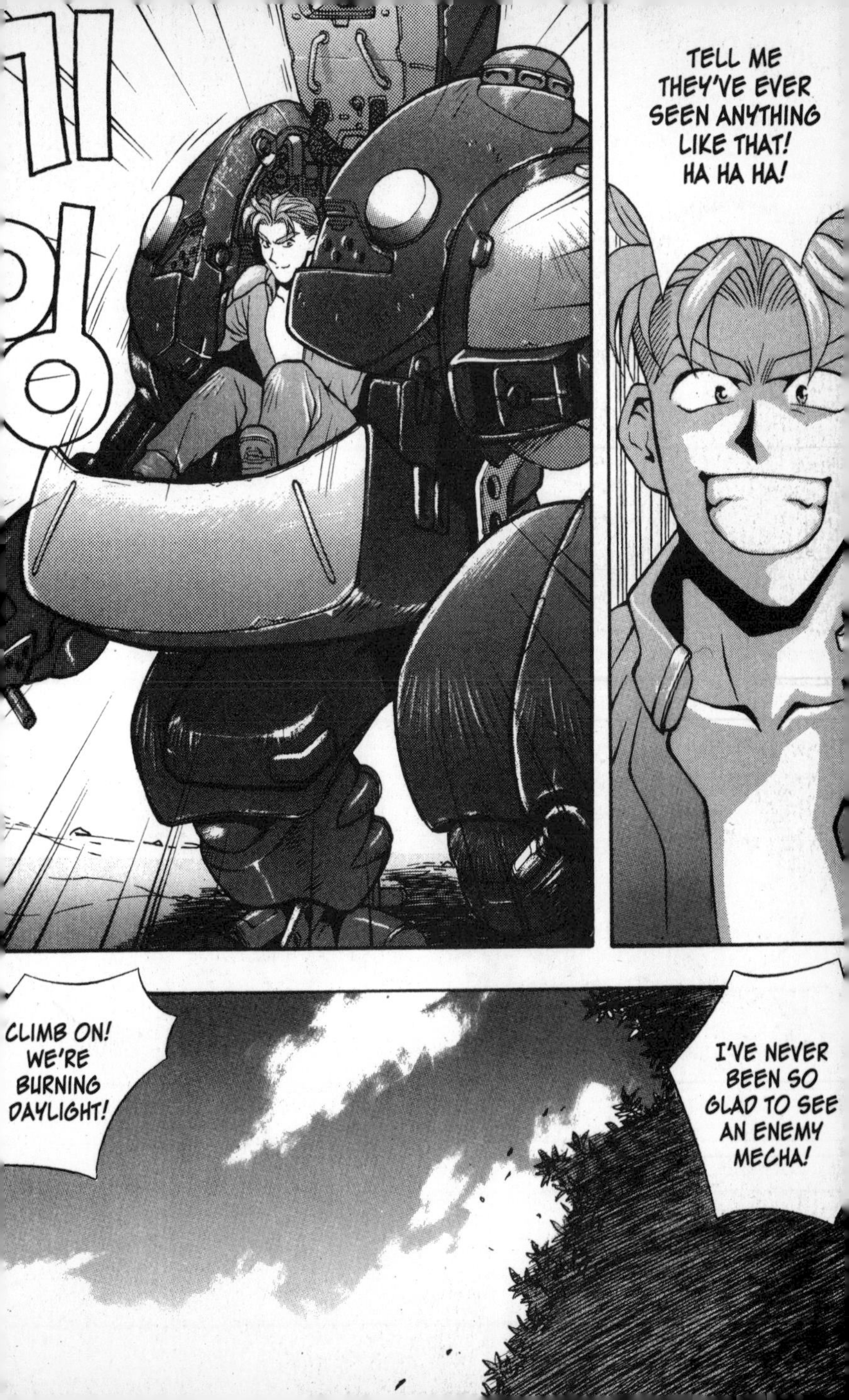
TELL ME THEY'VE EVER SEEN ANYTHING LIKE THAT! HA HA HA!
CLIMB ON! WE'RE BURNING DAYLIGHT!
I'VE NEVER BEEN SO GLAD TO SEE AN ENEMY MECHA!

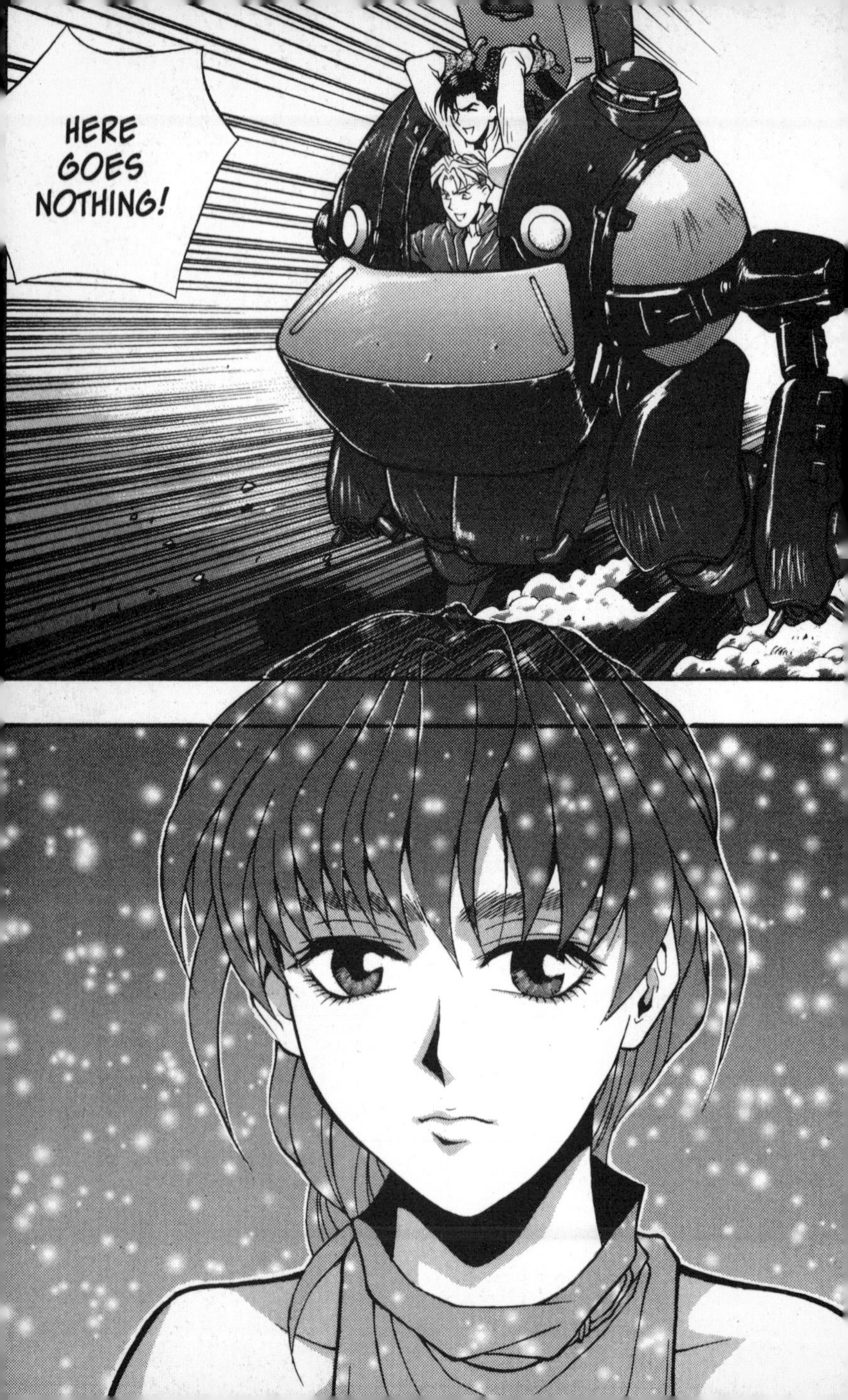
HERE GOES NOTHING!

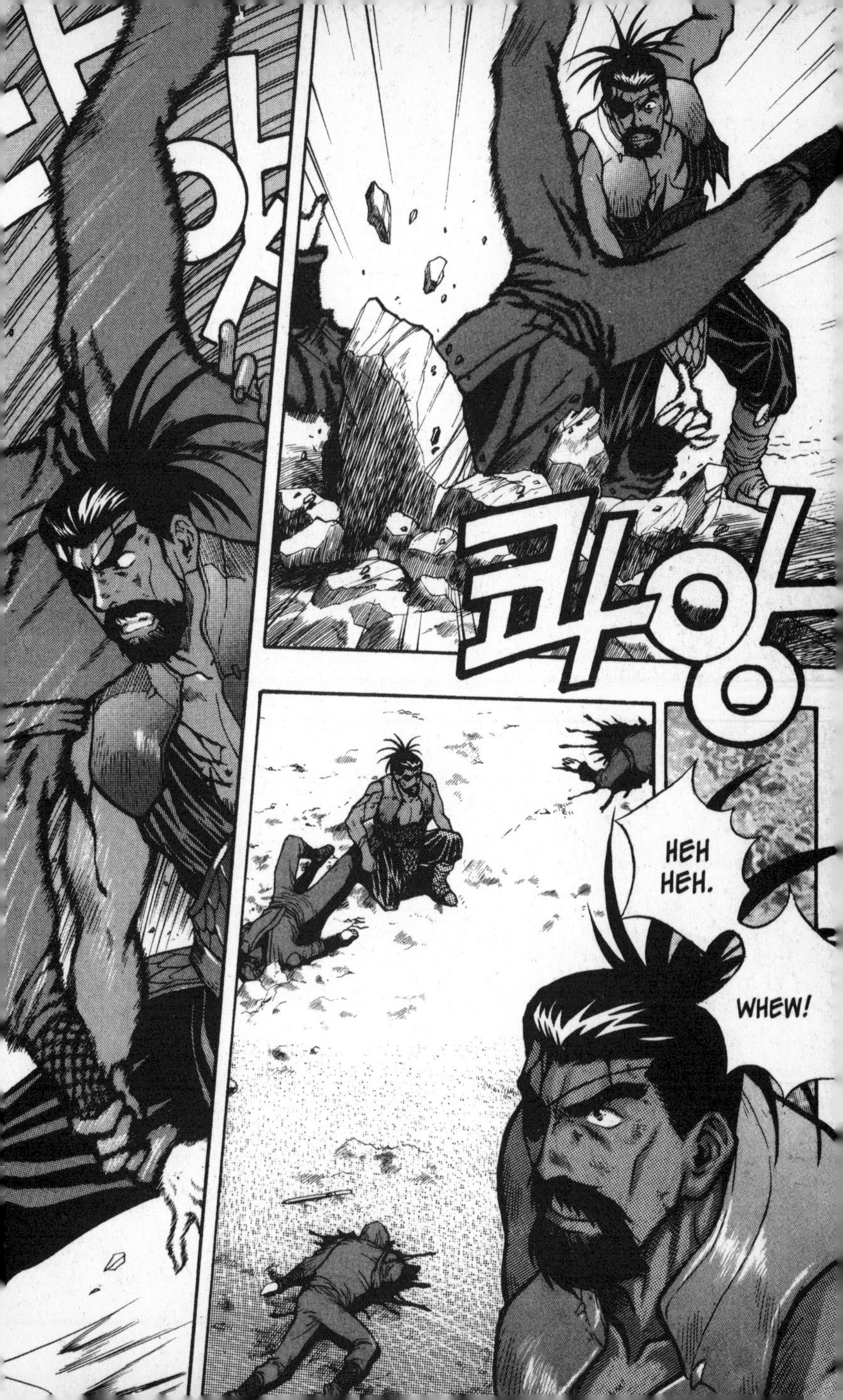
콰앙
HEH HEH.
WHEW!

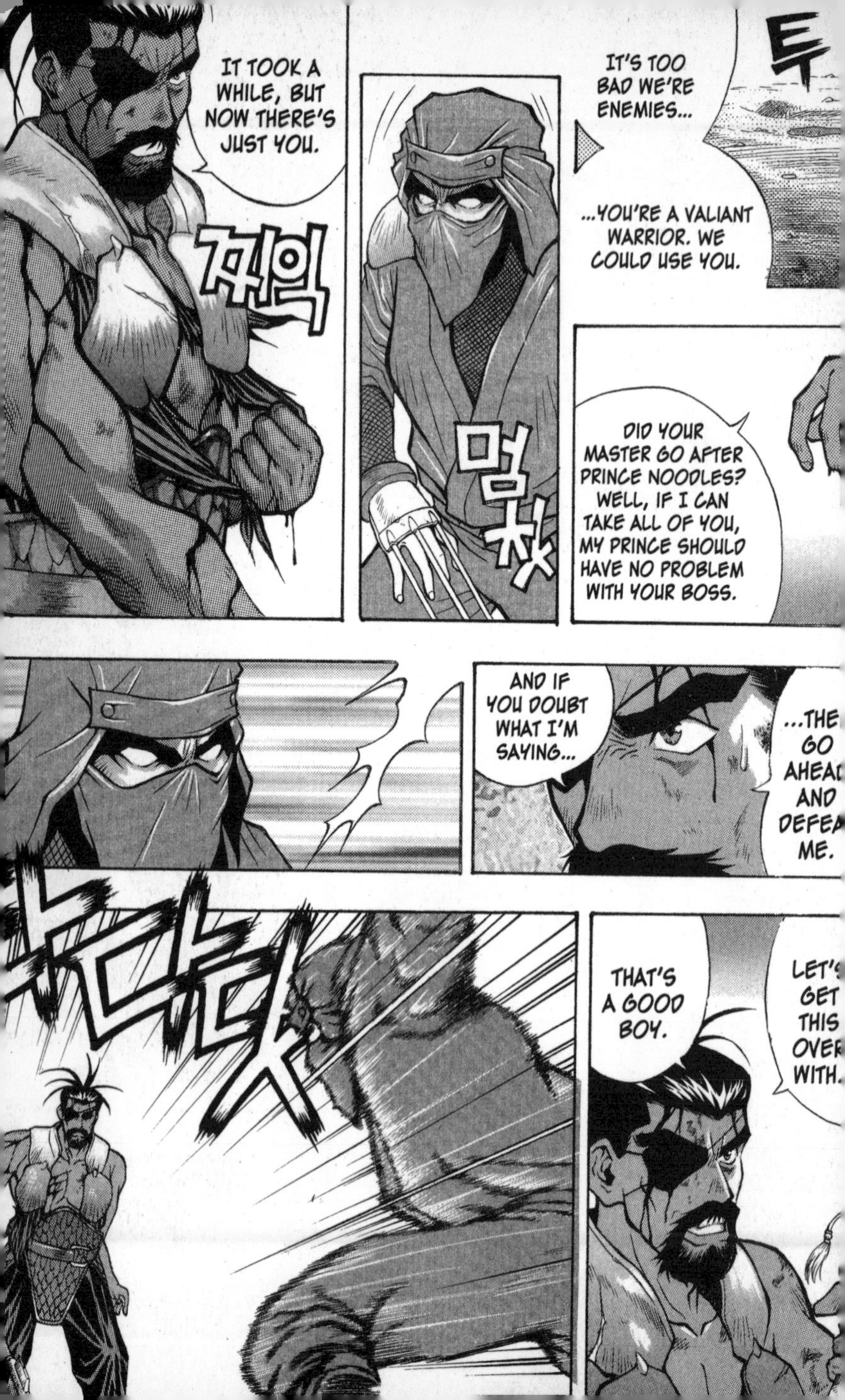
IT TOOK A WHILE, BUT NOW THERE'S JUST YOU.
쩌익
멈칫
IT'S TOO BAD WE'RE ENEMIES...
...YOU'RE A VALIANT WARRIOR. WE COULD USE YOU.
DID YOUR MASTER GO AFTER PRINCE NOODLES? WELL, IF I CAN TAKE ALL OF YOU, MY PRINCE SHOULD HAVE NO PROBLEM WITH YOUR BOSS.
AND IF YOU DOUBT WHAT I'M SAYING...
...THE GO AHEA AND DEFEA ME.
THAT'S A GOOD BOY.
LET'S GET THIS OVER WITH.

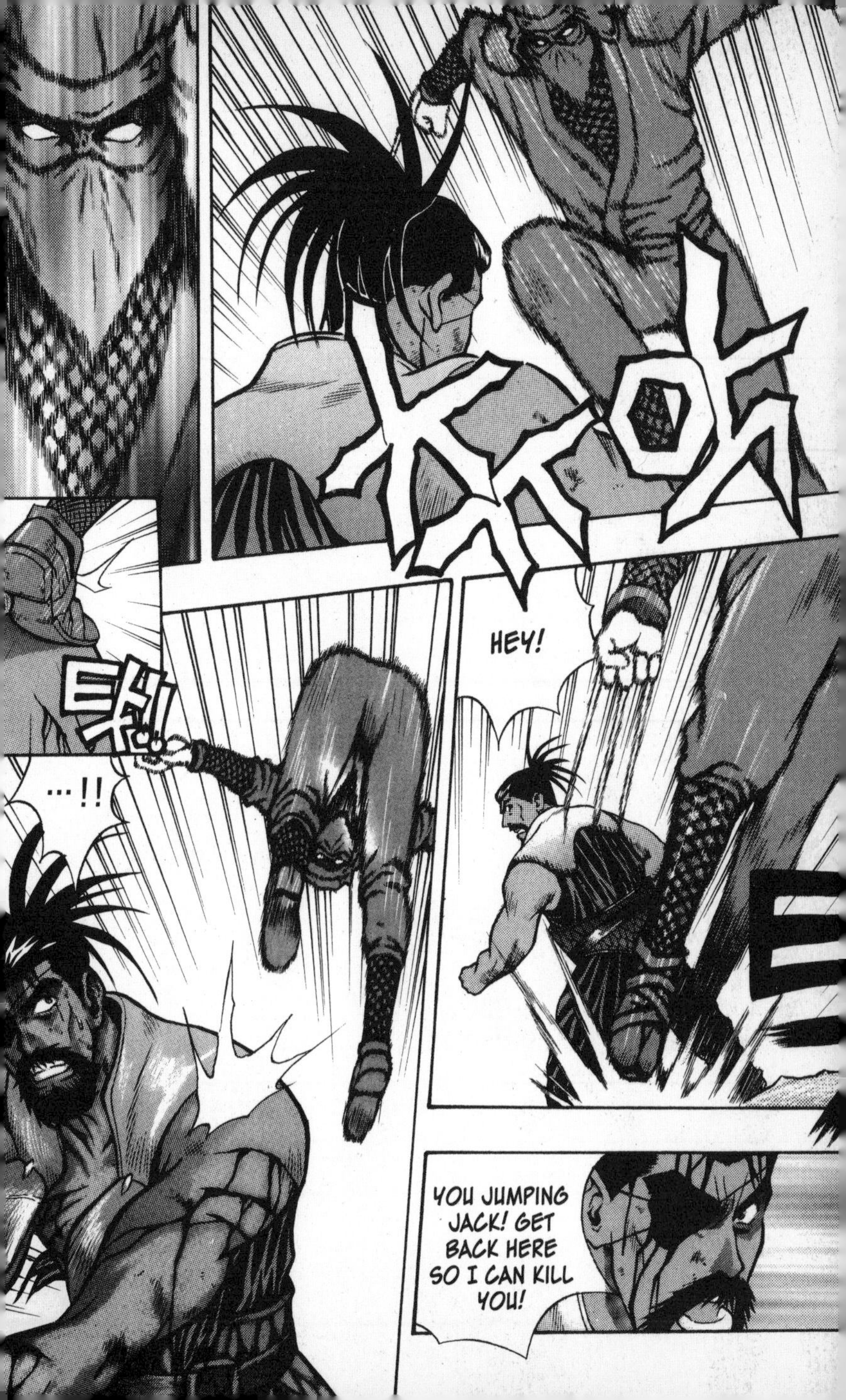

HEY!
...!!
YOU JUMPING JACK! GET BACK HERE SO I CAN KILL YOU!

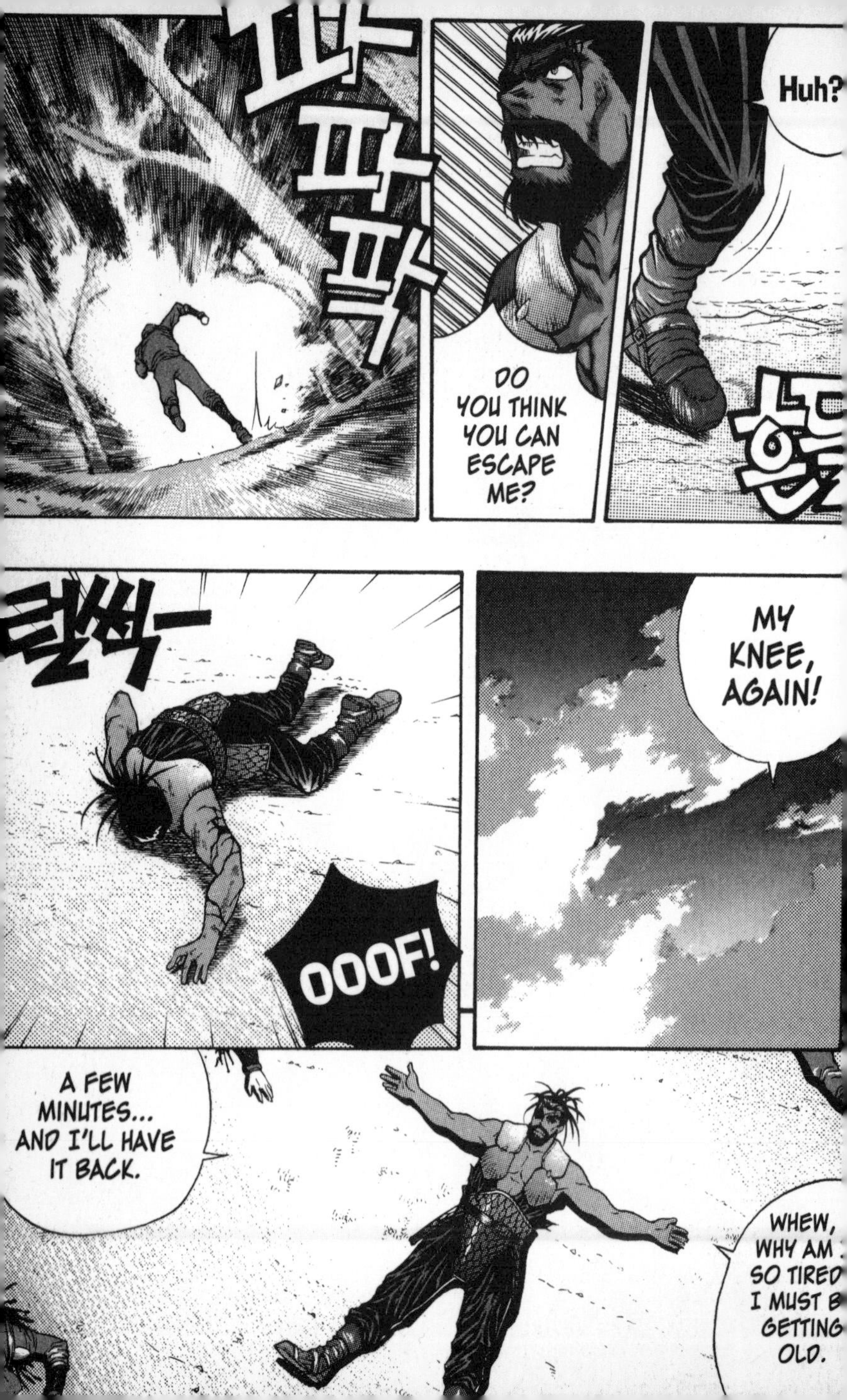
파파파팍
DO YOU THINK YOU CAN ESCAPE ME?
Huh?
OOOF!
MY KNEE, AGAIN!
A FEW MINUTES... AND I'LL HAVE IT BACK.
WHEW, WHY AM SO TIRED I MUST B GETTING OLD.

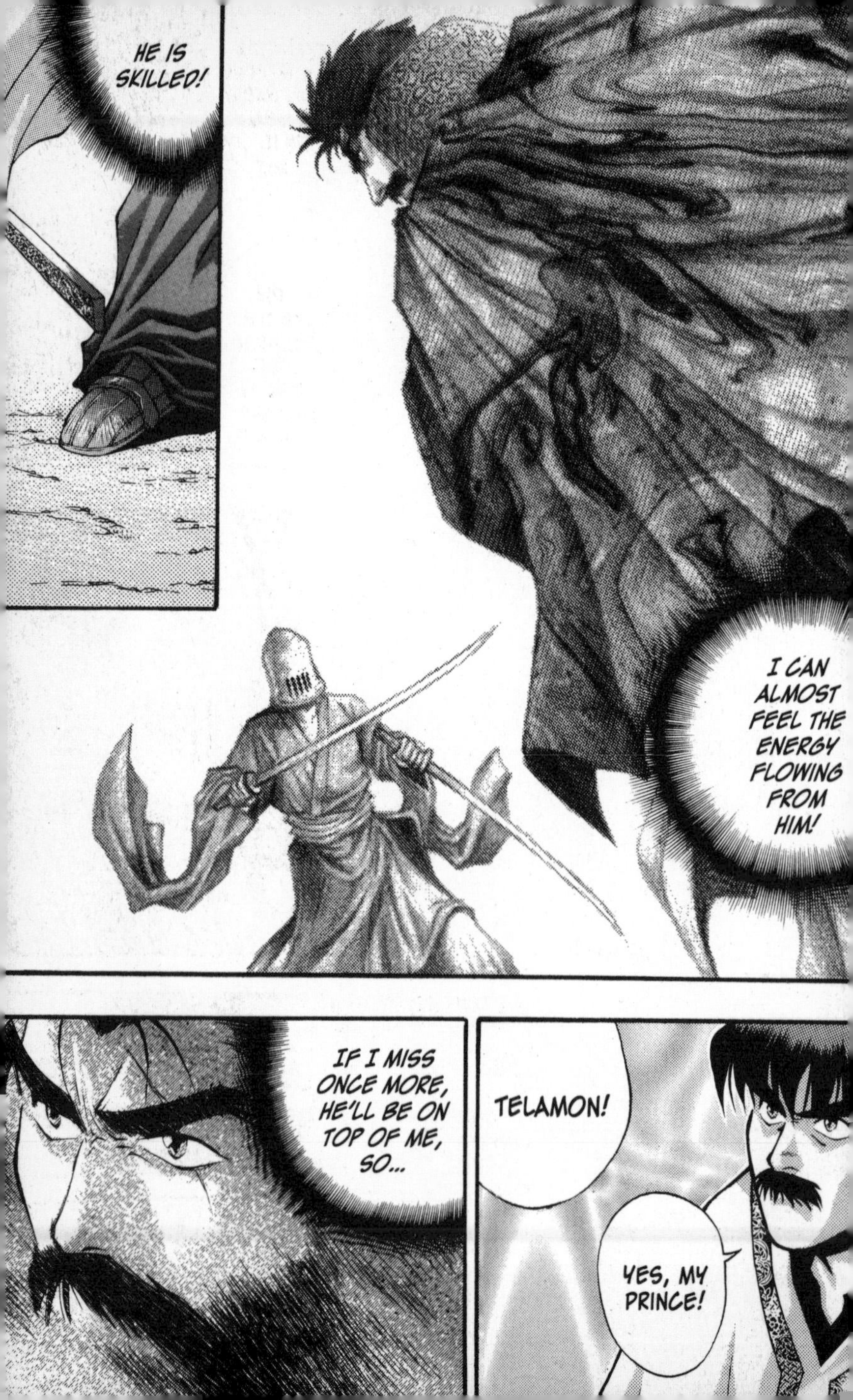
HE IS SKILLED!
I CAN ALMOST FEEL THE ENERGY FLOWING FROM HIM!
IF I MISS ONCE MORE, HE'LL BE ON TOP OF ME, SO...
TELAMON!
YES, MY PRINCE!

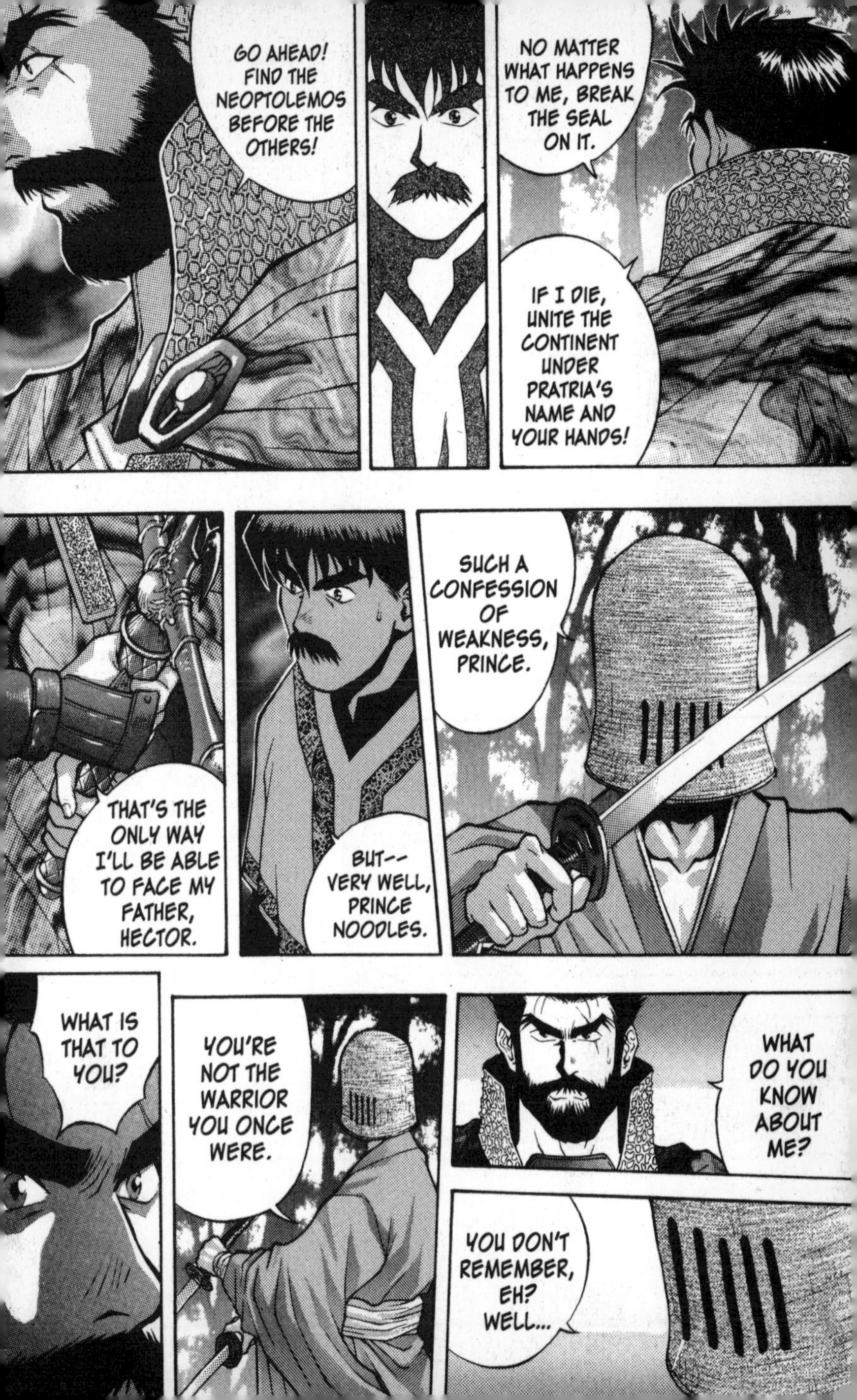
GO AHEAD! FIND THE NEOPTOLEMOS BEFORE THE OTHERS!
NO MATTER WHAT HAPPENS TO ME, BREAK THE SEAL ON IT.
IF I DIE, UNITE THE CONTINENT UNDER PRATRIA'S NAME AND YOUR HANDS!
THAT'S THE ONLY WAY I'LL BE ABLE TO FACE MY FATHER, HECTOR.
BUT-- VERY WELL, PRINCE NOODLES.
SUCH A CONFESSION OF WEAKNESS, PRINCE.
WHAT IS THAT TO YOU?
YOU'RE NOT THE WARRIOR YOU ONCE WERE.
WHAT DO YOU KNOW ABOUT ME?
YOU DON'T REMEMBER, EH? WELL...

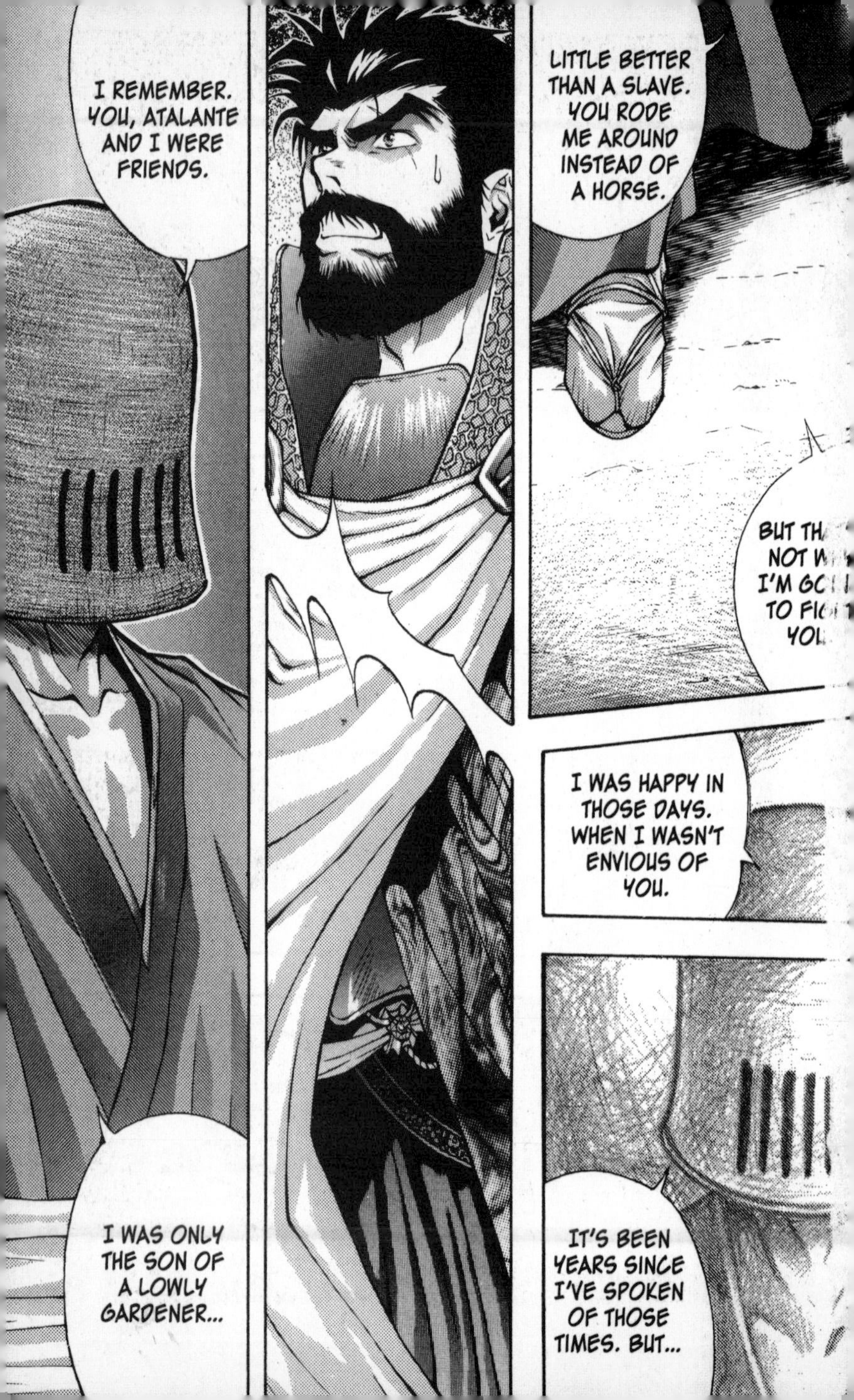
I REMEMBER. YOU, ATALANTE AND I WERE FRIENDS.
I WAS ONLY THE SON OF A LOWLY GARDENER...
LITTLE BETTER THAN A SLAVE. YOU RODE ME AROUND INSTEAD OF A HORSE.
I WAS HAPPY IN THOSE DAYS. WHEN I WASN'T ENVIOUS OF YOU.
IT'S BEEN YEARS SINCE I'VE SPOKEN OF THOSE TIMES. BUT...

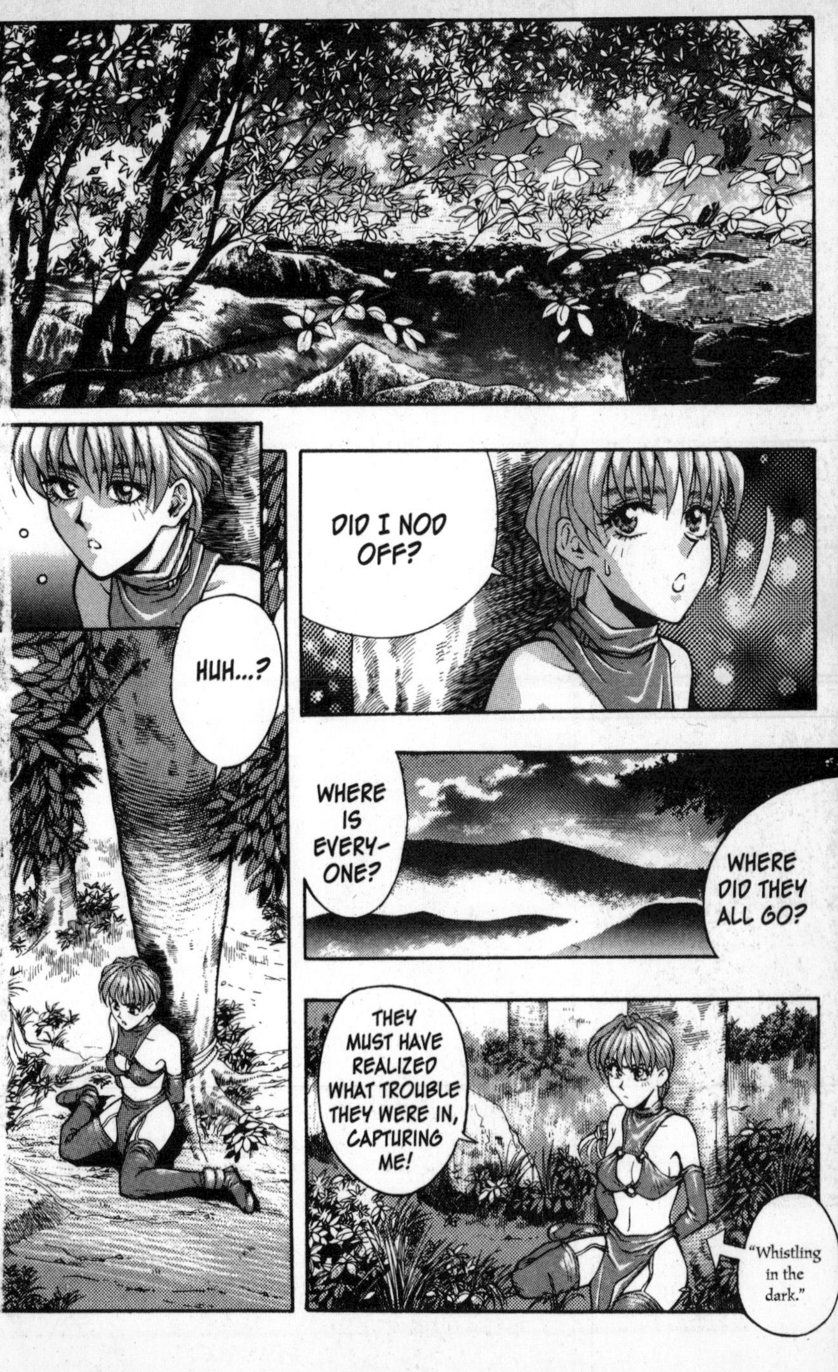
HUH...?
DID I NOD OFF?
WHERE IS EVERY-ONE?
WHERE DID THEY ALL GO?
THEY MUST HAVE REALIZED WHAT TROUBLE THEY WERE IN, CAPTURING ME!
"Whistling in the dark."

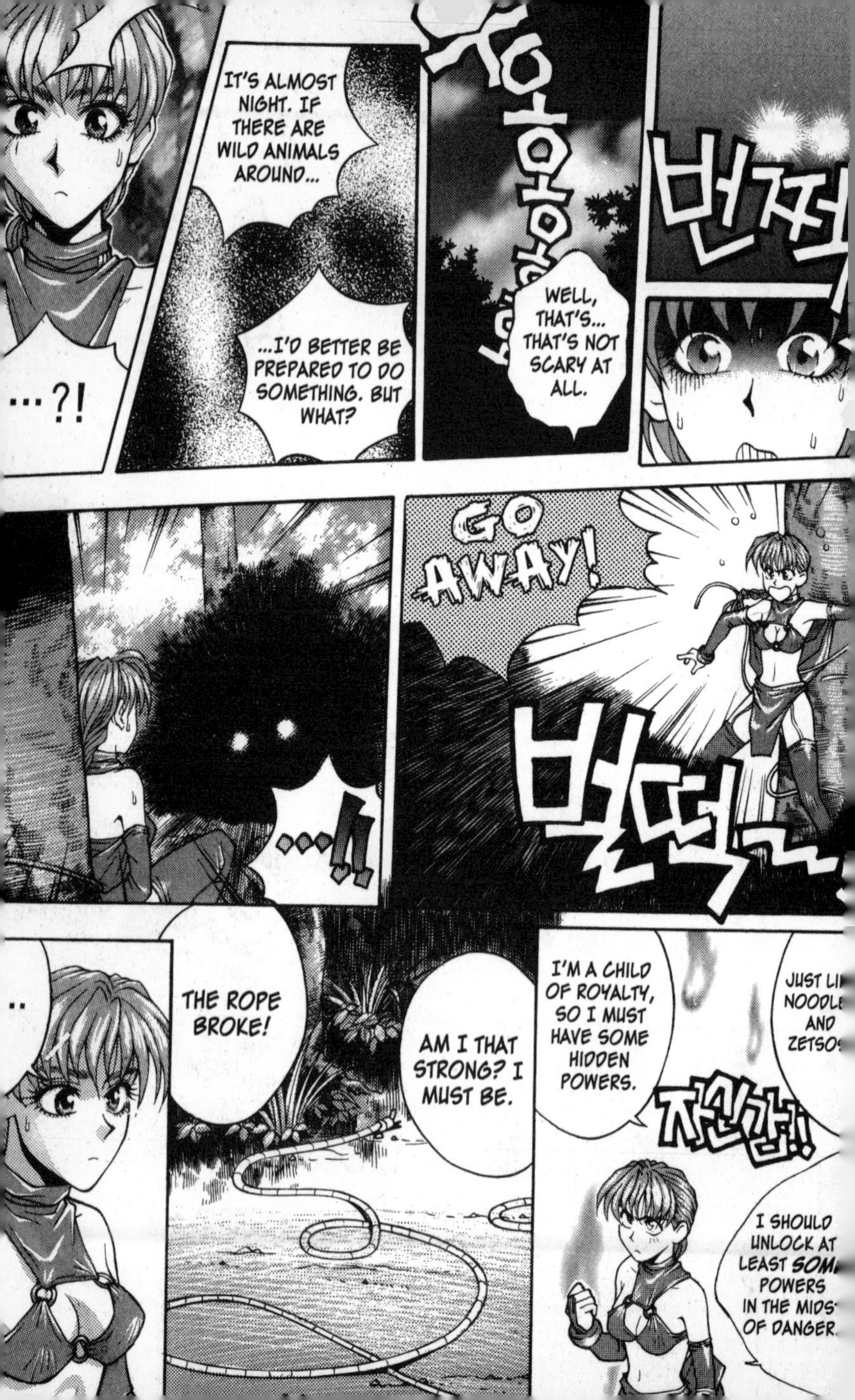
...?!
IT'S ALMOST NIGHT. IF THERE ARE WILD ANIMALS AROUND...
...I'D BETTER BE PREPARED TO DO SOMETHING. BUT WHAT?
WELL, THAT'S... THAT'S NOT SCARY AT ALL.
...!!
GO AWAY!
..
THE ROPE BROKE!
AM I THAT STRONG? I MUST BE.
I'M A CHILD OF ROYALTY, SO I MUST HAVE SOME HIDDEN POWERS.
JUST LI NOODLE AND ZETSO
I SHOULD UNLOCK AT LEAST SOM POWERS IN THE MIDS OF DANGER.

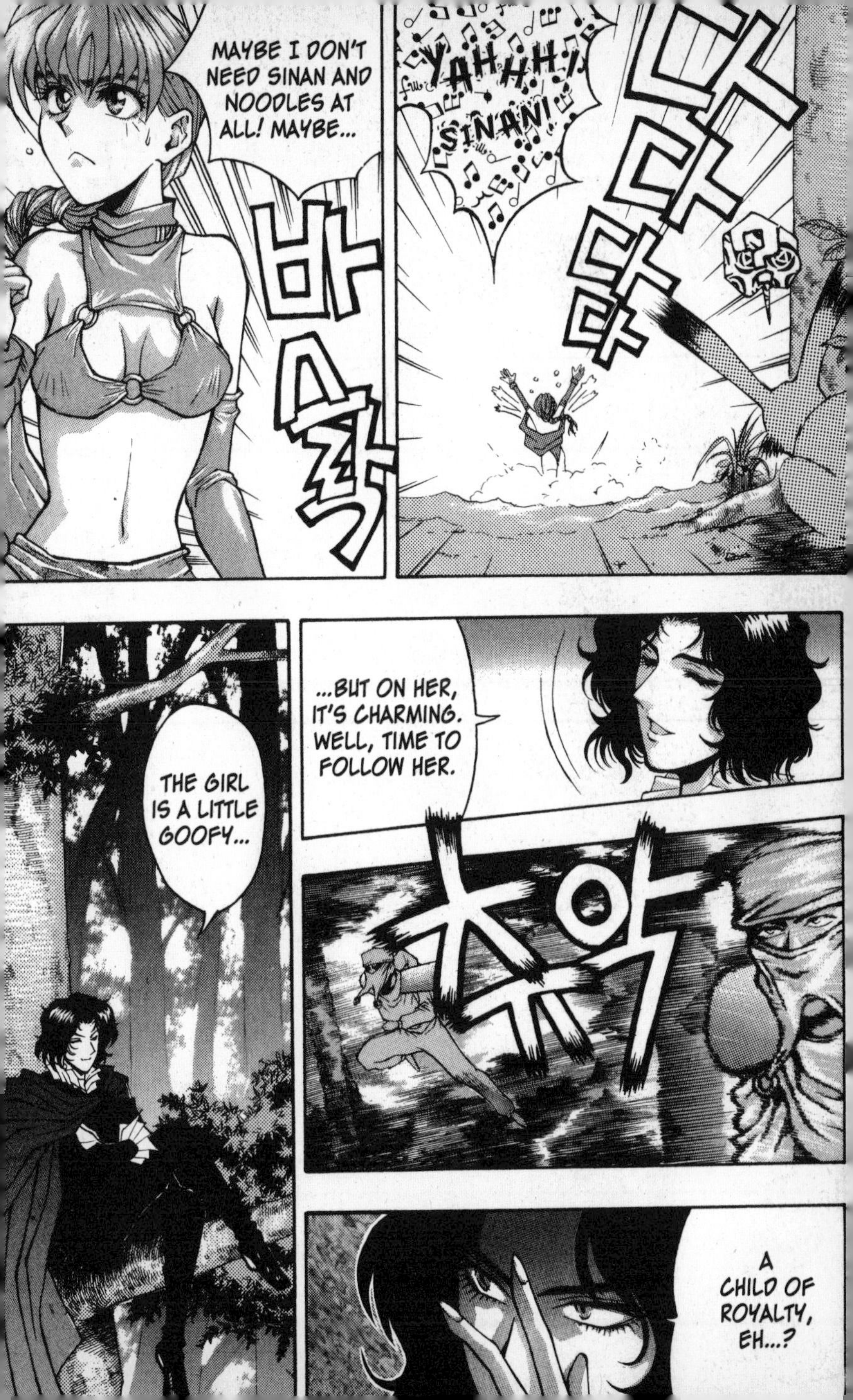

MAYBE I DON'T NEED SINAN AND NOODLES AT ALL! MAYBE...
바스칫
YAHHH! SINAN!
다다닥
THE GIRL IS A LITTLE GOOFY...
...BUT ON HER, IT'S CHARMING. WELL, TIME TO FOLLOW HER.
A CHILD OF ROYALTY, EH...?

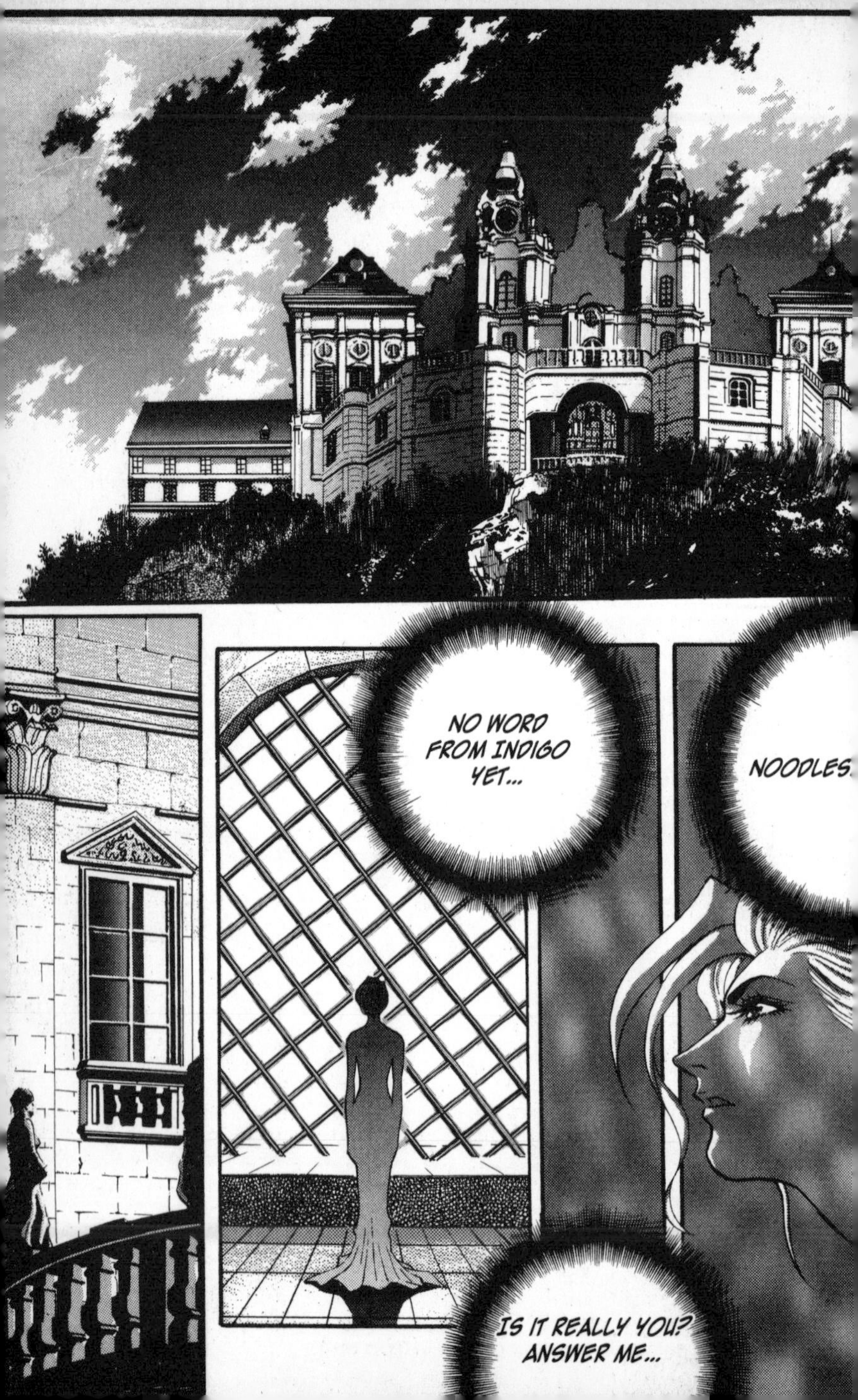
NO WORD FROM INDIGO YET...
NOODLES.
IS IT REALLY YOU? ANSWER ME...

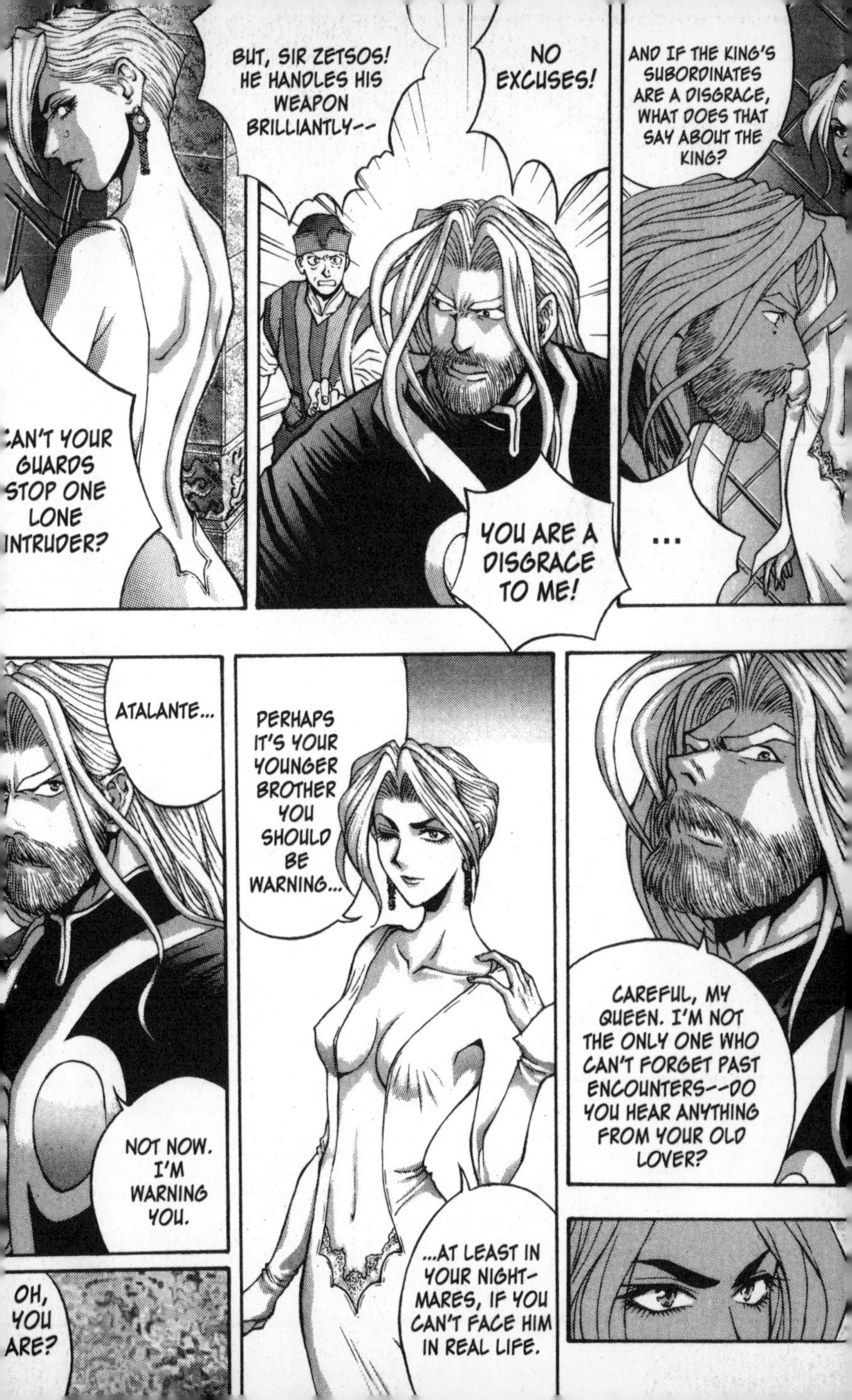
BUT, SIR ZETSOS! HE HANDLES HIS WEAPON BRILLIANTLY--
NO EXCUSES!
AND IF THE KING'S SUBORDINATES ARE A DISGRACE, WHAT DOES THAT SAY ABOUT THE KING?
CAN'T YOUR GUARDS STOP ONE LONE INTRUDER?
YOU ARE A DISGRACE TO ME!
...
ATALANTE...
NOT NOW. I'M WARNING YOU.
OH, YOU ARE?
PERHAPS IT'S YOUR YOUNGER BROTHER YOU SHOULD BE WARNING...
...AT LEAST IN YOUR NIGHT-MARES, IF YOU CAN'T FACE HIM IN REAL LIFE.
CAREFUL, MY QUEEN. I'M NOT THE ONLY ONE WHO CAN'T FORGET PAST ENCOUNTERS--DO YOU HEAR ANYTHING FROM YOUR OLD LOVER?

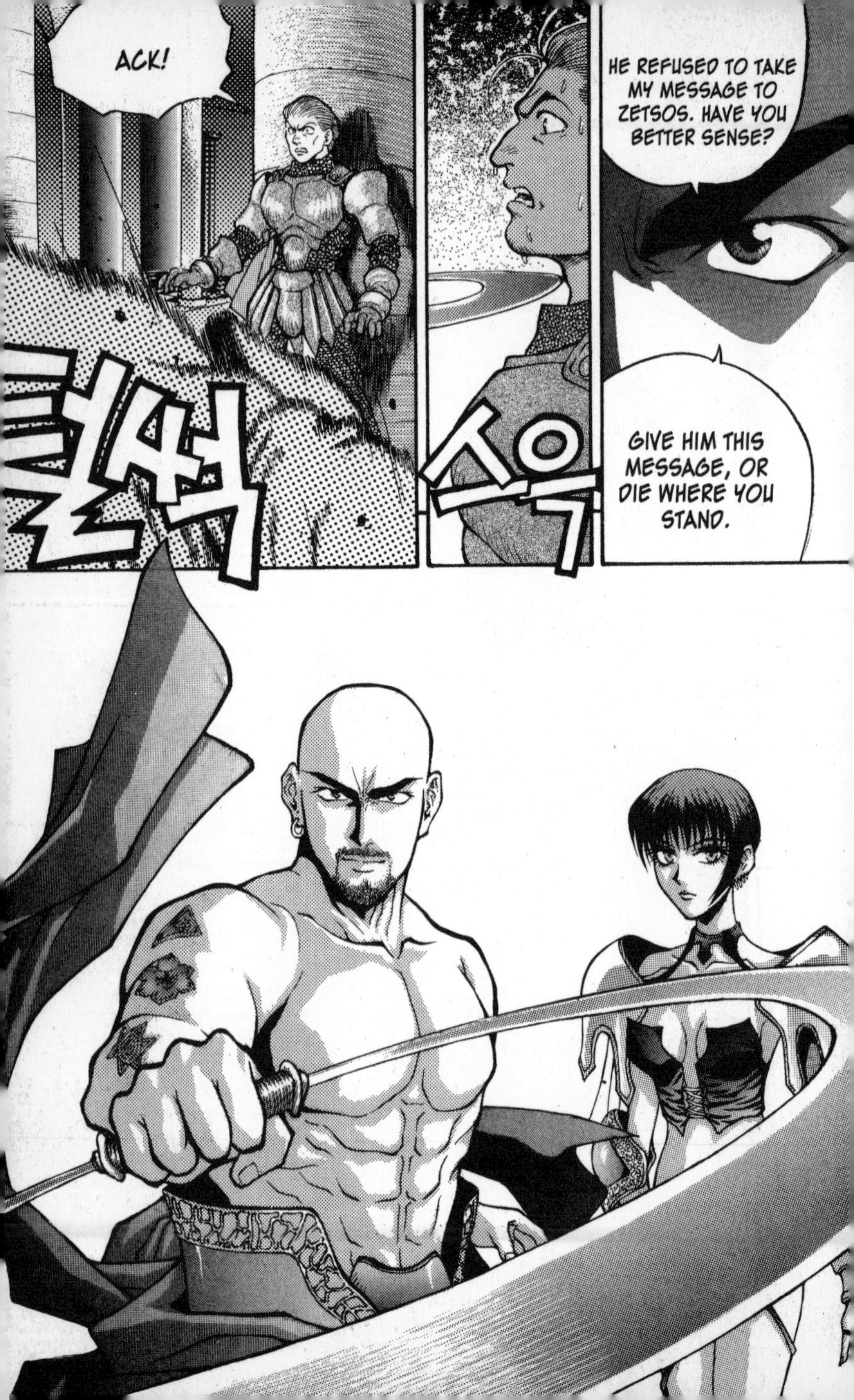
ACK!
HE REFUSED TO TAKE MY MESSAGE TO ZETSOS. HAVE YOU BETTER SENSE?
GIVE HIM THIS MESSAGE, OR DIE WHERE YOU STAND.

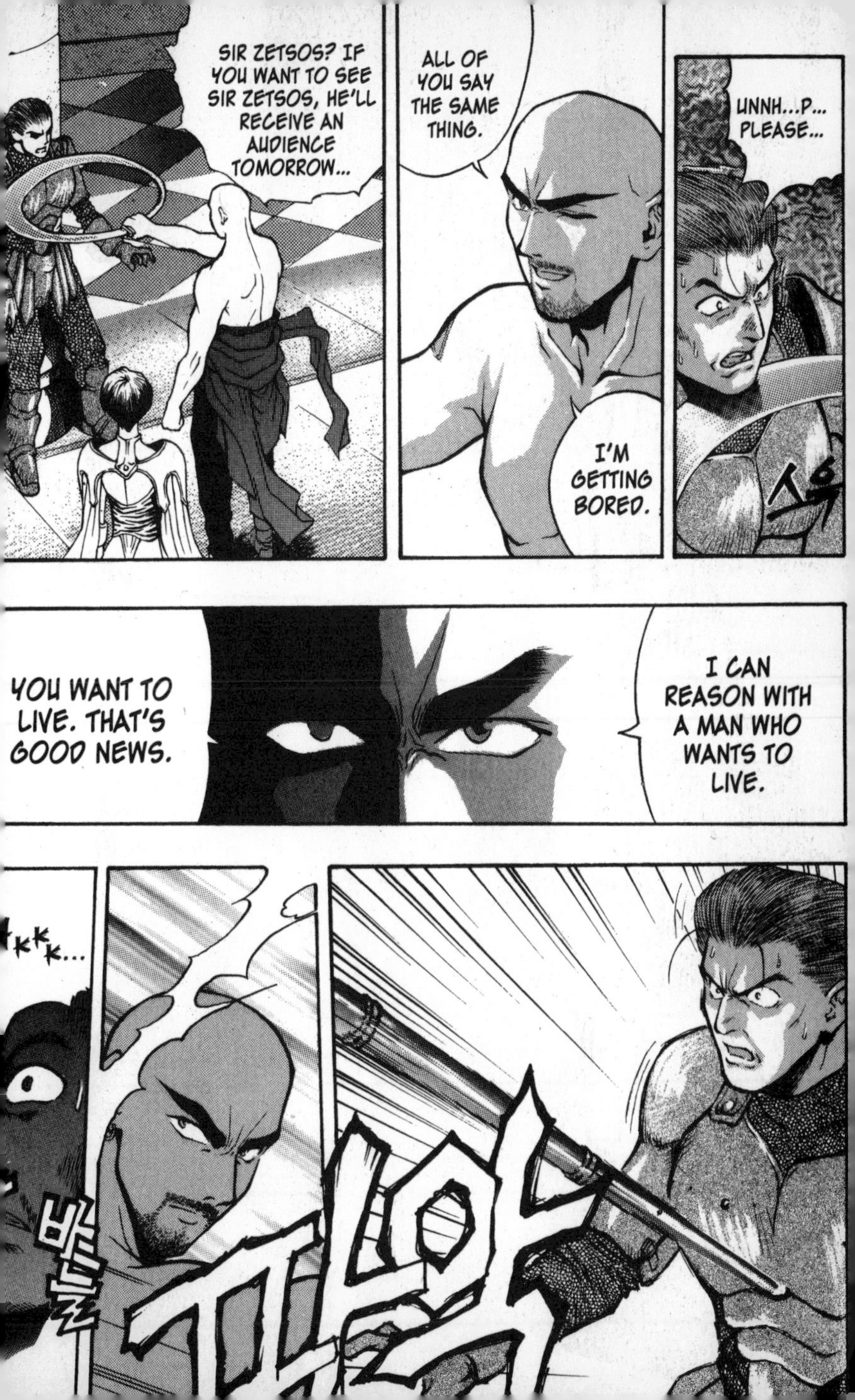
SIR ZETSOS? IF YOU WANT TO SEE SIR ZETSOS, HE'LL RECEIVE AN AUDIENCE TOMORROW...
ALL OF YOU SAY THE SAME THING.
I'M GETTING BORED.
UNNH...P... PLEASE...
YOU WANT TO LIVE. THAT'S GOOD NEWS.
I CAN REASON WITH A MAN WHO WANTS TO LIVE.
KKK...

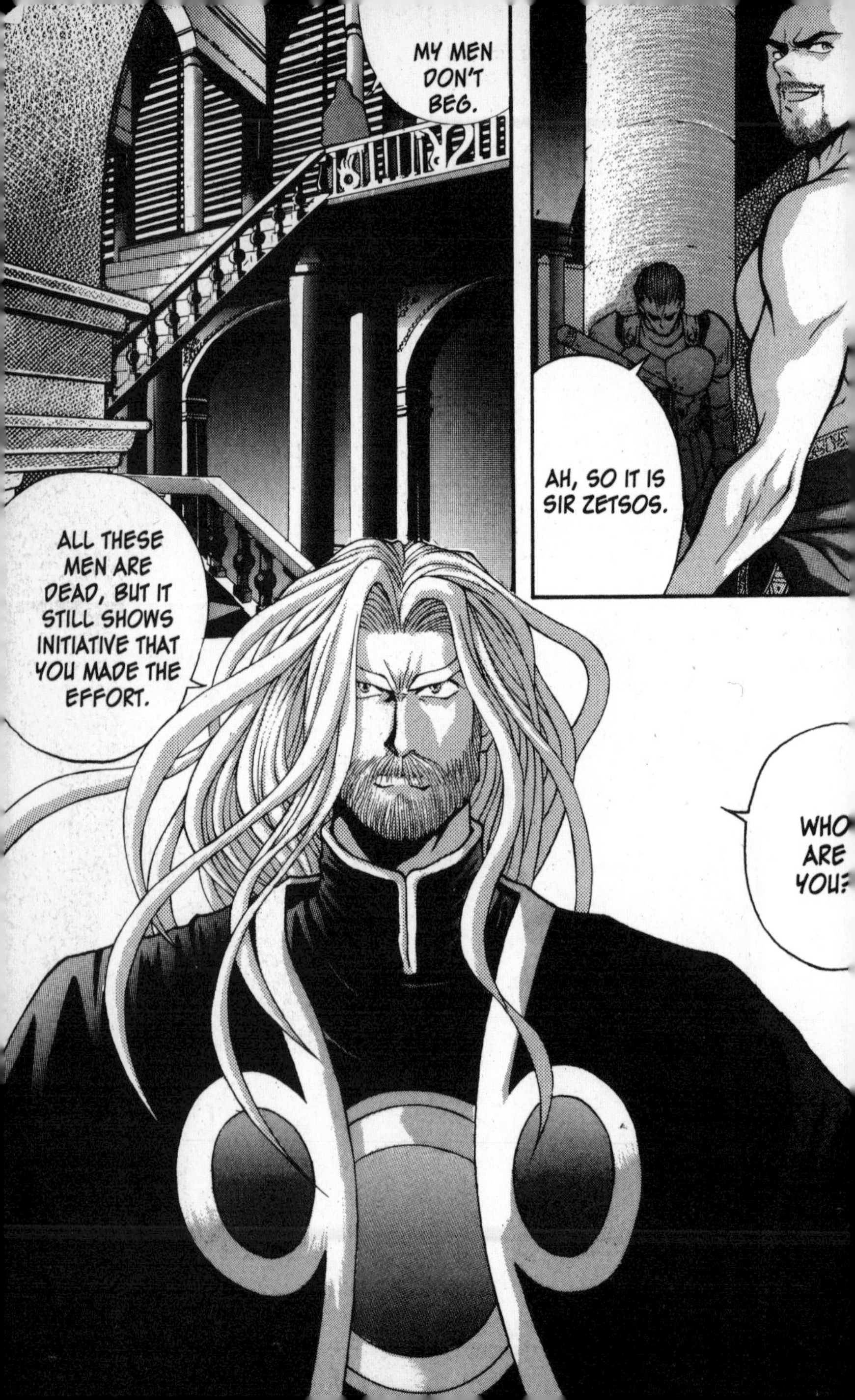
MY MEN DON'T BEG.
AH, SO IT IS SIR ZETSOS.
ALL THESE MEN ARE DEAD, BUT IT STILL SHOWS INITIATIVE THAT YOU MADE THE EFFORT.
WHO ARE YOU?

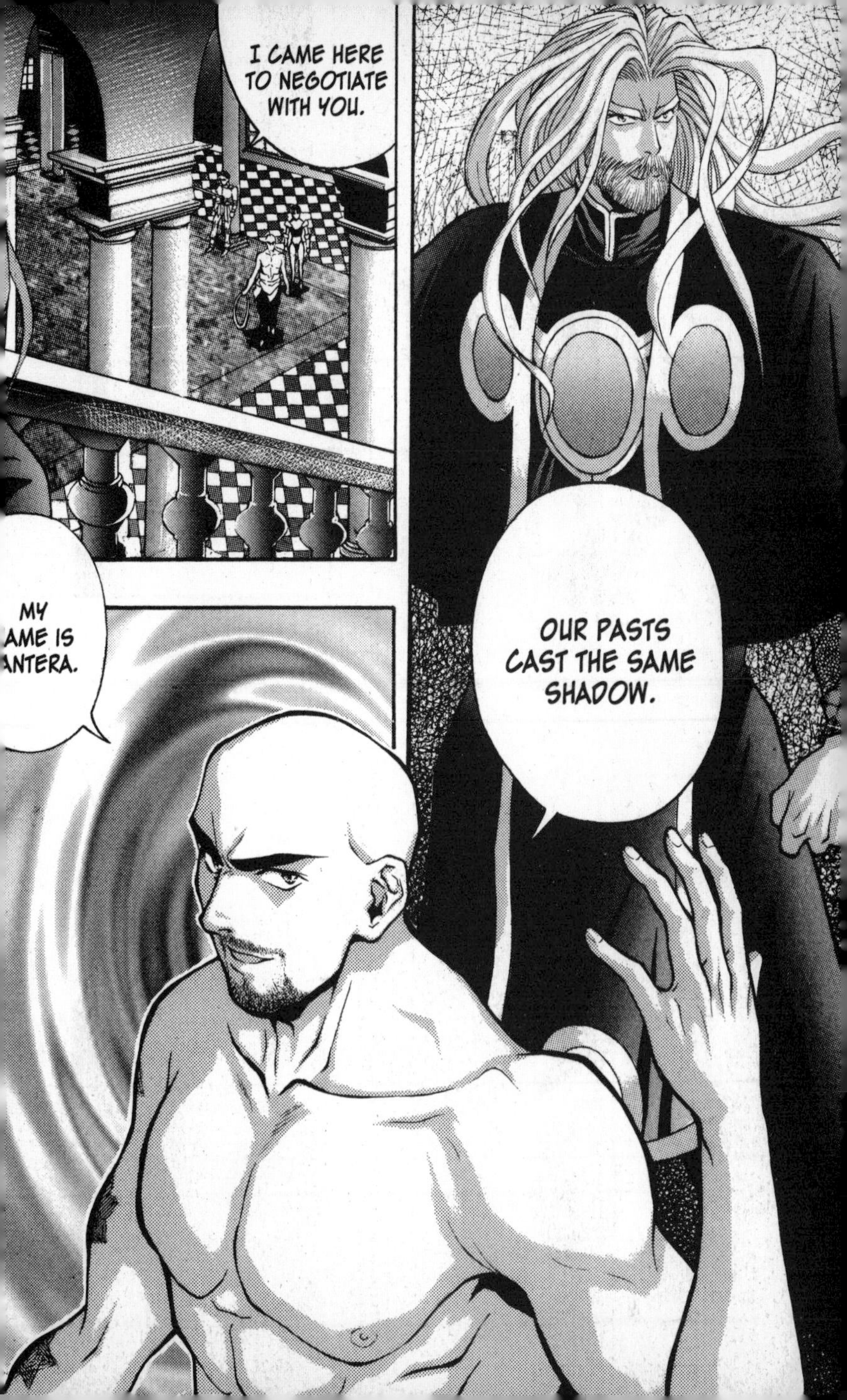
I CAME HERE TO NEGOTIATE WITH YOU.
MY AME IS ANTERA.
OUR PASTS CAST THE SAME SHADOW.

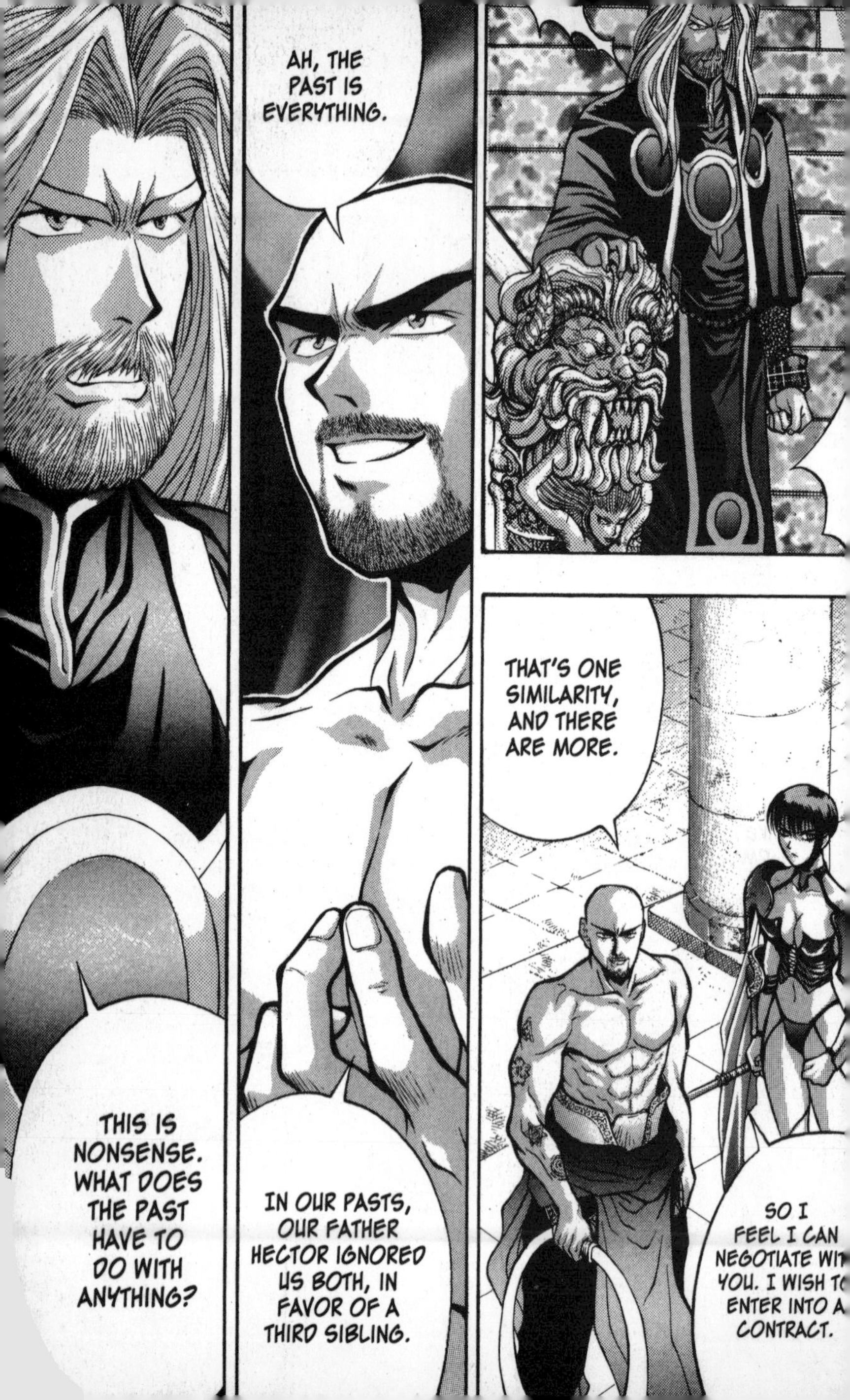
THIS IS NONSENSE. WHAT DOES THE PAST HAVE TO DO WITH ANYTHING?
AH, THE PAST IS EVERYTHING.
IN OUR PASTS, OUR FATHER HECTOR IGNORED US BOTH, IN FAVOR OF A THIRD SIBLING.
THAT'S ONE SIMILARITY, AND THERE ARE MORE.
SO I FEEL I CAN NEGOTIATE WIT YOU. I WISH T ENTER INTO A CONTRACT.

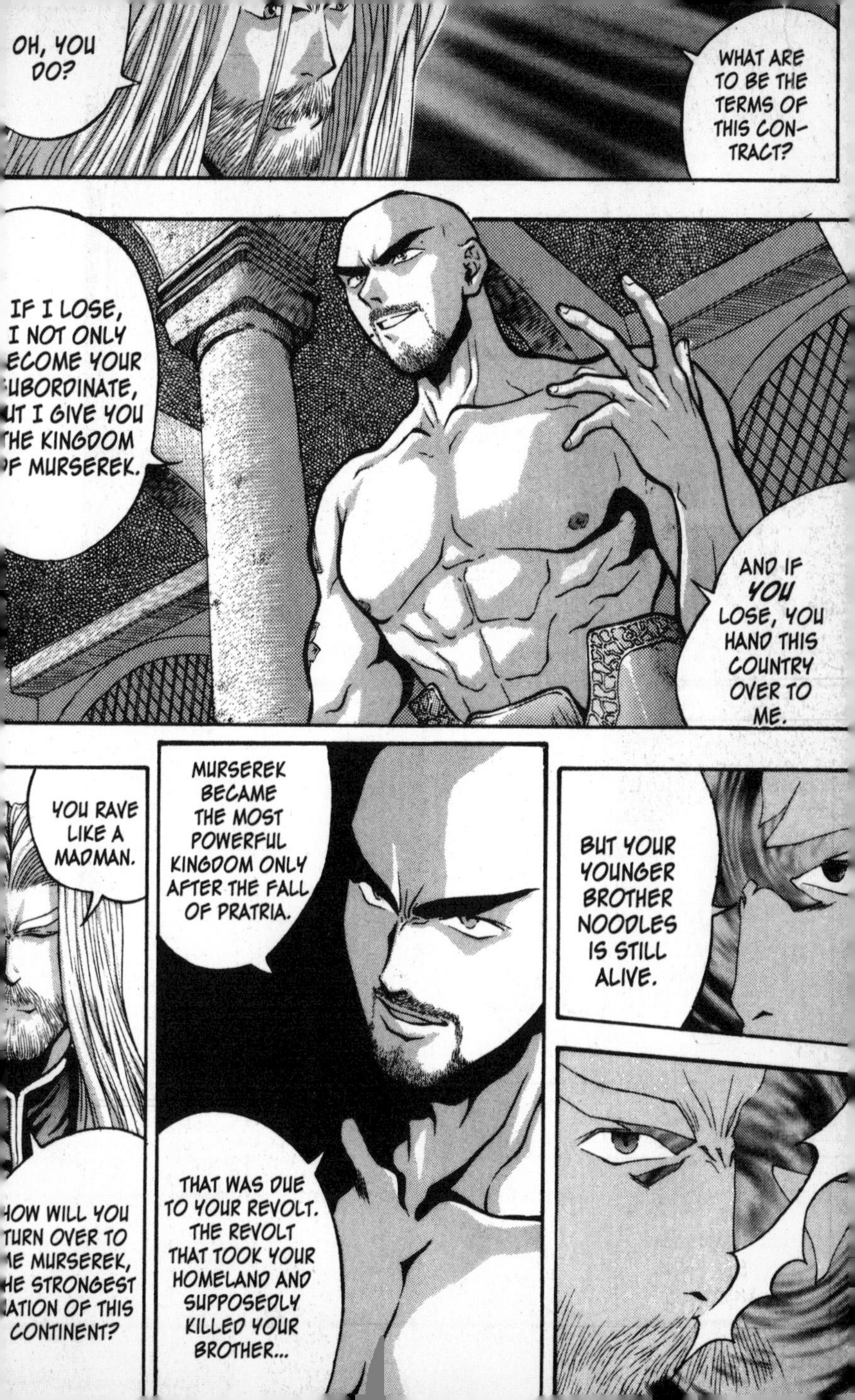
OH, YOU DO?
WHAT ARE TO BE THE TERMS OF THIS CON-TRACT?
IF I LOSE, I NOT ONLY ECOME YOUR UBORDINATE, UT I GIVE YOU HE KINGDOM F MURSEREK.
AND IF YOU LOSE, YOU HAND THIS COUNTRY OVER TO ME.
YOU RAVE LIKE A MADMAN.
HOW WILL YOU URN OVER TO E MURSEREK, HE STRONGEST ATION OF THIS CONTINENT?
MURSEREK BECAME THE MOST POWERFUL KINGDOM ONLY AFTER THE FALL OF PRATRIA.
THAT WAS DUE TO YOUR REVOLT. THE REVOLT THAT TOOK YOUR HOMELAND AND SUPPOSEDLY KILLED YOUR BROTHER...
BUT YOUR YOUNGER BROTHER NOODLES IS STILL ALIVE.

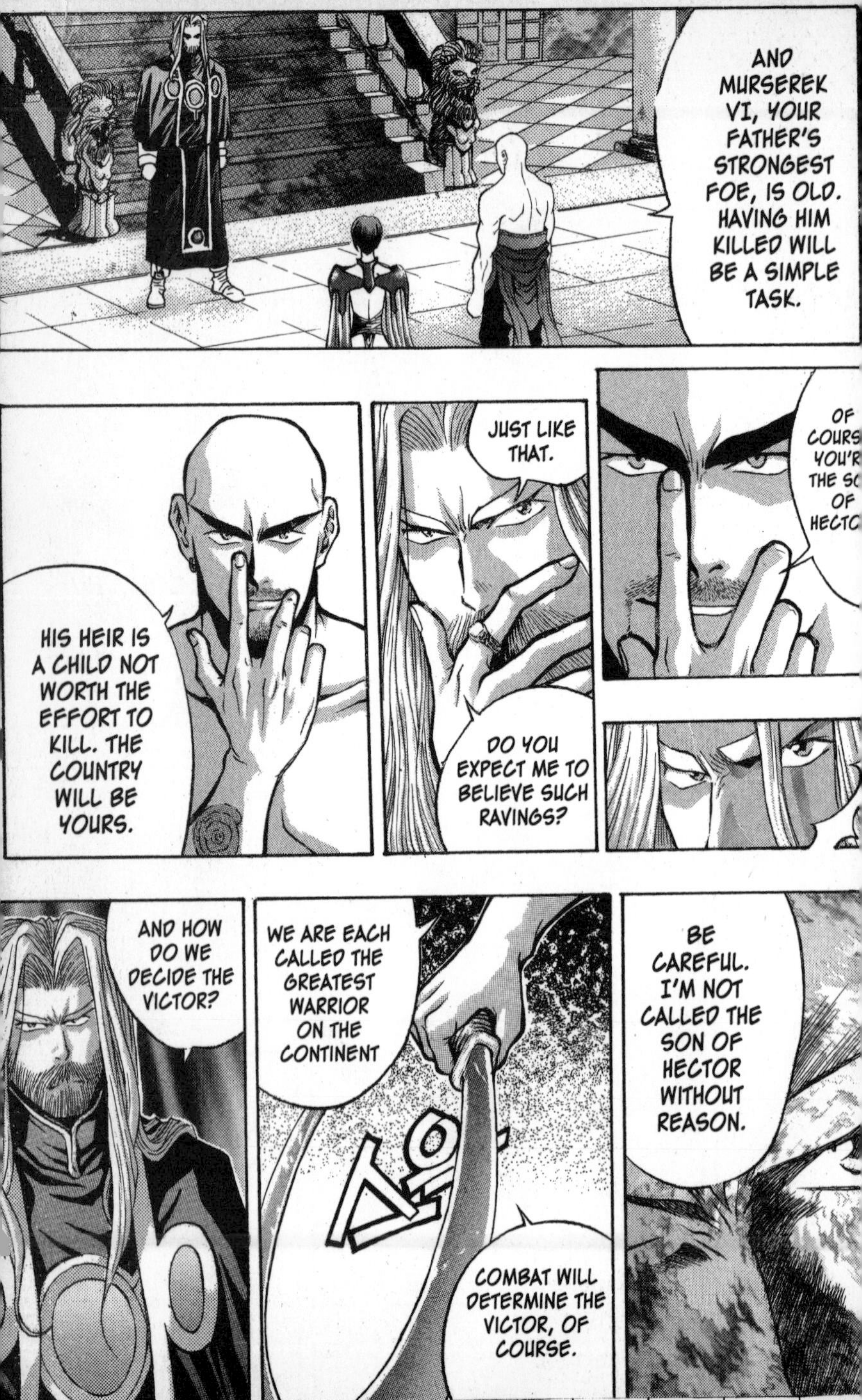
AND MURSEREK VI, YOUR FATHER'S STRONGEST FOE, IS OLD. HAVING HIM KILLED WILL BE A SIMPLE TASK.
HIS HEIR IS A CHILD NOT WORTH THE EFFORT TO KILL. THE COUNTRY WILL BE YOURS.
JUST LIKE THAT.
DO YOU EXPECT ME TO BELIEVE SUCH RAVINGS?
OF COURS YOU'R THE S OF HECT
AND HOW DO WE DECIDE THE VICTOR?
WE ARE EACH CALLED THE GREATEST WARRIOR ON THE CONTINENT
COMBAT WILL DETERMINE THE VICTOR, OF COURSE.
BE CAREFUL. I'M NOT CALLED THE SON OF HECTOR WITHOUT REASON.

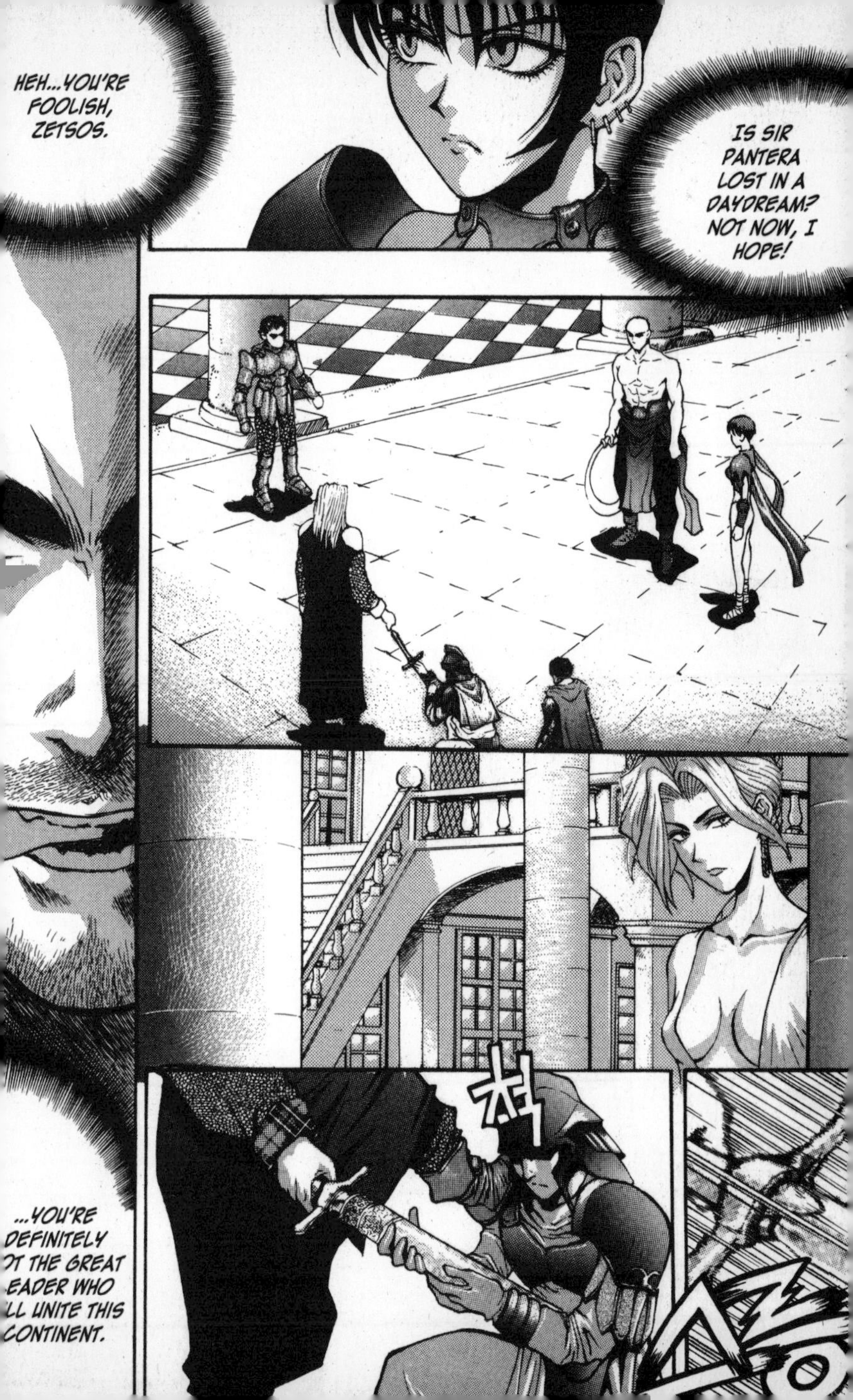
HEH...YOU'RE FOOLISH, ZETSOS.
IS SIR PANTERA LOST IN A DAYDREAM? NOT NOW, I HOPE!
...YOU'RE
DEFINITELY
OT THE GREAT
EADER WHO
LL UNITE THIS
CONTINENT.

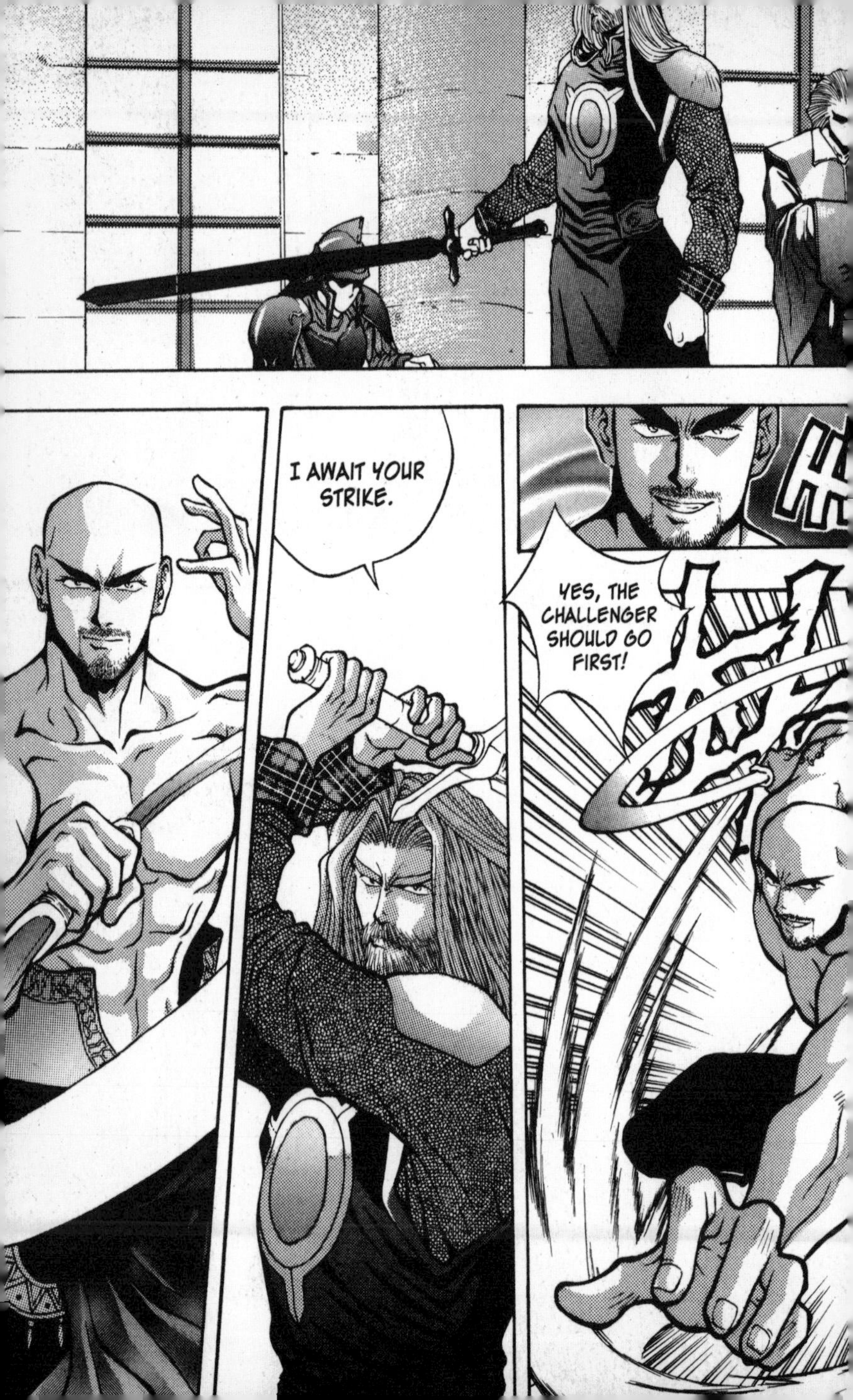
I AWAIT YOUR STRIKE.
YES, THE CHALLENGER SHOULD GO FIRST!

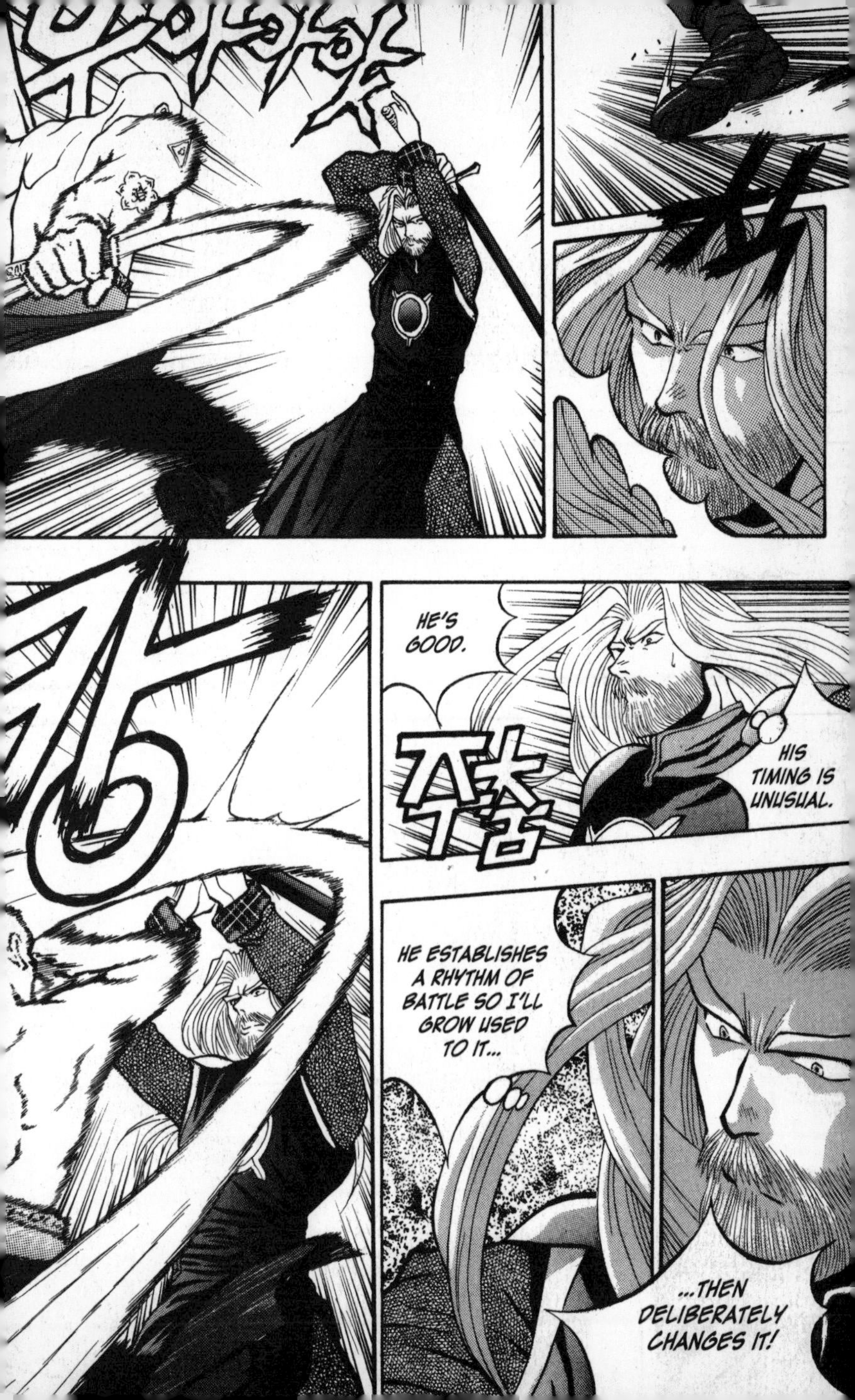
HE'S GOOD.
HIS TIMING IS UNUSUAL.
HE ESTABLISHES A RHYTHM OF BATTLE SO I'LL GROW USED TO IT...
...THEN DELIBERATELY CHANGES IT!

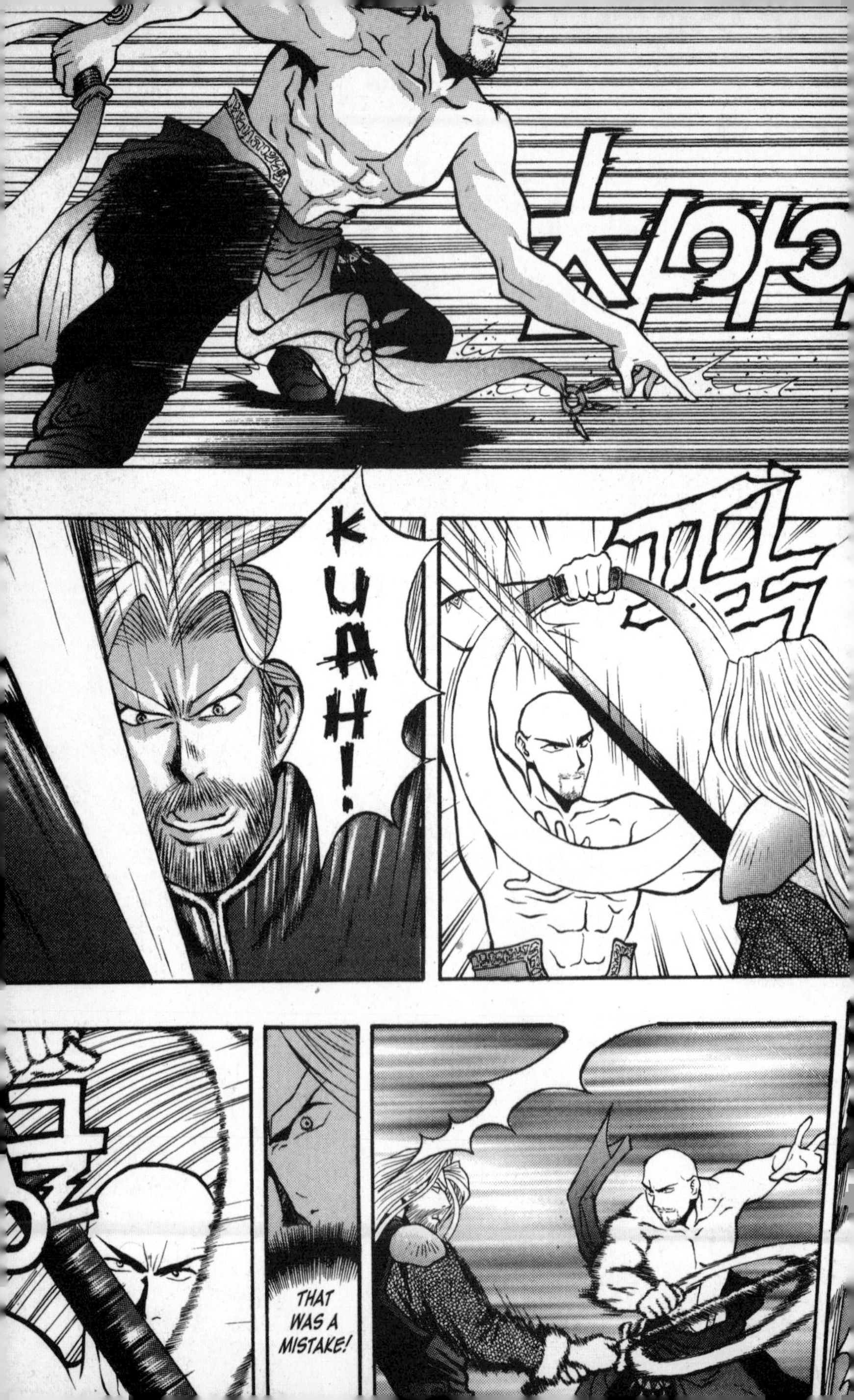
KUAH!
THAT WAS A MISTAKE!

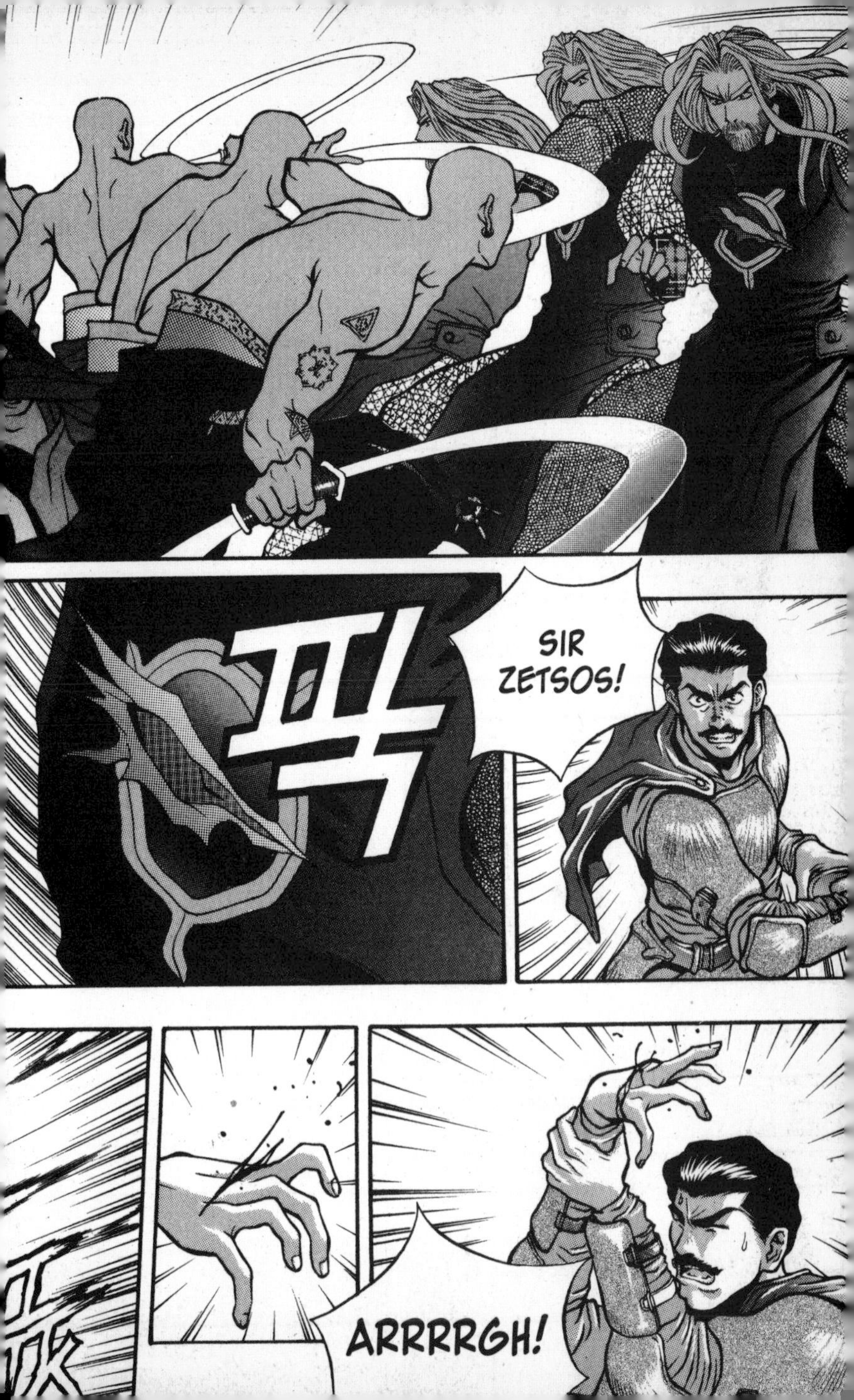

퍽
SIR ZETSOS!
ARRRRGH!

THIS DUEL IS BETWEEN THEM. AND NO ONE ELSE.

BEGONE!

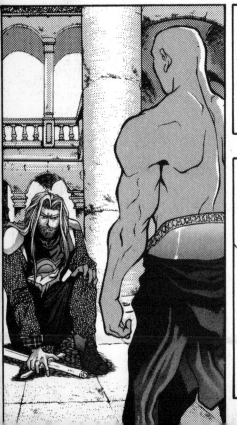

INTERESTING. I WAS DEFENSELESS JUST THEN, AND HE DIDN'T ATTACK.

B...
WHY

YOU'RE NOT PAYING ATTENTION. THAT'S A MISTAKE A BEGINNER MAKES.

BUT I'L GIVE YO ANOTHE CHANCE

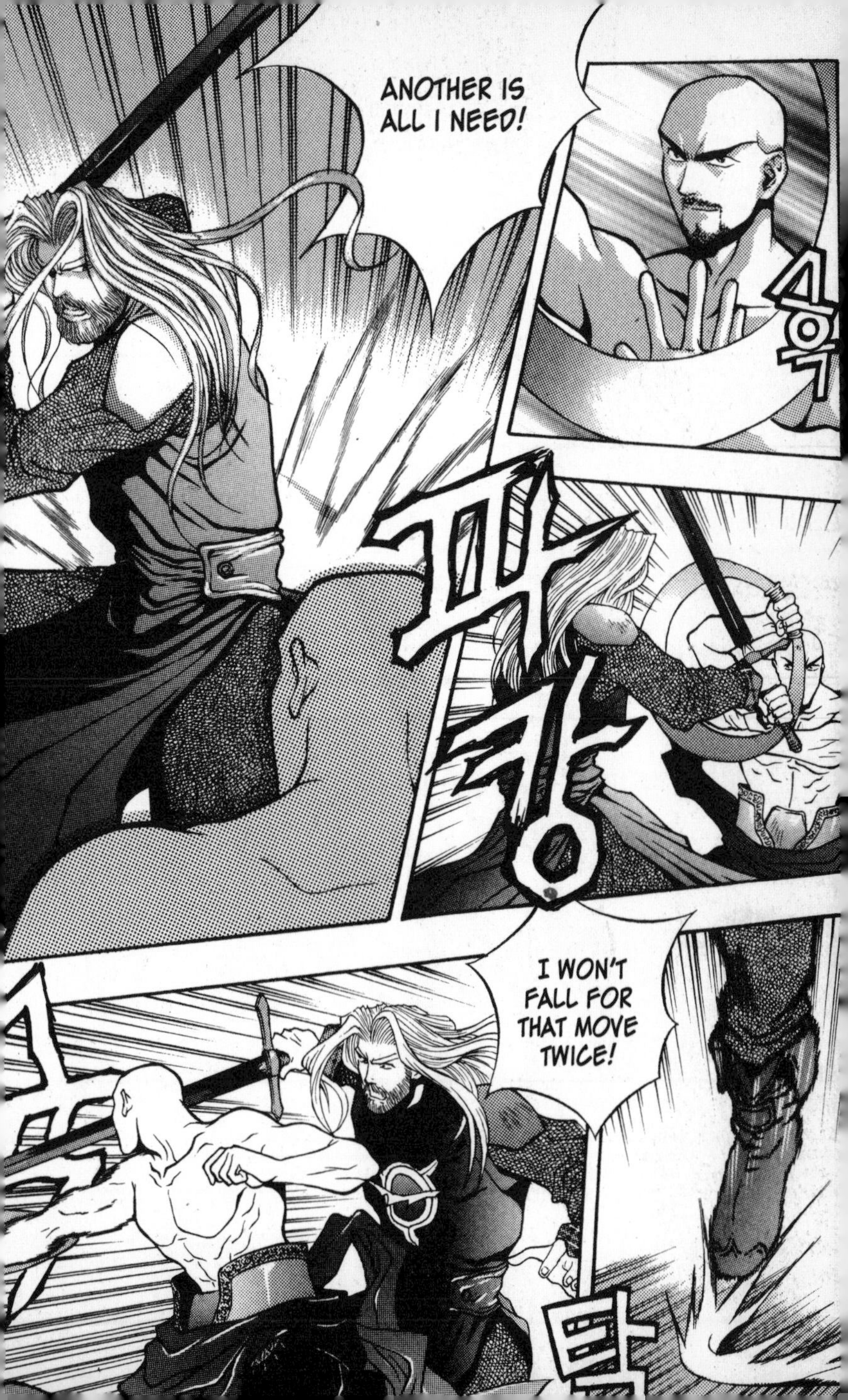
ANOTHER IS ALL I NEED!
스윽
파캉
I WON'T FALL FOR THAT MOVE TWICE!
탁

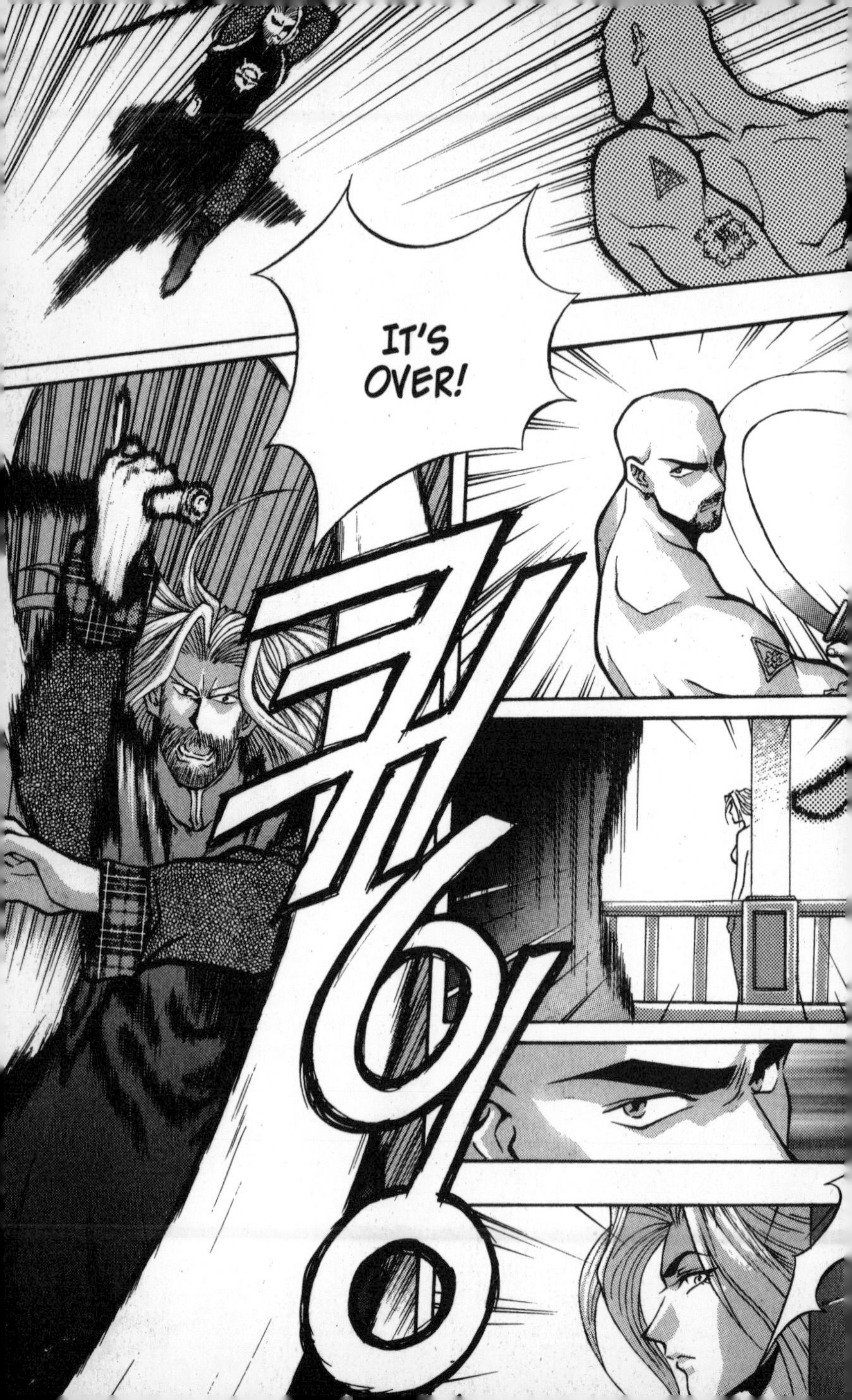

IT'S OVER!

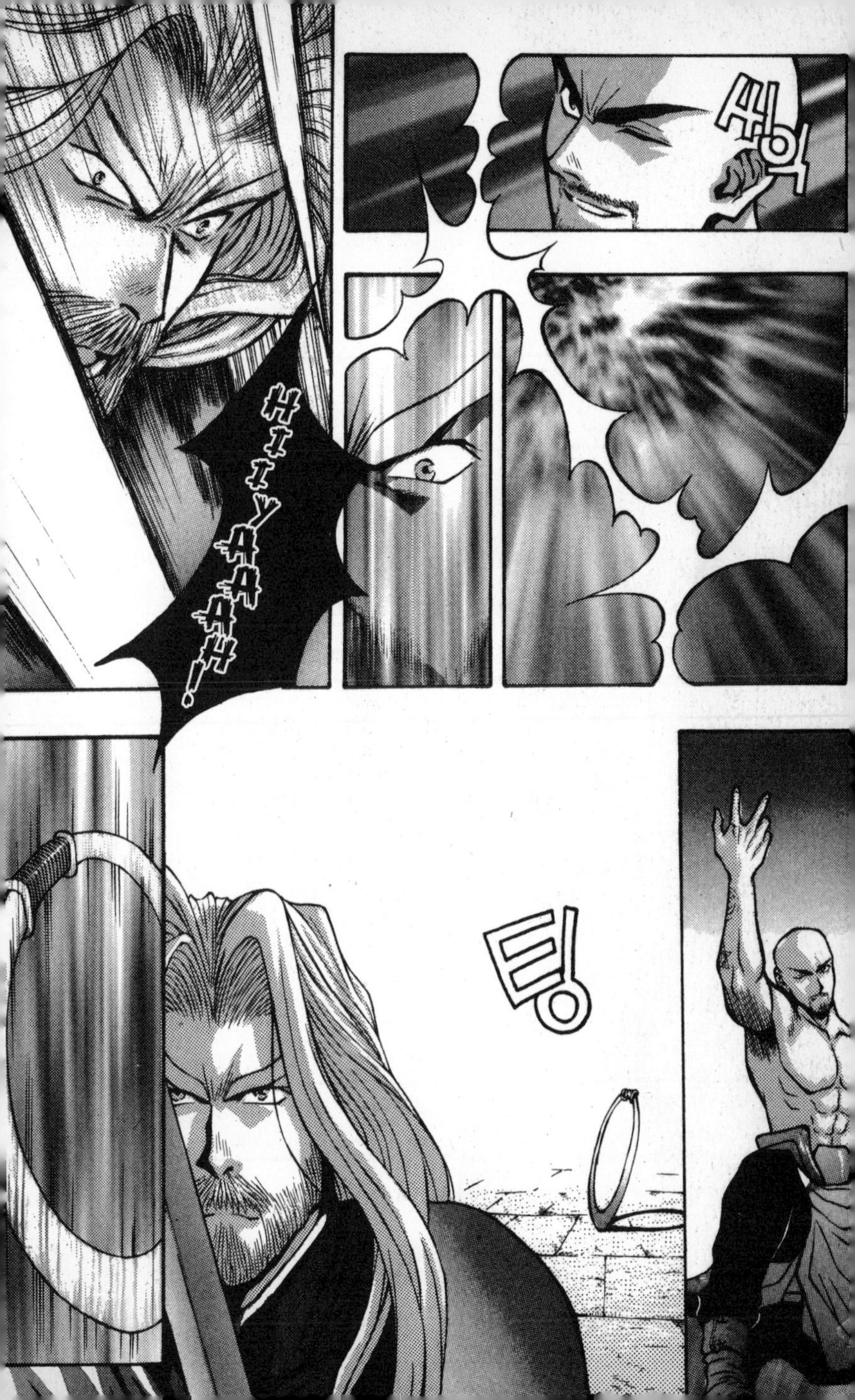
HIIYAAAH!
쉬익
팅

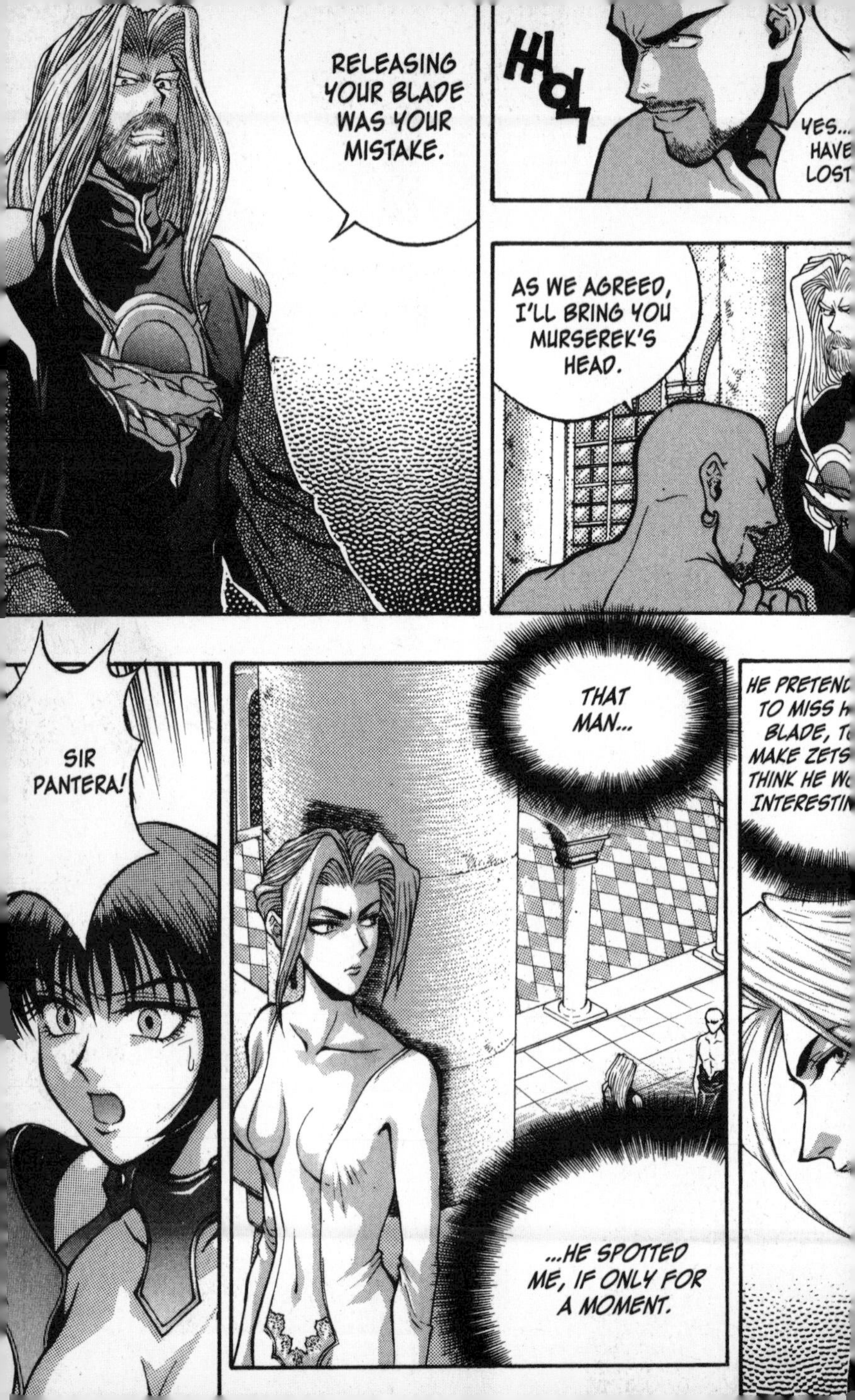
RELEASING YOUR BLADE WAS YOUR MISTAKE.
HOLD
YES... HAVE LOST
AS WE AGREED, I'LL BRING YOU MURSEREK'S HEAD.
SIR PANTERA!
THAT MAN...
...HE SPOTTED ME, IF ONLY FOR A MOMENT.
HE PRETEND TO MISS H BLADE, TO MAKE ZETS THINK HE WO INTERESTIN

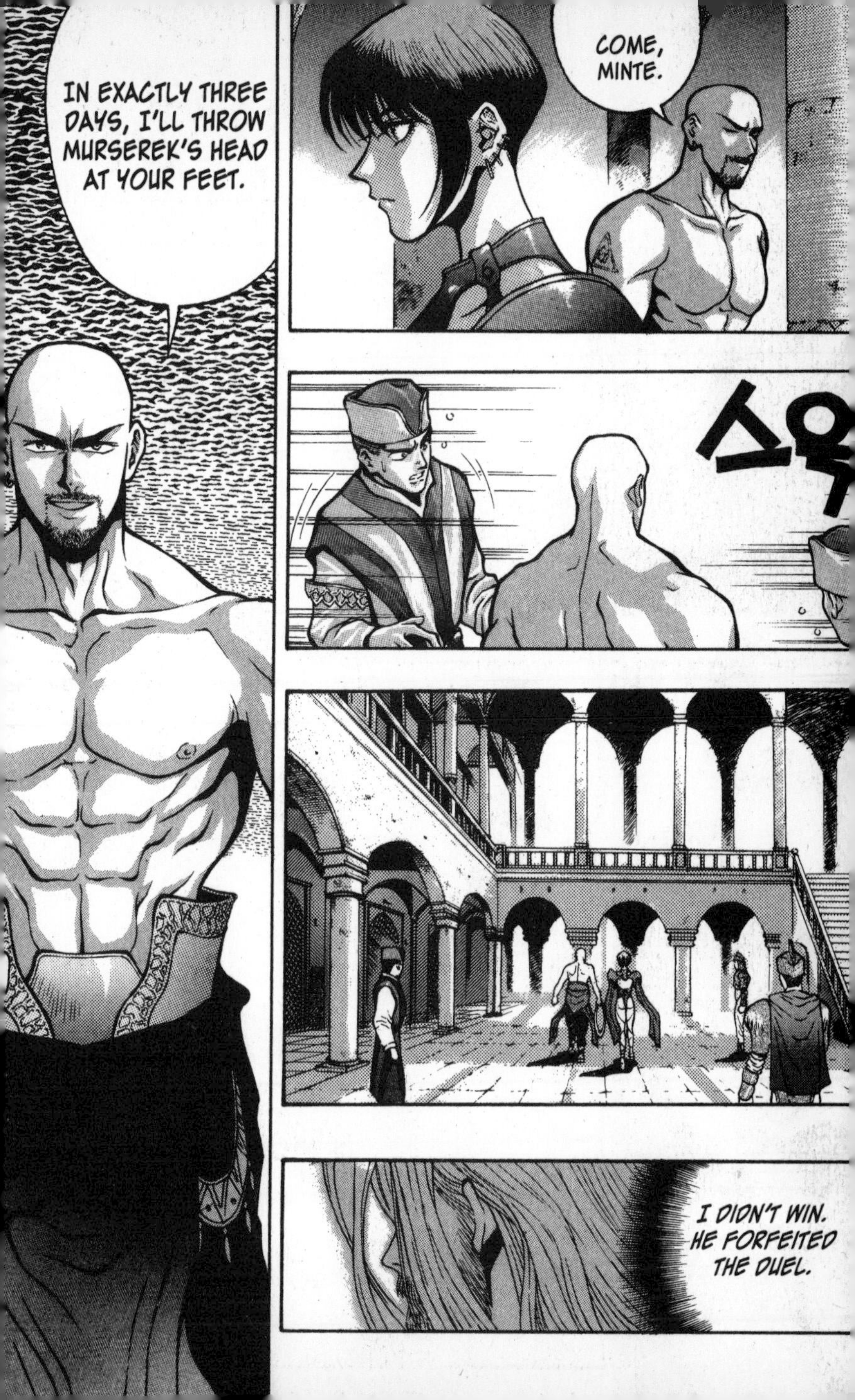
IN EXACTLY THREE DAYS, I'LL THROW MURSEREK'S HEAD AT YOUR FEET.
COME, MINTE.
I DIDN'T WIN. HE FORFEITED THE DUEL.

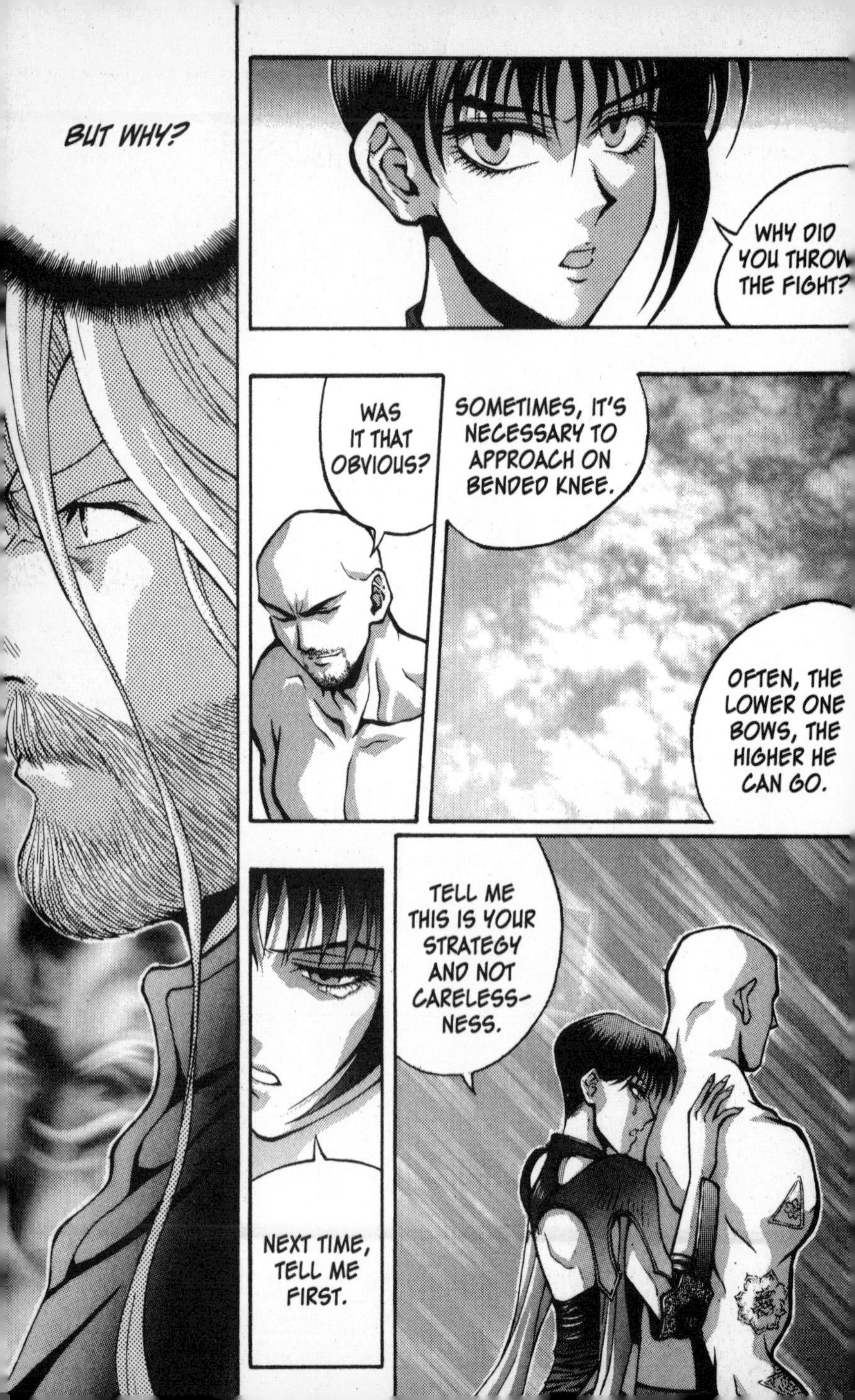
BUT WHY?
WHY DID YOU THROW THE FIGHT?
WAS IT THAT OBVIOUS?
SOMETIMES, IT'S NECESSARY TO APPROACH ON BENDED KNEE.
OFTEN, THE LOWER ONE BOWS, THE HIGHER HE CAN GO.
TELL ME THIS IS YOUR STRATEGY AND NOT CARELESS-NESS.
NEXT TIME, TELL ME FIRST.

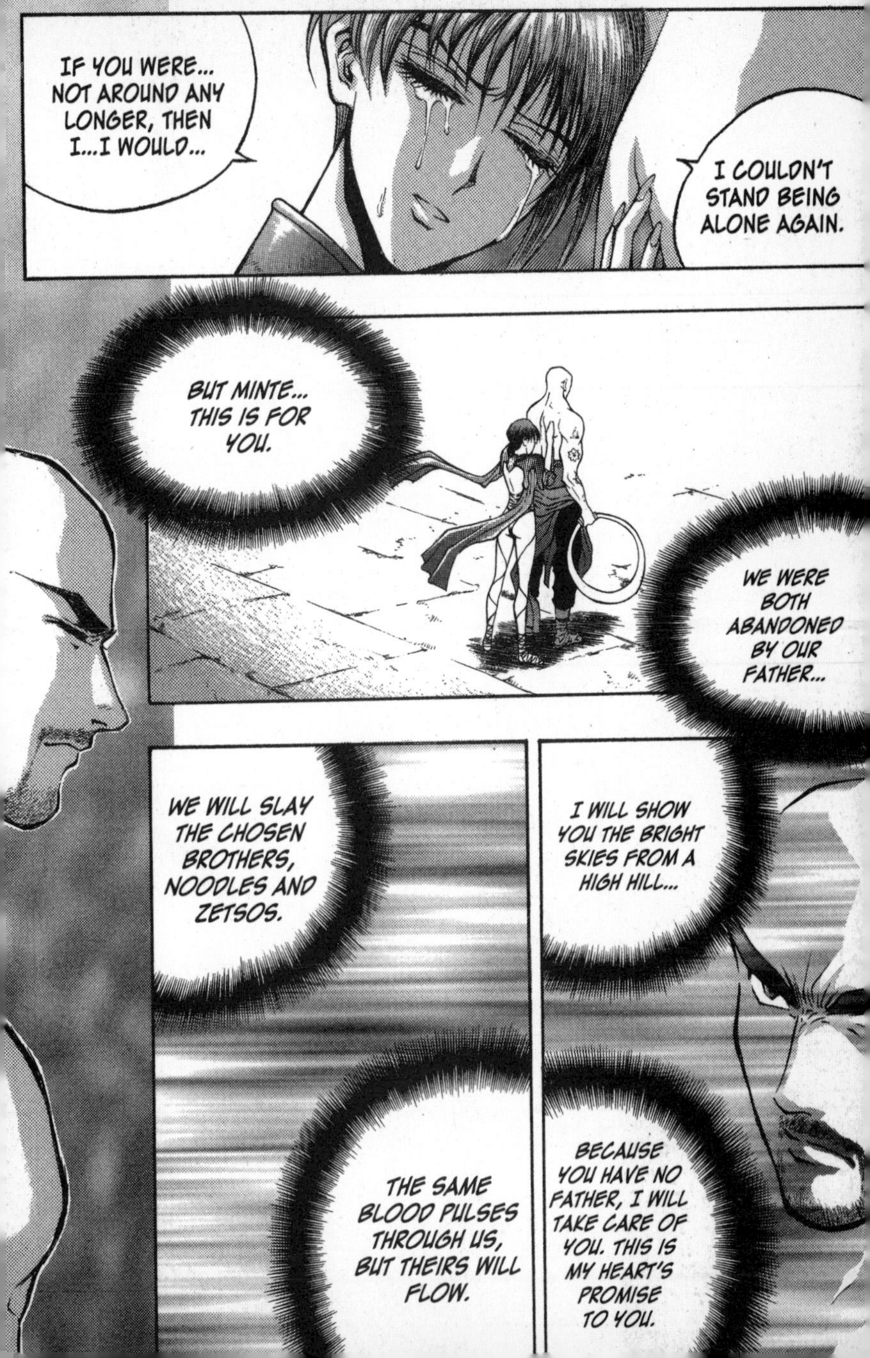
IF YOU WERE... NOT AROUND ANY LONGER, THEN I...I WOULD...
I COULDN'T STAND BEING ALONE AGAIN.
BUT MINTE... THIS IS FOR YOU.
WE WERE BOTH ABANDONED BY OUR FATHER...
WE WILL SLAY THE CHOSEN BROTHERS, NOODLES AND ZETSOS.
THE SAME BLOOD PULSES THROUGH US, BUT THEIRS WILL FLOW.
I WILL SHOW YOU THE BRIGHT SKIES FROM A HIGH HILL...
BECAUSE YOU HAVE NO FATHER, I WILL TAKE CARE OF YOU. THIS IS MY HEART'S PROMISE TO YOU.

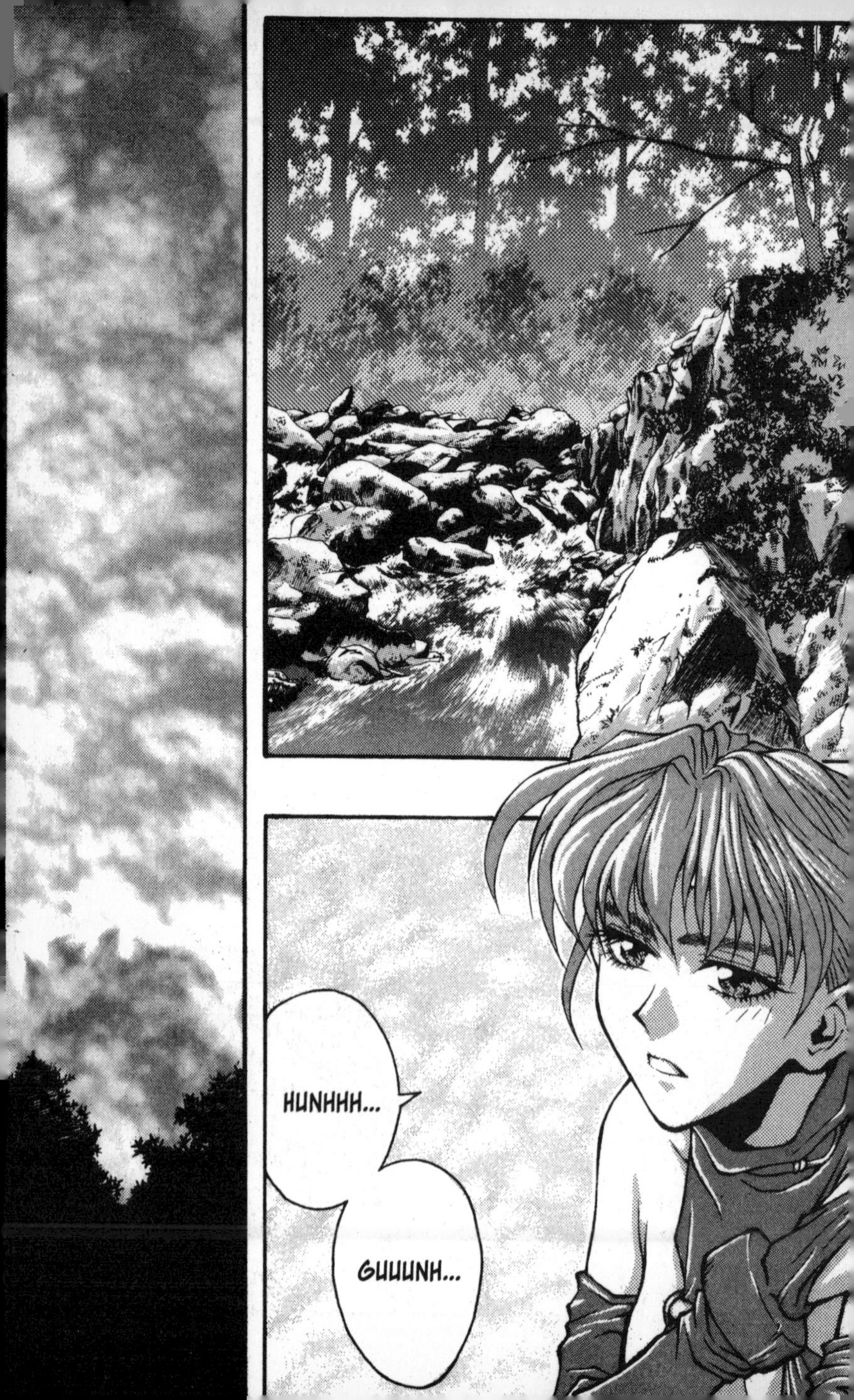
HUNHHH...
GUUUNH...

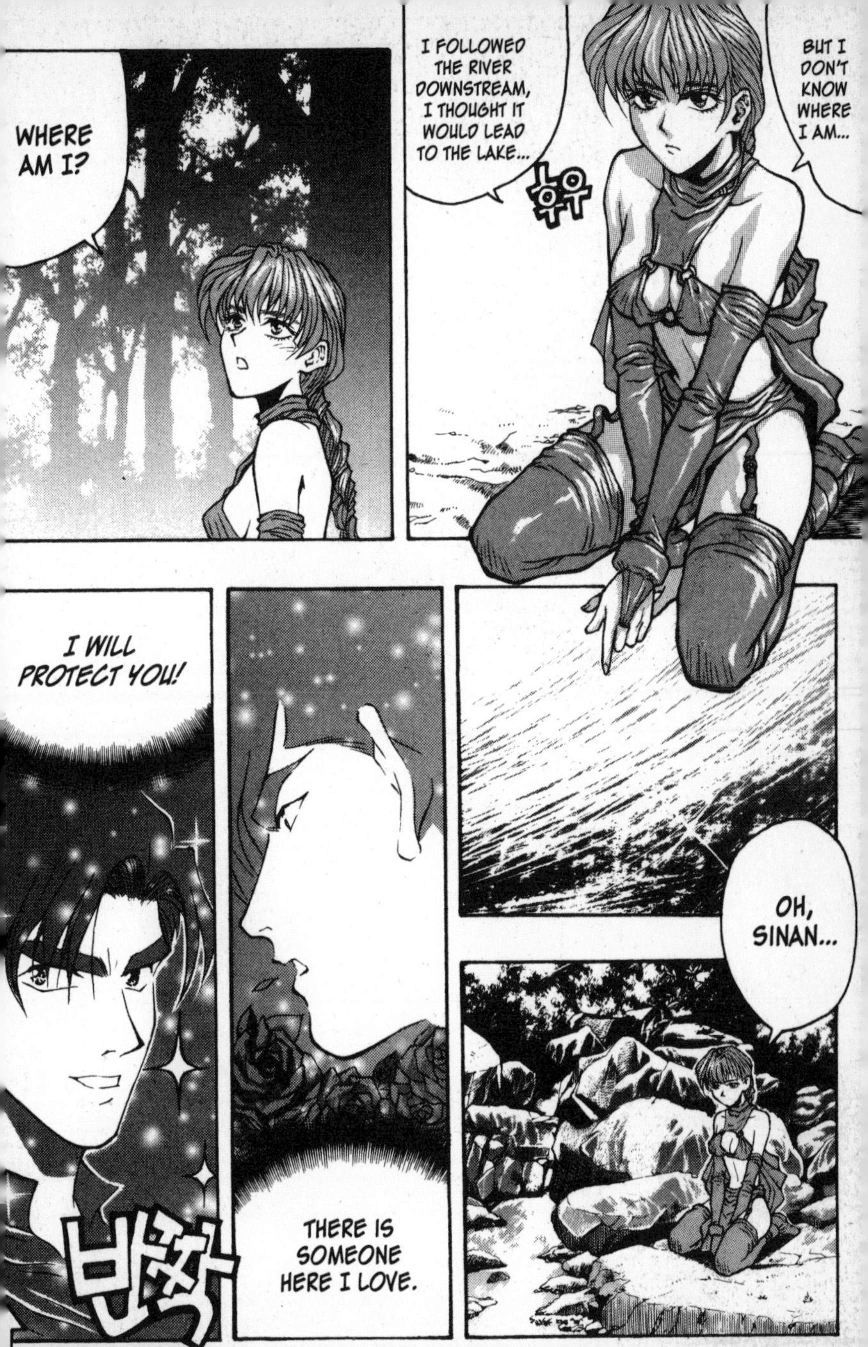
WHERE AM I?
I FOLLOWED THE RIVER DOWNSTREAM, I THOUGHT IT WOULD LEAD TO THE LAKE...
BUT I DON'T KNOW WHERE I AM...
I WILL PROTECT YOU!
반짝
THERE IS SOMEONE HERE I LOVE.
OH, SINAN...

The stars are in Mayi's eyes.

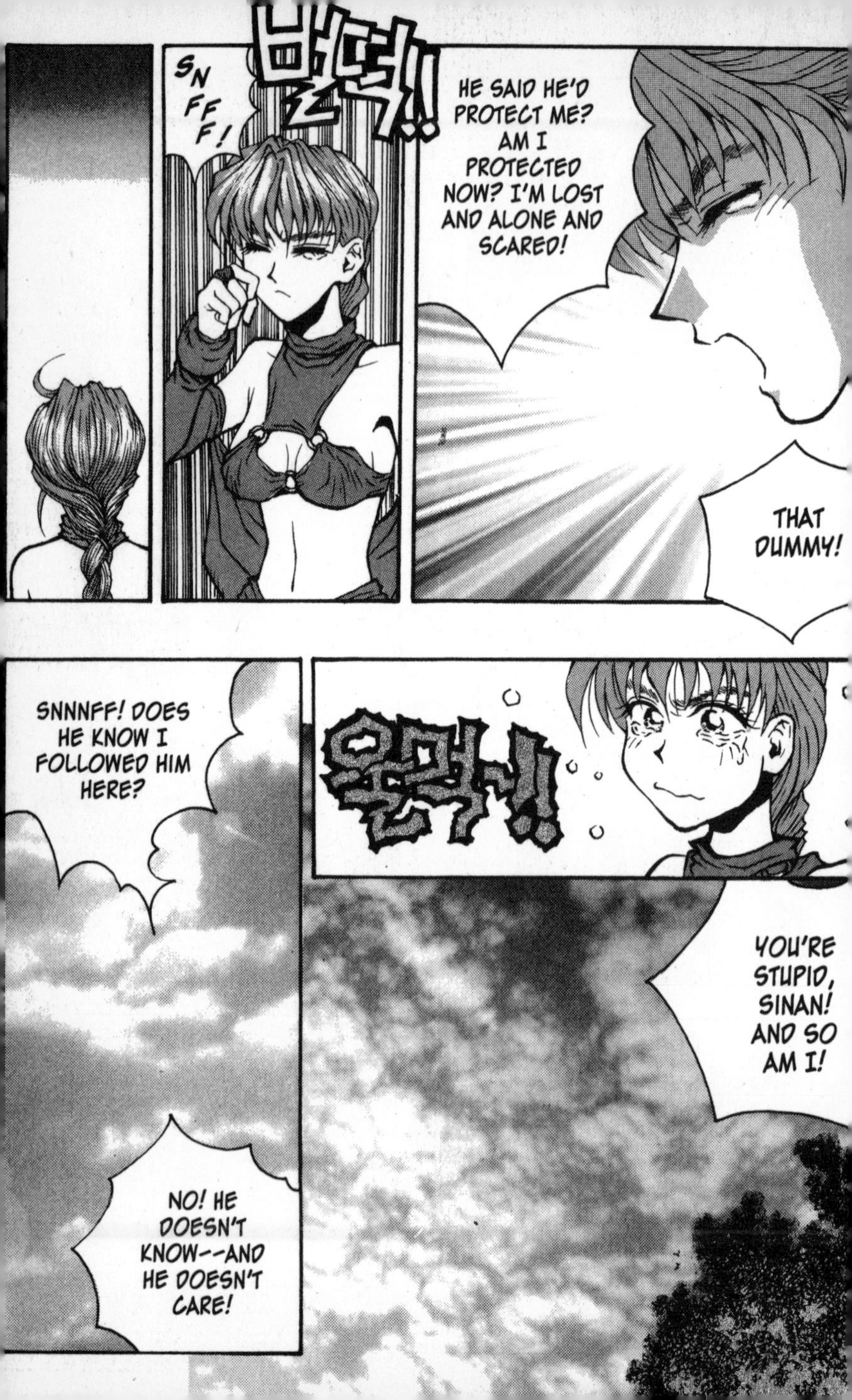

SNFFF!
벌떡!!
HE SAID HE'D PROTECT ME? AM I PROTECTED NOW? I'M LOST AND ALONE AND SCARED!
THAT DUMMY!
SNNNFF! DOES HE KNOW I FOLLOWED HIM HERE?
NO! HE DOESN'T KNOW--AND HE DOESN'T CARE!
울컥!!
YOU'RE STUPID, SINAN! AND SO AM I!

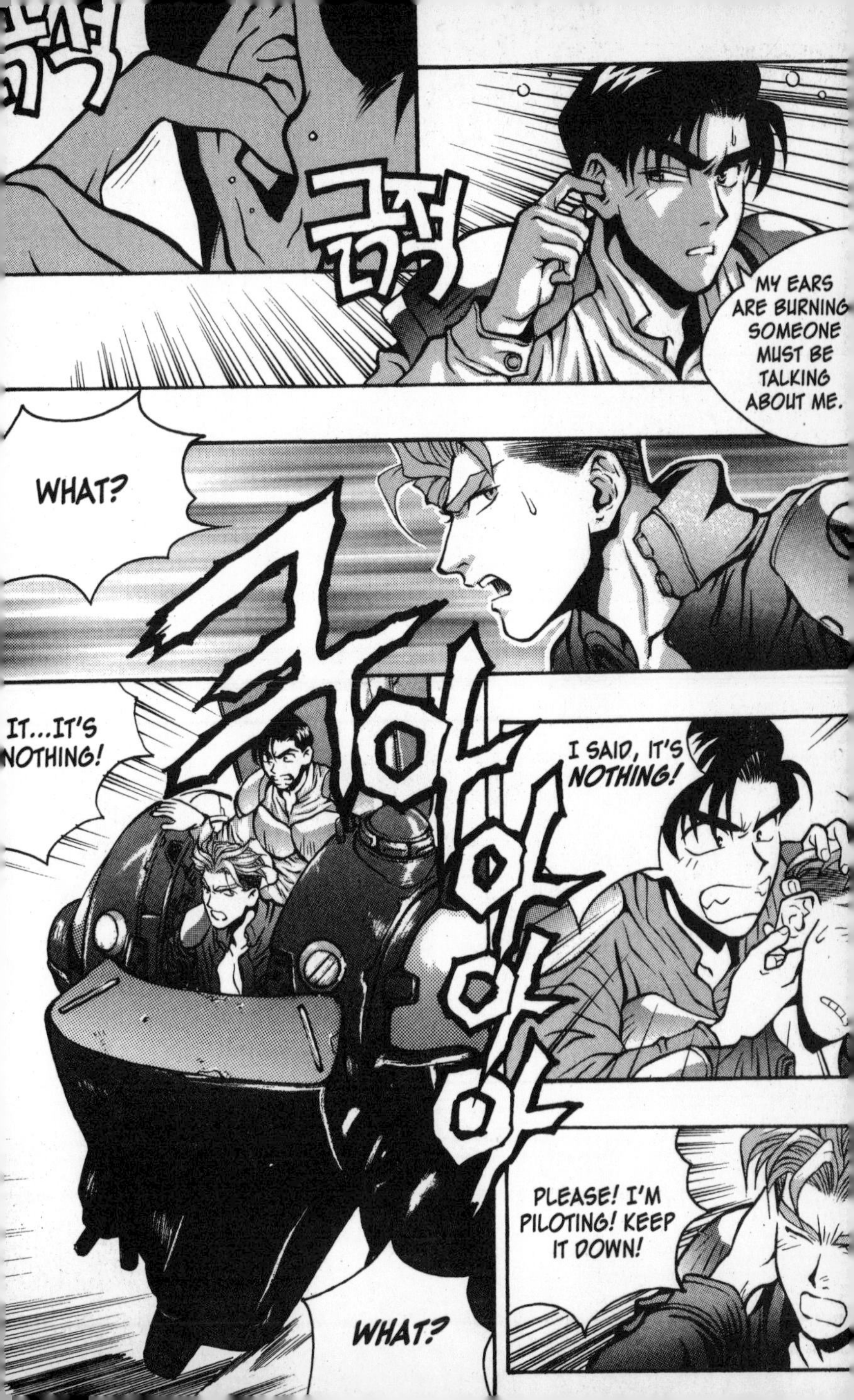
MY EARS ARE BURNING SOMEONE MUST BE TALKING ABOUT ME.
WHAT?
IT...IT'S NOTHING!
WHAT?
I SAID, IT'S NOTHING!
PLEASE! I'M PILOTING! KEEP IT DOWN!

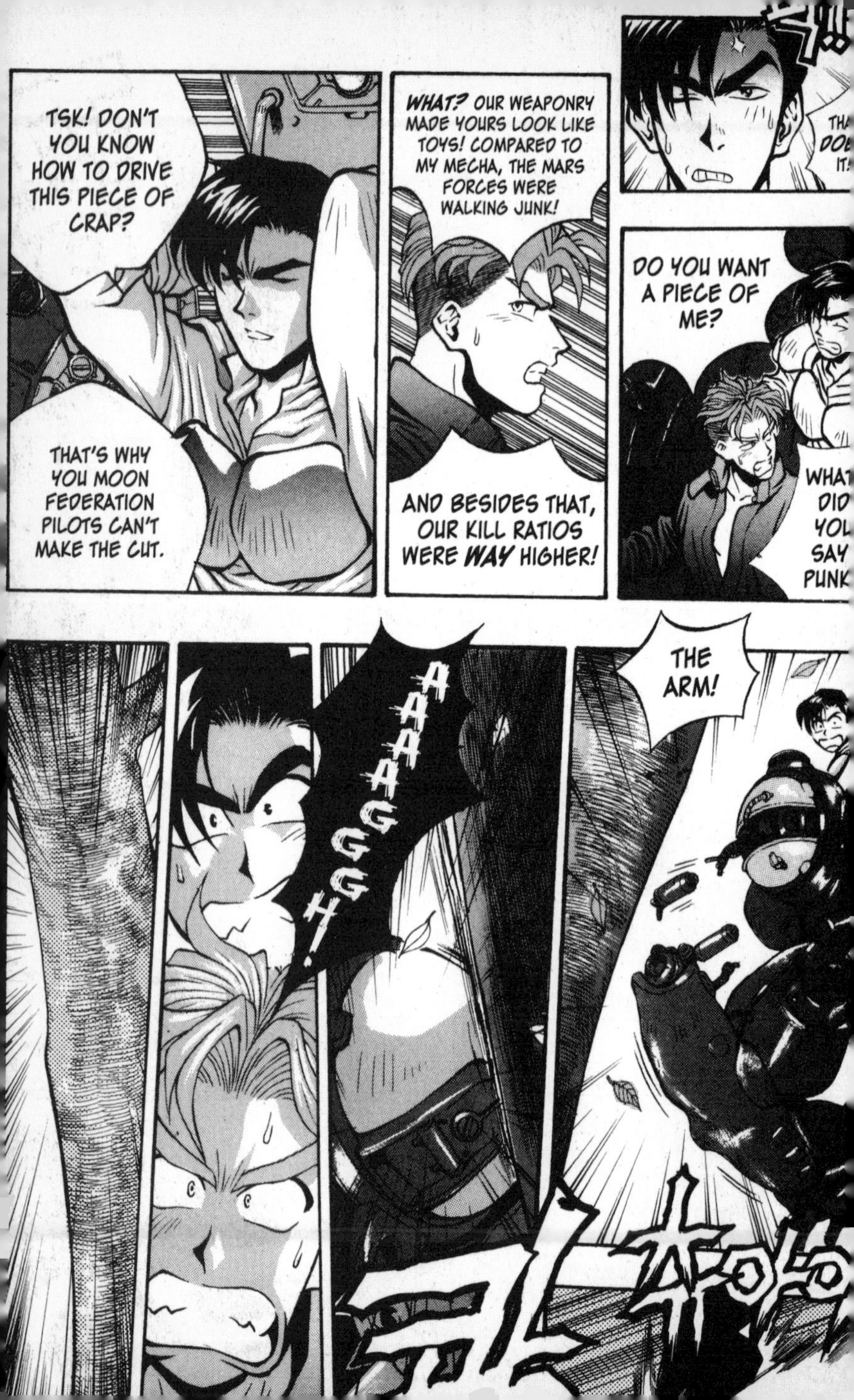
TSK! DON'T YOU KNOW HOW TO DRIVE THIS PIECE OF CRAP?
THAT'S WHY YOU MOON FEDERATION PILOTS CAN'T MAKE THE CUT.
WHAT? OUR WEAPONRY MADE YOURS LOOK LIKE TOYS! COMPARED TO MY MECHA, THE MARS FORCES WERE WALKING JUNK!
AND BESIDES THAT, OUR KILL RATIOS WERE WAY HIGHER!
DO YOU WANT A PIECE OF ME?
WHAT DID YOU SAY PUNK
AAAAAGGGH!
THE ARM!

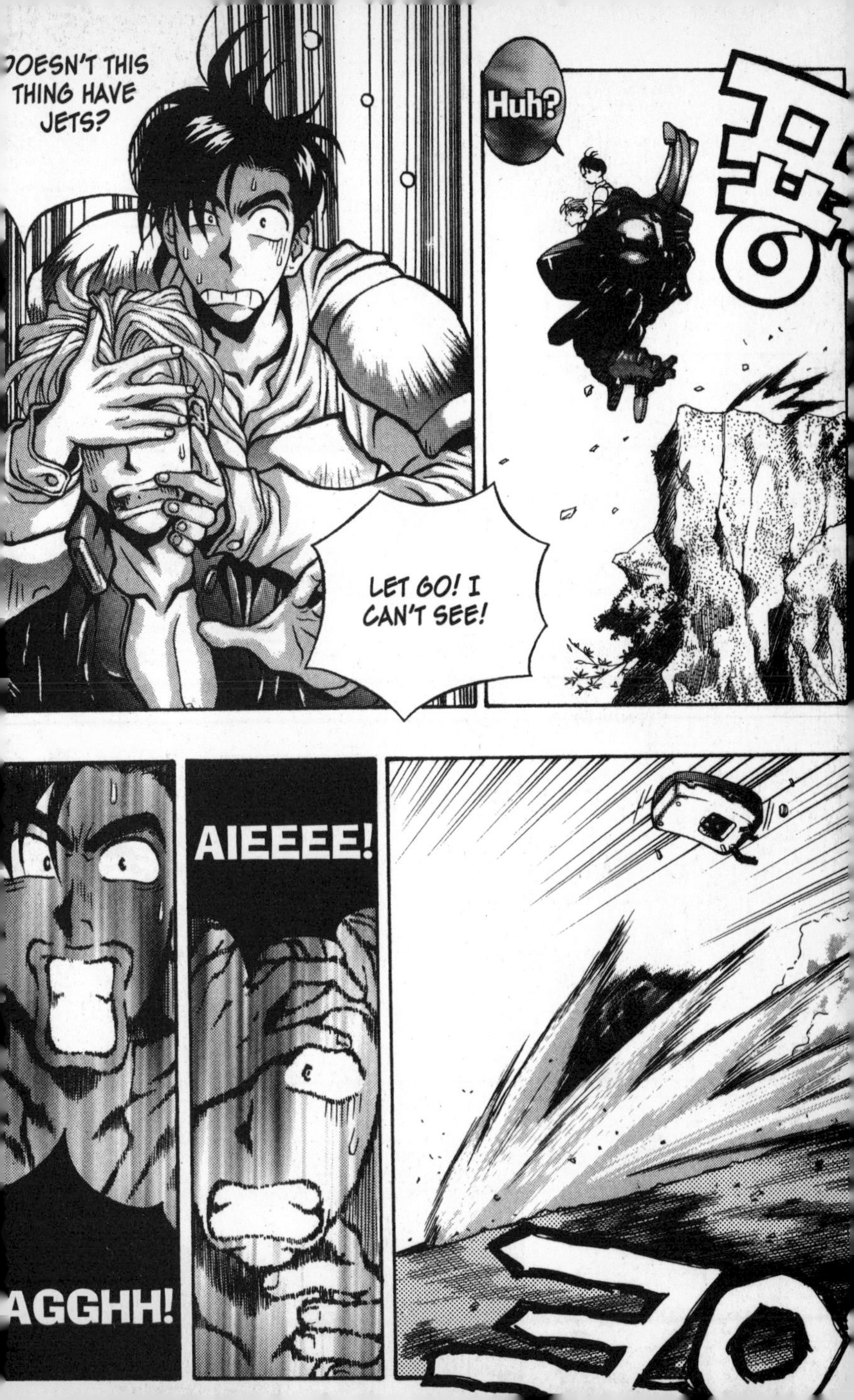
DOESN'T THIS THING HAVE JETS?
LET GO! I CAN'T SEE!
Huh?
AGGHH!
AIEEEE!

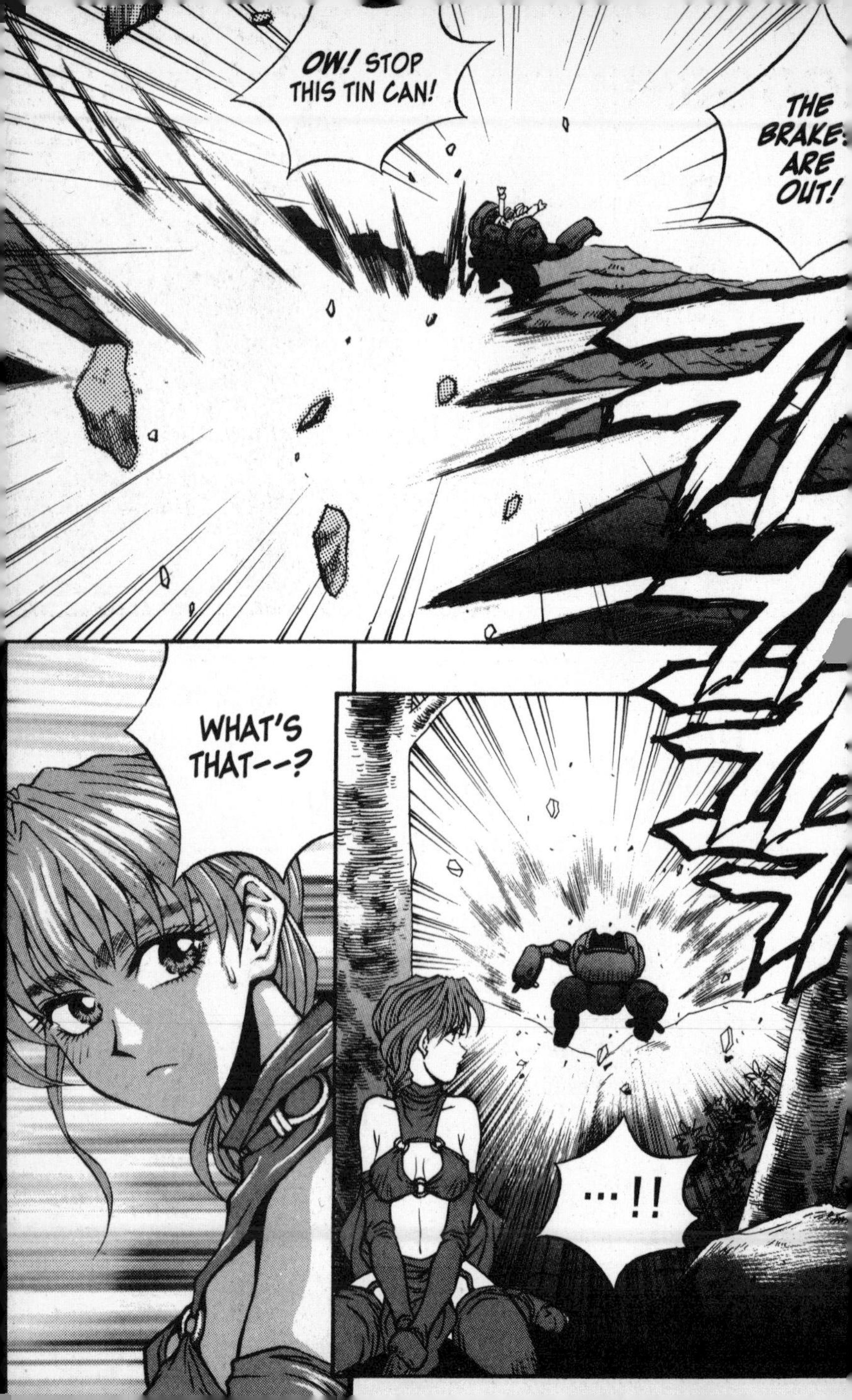

OW! STOP THIS TIN CAN!
THE BRAKES ARE OUT!
WHAT'S THAT--?
...!!

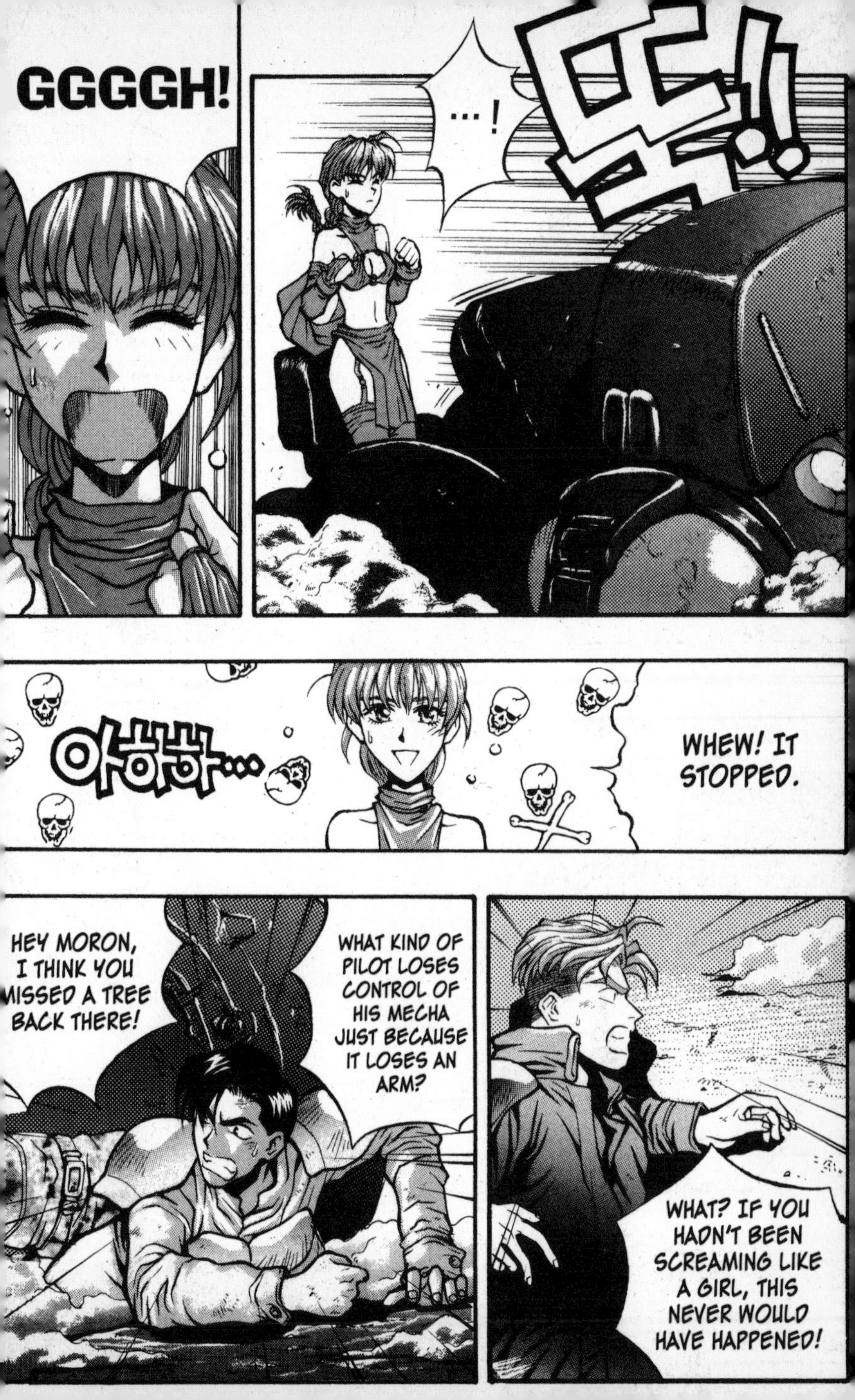
GGGGH!
...!
아하하...
WHEW! IT STOPPED.
HEY MORON, I THINK YOU MISSED A TREE BACK THERE!
WHAT KIND OF PILOT LOSES CONTROL OF HIS MECHA JUST BECAUSE IT LOSES AN ARM?
WHAT? IF YOU HADN'T BEEN SCREAMING LIKE A GIRL, THIS NEVER WOULD HAVE HAPPENED!

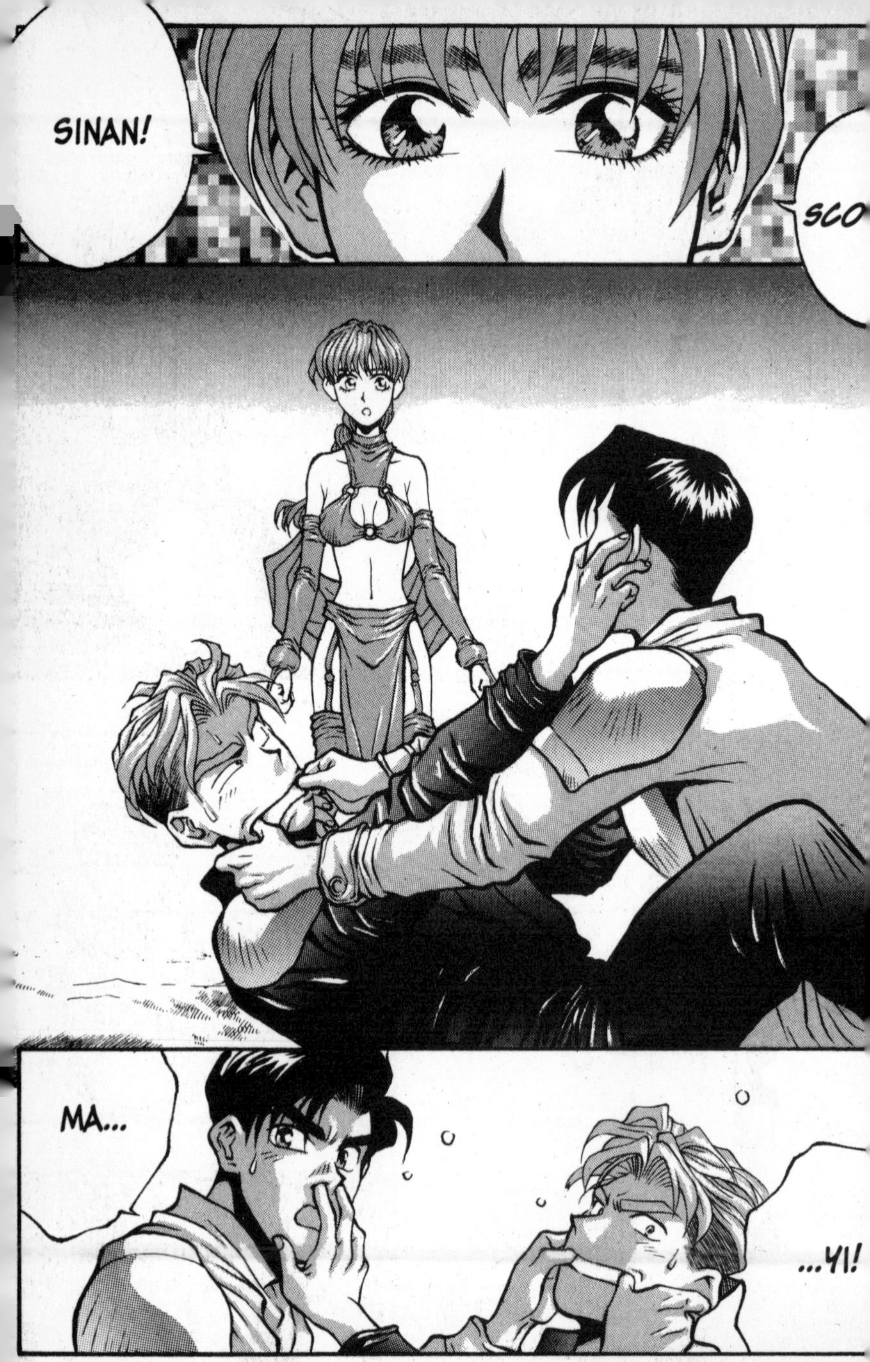
SINAN!
SCO
MA...
...YI!

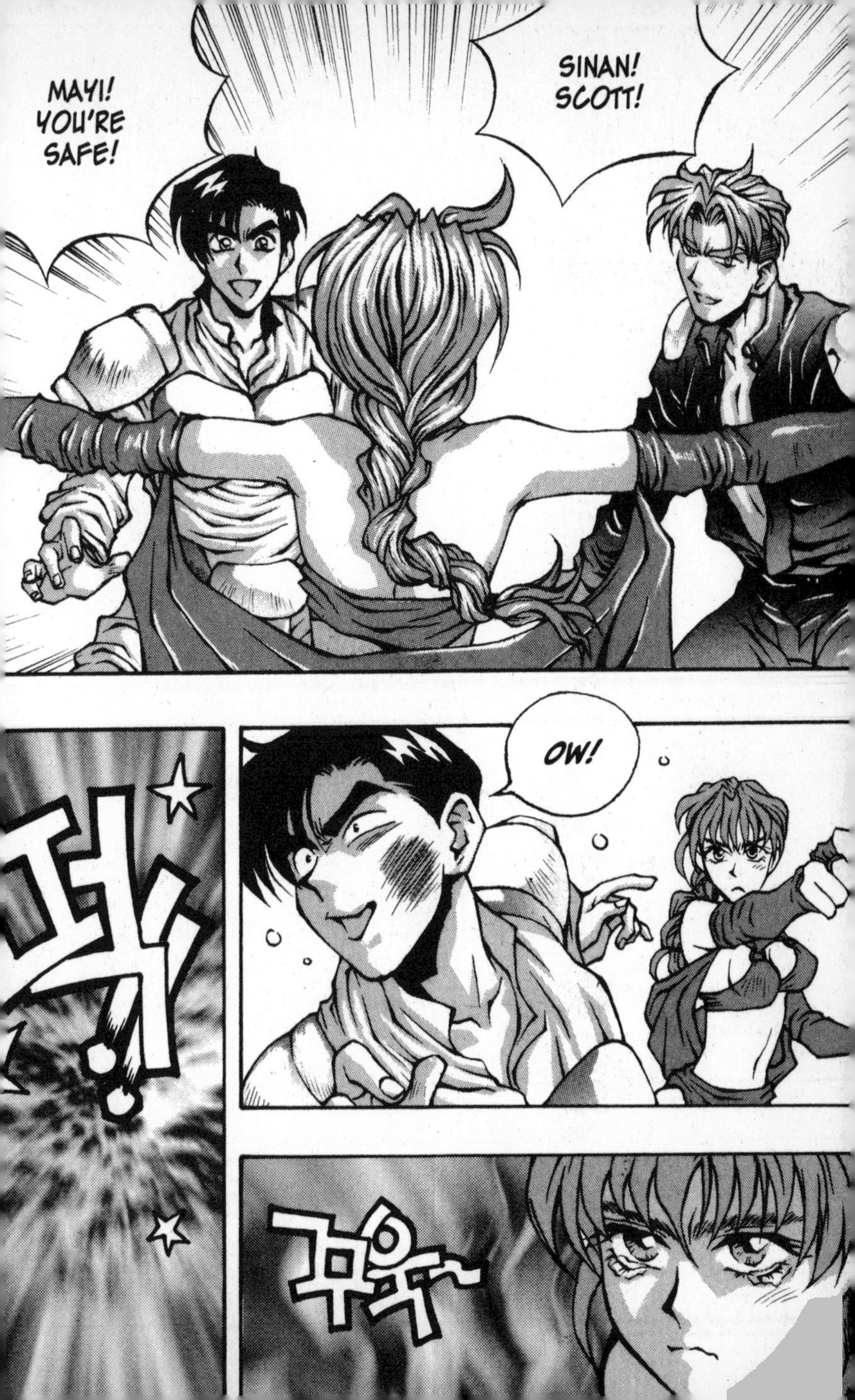
MAYI! YOU'RE SAFE!
SINAN! SCOTT!
OW!

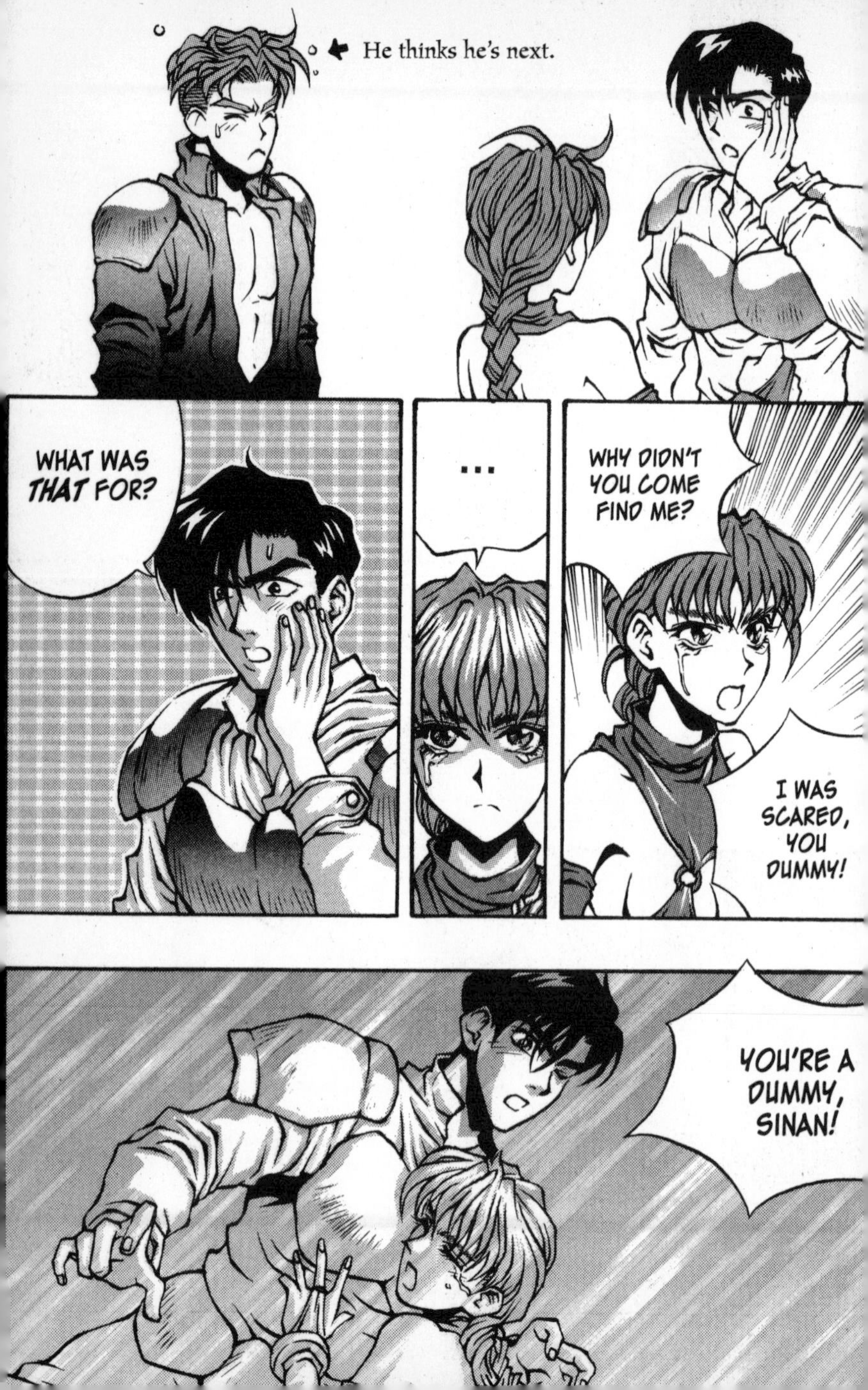
He thinks he's next.
WHAT WAS *THAT* FOR?
...
WHY DIDN'T YOU COME FIND ME?
I WAS SCARED, YOU DUMMY!
YOU'RE A DUMMY, SINAN!

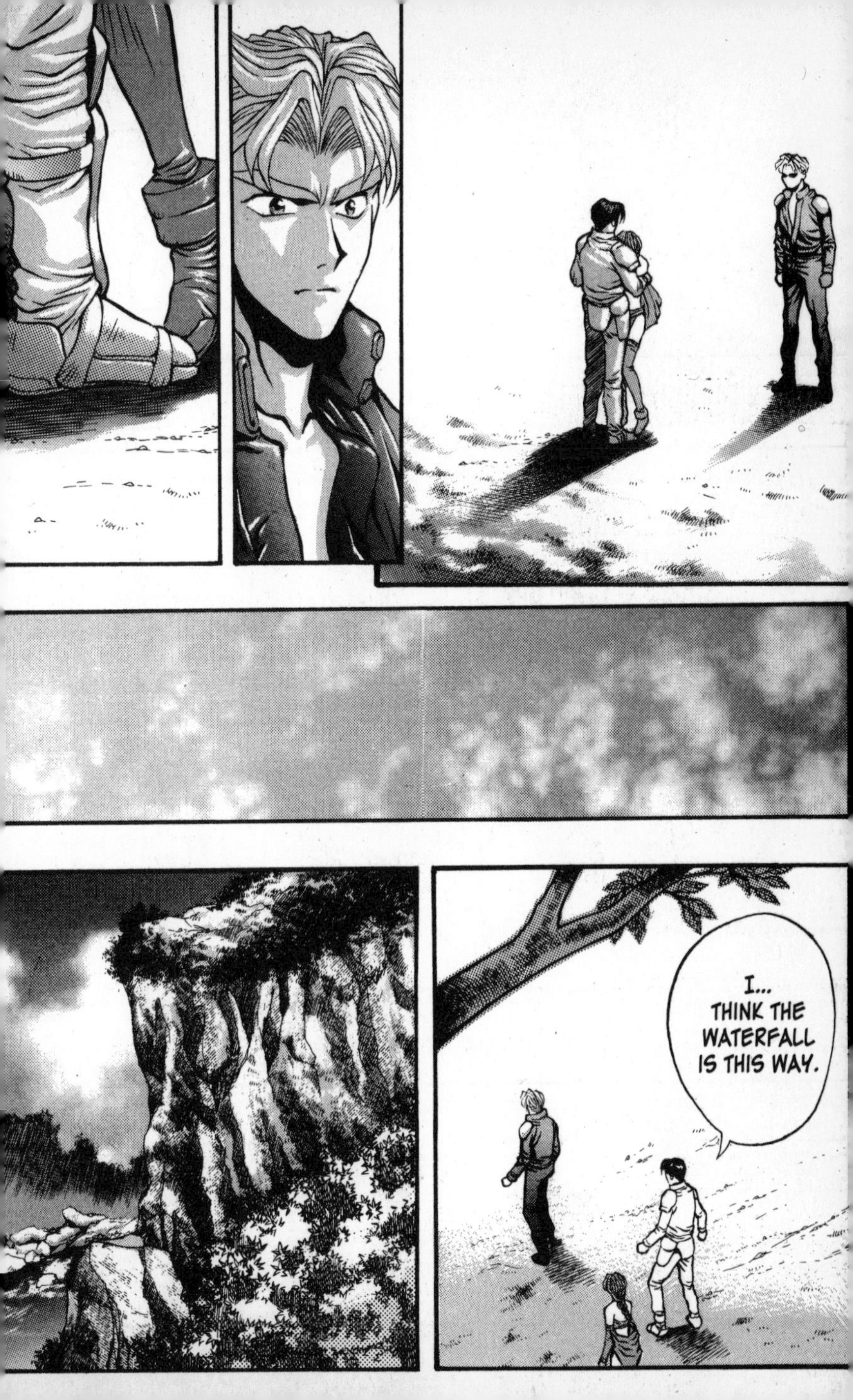
I... THINK THE WATERFALL IS THIS WAY.

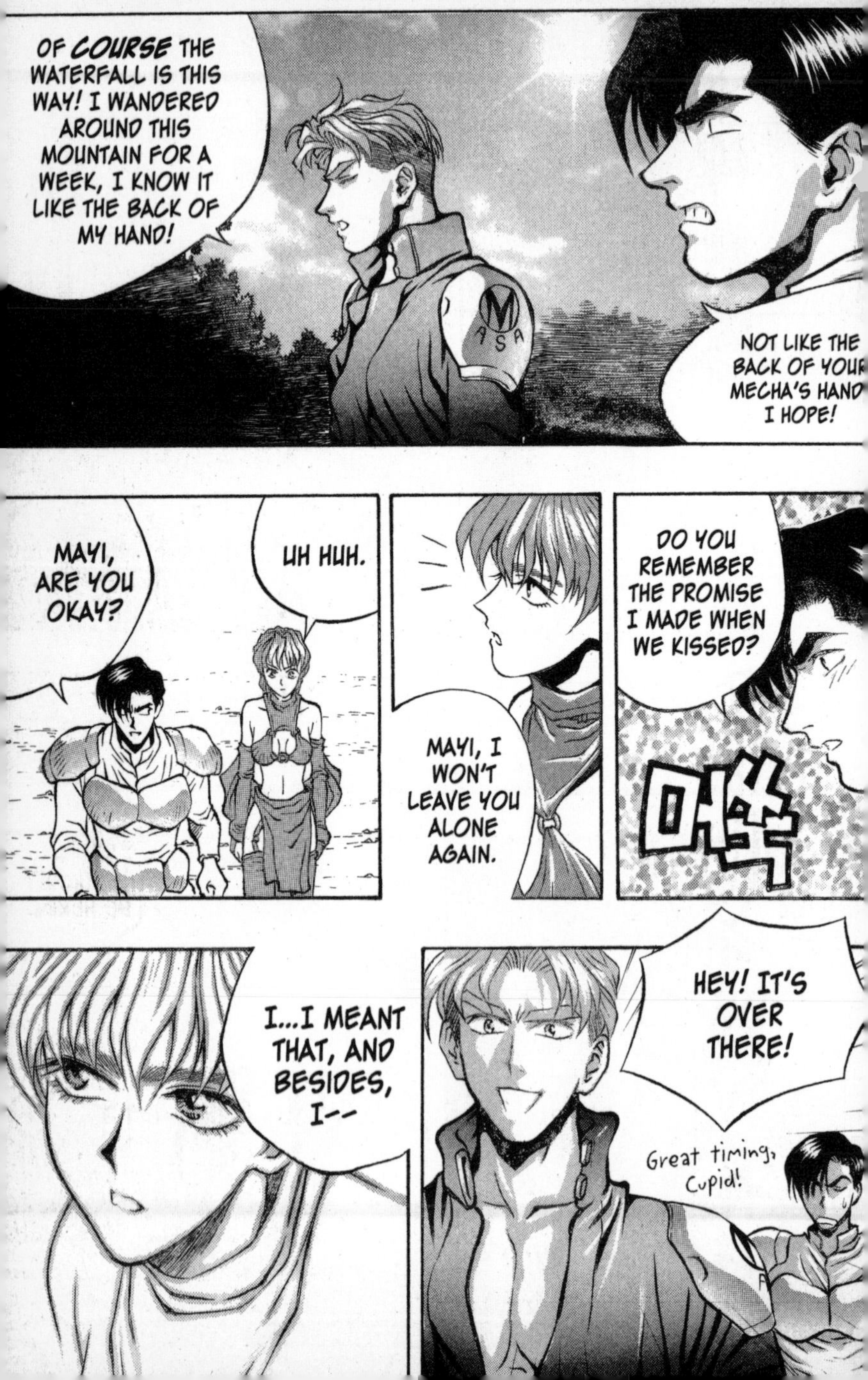
OF COURSE THE WATERFALL IS THIS WAY! I WANDERED AROUND THIS MOUNTAIN FOR A WEEK, I KNOW IT LIKE THE BACK OF MY HAND!
NOT LIKE THE BACK OF YOUR MECHA'S HAND I HOPE!
MAYI, ARE YOU OKAY?
UH HUH.
MAYI, I WON'T LEAVE YOU ALONE AGAIN.
DO YOU REMEMBER THE PROMISE I MADE WHEN WE KISSED?
머쓱
I...I MEANT THAT, AND BESIDES, I--
HEY! IT'S OVER THERE!
Great timing, Cupid!

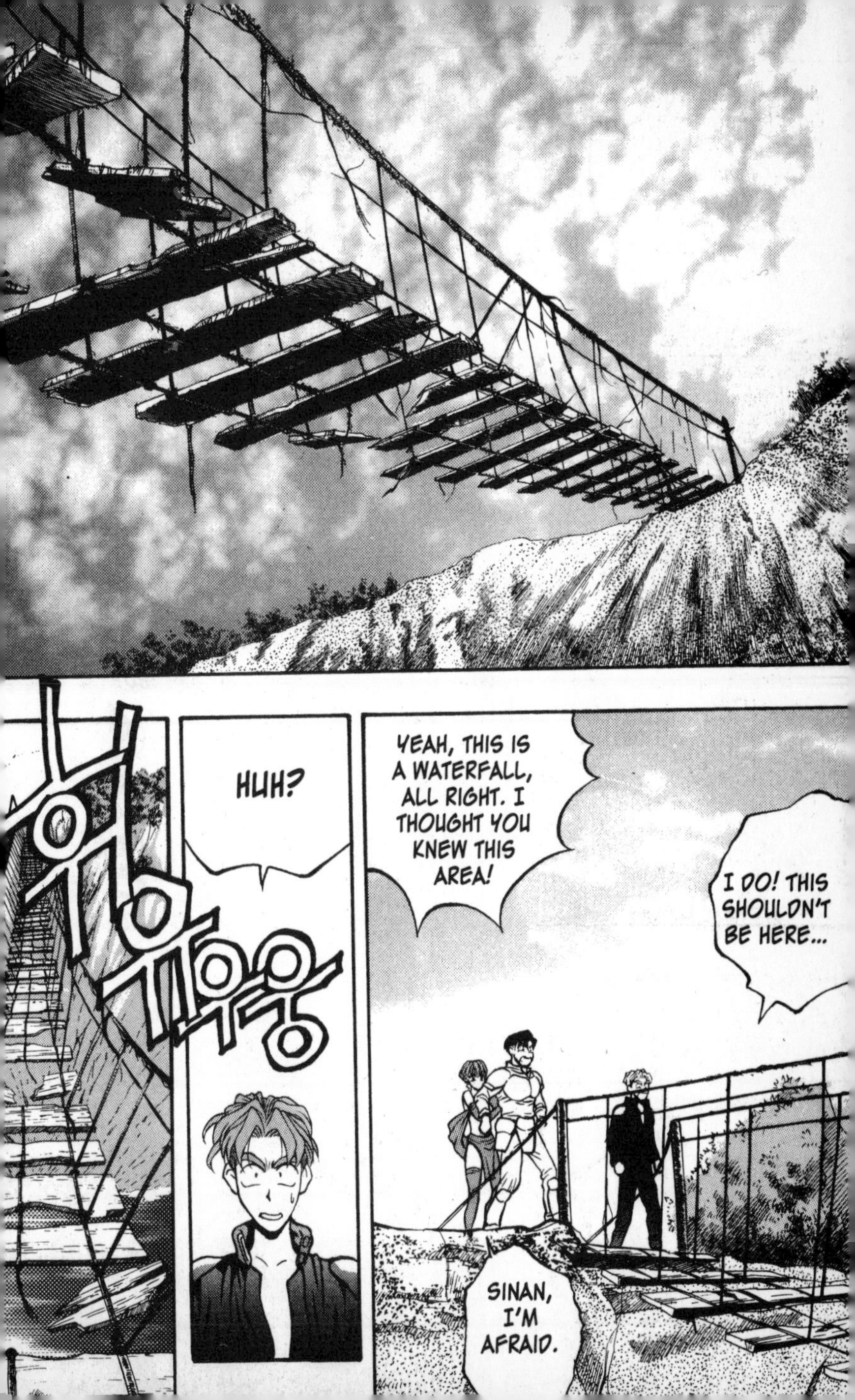
HUH?
YEAH, THIS IS A WATERFALL, ALL RIGHT. I THOUGHT YOU KNEW THIS AREA!
I DO! THIS SHOULDN'T BE HERE...
SINAN, I'M AFRAID.

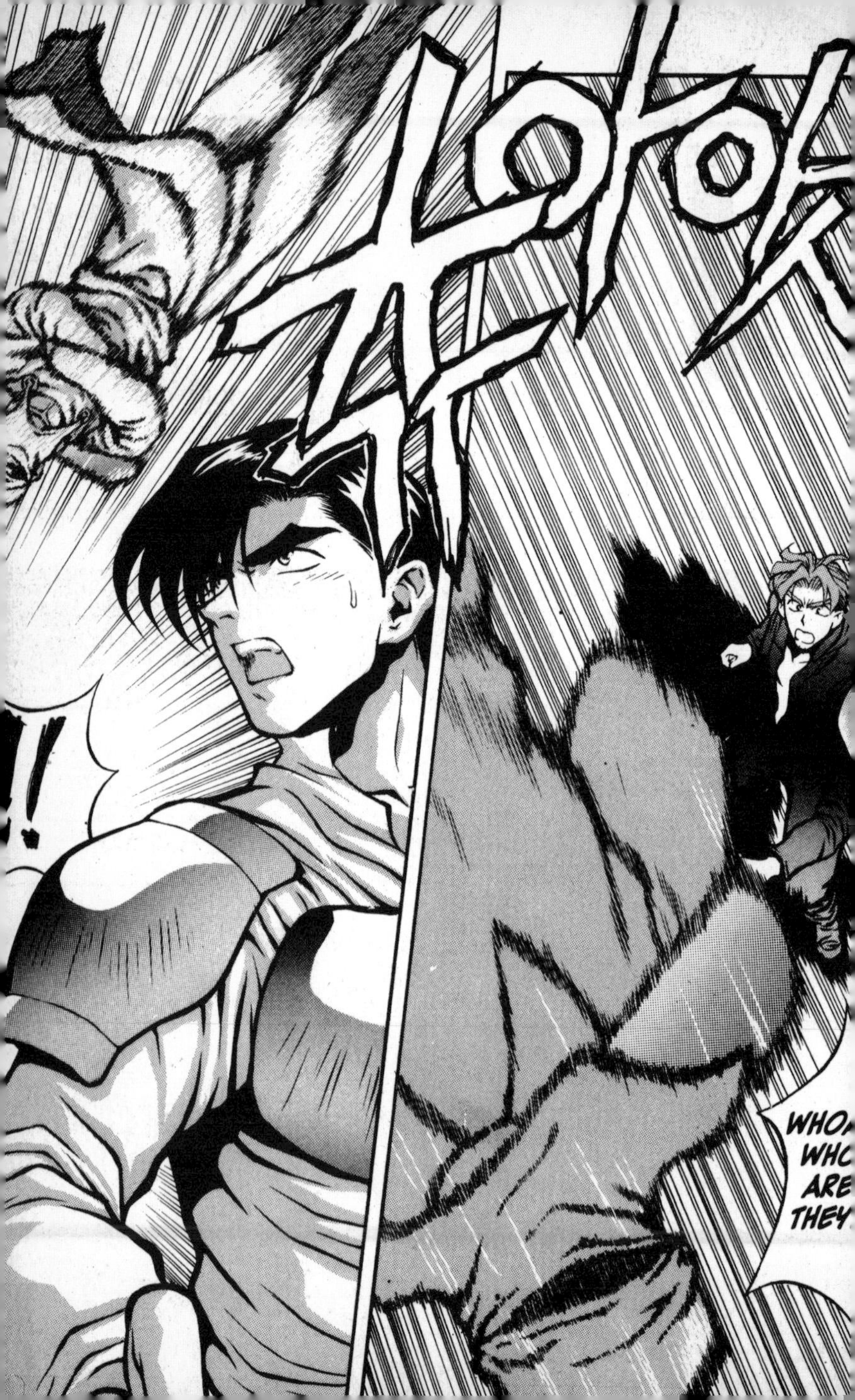
!!
WHOA
WHO
ARE
THEY

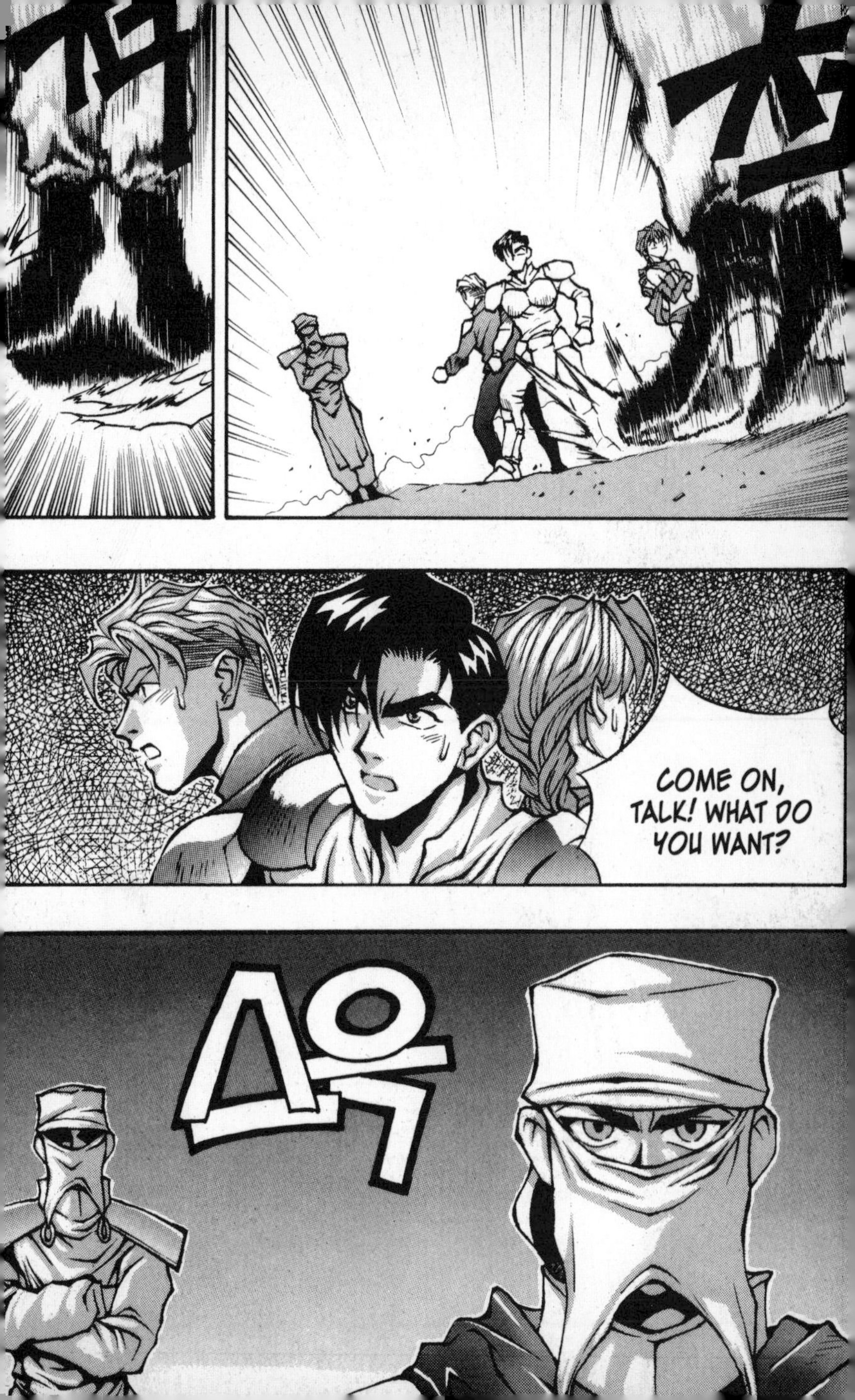
COME ON, TALK! WHAT DO YOU WANT?

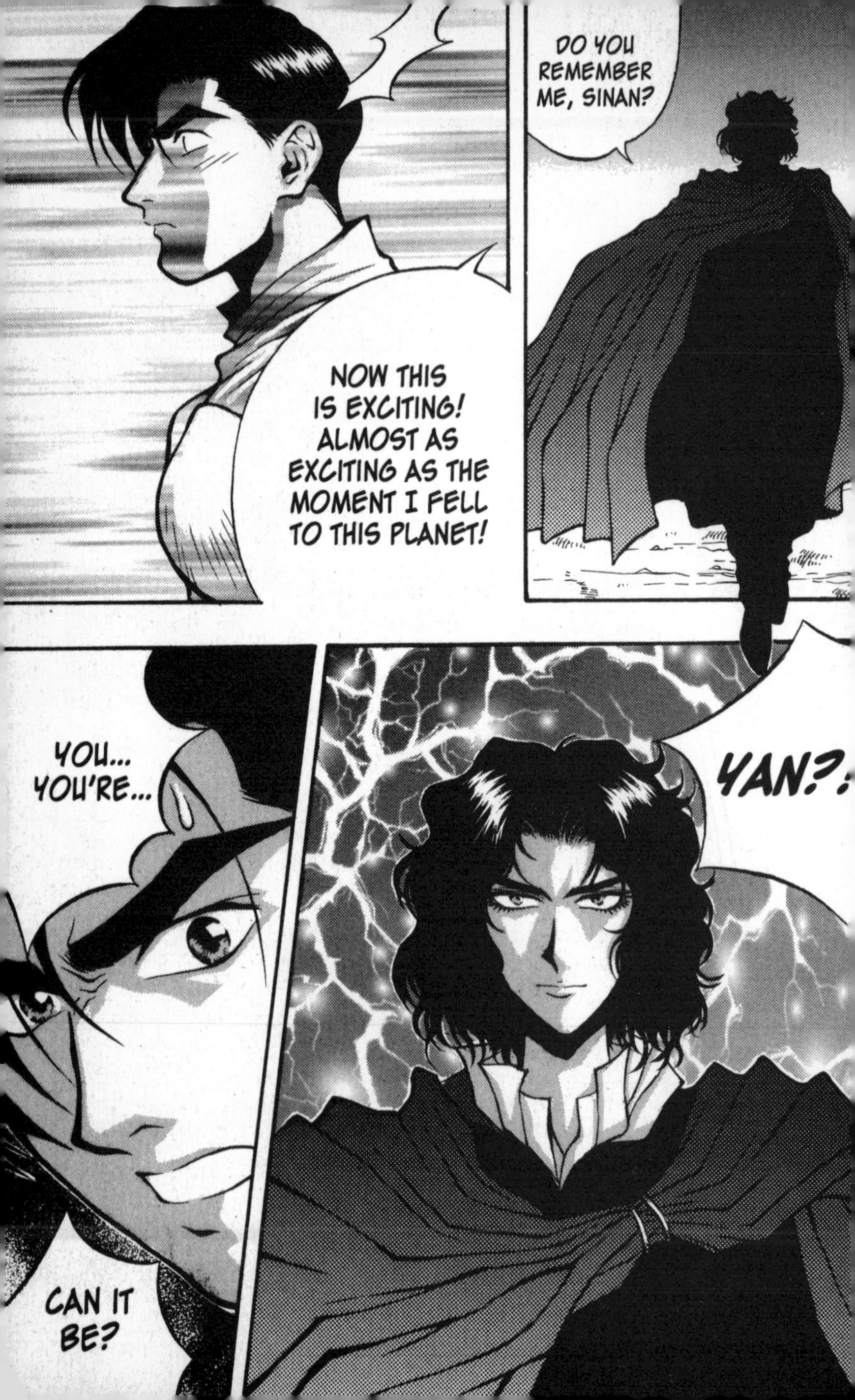
NOW THIS IS EXCITING! ALMOST AS EXCITING AS THE MOMENT I FELL TO THIS PLANET!
DO YOU REMEMBER ME, SINAN?
YOU... YOU'RE...
CAN IT BE?
YAN?!

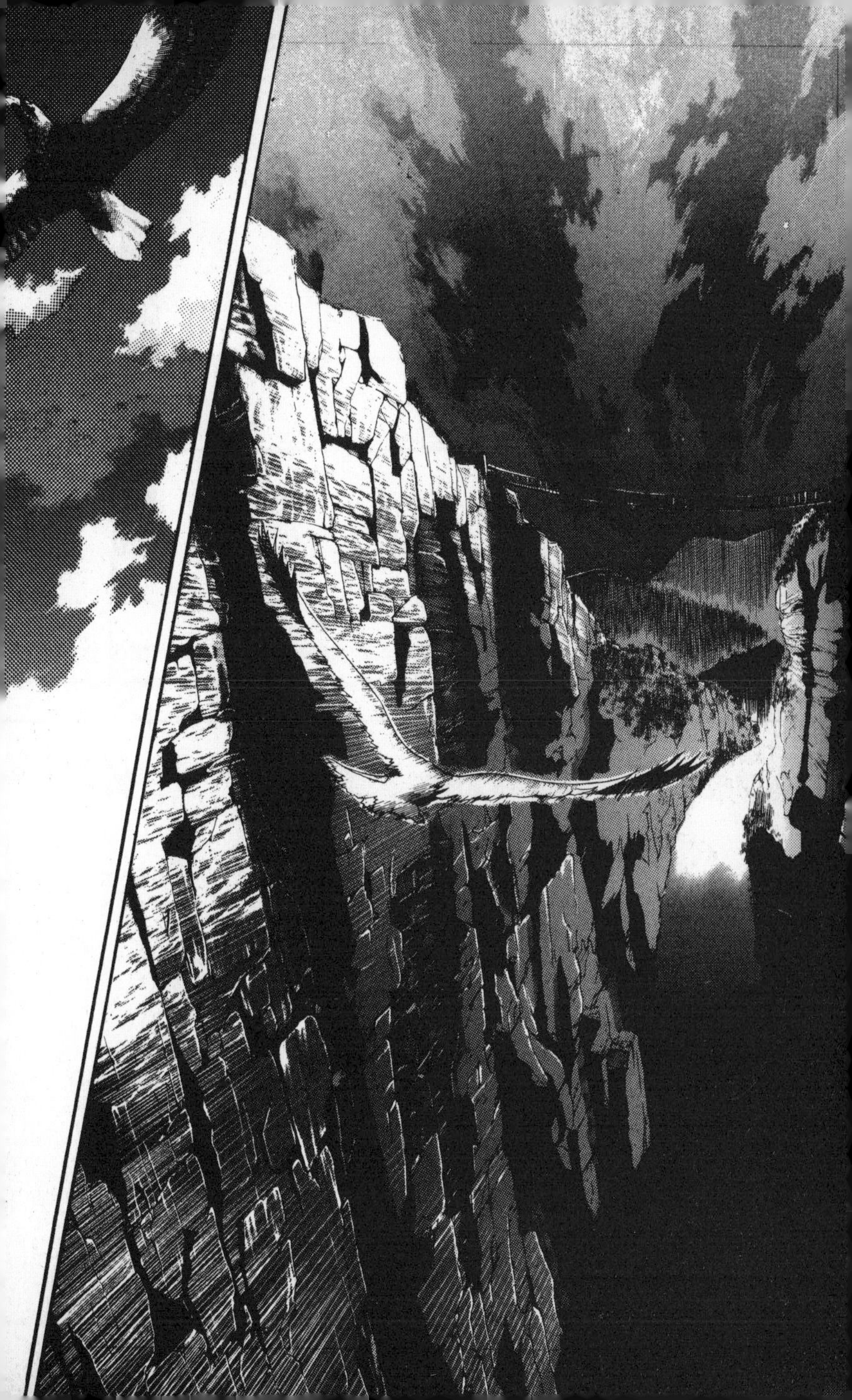

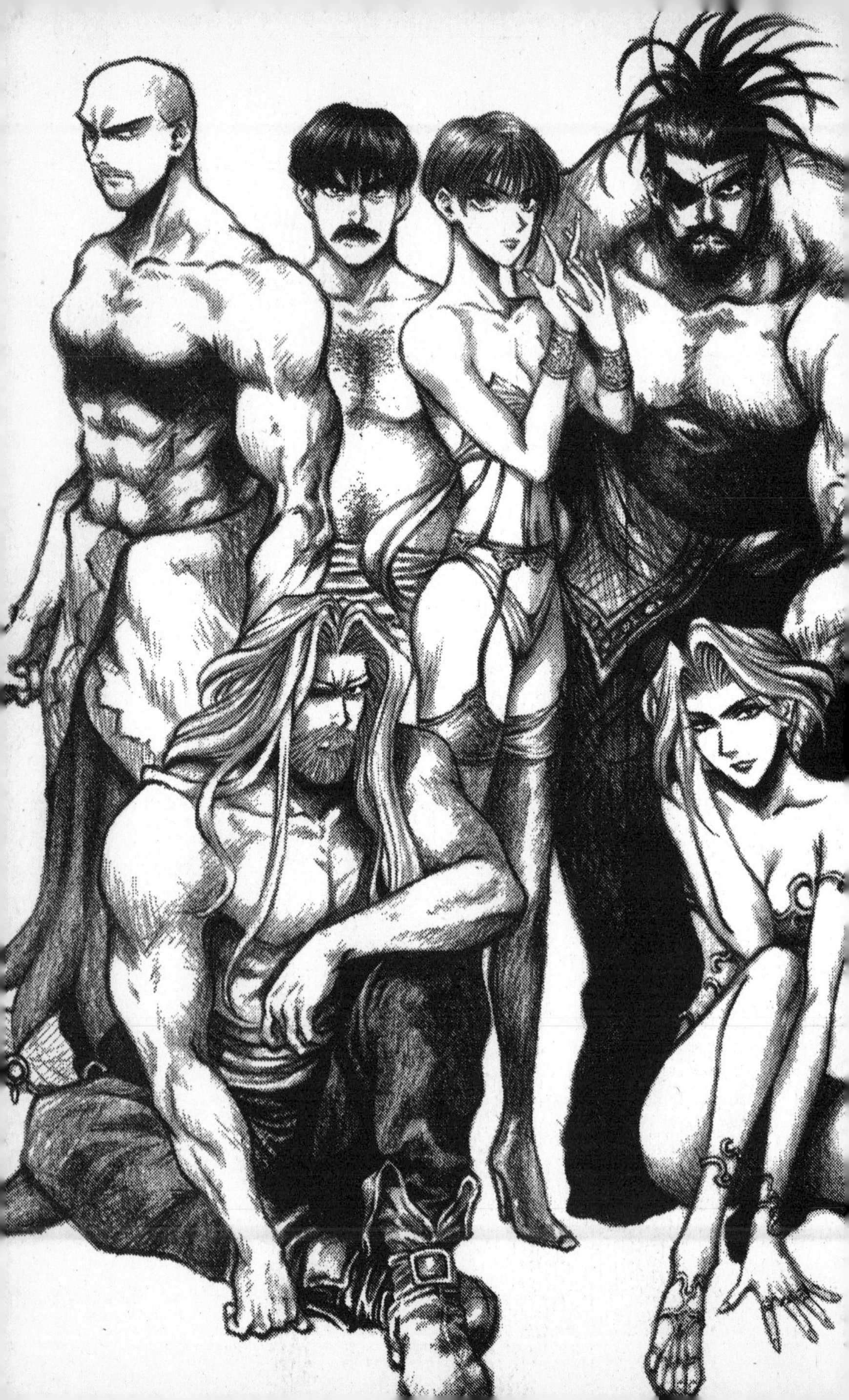

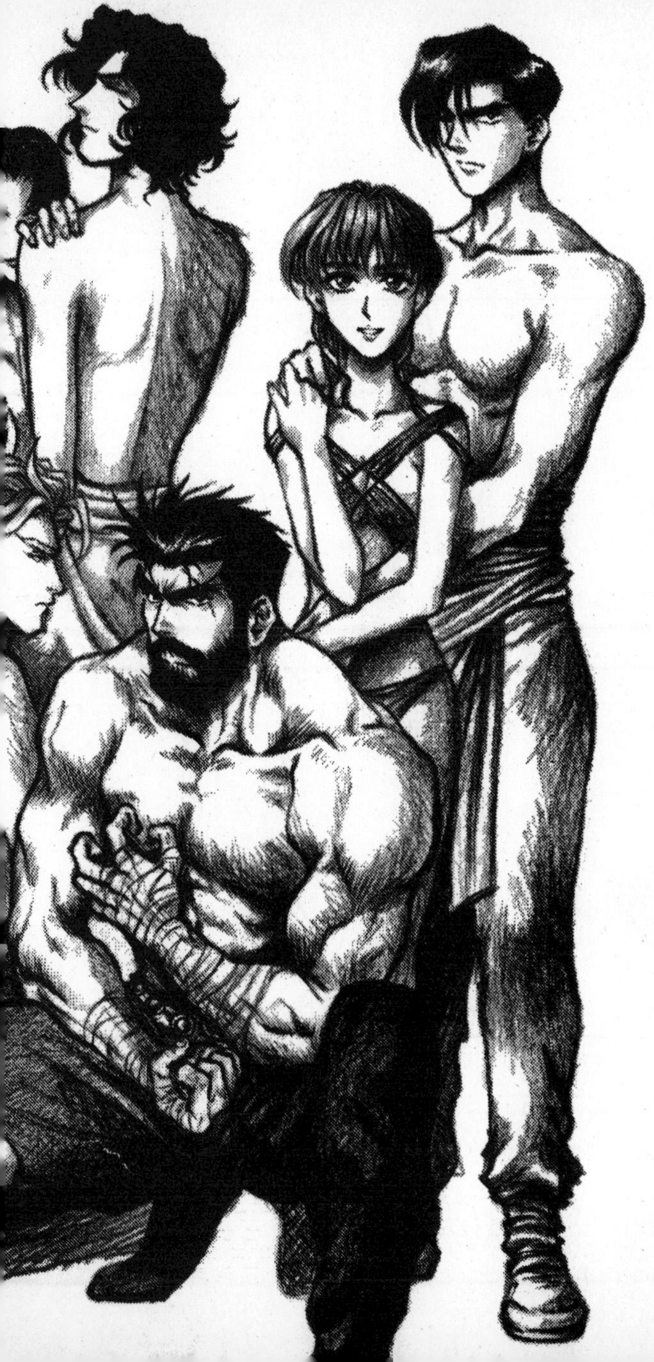

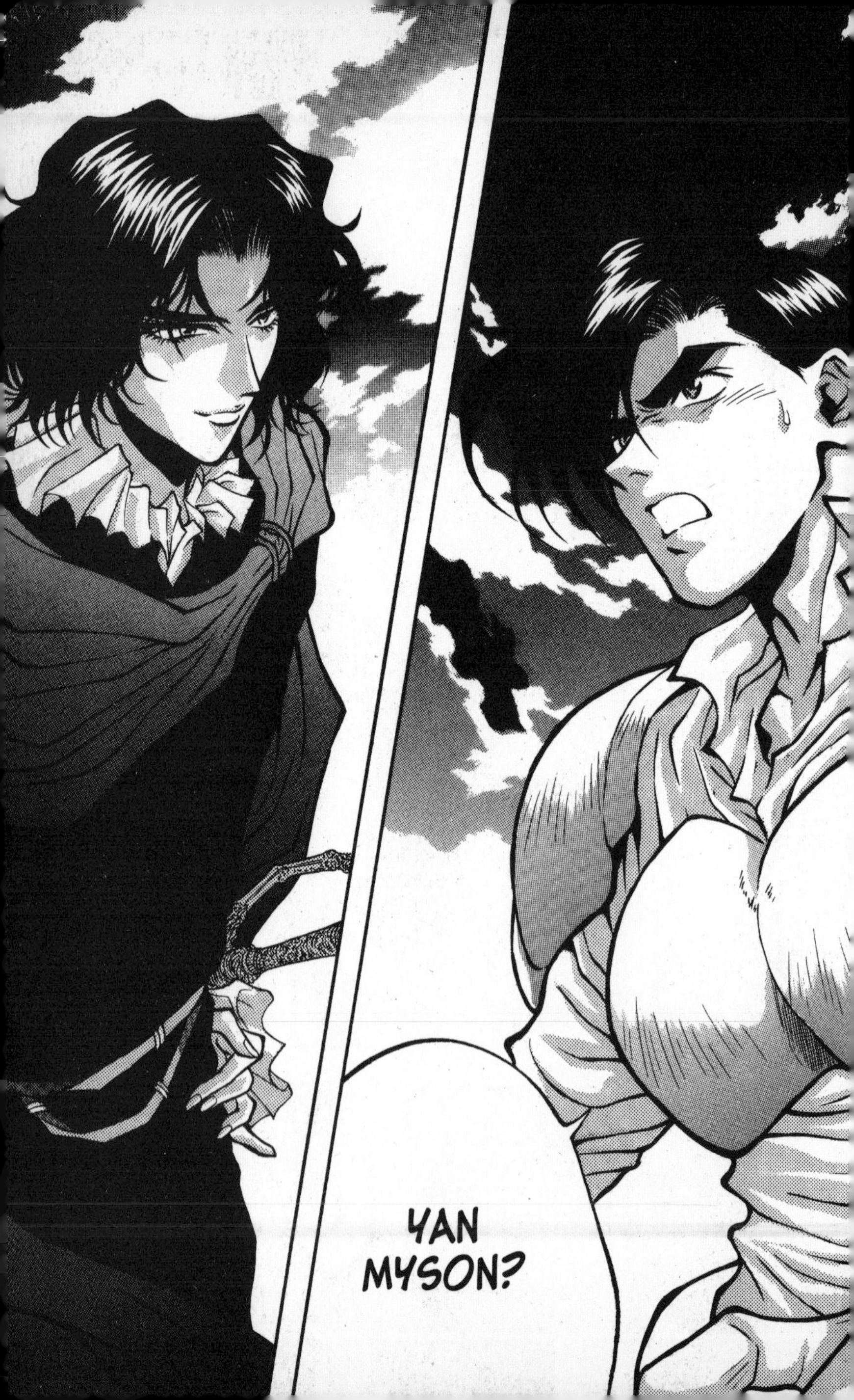
YAN MYSON?

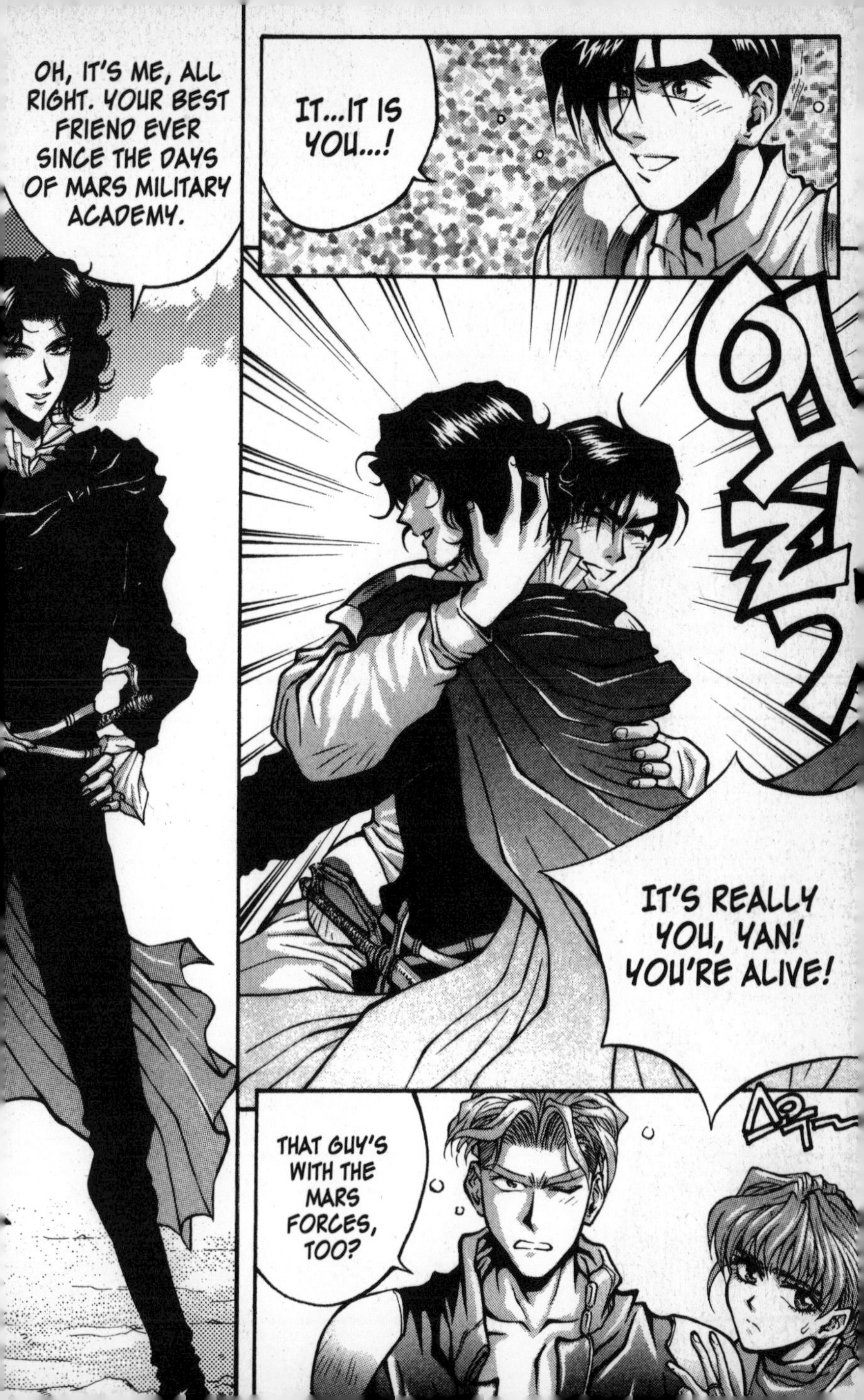
OH, IT'S ME, ALL RIGHT. YOUR BEST FRIEND EVER SINCE THE DAYS OF MARS MILITARY ACADEMY.
IT...IT IS YOU...!
IT'S REALLY YOU, YAN! YOU'RE ALIVE!
THAT GUY'S WITH THE MARS FORCES, TOO?

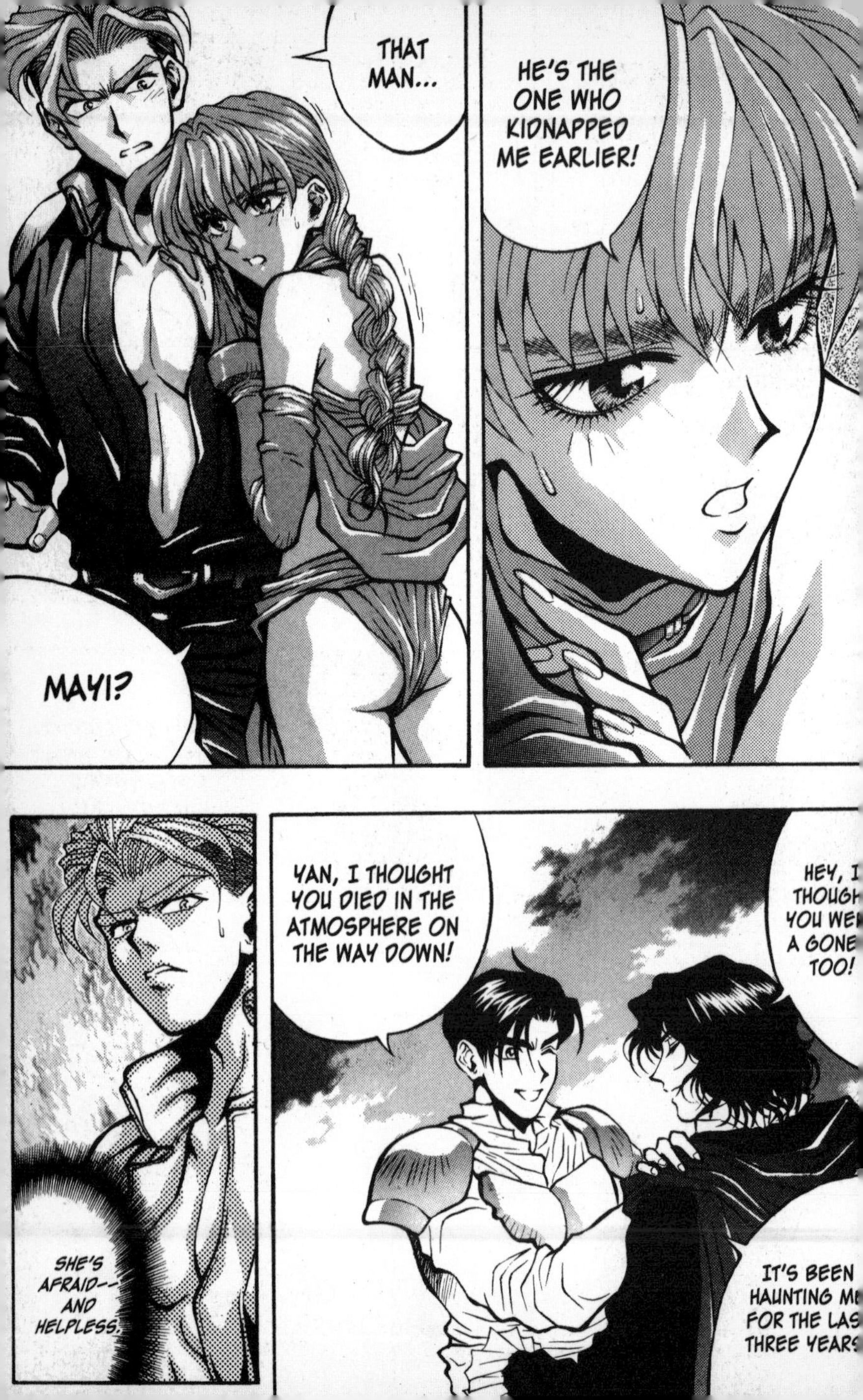
MAYI?
THAT MAN...
HE'S THE ONE WHO KIDNAPPED ME EARLIER!
SHE'S AFRAID-- AND HELPLESS.
YAN, I THOUGHT YOU DIED IN THE ATMOSPHERE ON THE WAY DOWN!
HEY, I THOUGH YOU WE A GONE TOO!
IT'S BEEN HAUNTING M FOR THE LAS THREE YEARS

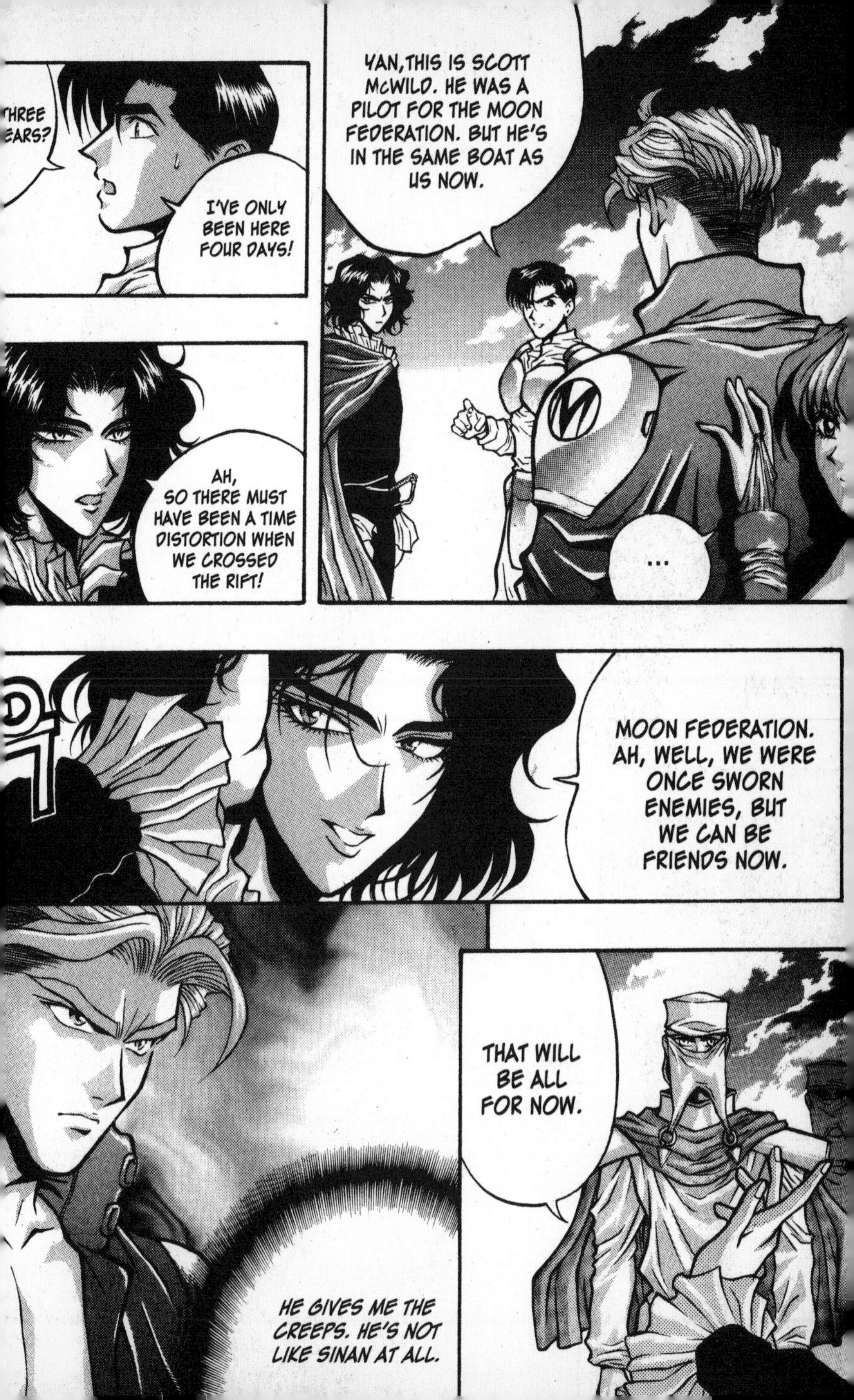
THREE
EARS?
I'VE ONLY BEEN HERE FOUR DAYS!
YAN, THIS IS SCOTT McWILD. HE WAS A PILOT FOR THE MOON FEDERATION. BUT HE'S IN THE SAME BOAT AS US NOW.
AH, SO THERE MUST HAVE BEEN A TIME DISTORTION WHEN WE CROSSED THE RIFT!
...
MOON FEDERATION. AH, WELL, WE WERE ONCE SWORN ENEMIES, BUT WE CAN BE FRIENDS NOW.
THAT WILL BE ALL FOR NOW.
HE GIVES ME THE CREEPS. HE'S NOT LIKE SINAN AT ALL.

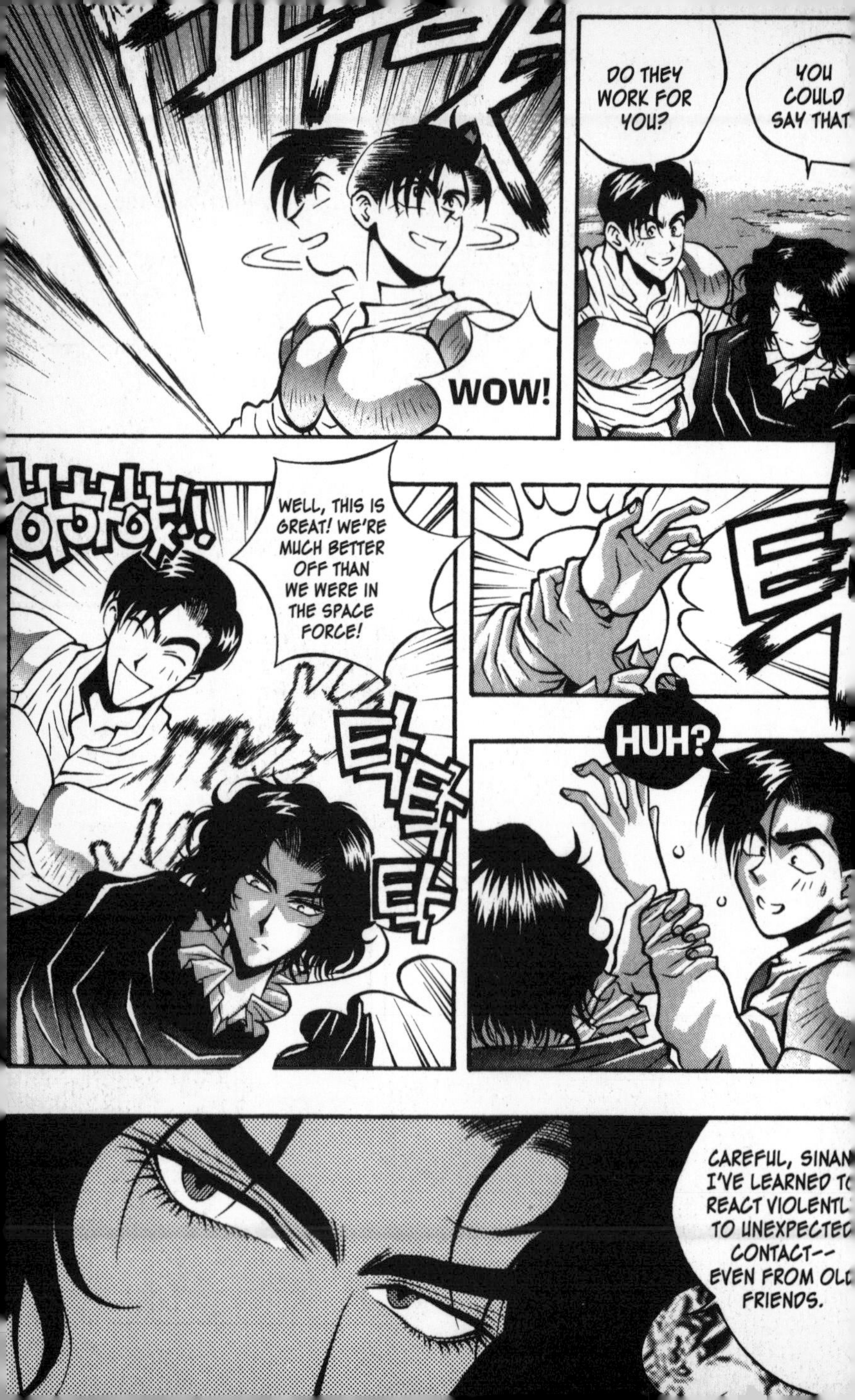
WOW!
DO THEY WORK FOR YOU?
YOU COULD SAY THAT
하하핫!!
WELL, THIS IS GREAT! WE'RE MUCH BETTER OFF THAN WE WERE IN THE SPACE FORCE!
HUH?
CAREFUL, SINAN I'VE LEARNED TO REACT VIOLENTL TO UNEXPECTED CONTACT-- EVEN FROM OLD FRIENDS.

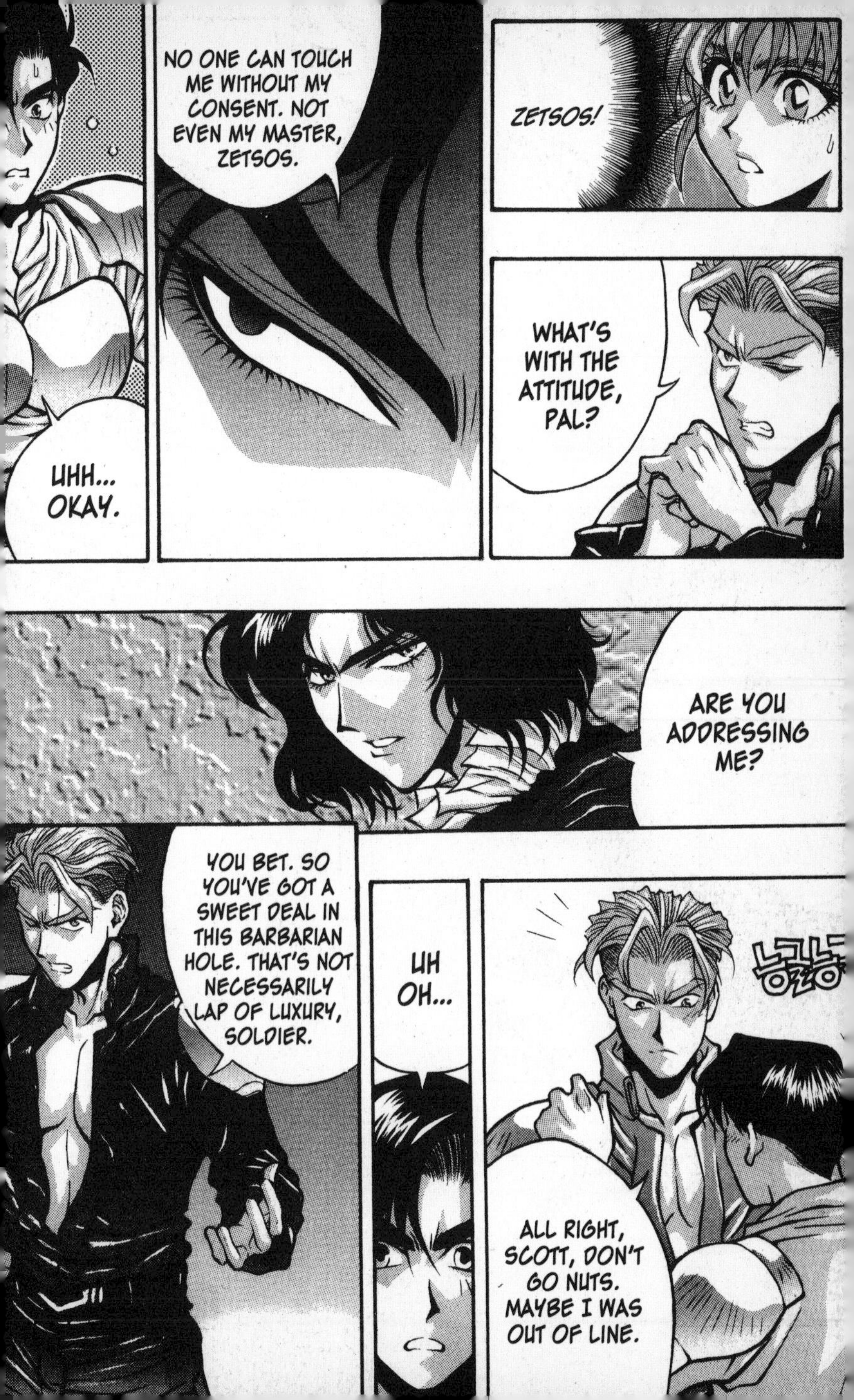
UHH... OKAY.
NO ONE CAN TOUCH ME WITHOUT MY CONSENT. NOT EVEN MY MASTER, ZETSOS.
ZETSOS!
WHAT'S WITH THE ATTITUDE, PAL?
ARE YOU ADDRESSING ME?
YOU BET. SO YOU'VE GOT A SWEET DEAL IN THIS BARBARIAN HOLE. THAT'S NOT NECESSARILY LAP OF LUXURY, SOLDIER.
UH OH...
ALL RIGHT, SCOTT, DON'T GO NUTS. MAYBE I WAS OUT OF LINE.

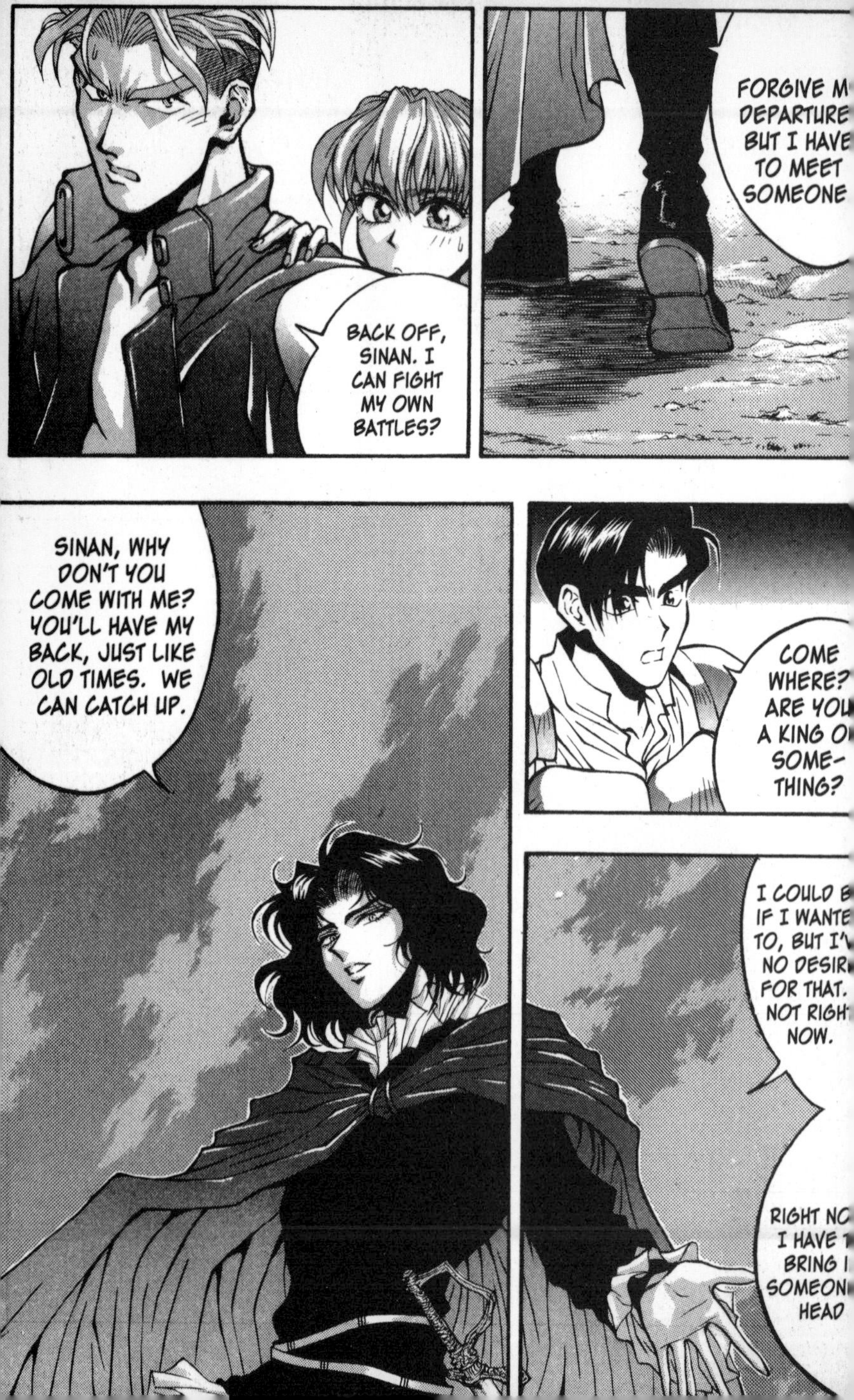
BACK OFF, SINAN. I CAN FIGHT MY OWN BATTLES?
FORGIVE M DEPARTURE BUT I HAVE TO MEET SOMEONE
SINAN, WHY DON'T YOU COME WITH ME? YOU'LL HAVE MY BACK, JUST LIKE OLD TIMES. WE CAN CATCH UP.
COME WHERE? ARE YOU A KING O SOME-THING?
I COULD B IF I WANTE TO, BUT I' NO DESIR FOR THAT. NOT RIGH NOW.
RIGHT NO I HAVE BRING I SOMEON HEAD

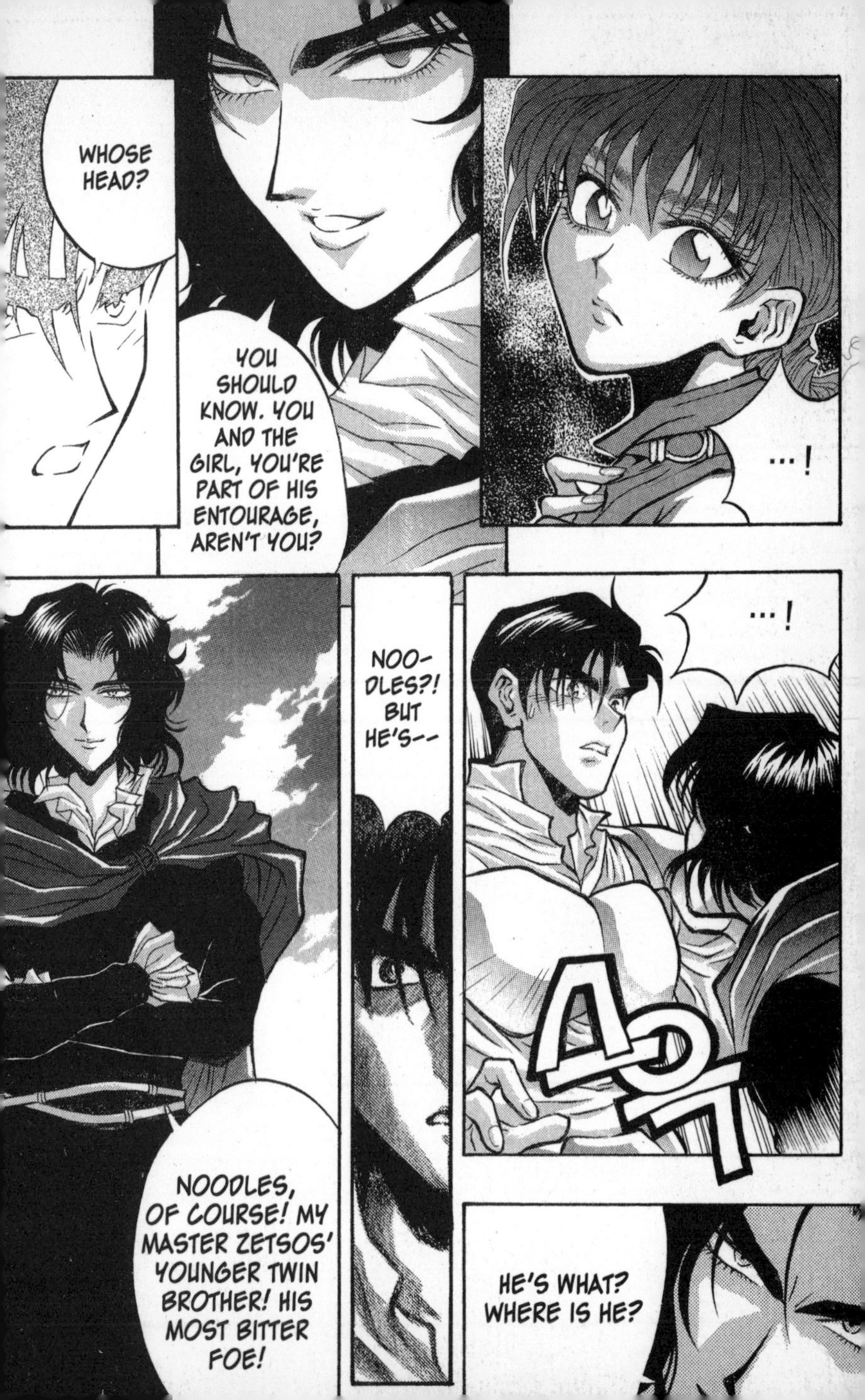

WHOSE HEAD?
YOU SHOULD KNOW. YOU AND THE GIRL, YOU'RE PART OF HIS ENTOURAGE, AREN'T YOU?
...!
NOODLES, OF COURSE! MY MASTER ZETSOS' YOUNGER TWIN BROTHER! HIS MOST BITTER FOE!
NOO-DLES?! BUT HE'S--
...!
HE'S WHAT? WHERE IS HE?

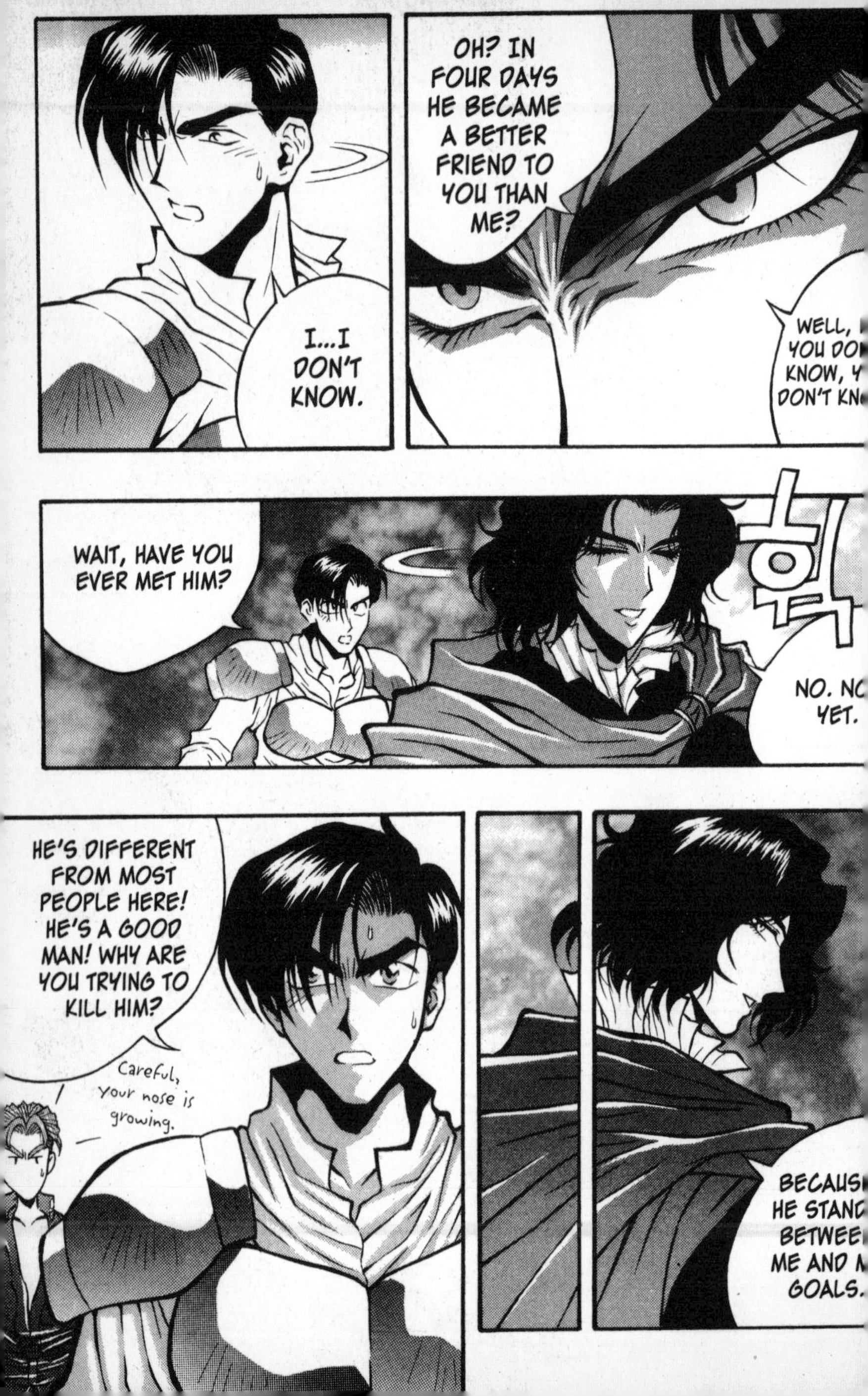
I...I DON'T KNOW.
OH? IN FOUR DAYS HE BECAME A BETTER FRIEND TO YOU THAN ME?
WELL, YOU DO KNOW, Y DON'T KN
WAIT, HAVE YOU EVER MET HIM?
휙
NO. NO YET.
HE'S DIFFERENT FROM MOST PEOPLE HERE! HE'S A GOOD MAN! WHY ARE YOU TRYING TO KILL HIM?
Careful, your nose is growing.
BECAUS HE STAND BETWEE ME AND M GOALS.

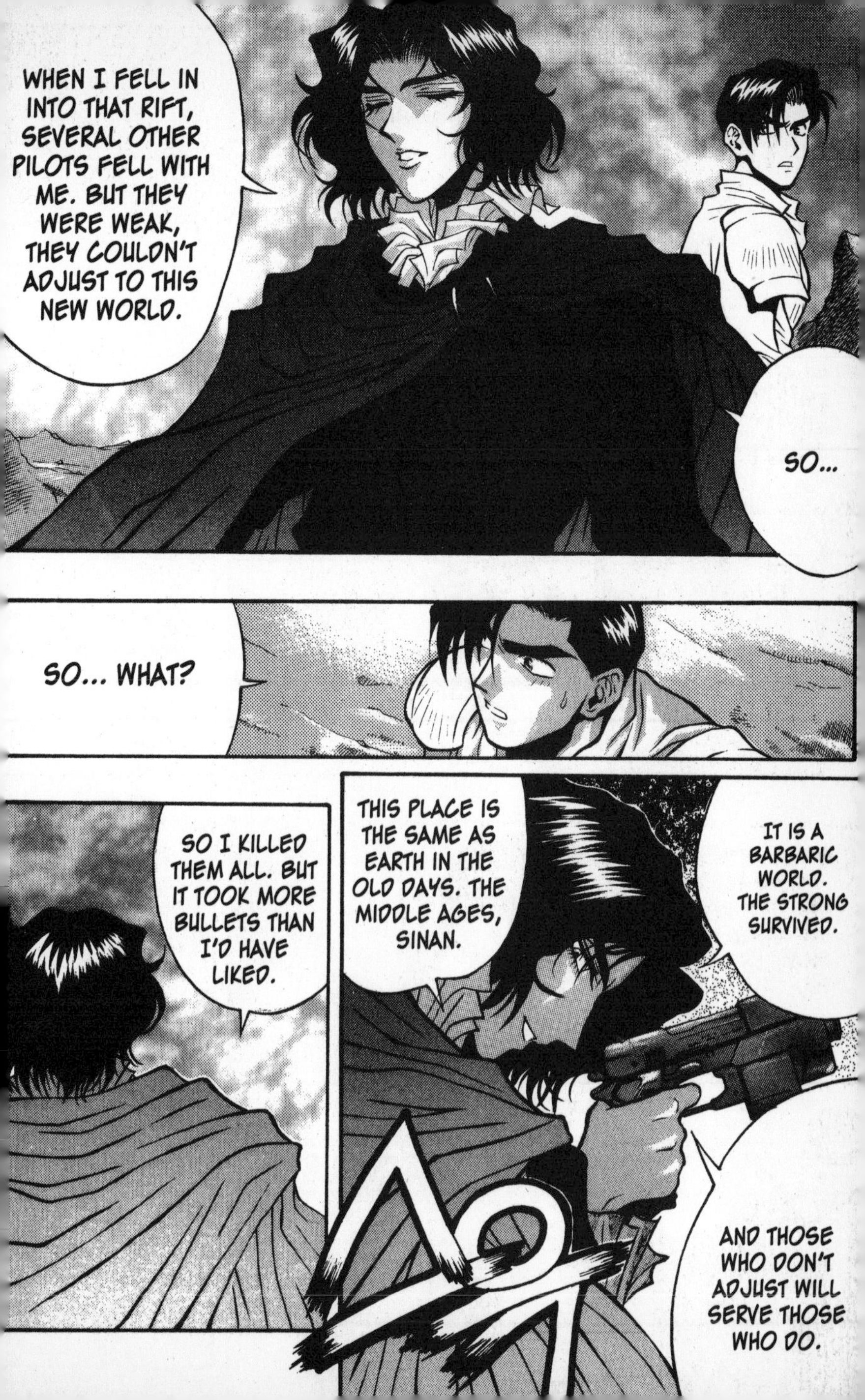
WHEN I FELL IN INTO THAT RIFT, SEVERAL OTHER PILOTS FELL WITH ME. BUT THEY WERE WEAK, THEY COULDN'T ADJUST TO THIS NEW WORLD.
SO...
SO... WHAT?
SO I KILLED THEM ALL. BUT IT TOOK MORE BULLETS THAN I'D HAVE LIKED.
THIS PLACE IS THE SAME AS EARTH IN THE OLD DAYS. THE MIDDLE AGES, SINAN.
IT IS A BARBARIC WORLD. THE STRONG SURVIVED.
AND THOSE WHO DON'T ADJUST WILL SERVE THOSE WHO DO.

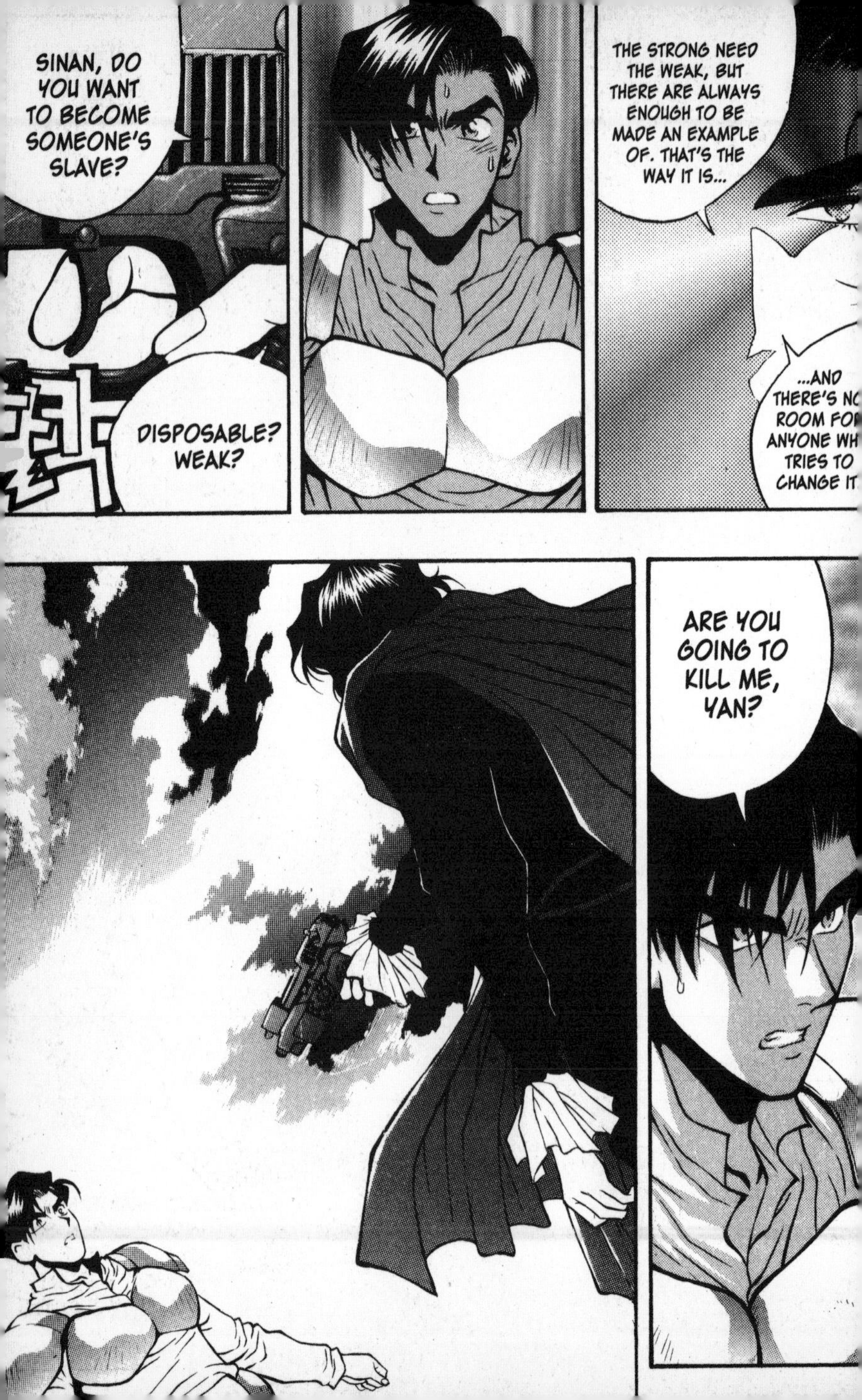
SINAN, DO YOU WANT TO BECOME SOMEONE'S SLAVE?
DISPOSABLE? WEAK?
THE STRONG NEED THE WEAK, BUT THERE ARE ALWAYS ENOUGH TO BE MADE AN EXAMPLE OF. THAT'S THE WAY IT IS...
...AND THERE'S NO ROOM FOR ANYONE WHO TRIES TO CHANGE IT.
ARE YOU GOING TO KILL ME, YAN?

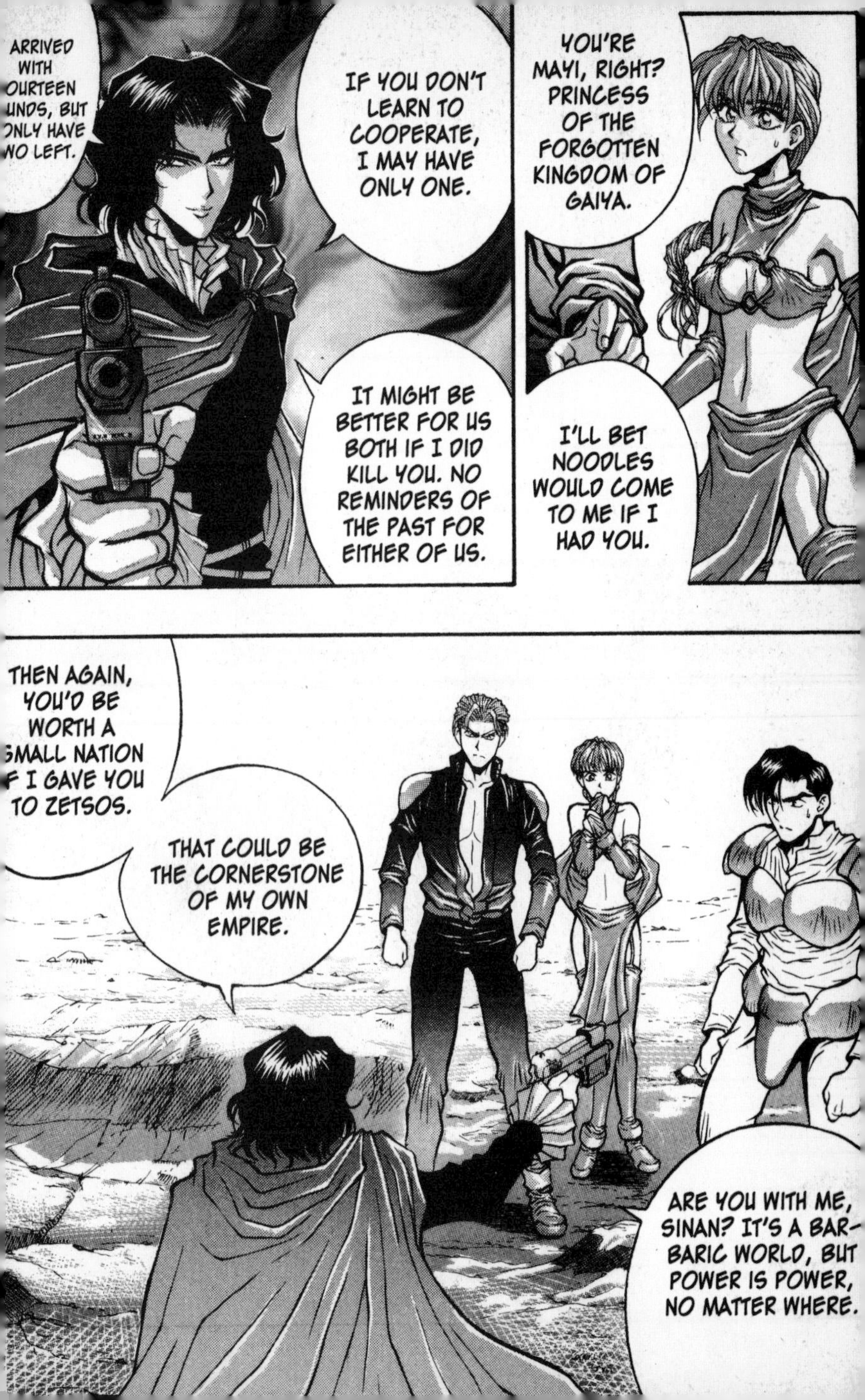
ARRIVED WITH OURTEEN UNDS, BUT NLY HAVE WO LEFT.
IF YOU DON'T LEARN TO COOPERATE, I MAY HAVE ONLY ONE.
IT MIGHT BE BETTER FOR US BOTH IF I DID KILL YOU. NO REMINDERS OF THE PAST FOR EITHER OF US.
YOU'RE MAYI, RIGHT? PRINCESS OF THE FORGOTTEN KINGDOM OF GAIYA.
I'LL BET NOODLES WOULD COME TO ME IF I HAD YOU.
THEN AGAIN, YOU'D BE WORTH A MALL NATION F I GAVE YOU TO ZETSOS.
THAT COULD BE THE CORNERSTONE OF MY OWN EMPIRE.
ARE YOU WITH ME, SINAN? IT'S A BAR-BARIC WORLD, BUT POWER IS POWER, NO MATTER WHERE.

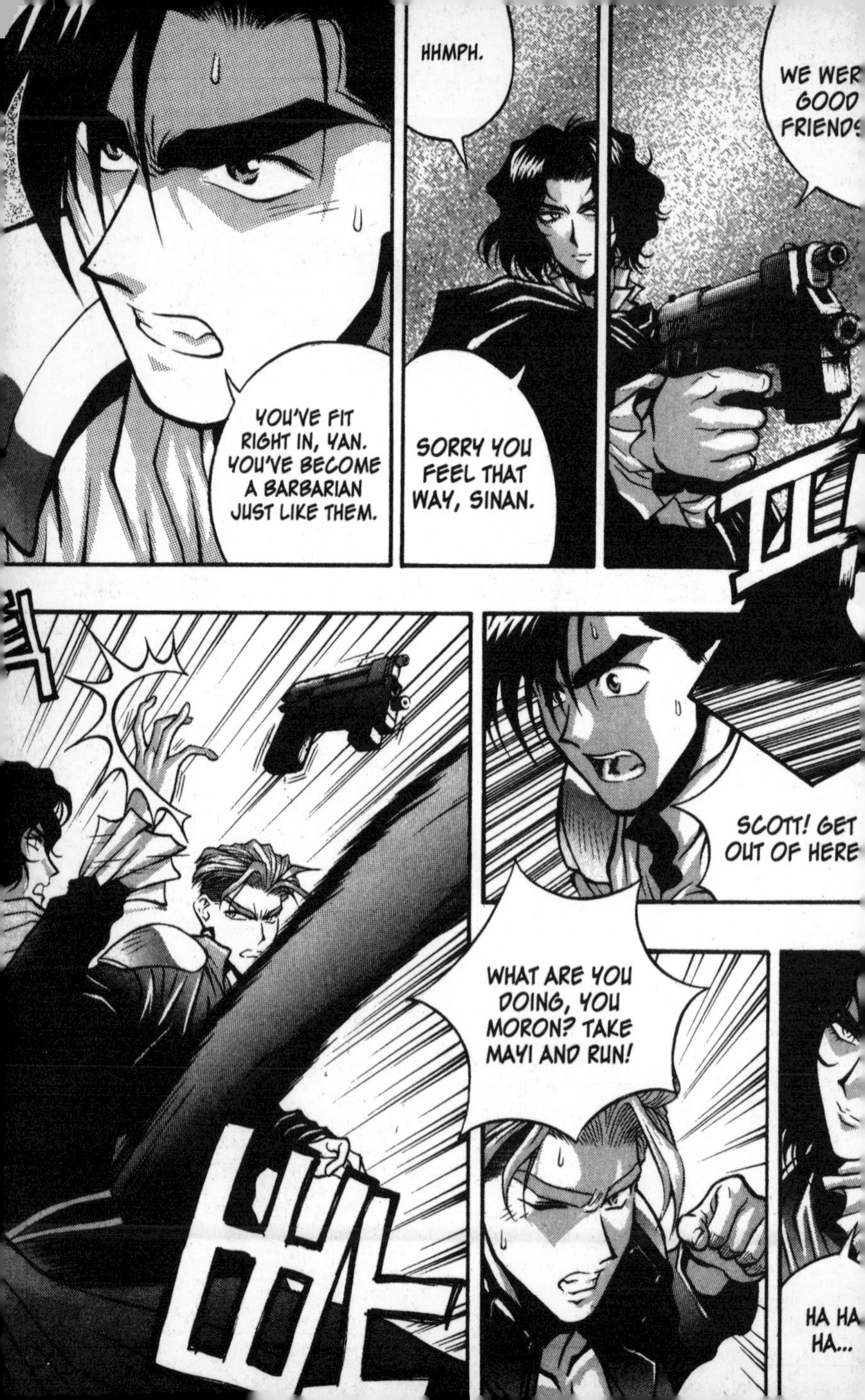
YOU'VE FIT RIGHT IN, YAN. YOU'VE BECOME A BARBARIAN JUST LIKE THEM.
HHMPH.
SORRY YOU FEEL THAT WAY, SINAN.
WE WER GOOD FRIENDS
SCOTT! GET OUT OF HERE
WHAT ARE YOU DOING, YOU MORON? TAKE MAYI AND RUN!
HA HA HA...

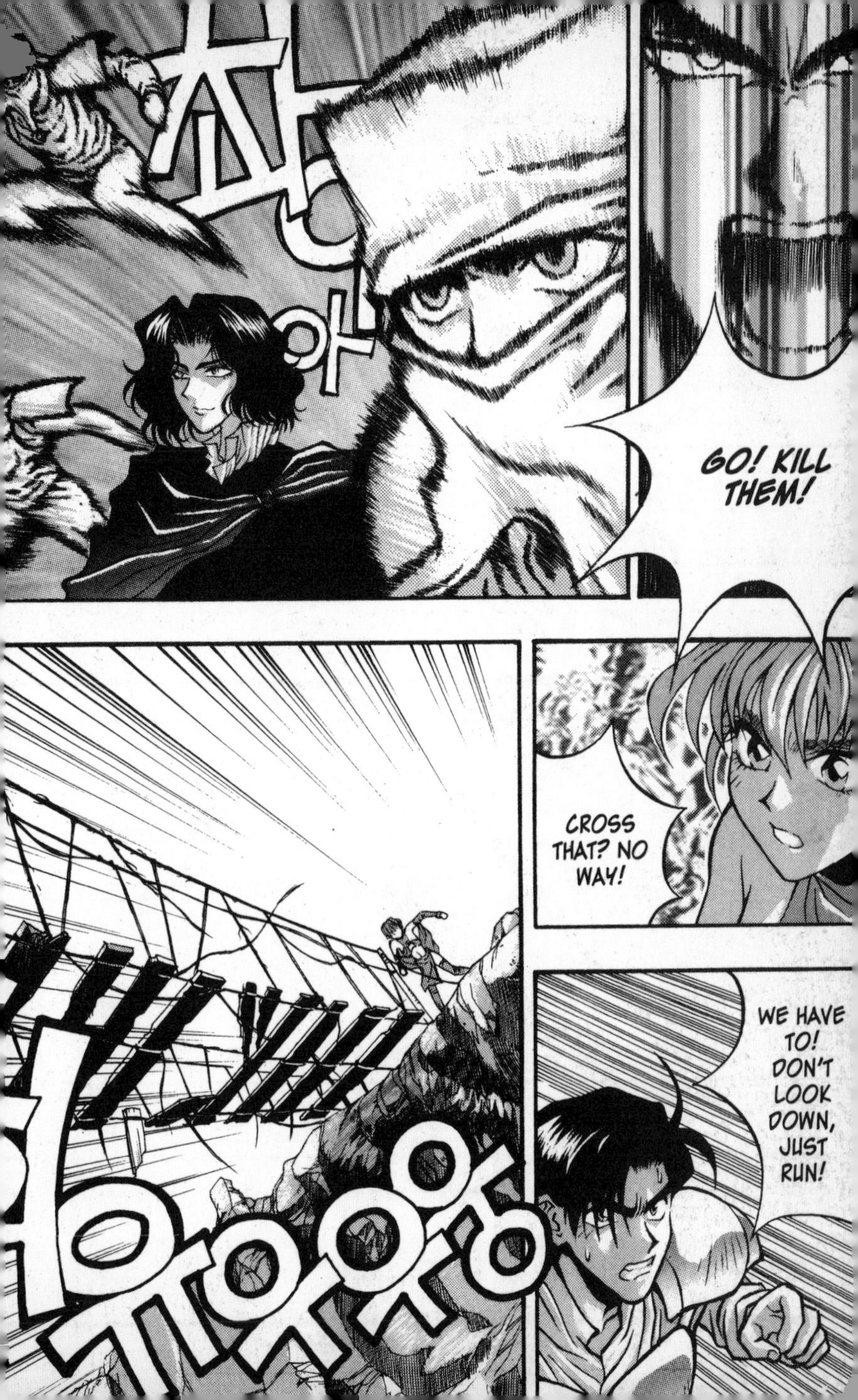
GO! KILL THEM!
CROSS THAT? NO WAY!
WE HAVE TO! DON'T LOOK DOWN, JUST RUN!

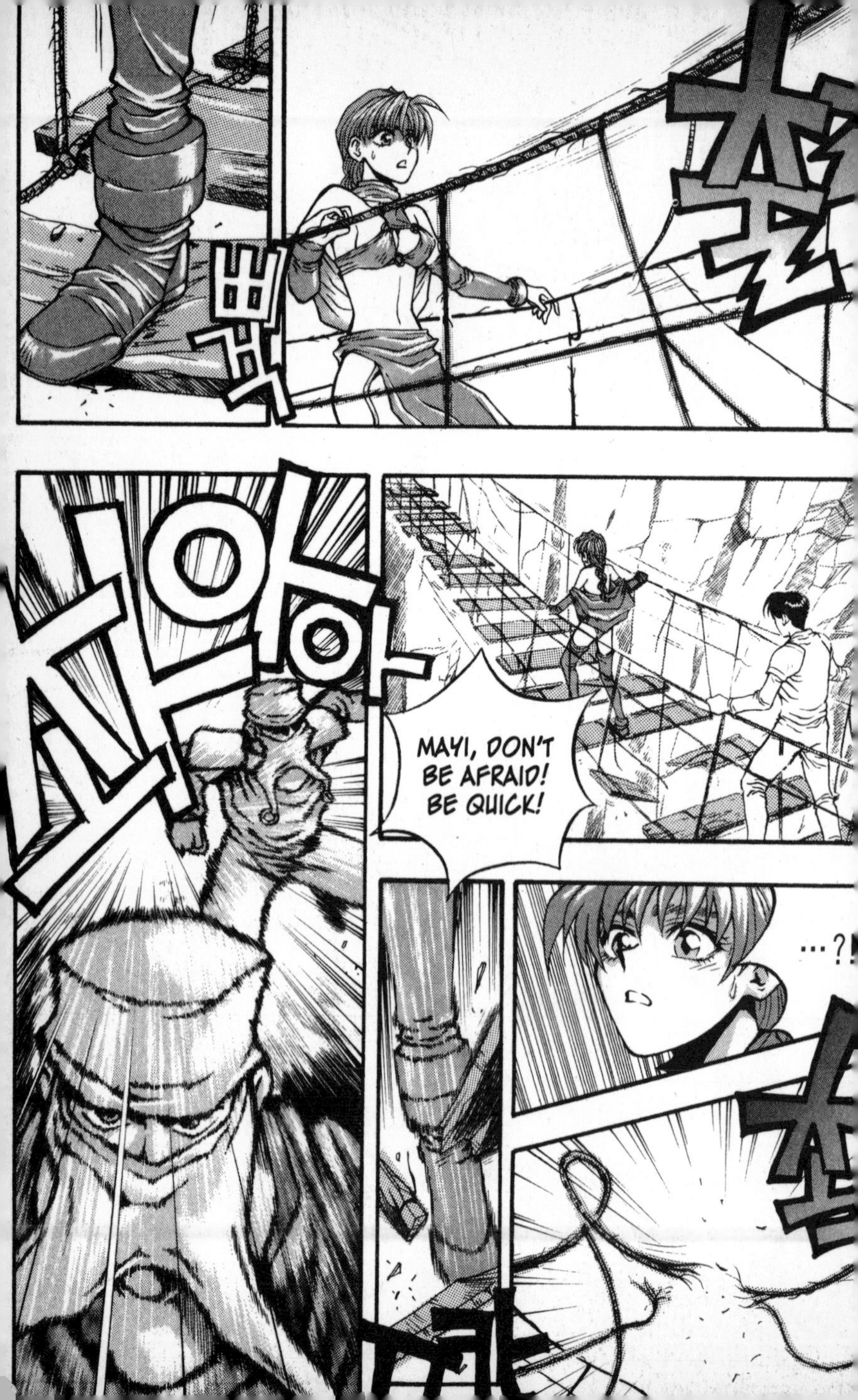
MAYI, DON'T BE AFRAID! BE QUICK!
...?!

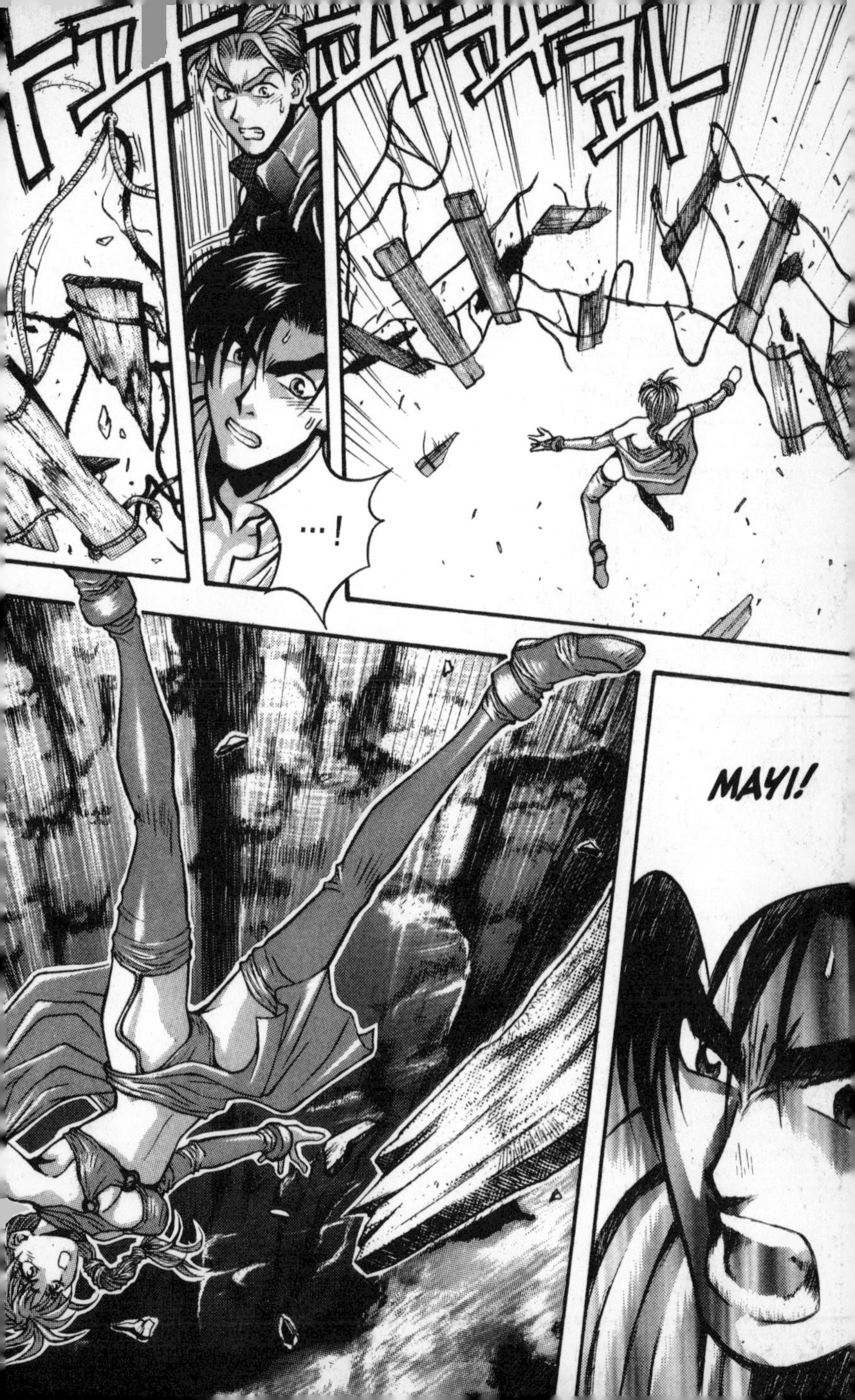
...!
MAYI!

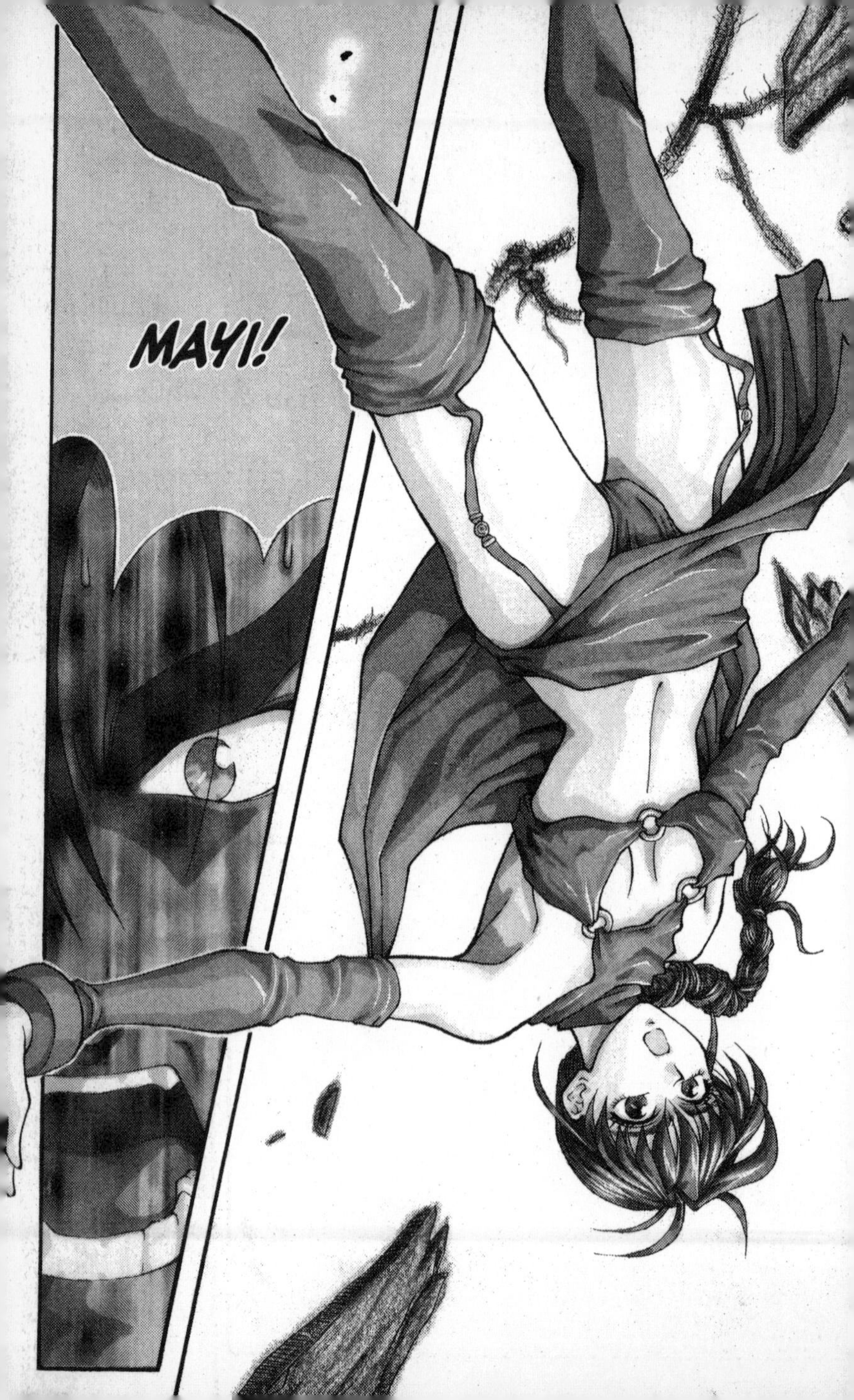
MAYI!

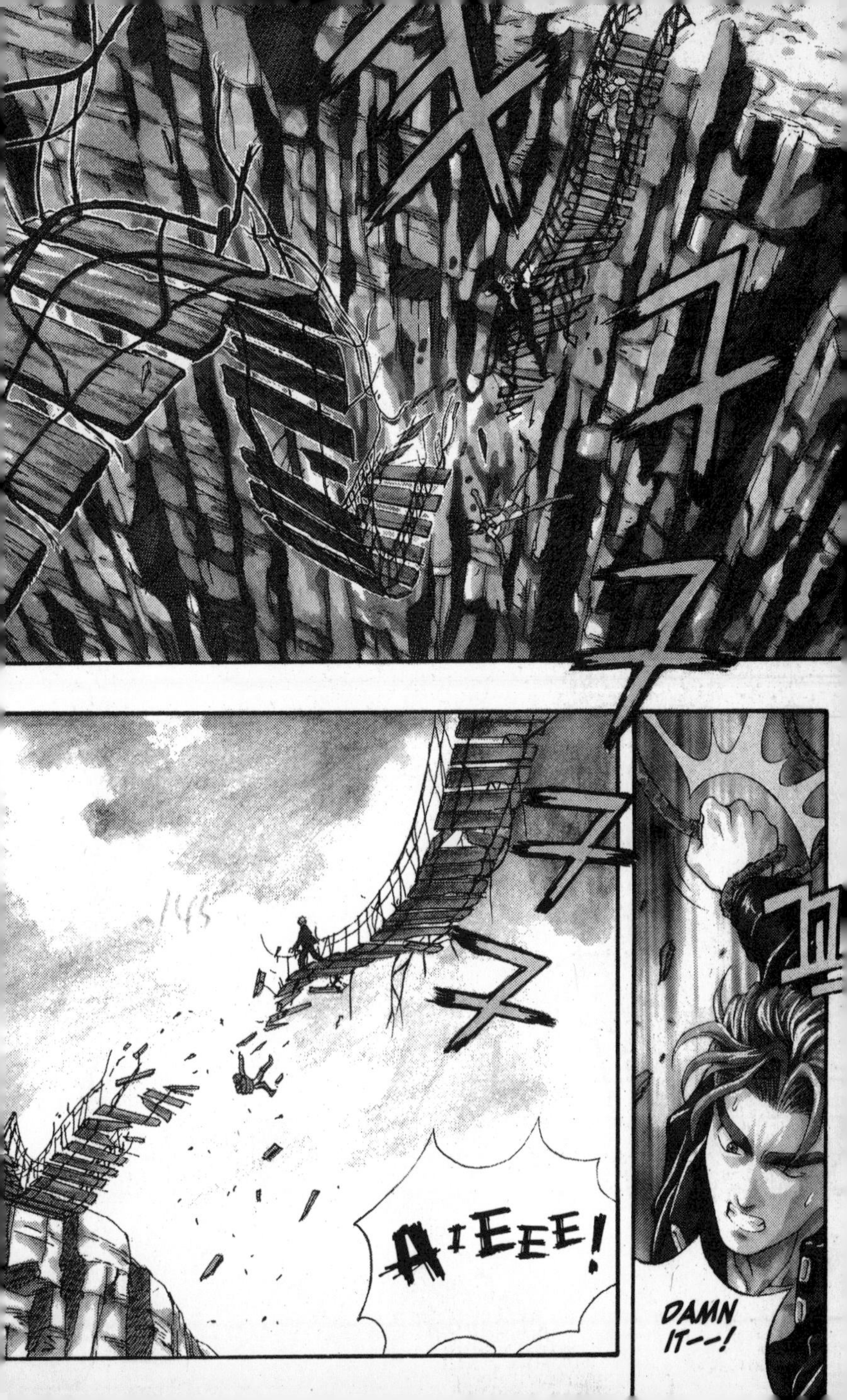
AIEEE!
DAMN IT--!

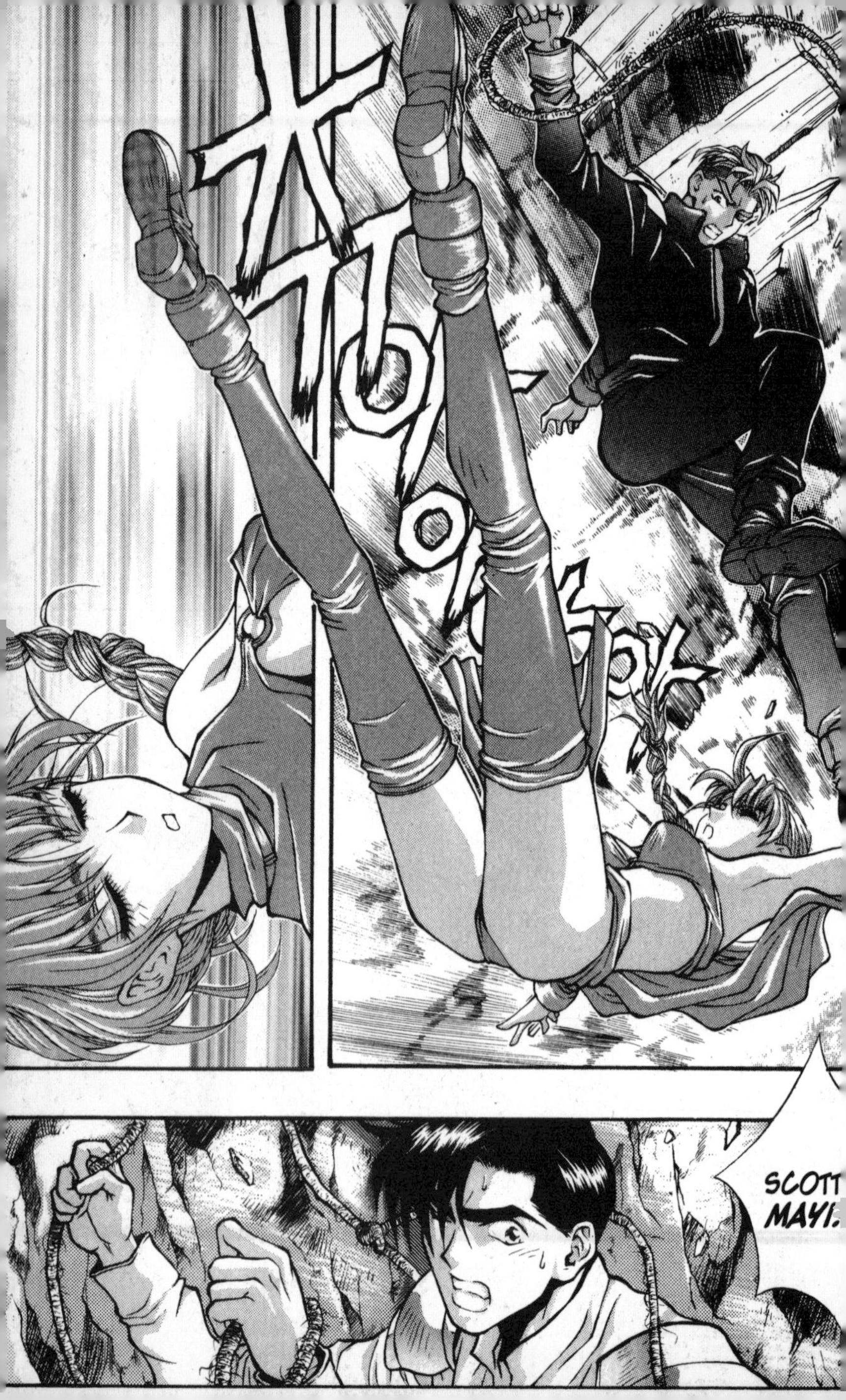
SCOTT
MAYI.

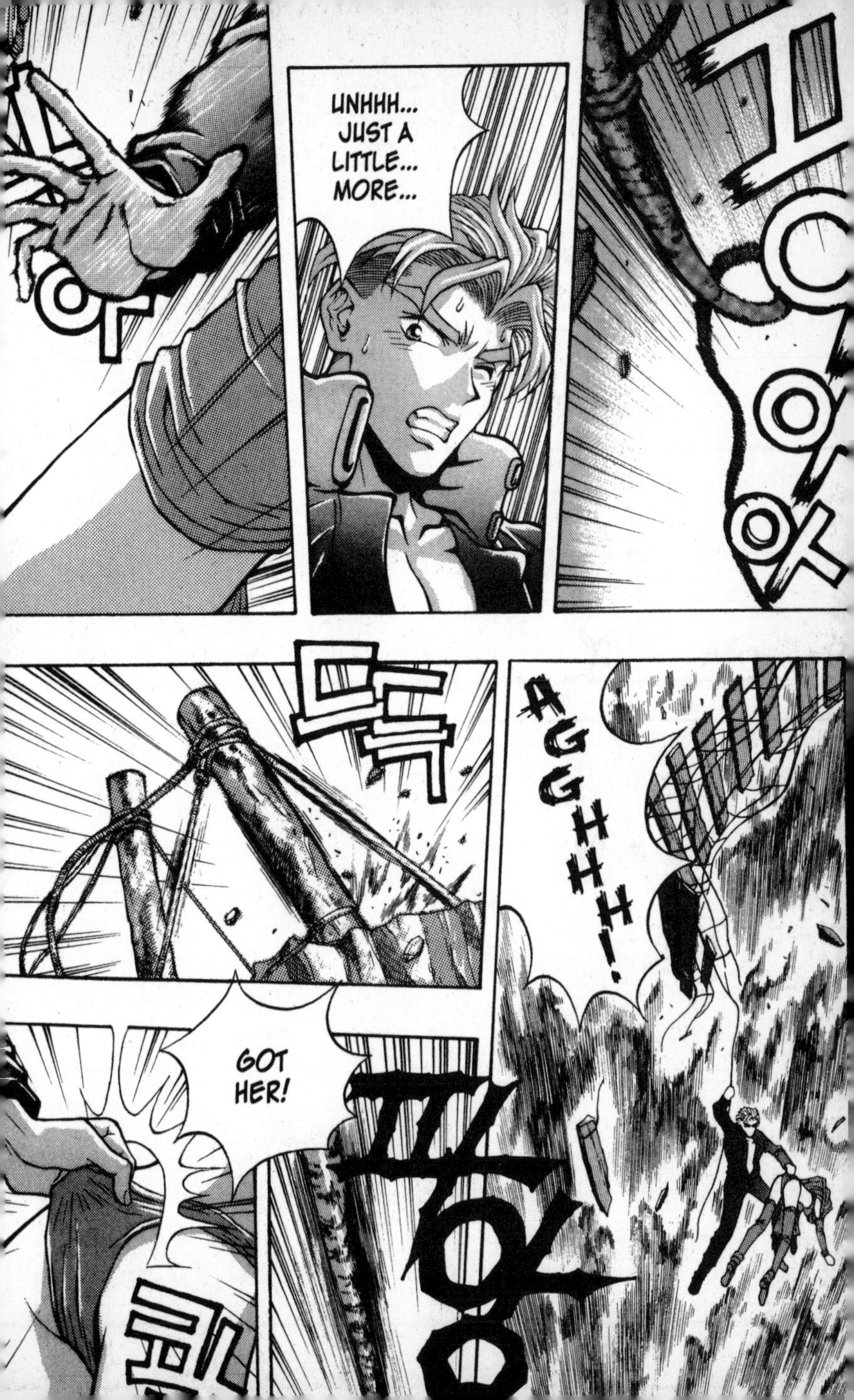
UNHHH... JUST A LITTLE... MORE...
GOT HER!
AGGHHH!

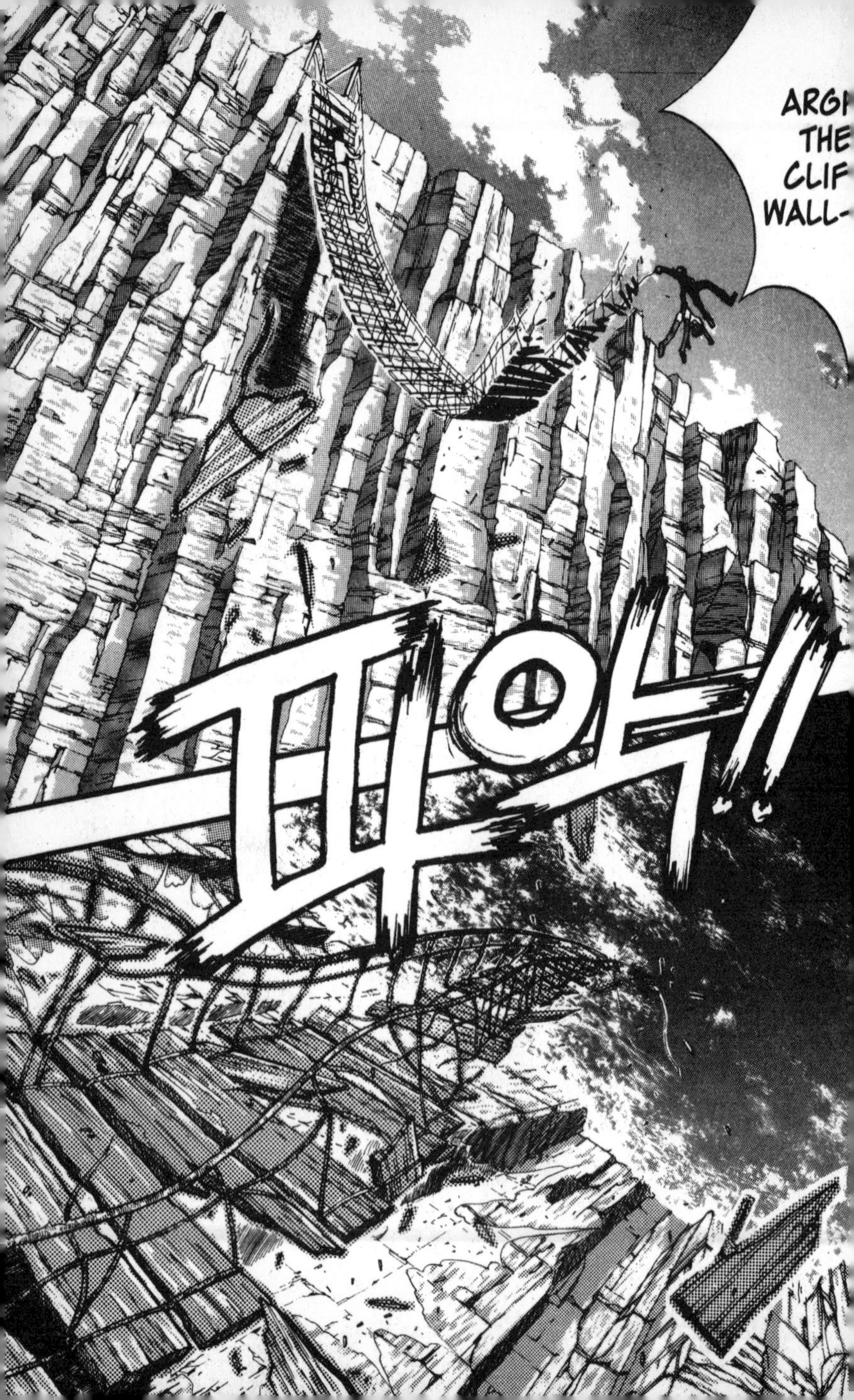
ARGH
THE
CLIF
WALL-
TTHOOM!!

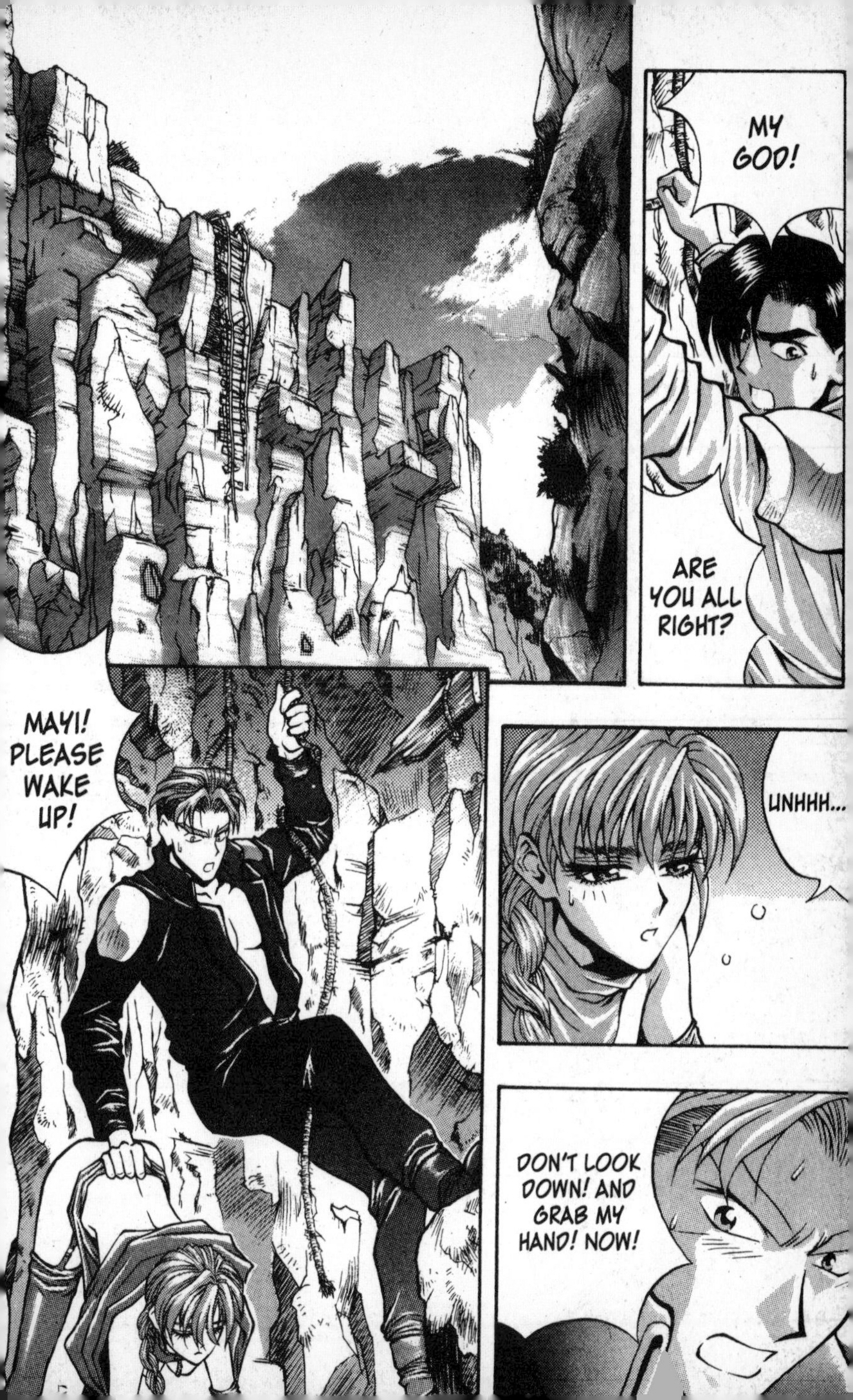
MY GOD!
ARE YOU ALL RIGHT?
MAYI! PLEASE WAKE UP!
UNHHH...
DON'T LOOK DOWN! AND GRAB MY HAND! NOW!

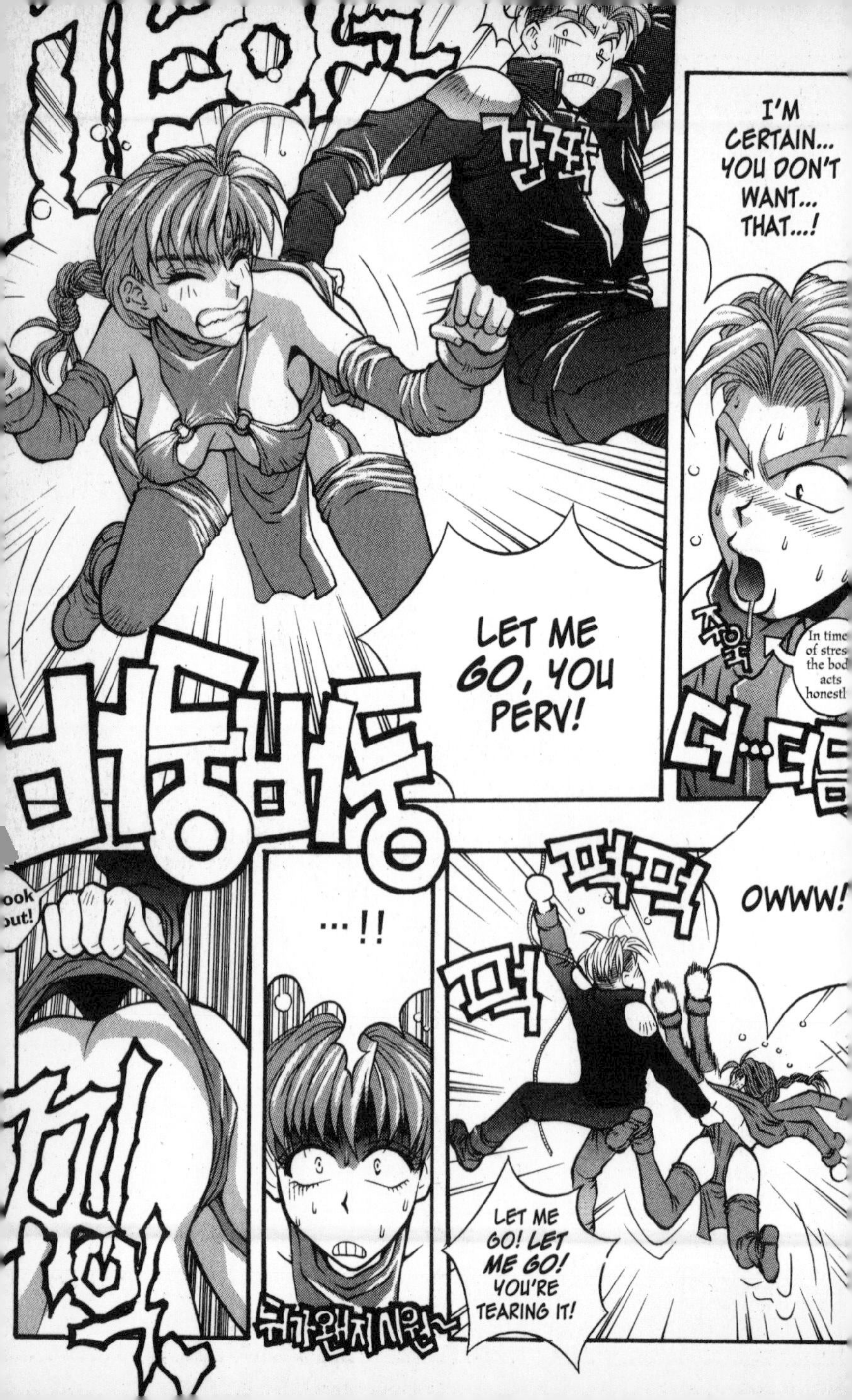
LET ME GO, YOU PERV!
I'M CERTAIN... YOU DON'T WANT... THAT...!
In time of stres the bod acts honestl
ook out!
...!!
OWWW!
LET ME GO! LET ME GO! YOU'RE TEARING IT!

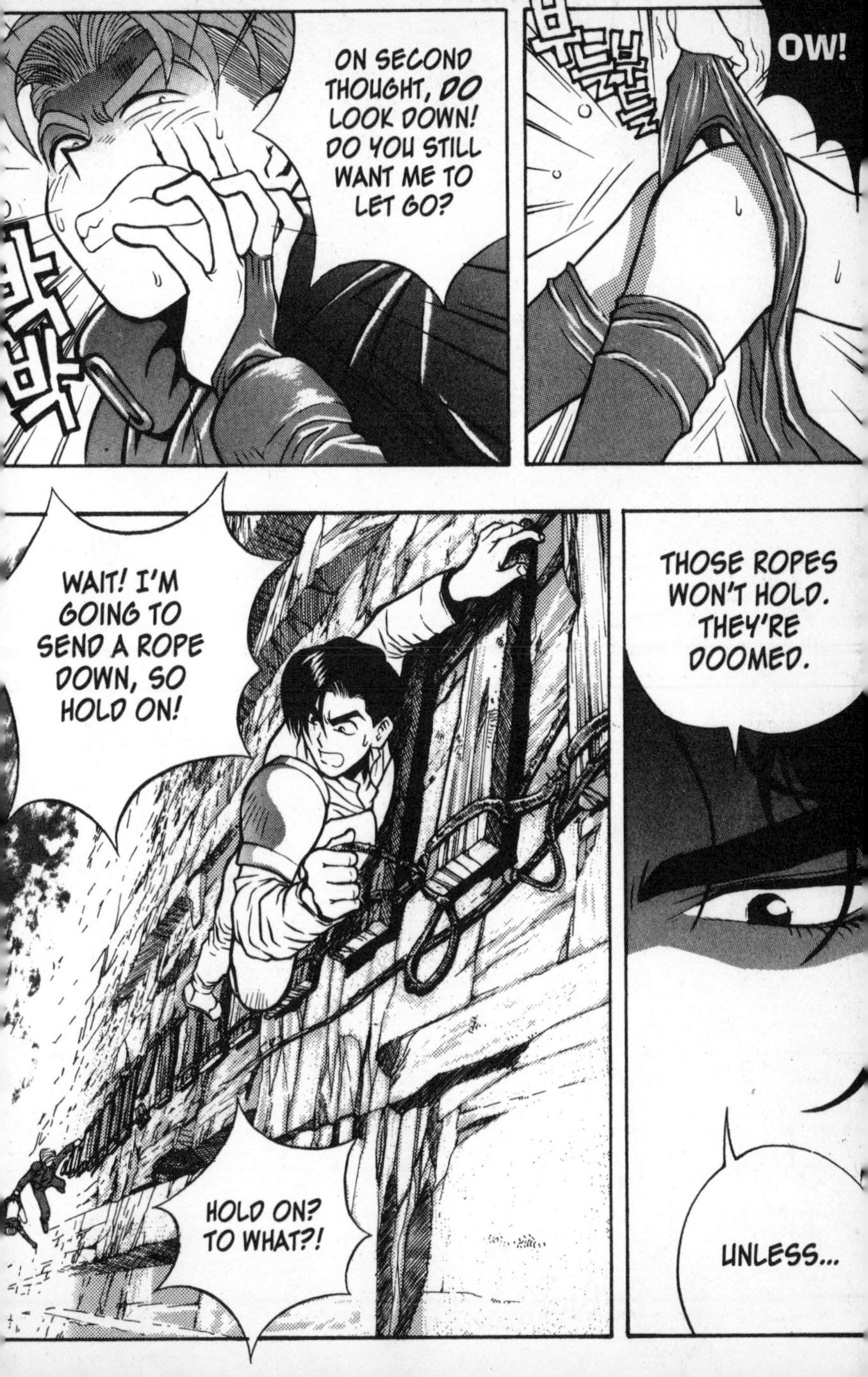
ON SECOND THOUGHT, DO LOOK DOWN! DO YOU STILL WANT ME TO LET GO?
OW!
WAIT! I'M GOING TO SEND A ROPE DOWN, SO HOLD ON!
HOLD ON? TO WHAT?!
THOSE ROPES WON'T HOLD. THEY'RE DOOMED.
UNLESS...

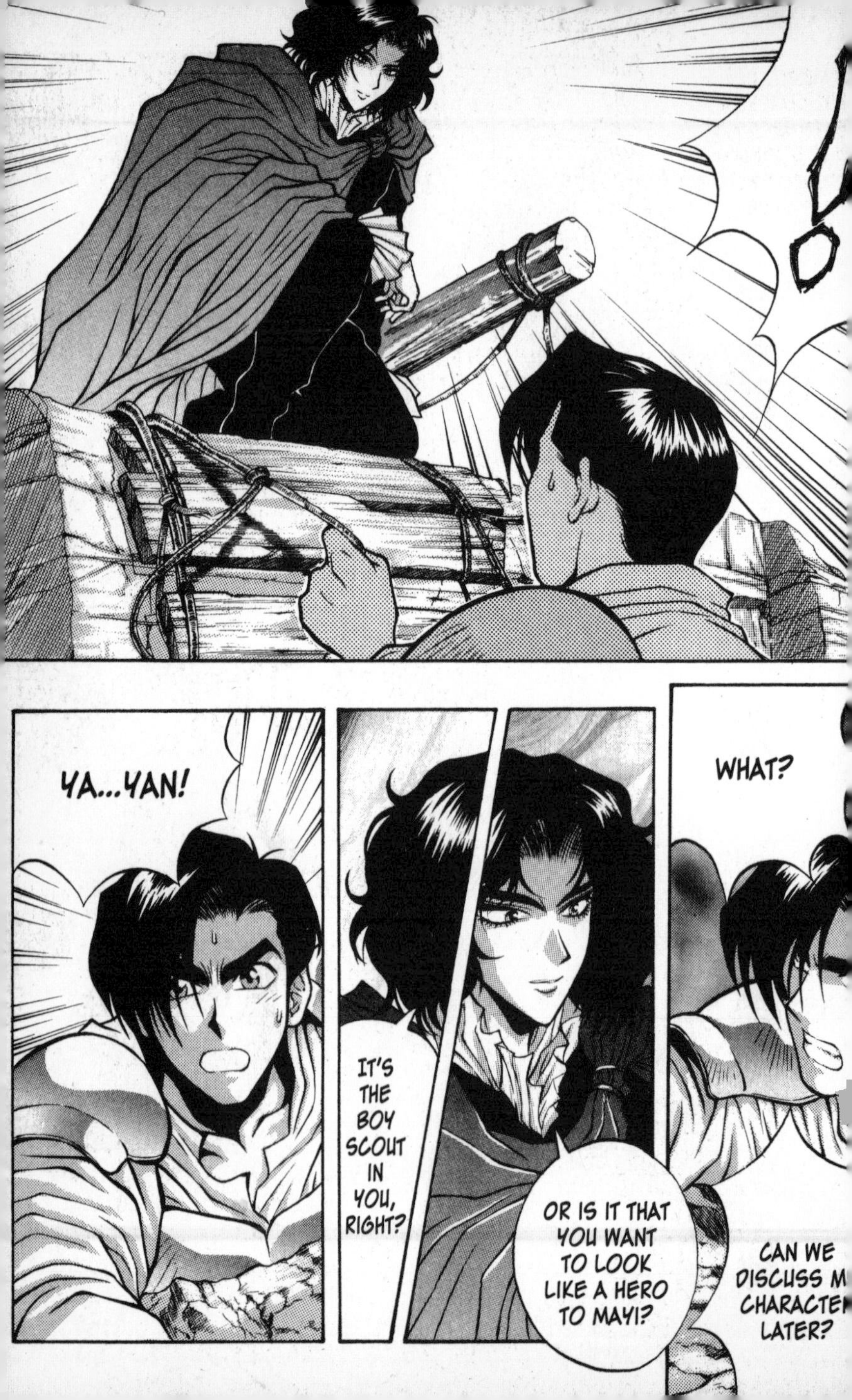
YA...YAN!
IT'S THE BOY SCOUT IN YOU, RIGHT?
OR IS IT THAT YOU WANT TO LOOK LIKE A HERO TO MAYI?
WHAT?
CAN WE DISCUSS M CHARACTE LATER?

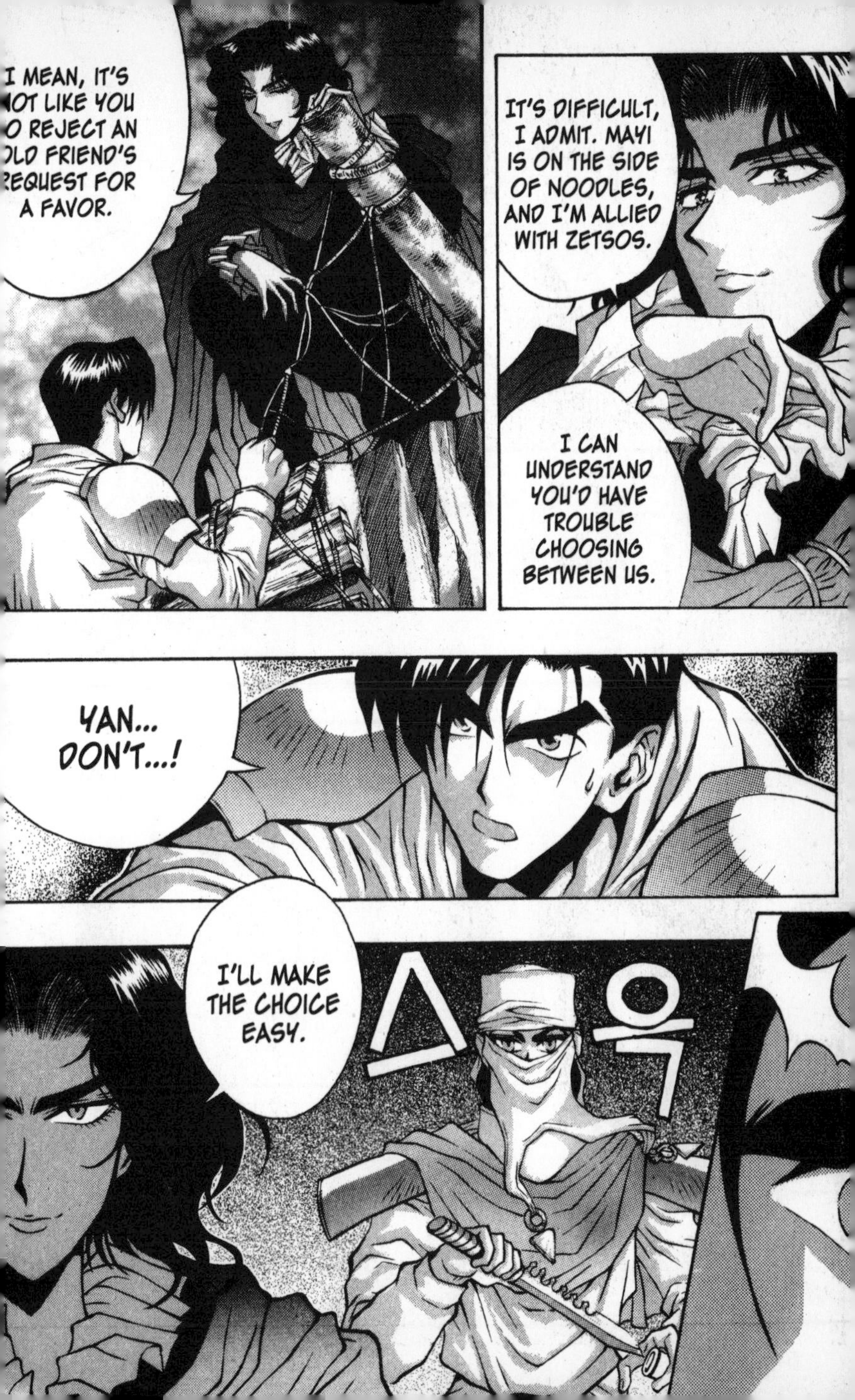
I MEAN, IT'S NOT LIKE YOU TO REJECT AN OLD FRIEND'S REQUEST FOR A FAVOR.
IT'S DIFFICULT, I ADMIT. MAYI IS ON THE SIDE OF NOODLES, AND I'M ALLIED WITH ZETSOS.
I CAN UNDERSTAND YOU'D HAVE TROUBLE CHOOSING BETWEEN US.
YAN... DON'T...!
I'LL MAKE THE CHOICE EASY.
스윽

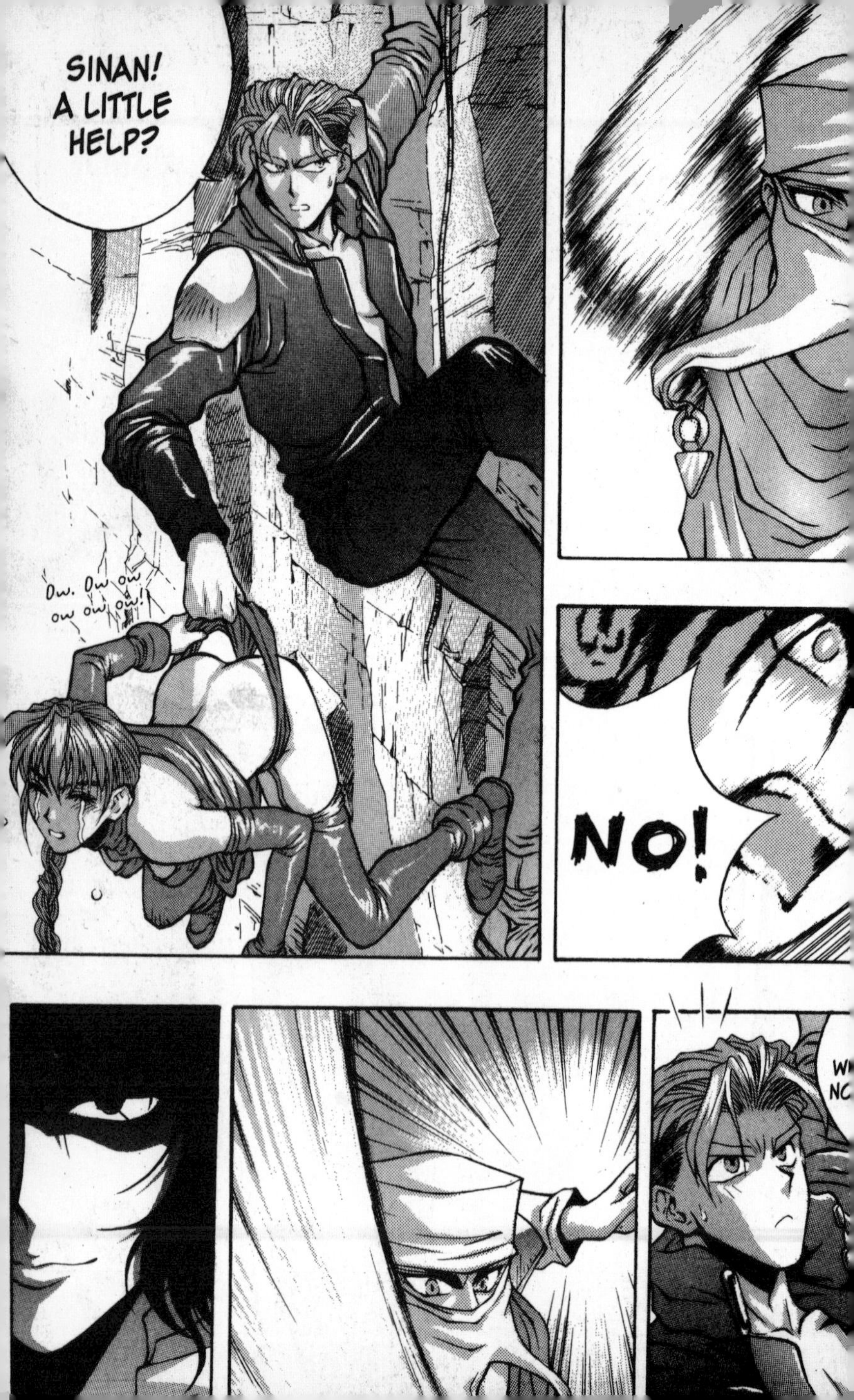
SINAN! A LITTLE HELP?
Ow. Ow ow ow ow ow!
NO!

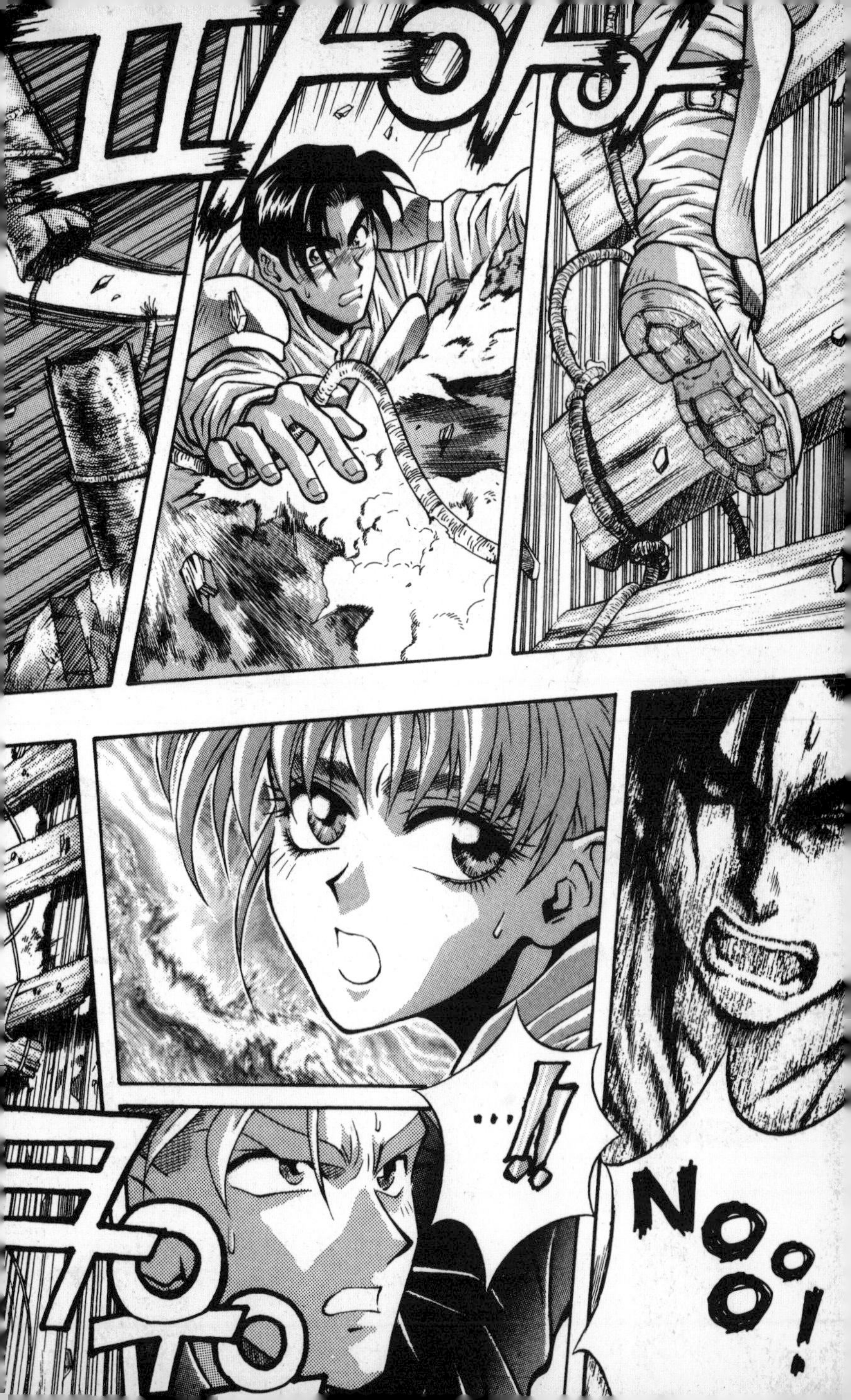
...!
NOOO!

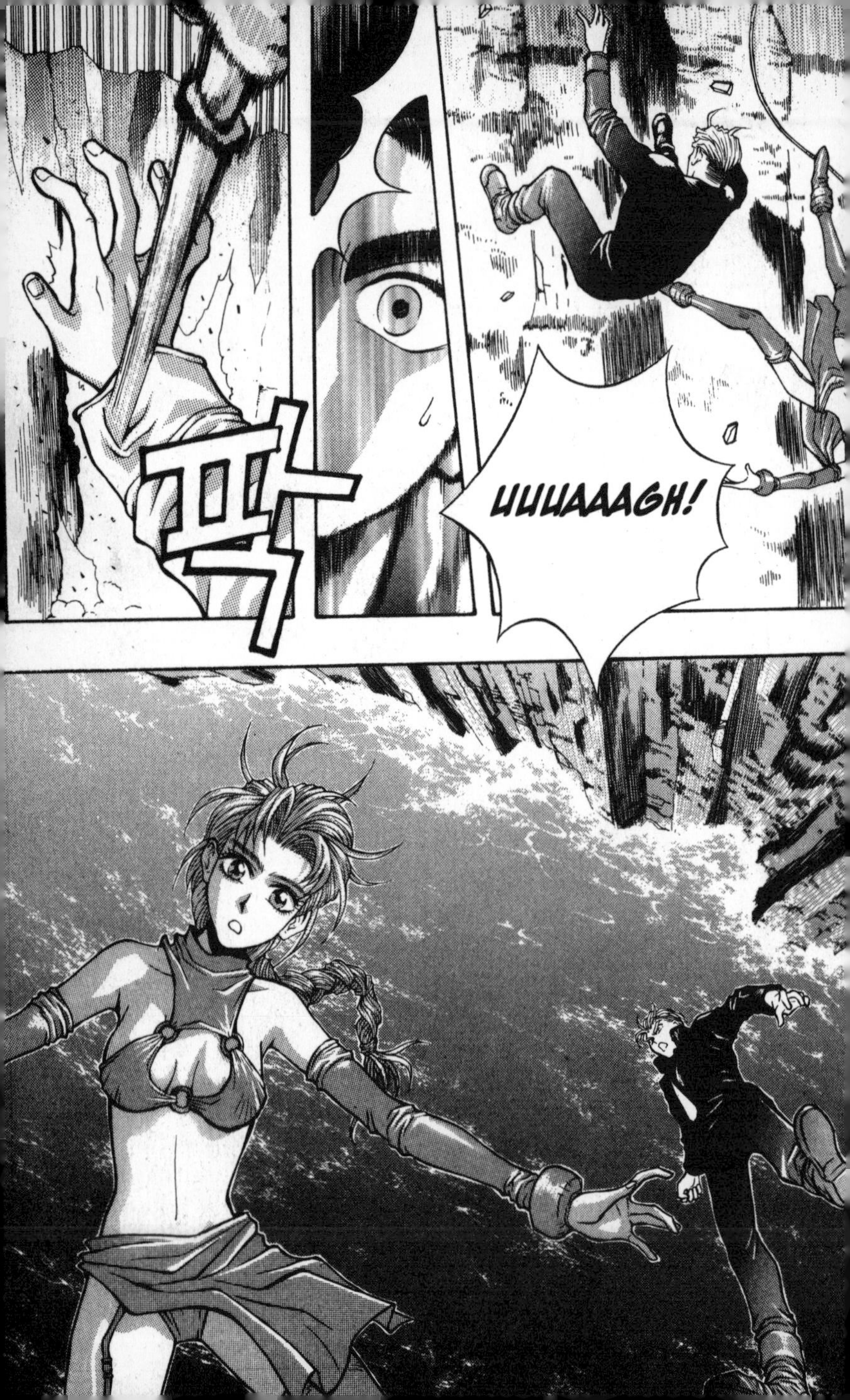
팍
UUUAAAGH!

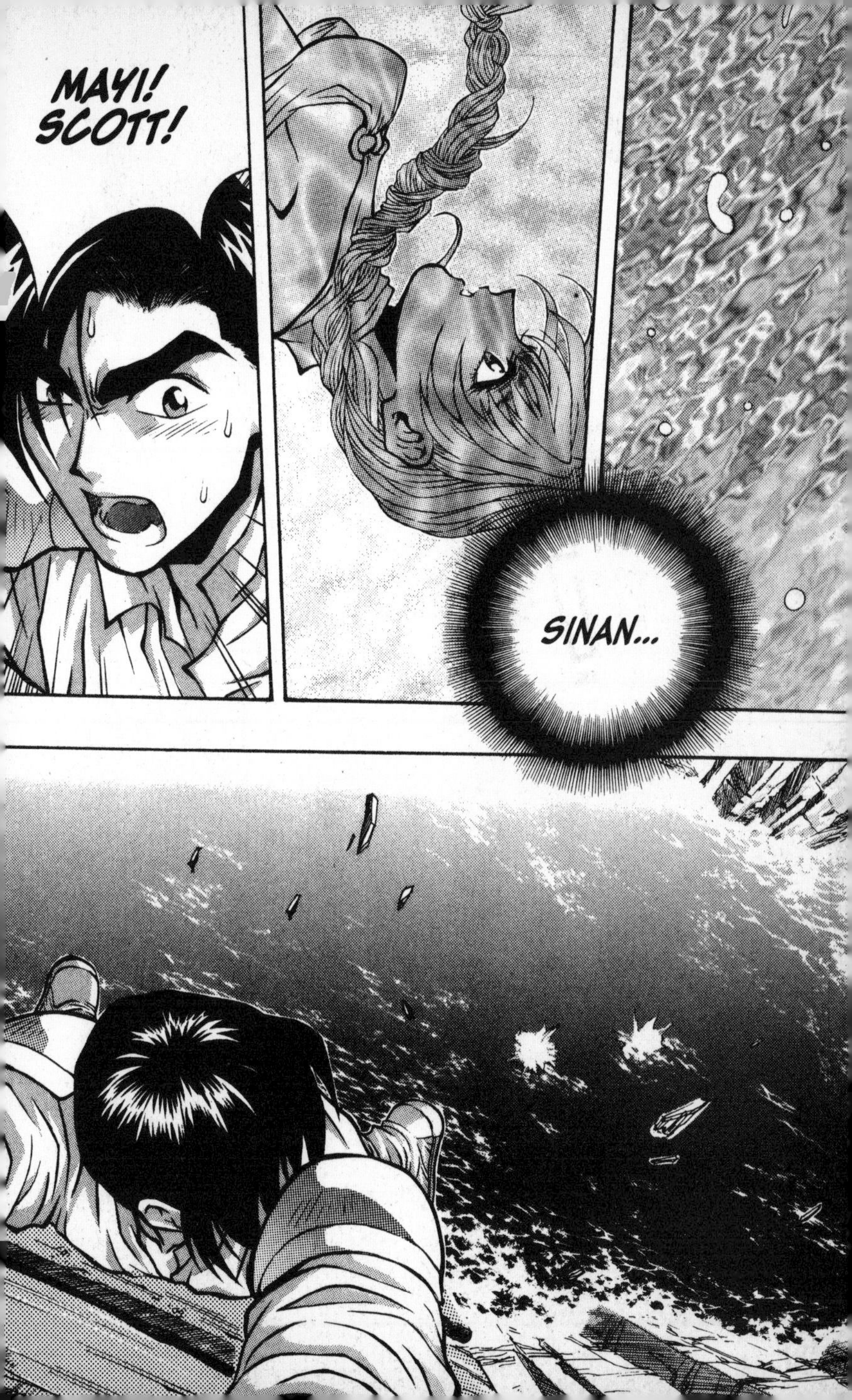
MAYI! SCOTT!
SINAN...

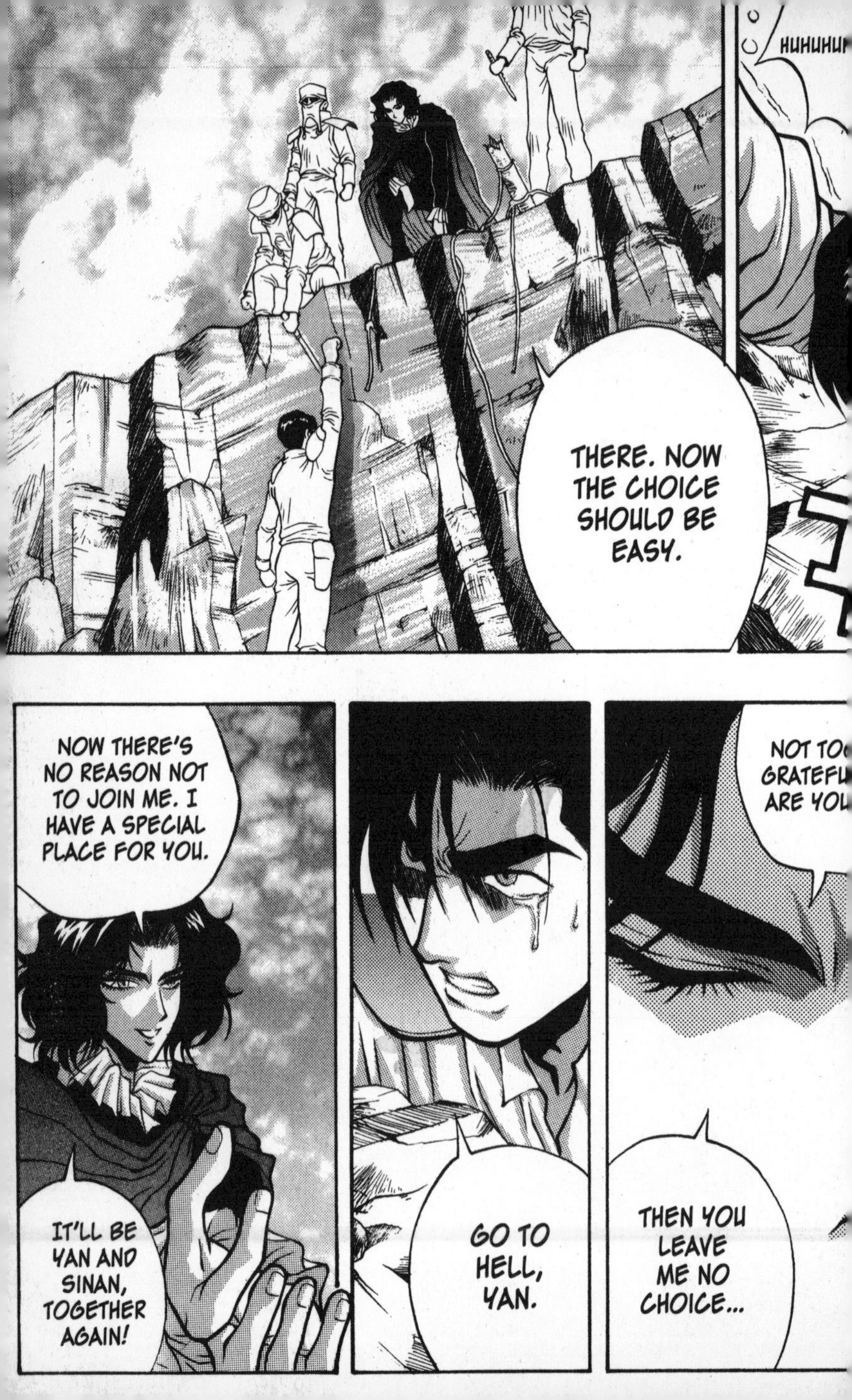
THERE. NOW THE CHOICE SHOULD BE EASY.
HUHUHU
NOW THERE'S NO REASON NOT TO JOIN ME. I HAVE A SPECIAL PLACE FOR YOU.
IT'LL BE YAN AND SINAN, TOGETHER AGAIN!
GO TO HELL, YAN.
NOT TO GRATEF ARE YO
THEN YOU LEAVE ME NO CHOICE...

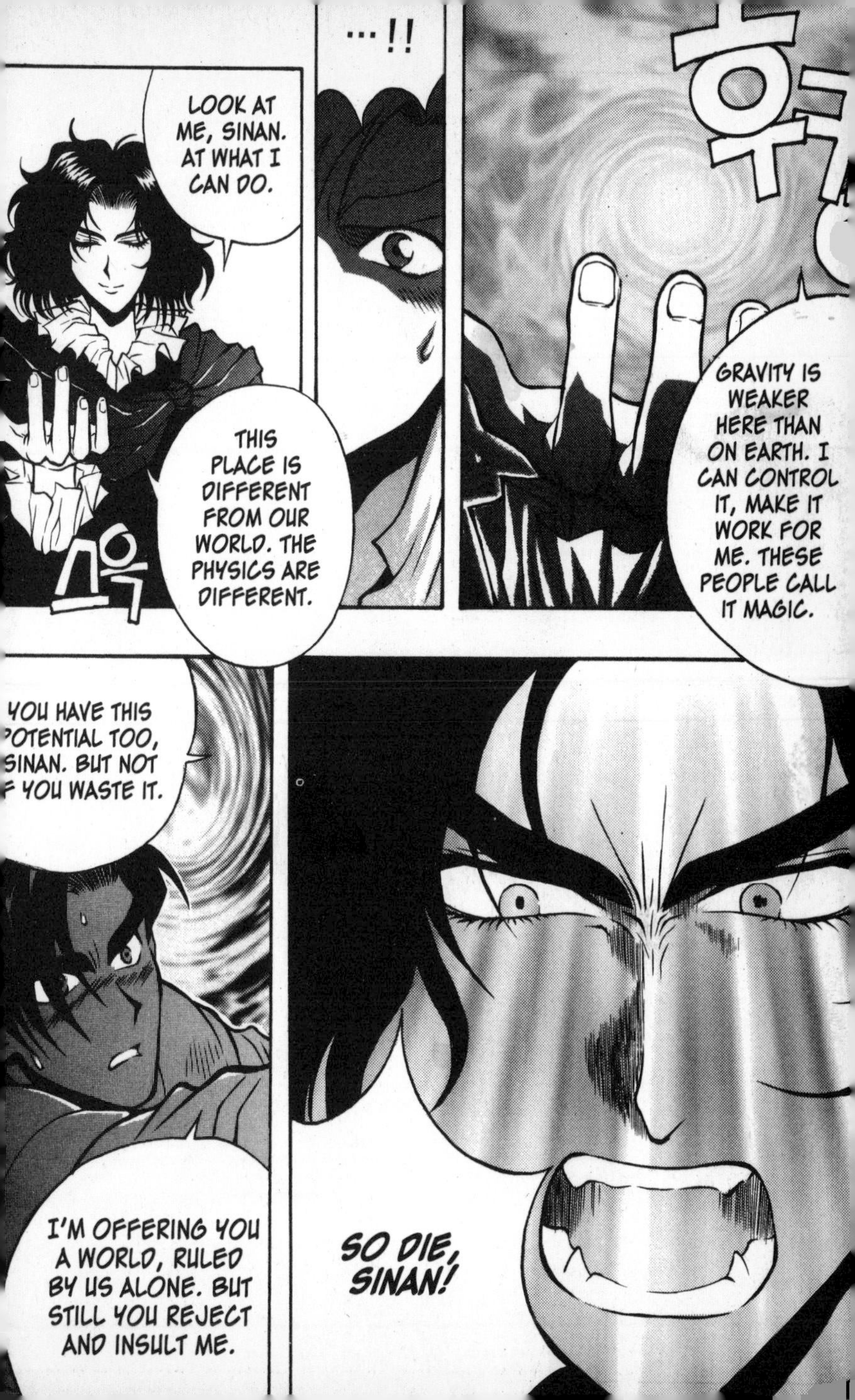
LOOK AT ME, SINAN. AT WHAT I CAN DO.
THIS PLACE IS DIFFERENT FROM OUR WORLD. THE PHYSICS ARE DIFFERENT.
...!!
GRAVITY IS WEAKER HERE THAN ON EARTH. I CAN CONTROL IT, MAKE IT WORK FOR ME. THESE PEOPLE CALL IT MAGIC.
YOU HAVE THIS POTENTIAL TOO, SINAN. BUT NOT YOU WASTE IT.
I'M OFFERING YOU A WORLD, RULED BY US ALONE. BUT STILL YOU REJECT AND INSULT ME.
SO DIE, SINAN!

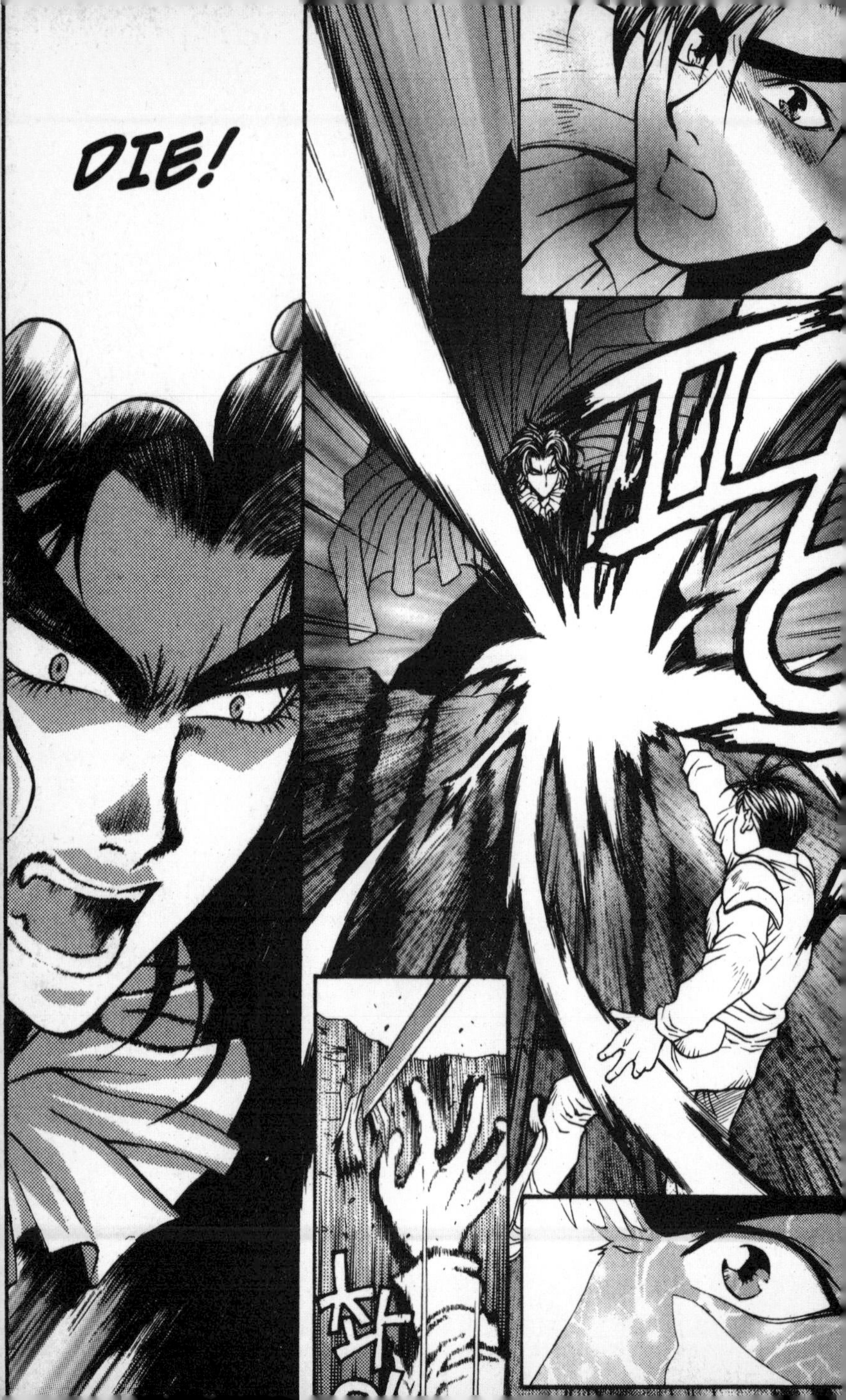
DIE!

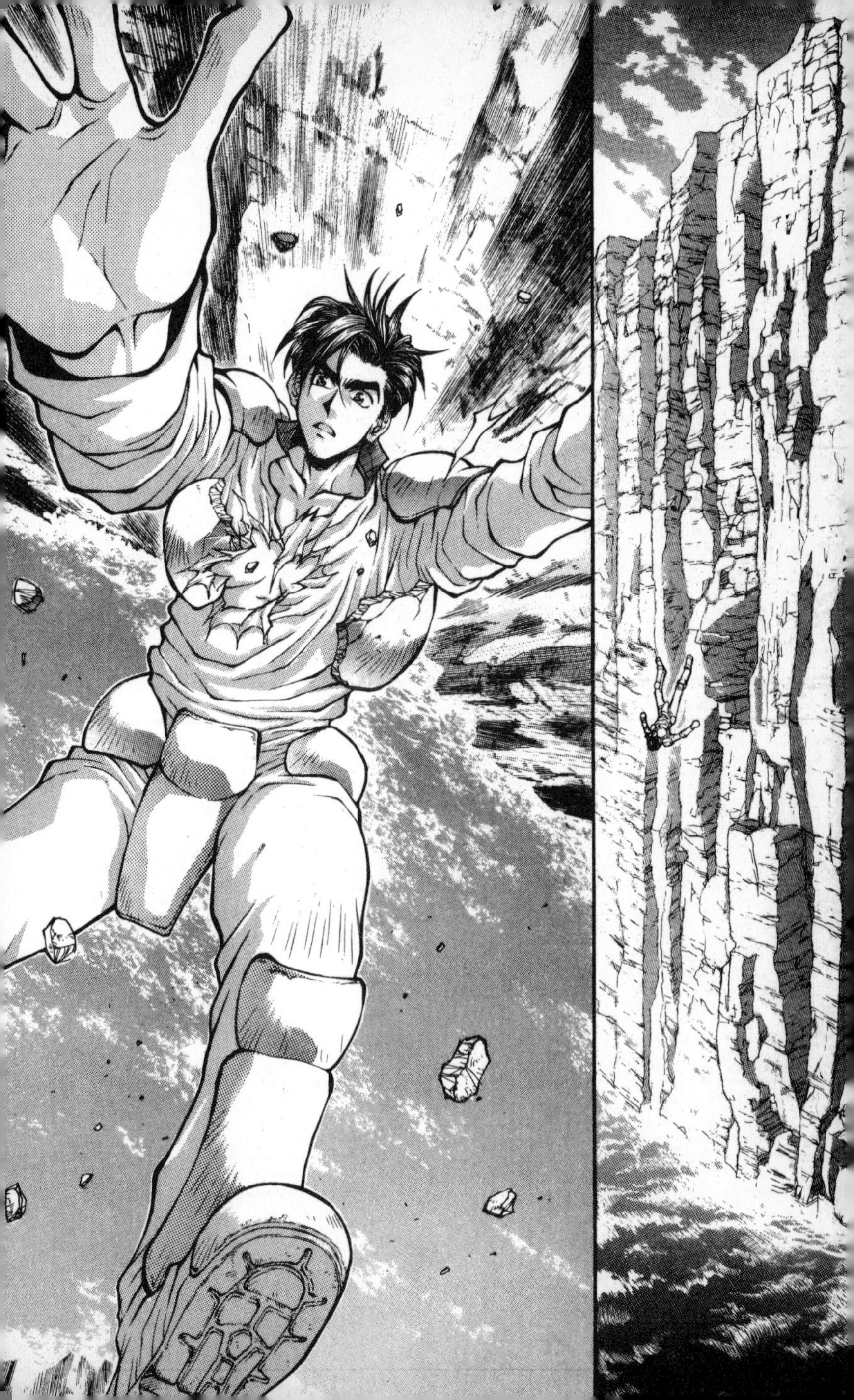

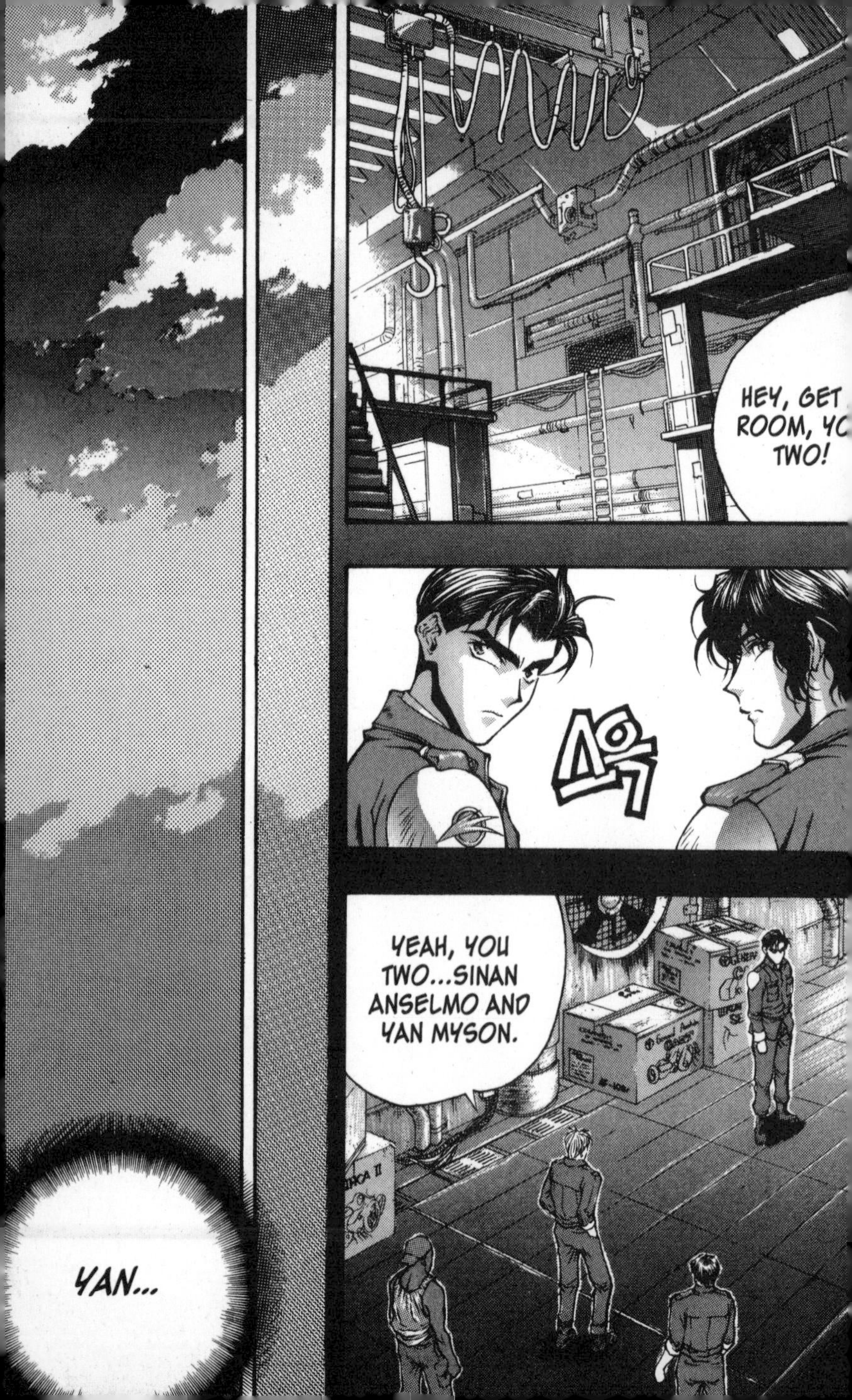
YAN...
HEY, GET ROOM, YO TWO!
YEAH, YOU TWO...SINAN ANSELMO AND YAN MYSON.

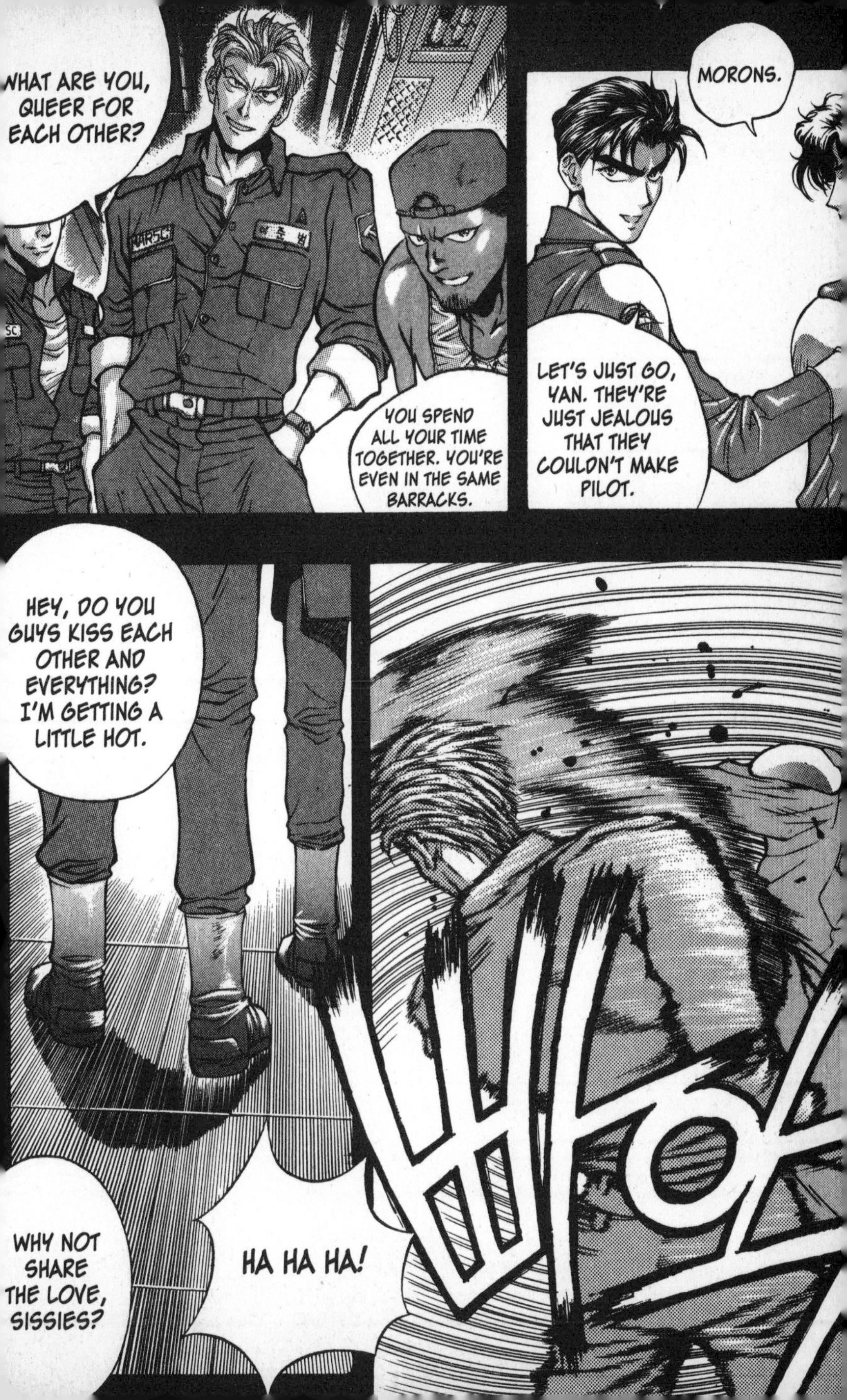
WHAT ARE YOU, QUEER FOR EACH OTHER?
YOU SPEND ALL YOUR TIME TOGETHER. YOU'RE EVEN IN THE SAME BARRACKS.
MORONS.
LET'S JUST GO, YAN. THEY'RE JUST JEALOUS THAT THEY COULDN'T MAKE PILOT.
HEY, DO YOU GUYS KISS EACH OTHER AND EVERYTHING? I'M GETTING A LITTLE HOT.
WHY NOT SHARE THE LOVE, SISSIES?
HA HA HA!

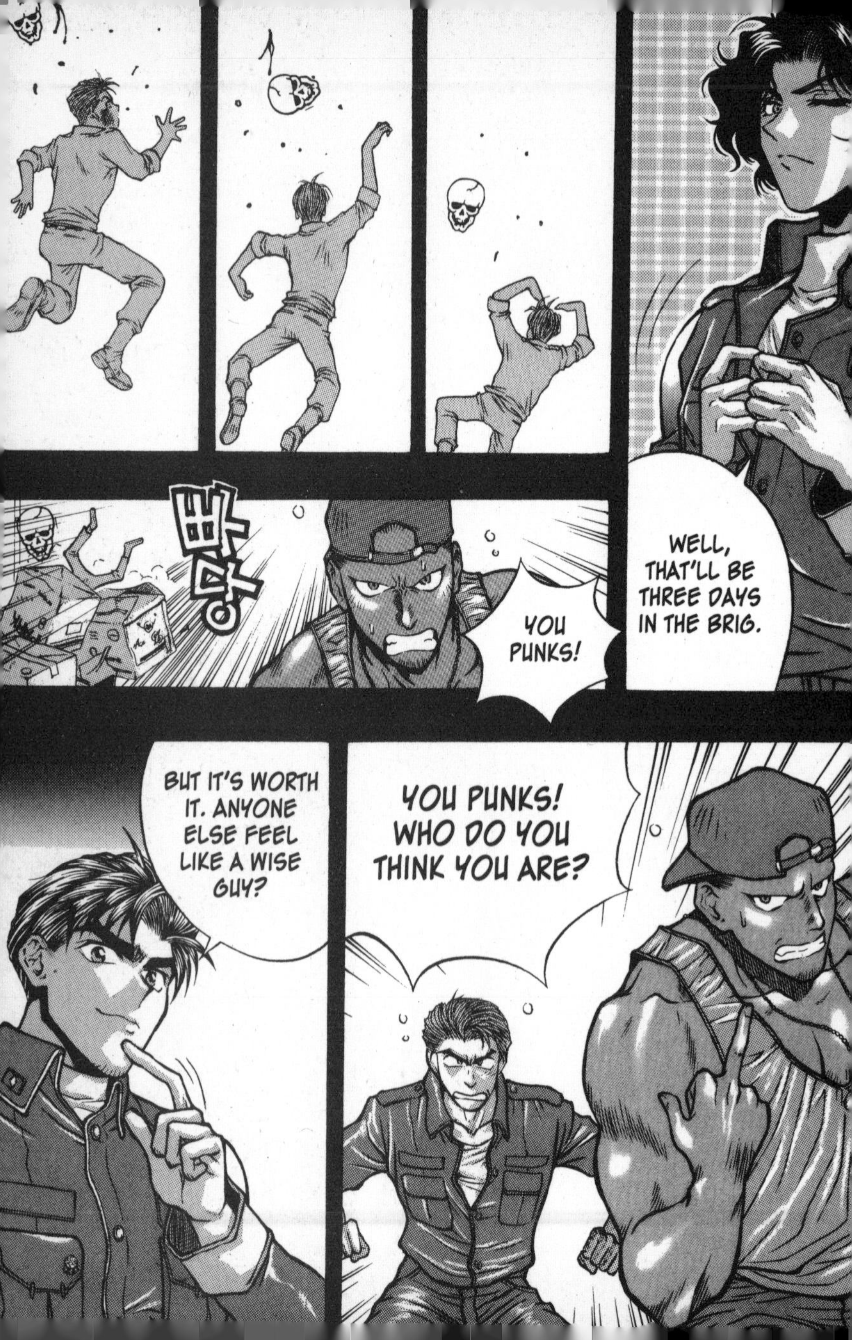
YOU PUNKS!
WELL, THAT'LL BE THREE DAYS IN THE BRIG.
BUT IT'S WORTH IT. ANYONE ELSE FEEL LIKE A WISE GUY?
YOU PUNKS! WHO DO YOU THINK YOU ARE?

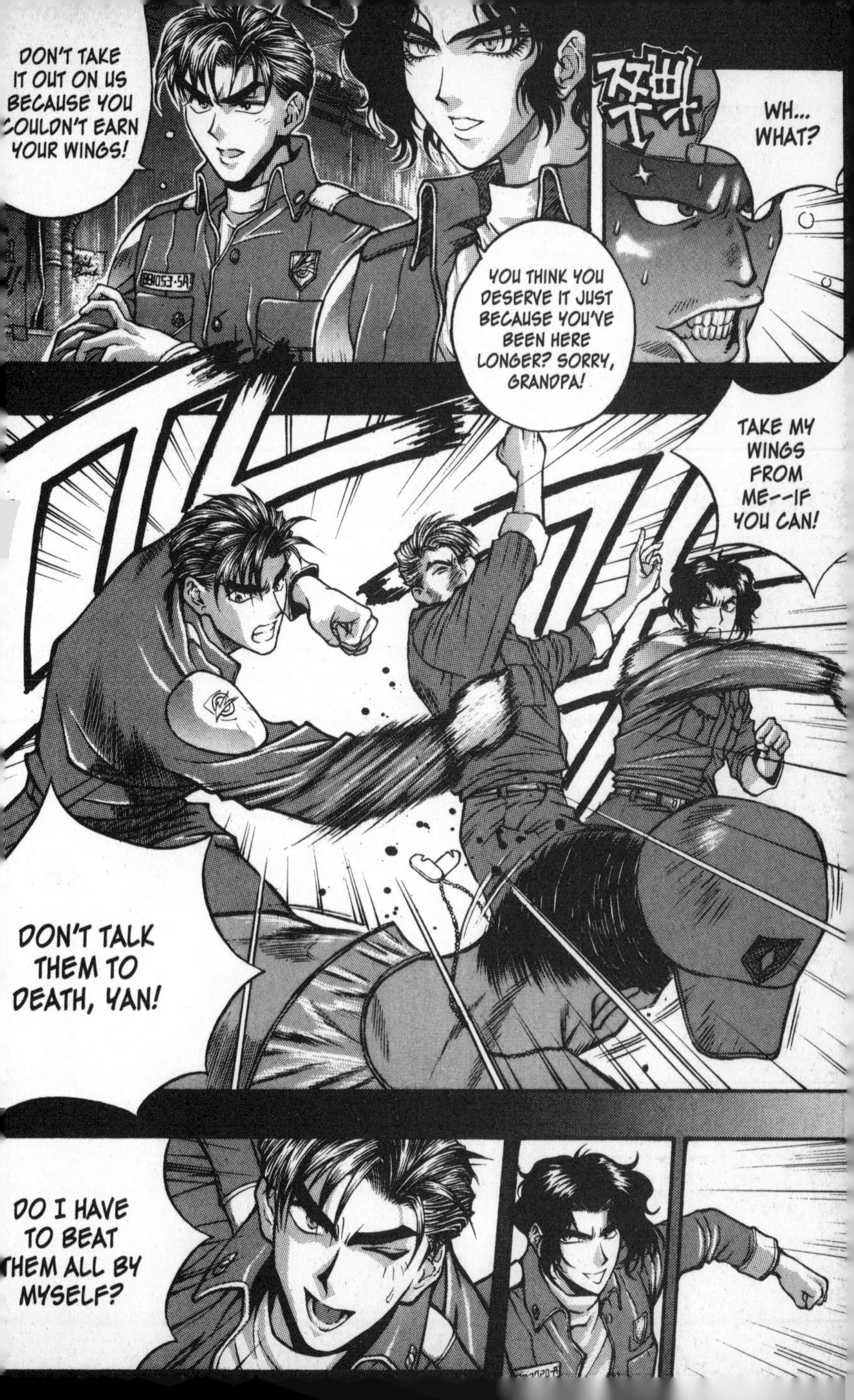
DON'T TAKE IT OUT ON US BECAUSE YOU COULDN'T EARN YOUR WINGS!
WH... WHAT?
YOU THINK YOU DESERVE IT JUST BECAUSE YOU'VE BEEN HERE LONGER? SORRY, GRANDPA!
TAKE MY WINGS FROM ME--IF YOU CAN!
DON'T TALK THEM TO DEATH, YAN!
DO I HAVE TO BEAT THEM ALL BY MYSELF?

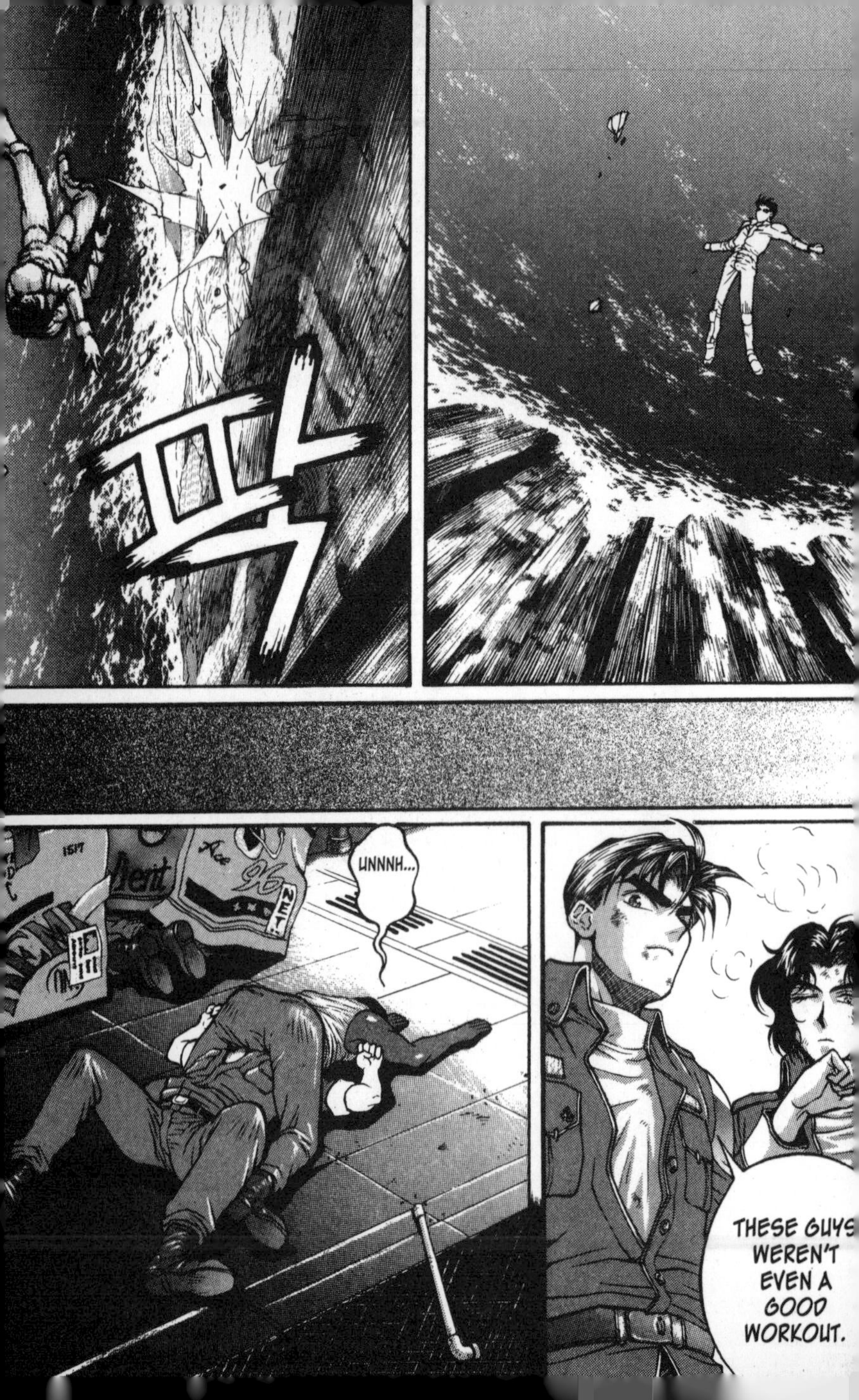
UNNNH...
THESE GUYS WEREN'T EVEN A GOOD WORKOUT.

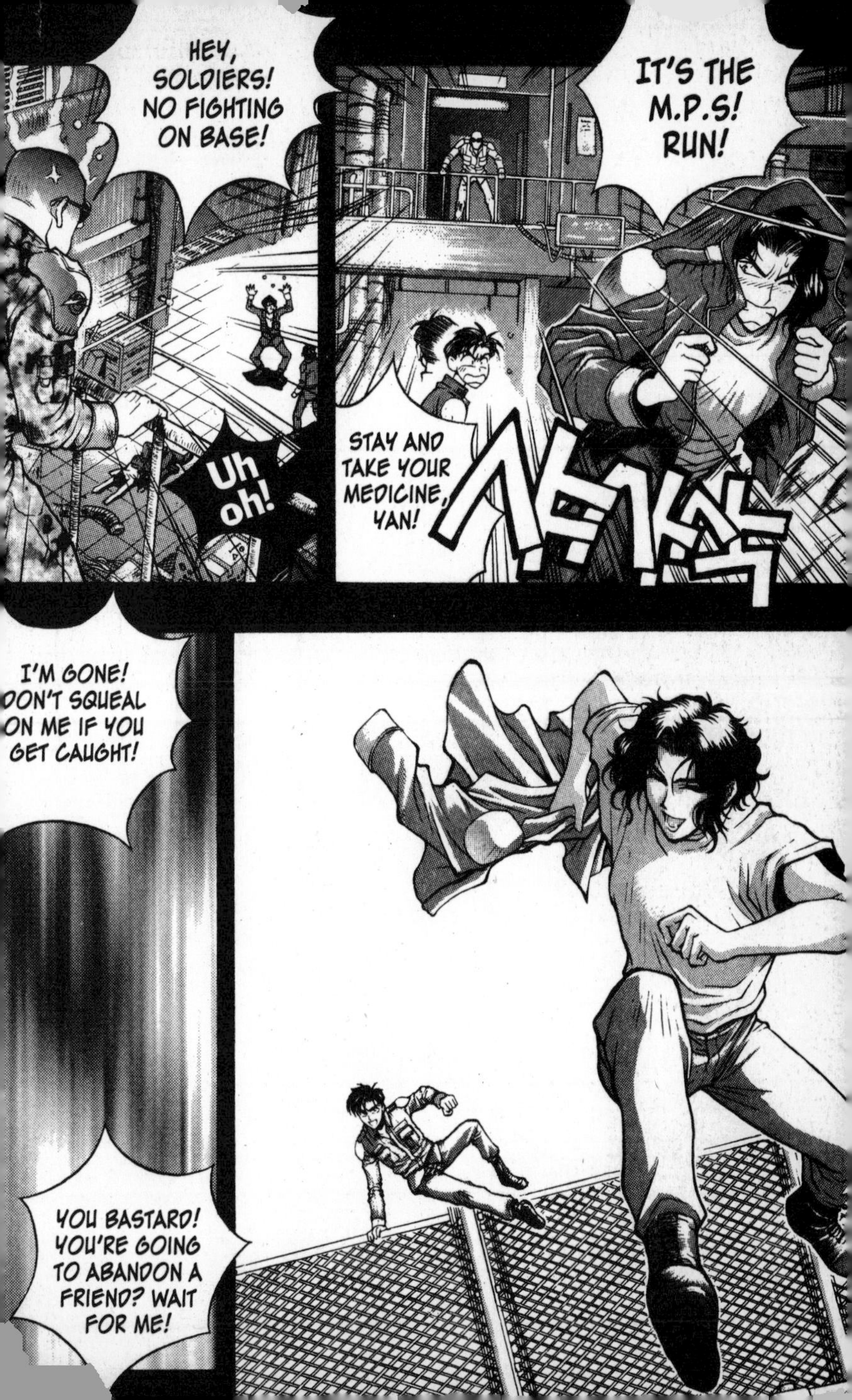
HEY, SOLDIERS! NO FIGHTING ON BASE!
Uh oh!
IT'S THE M.P.S! RUN!
STAY AND TAKE YOUR MEDICINE, YAN!
I'M GONE! DON'T SQUEAL ON ME IF YOU GET CAUGHT!
YOU BASTARD! YOU'RE GOING TO ABANDON A FRIEND? WAIT FOR ME!

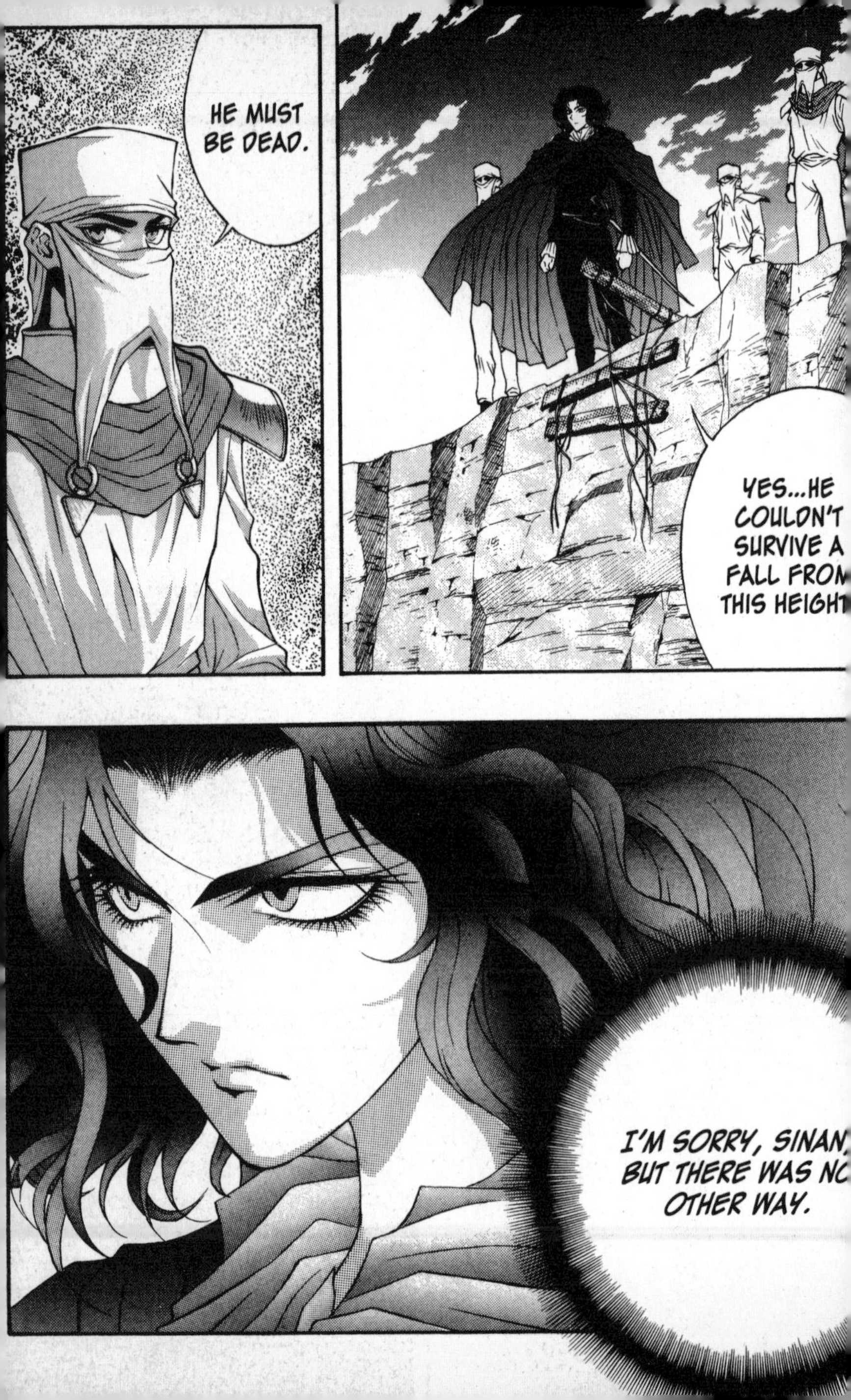
HE MUST BE DEAD.
YES...HE COULDN'T SURVIVE A FALL FROM THIS HEIGHT
I'M SORRY, SINAN, BUT THERE WAS NO OTHER WAY.

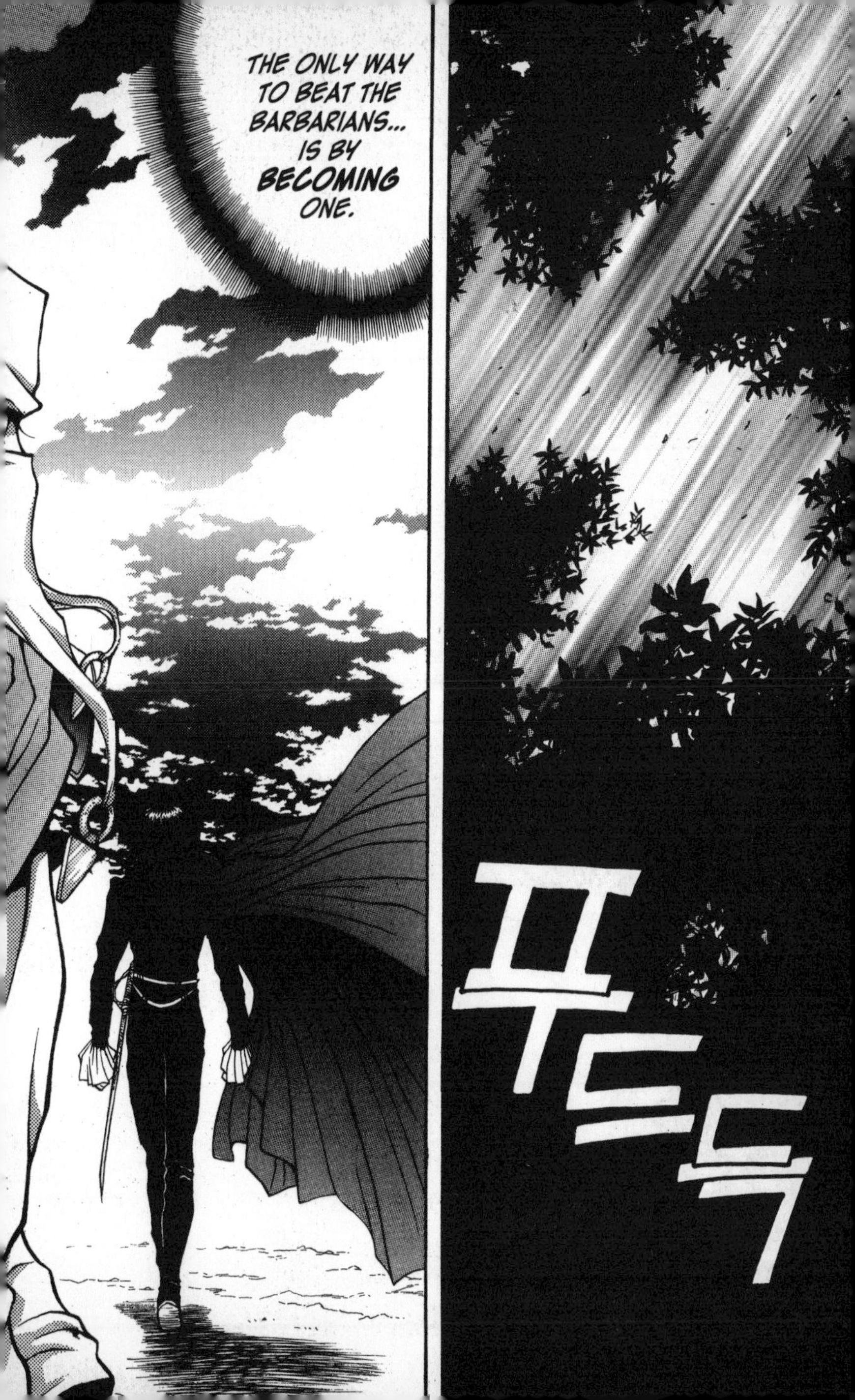
THE ONLY WAY TO BEAT THE BARBARIANS... IS BY BECOMING ONE.

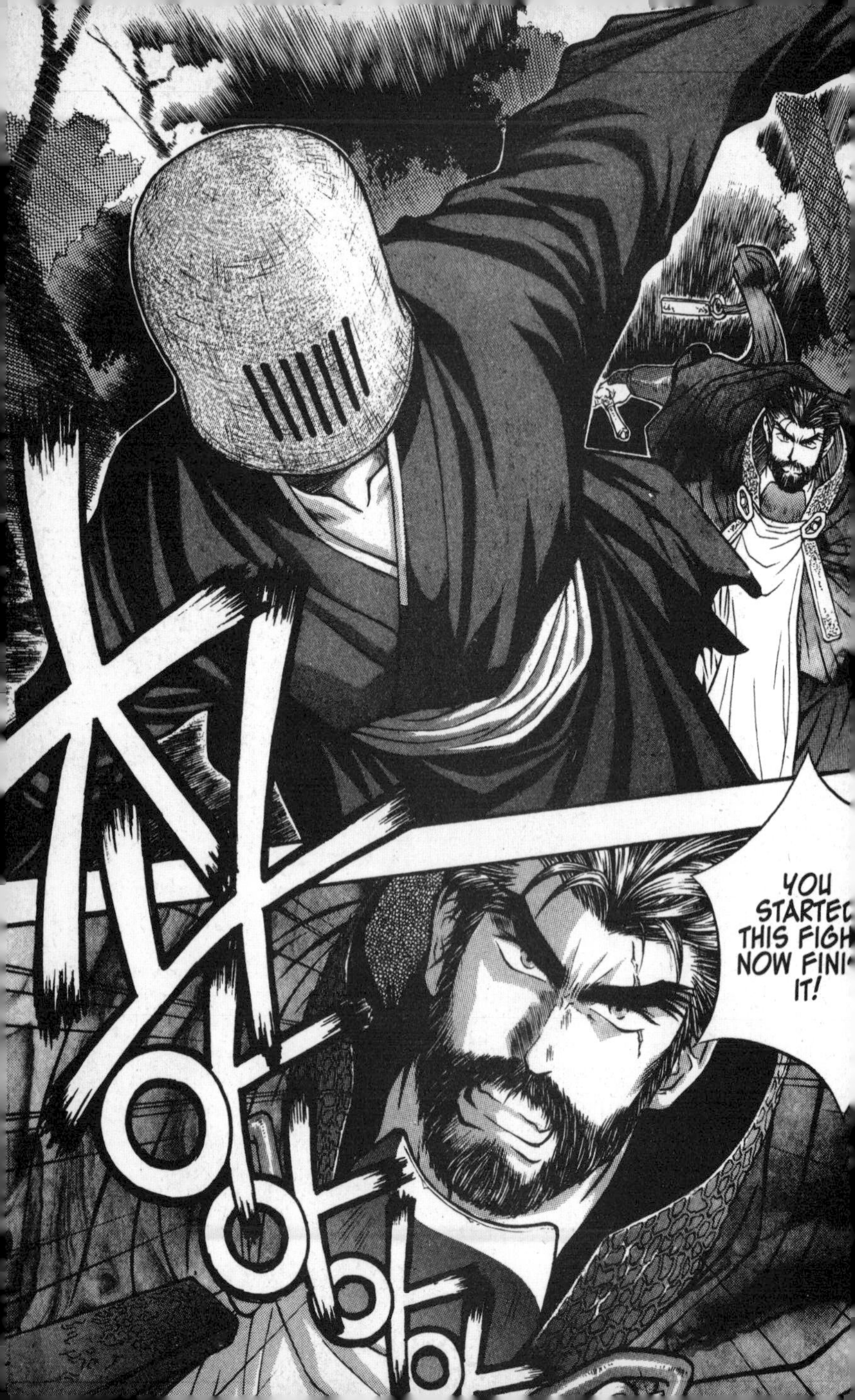
YOU STARTED THIS FIGH NOW FINI- IT!

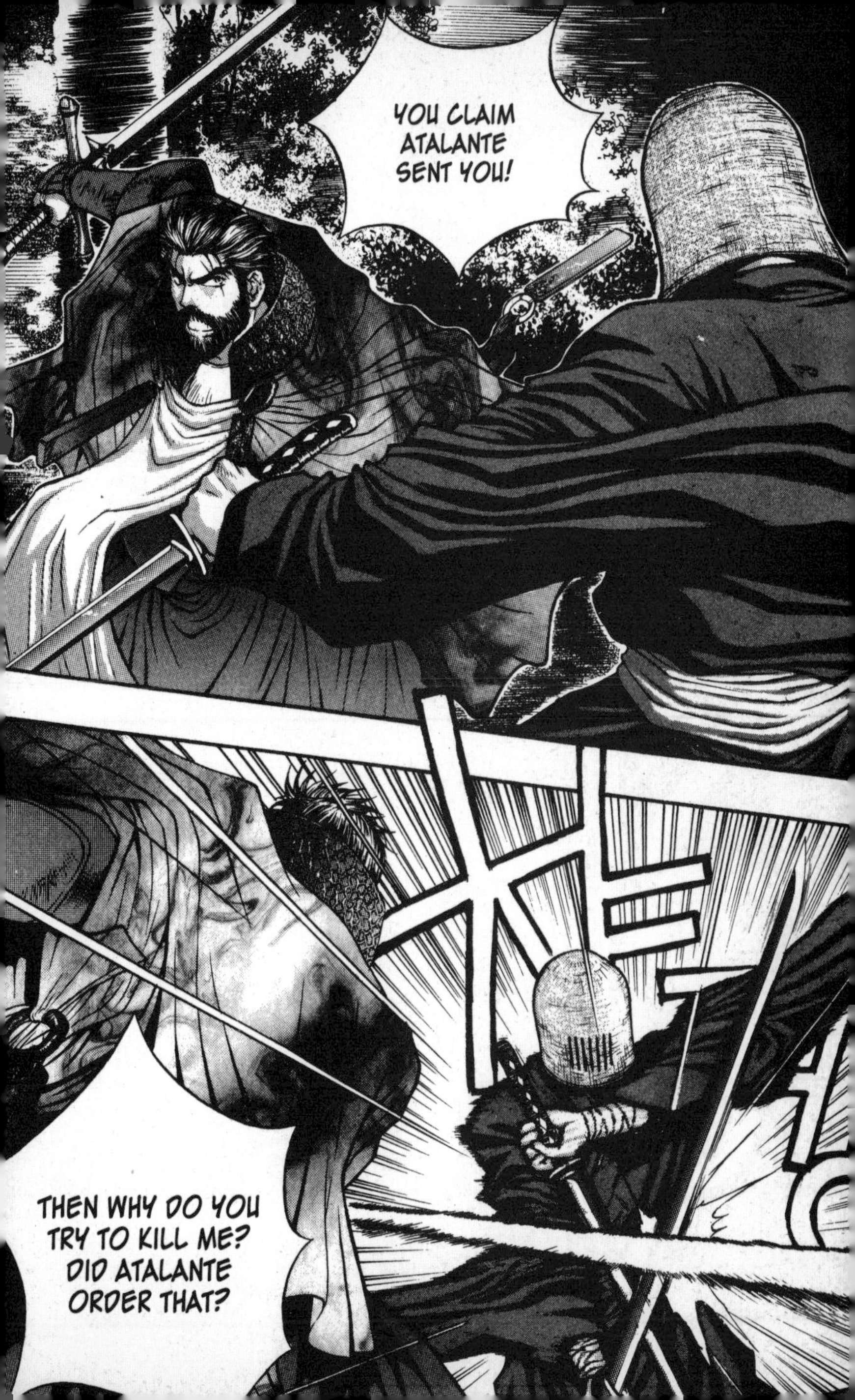
YOU CLAIM ATALANTE SENT YOU!
THEN WHY DO YOU TRY TO KILL ME? DID ATALANTE ORDER THAT?

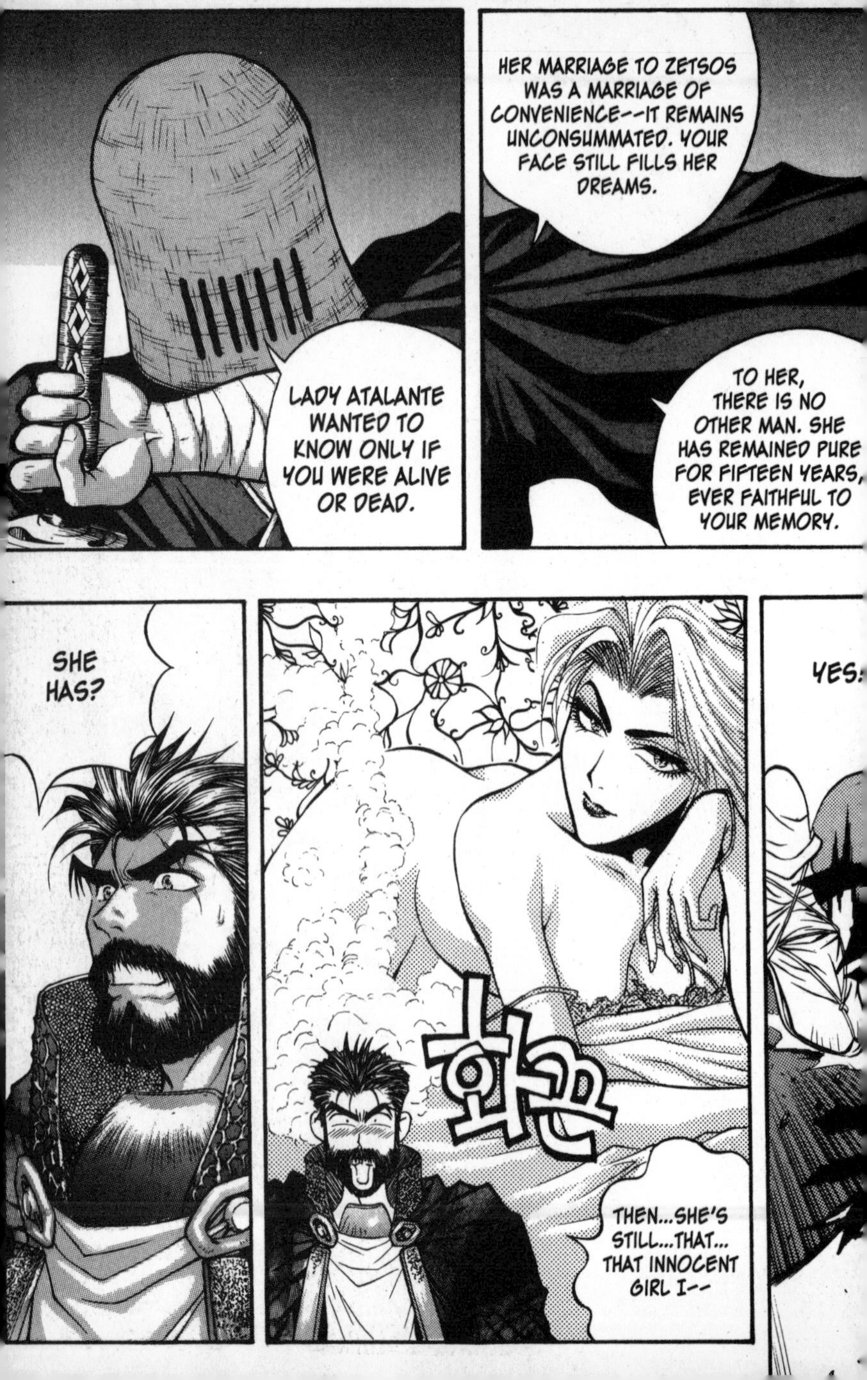
LADY ATALANTE WANTED TO KNOW ONLY IF YOU WERE ALIVE OR DEAD.
HER MARRIAGE TO ZETSOS WAS A MARRIAGE OF CONVENIENCE--IT REMAINS UNCONSUMMATED. YOUR FACE STILL FILLS HER DREAMS.
TO HER, THERE IS NO OTHER MAN. SHE HAS REMAINED PURE FOR FIFTEEN YEARS, EVER FAITHFUL TO YOUR MEMORY.
SHE HAS?
THEN...SHE'S STILL...THAT... THAT INNOCENT GIRL I--
YES.

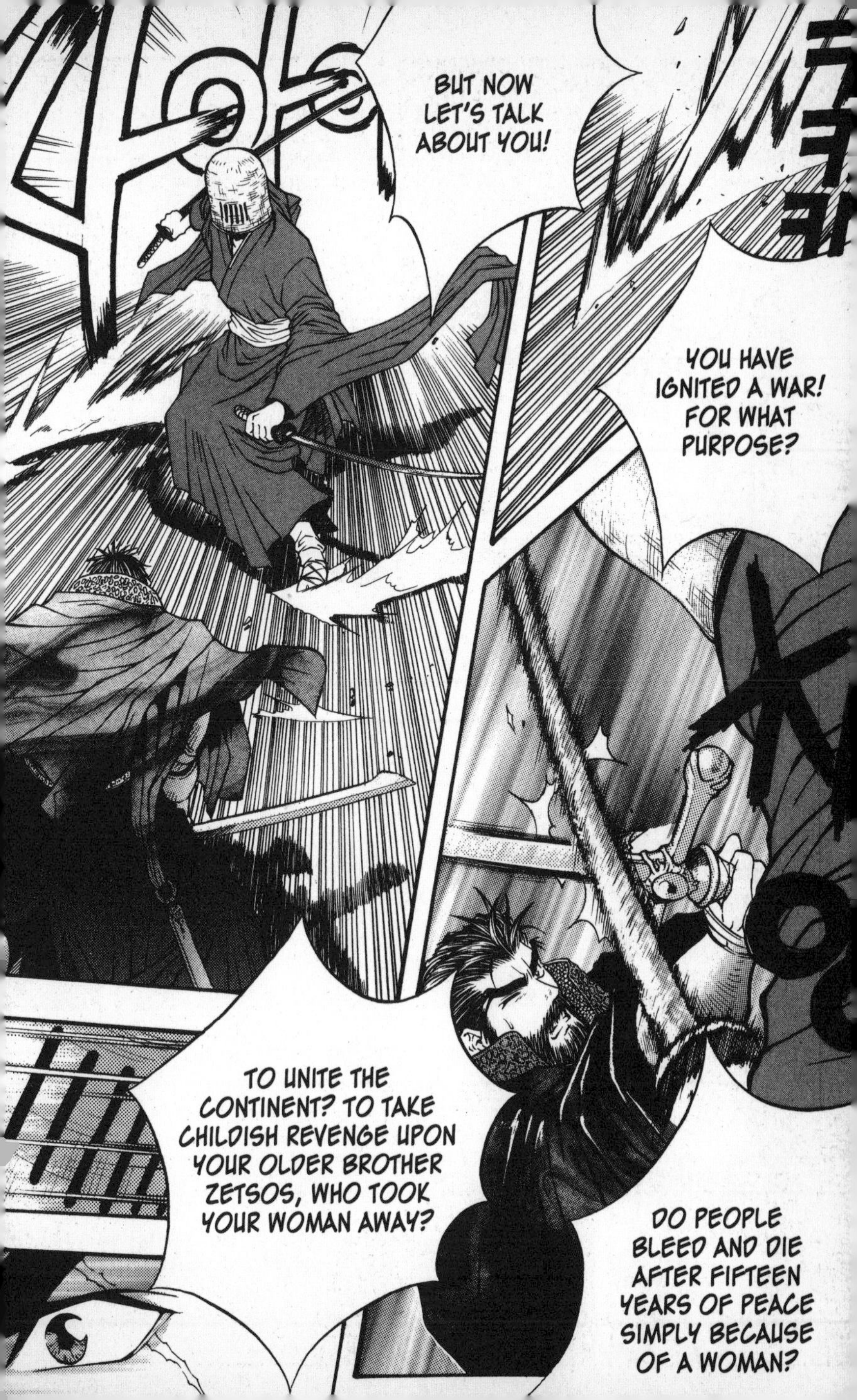
BUT NOW LET'S TALK ABOUT YOU!
YOU HAVE IGNITED A WAR! FOR WHAT PURPOSE?
TO UNITE THE CONTINENT? TO TAKE CHILDISH REVENGE UPON YOUR OLDER BROTHER ZETSOS, WHO TOOK YOUR WOMAN AWAY?
DO PEOPLE BLEED AND DIE AFTER FIFTEEN YEARS OF PEACE SIMPLY BECAUSE OF A WOMAN?

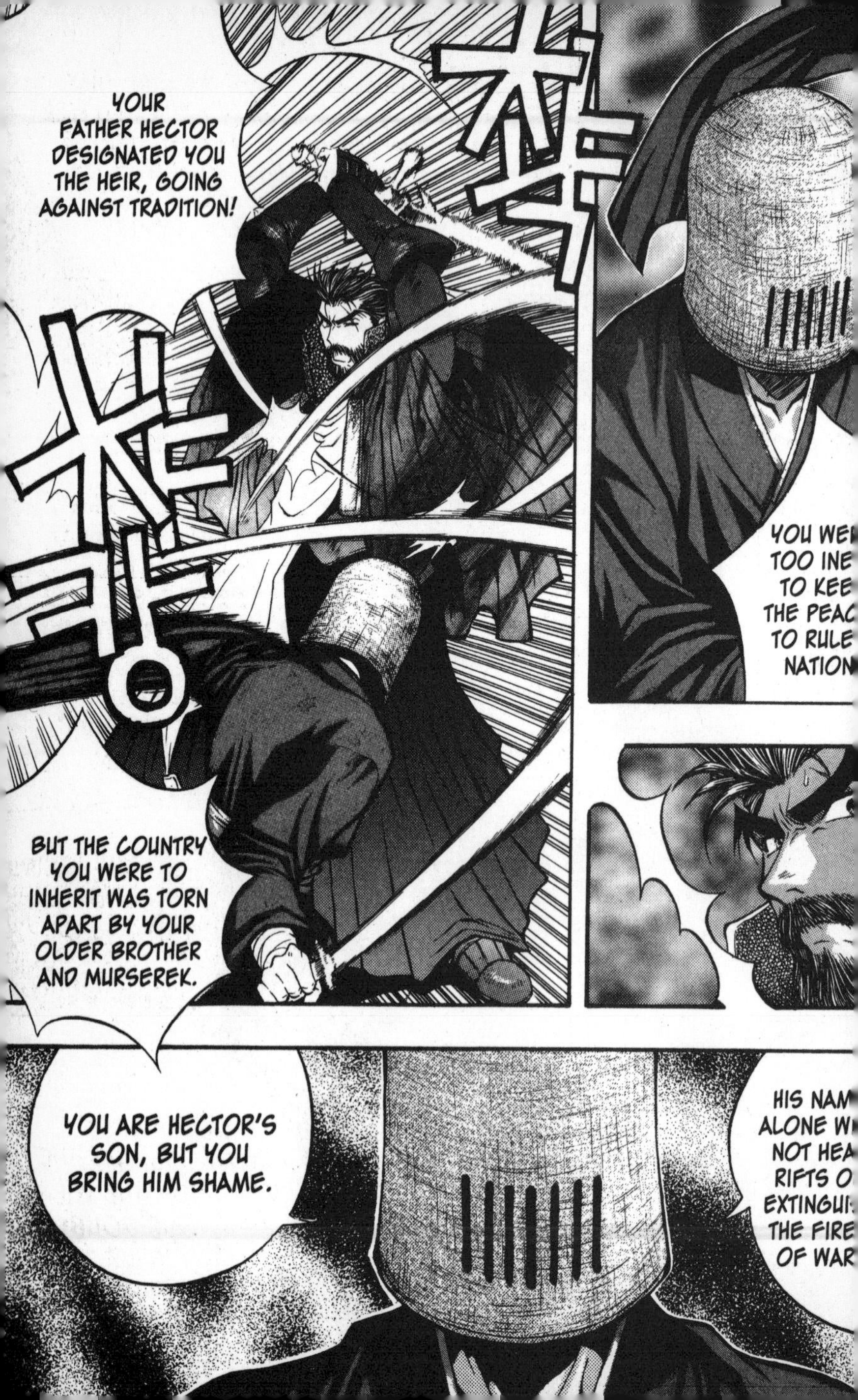
YOUR FATHER HECTOR DESIGNATED YOU THE HEIR, GOING AGAINST TRADITION!
BUT THE COUNTRY YOU WERE TO INHERIT WAS TORN APART BY YOUR OLDER BROTHER AND MURSEREK.
YOU WE TOO INE TO KEE THE PEAC TO RULE NATION
YOU ARE HECTOR'S SON, BUT YOU BRING HIM SHAME.
HIS NAM ALONE W NOT HEA RIFTS O EXTINGUI THE FIRE OF WAR

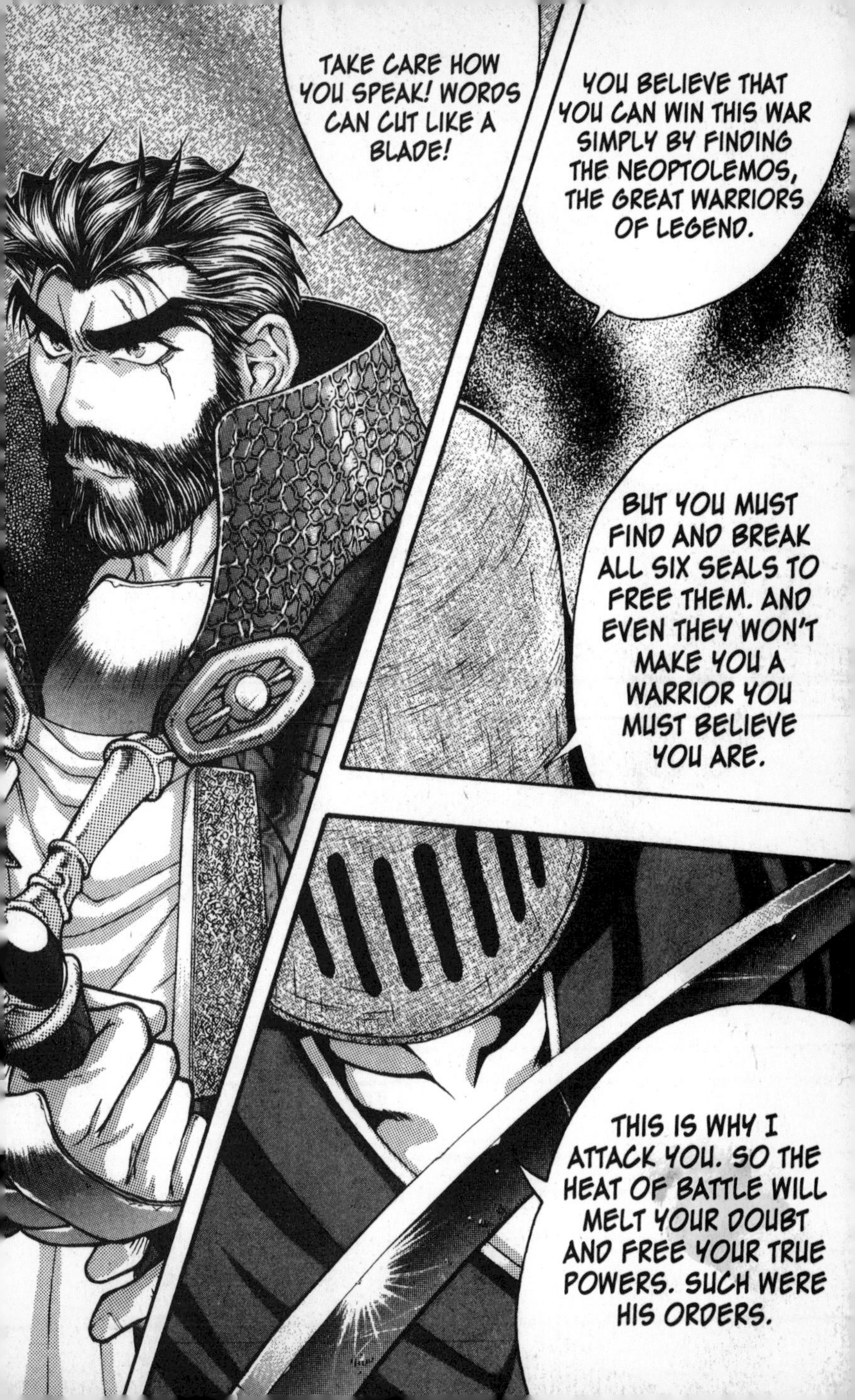
TAKE CARE HOW YOU SPEAK! WORDS CAN CUT LIKE A BLADE!
YOU BELIEVE THAT YOU CAN WIN THIS WAR SIMPLY BY FINDING THE NEOPTOLEMOS, THE GREAT WARRIORS OF LEGEND.
BUT YOU MUST FIND AND BREAK ALL SIX SEALS TO FREE THEM. AND EVEN THEY WON'T MAKE YOU A WARRIOR YOU MUST BELIEVE YOU ARE.
THIS IS WHY I ATTACK YOU. SO THE HEAT OF BATTLE WILL MELT YOUR DOUBT AND FREE YOUR TRUE POWERS. SUCH WERE HIS ORDERS.

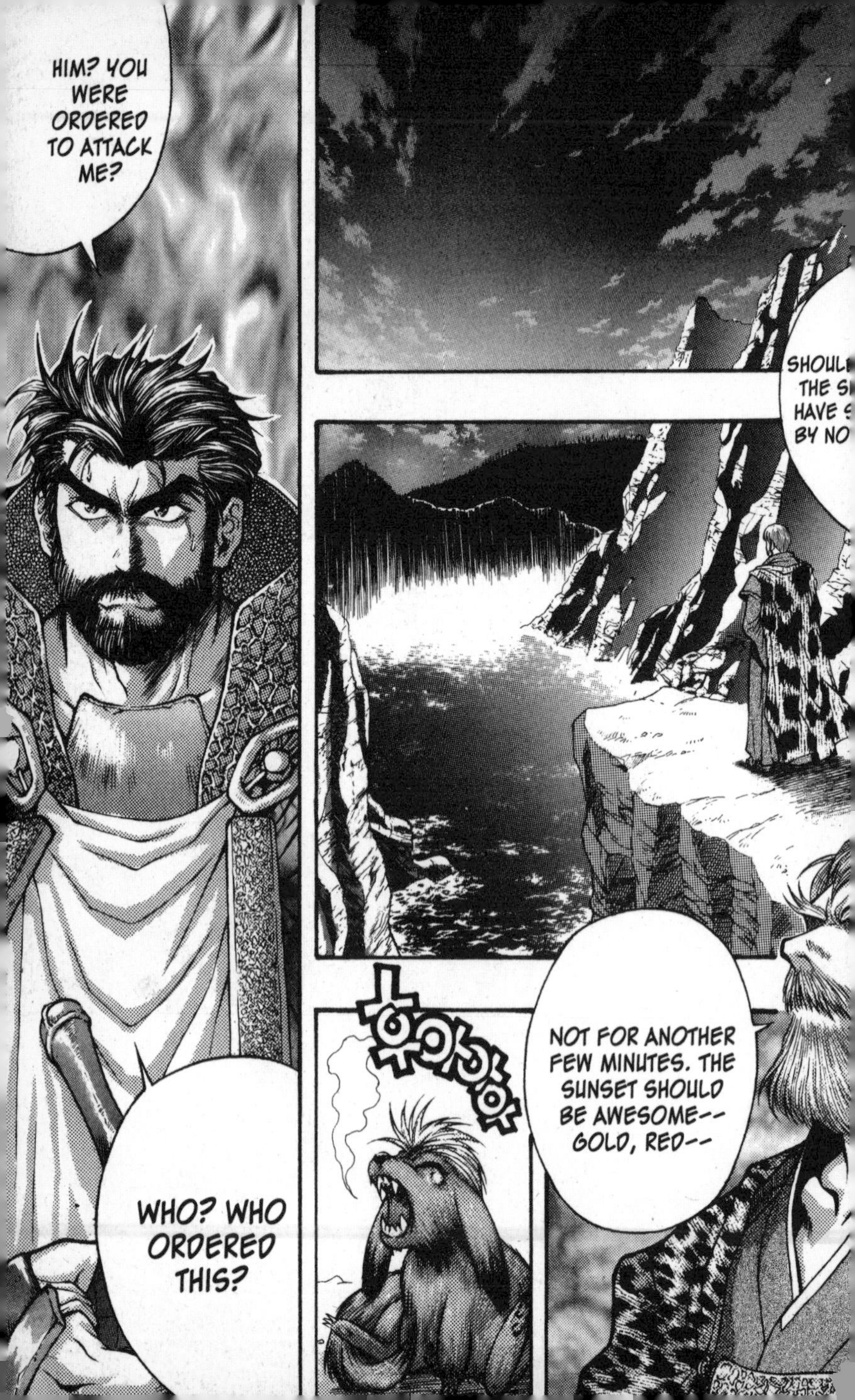
HIM? YOU WERE ORDERED TO ATTACK ME?
WHO? WHO ORDERED THIS?
SHOUL THE S HAVE S BY NO
NOT FOR ANOTHER FEW MINUTES. THE SUNSET SHOULD BE AWESOME-- GOLD, RED--

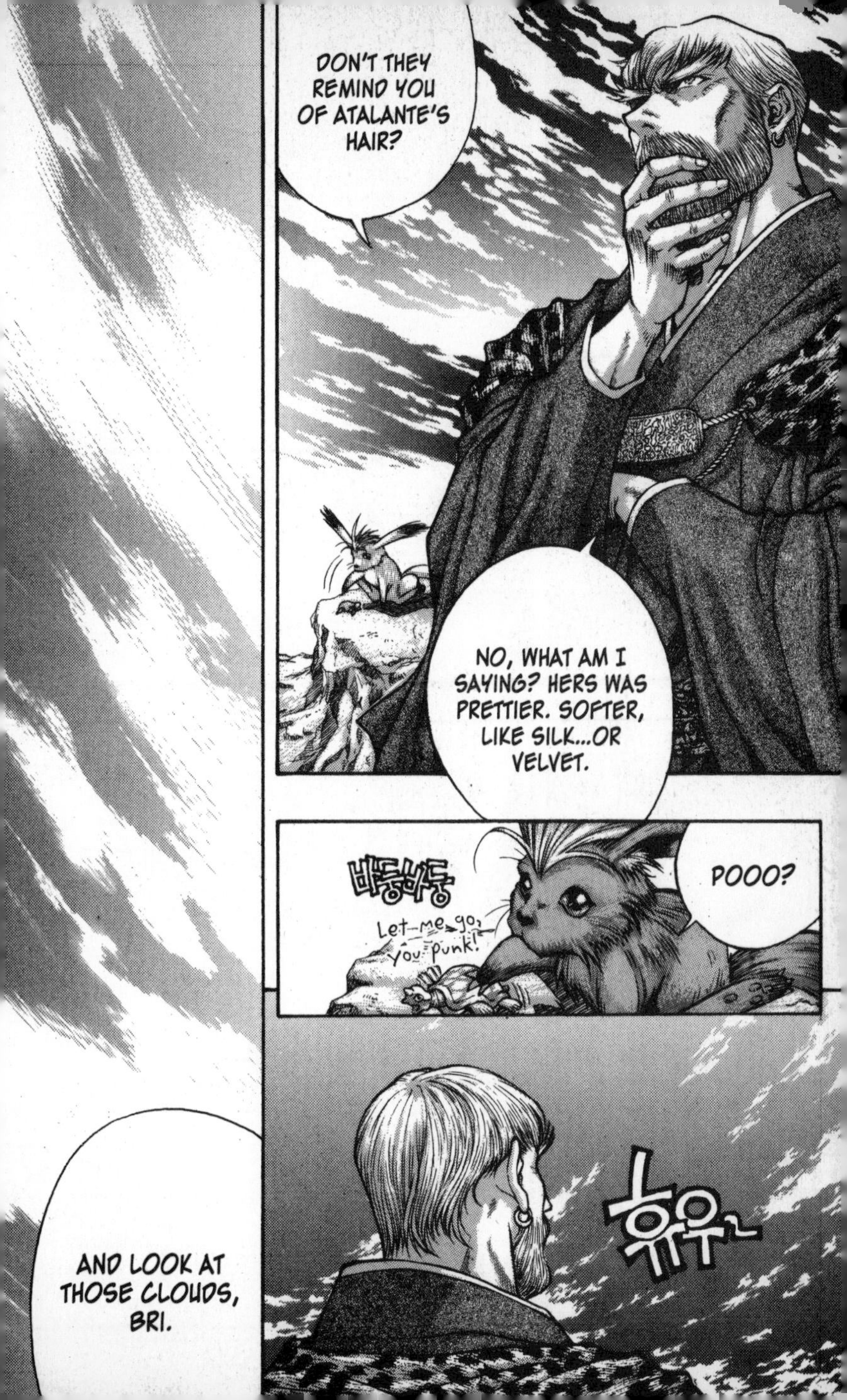
AND LOOK AT THOSE CLOUDS, BRI.
DON'T THEY REMIND YOU OF ATALANTE'S HAIR?
NO, WHAT AM I SAYING? HERS WAS PRETTIER. SOFTER, LIKE SILK...OR VELVET.
Let me go, you punk!
POOO?

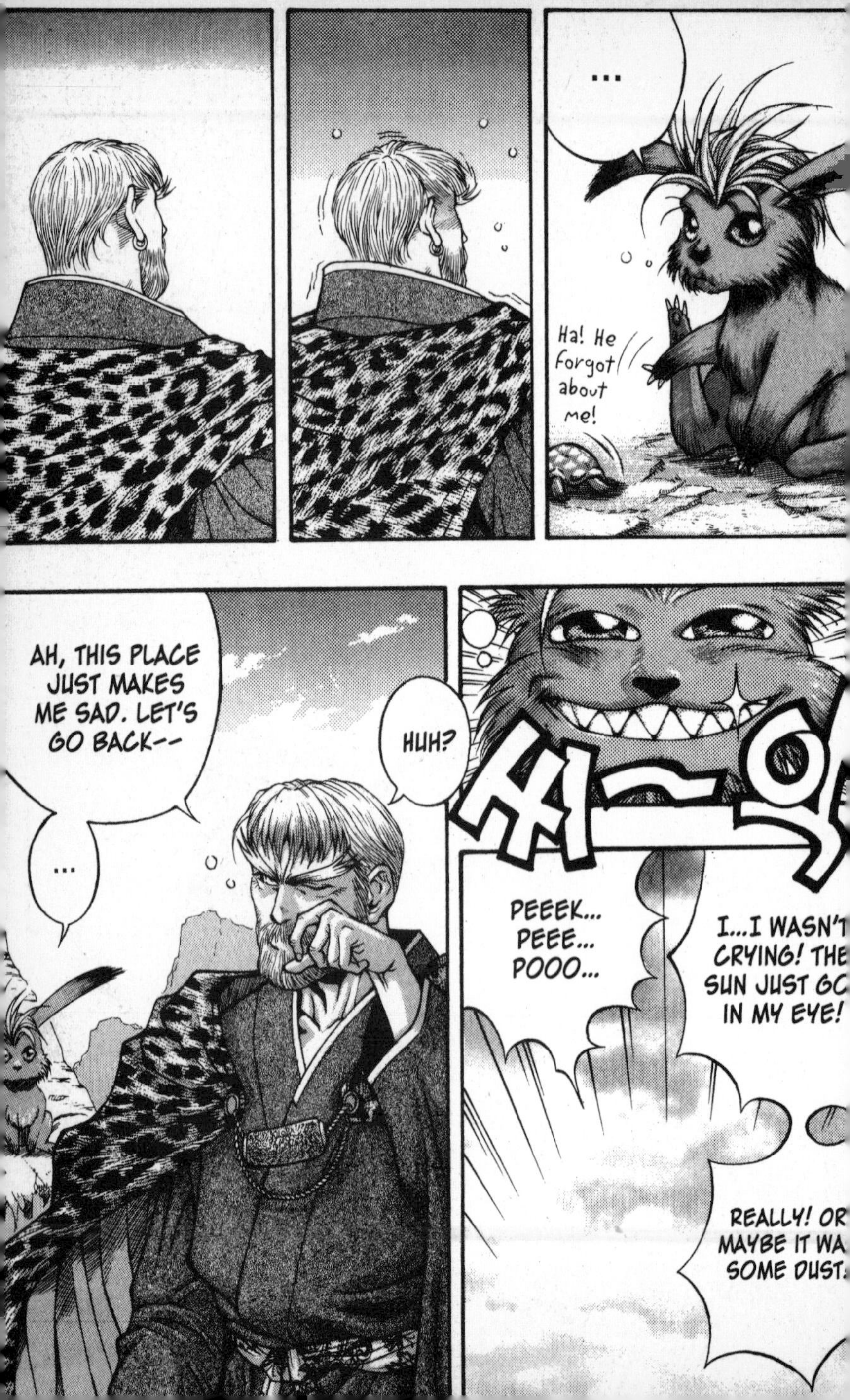
...
Ha! He forgot about me!
AH, THIS PLACE JUST MAKES ME SAD. LET'S GO BACK--
...
HUH?
PEEEK... PEEE... POOO...
I...I WASN'T CRYING! THE SUN JUST GO IN MY EYE!
REALLY! OR MAYBE IT WA SOME DUST.

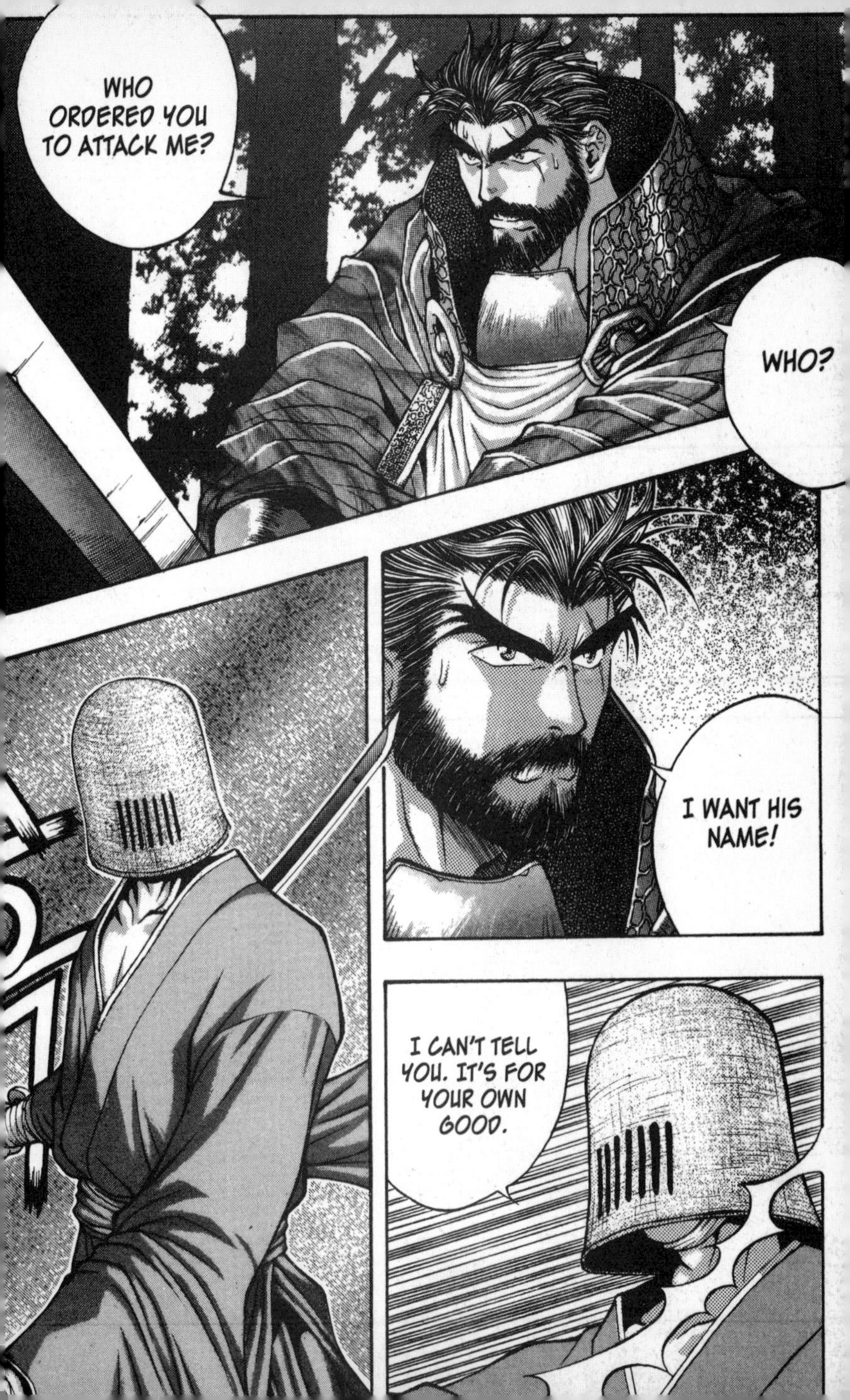
WHO ORDERED YOU TO ATTACK ME?
WHO?
I WANT HIS NAME!
I CAN'T TELL YOU. IT'S FOR YOUR OWN GOOD.

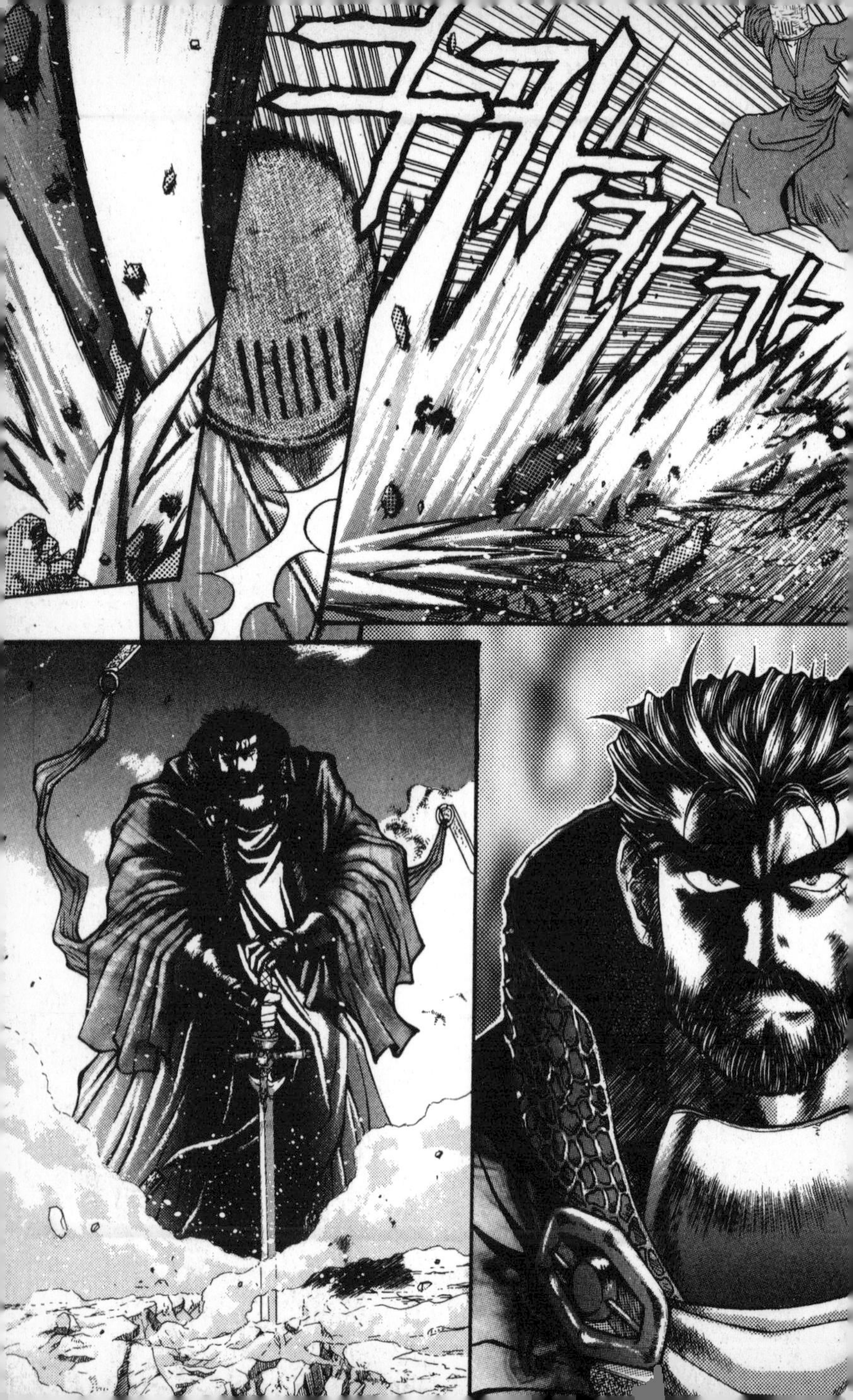

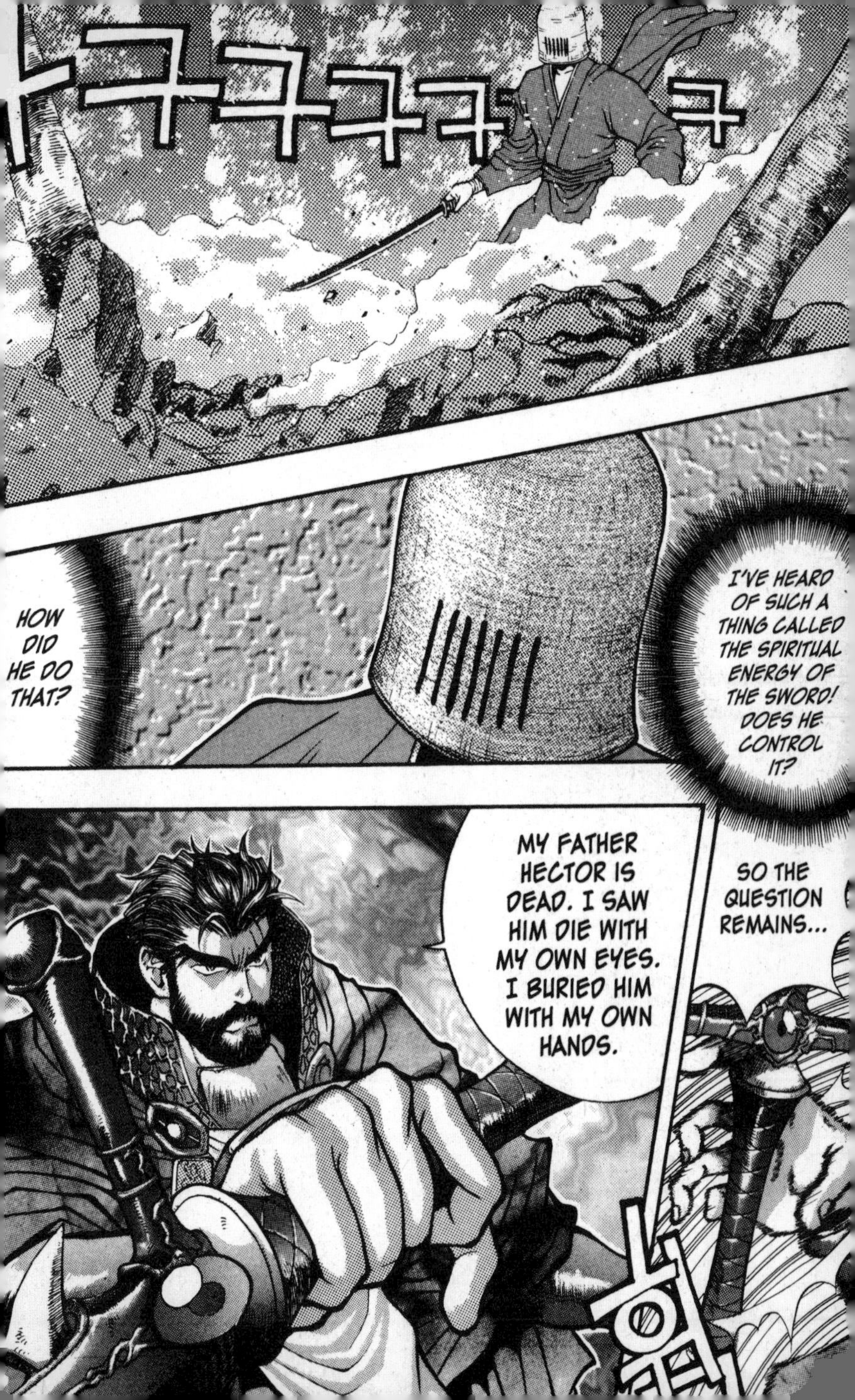
HOW DID HE DO THAT?
I'VE HEARD OF SUCH A THING CALLED THE SPIRITUAL ENERGY OF THE SWORD! DOES HE CONTROL IT?
MY FATHER HECTOR IS DEAD. I SAW HIM DIE WITH MY OWN EYES. I BURIED HIM WITH MY OWN HANDS.
SO THE QUESTION REMAINS...

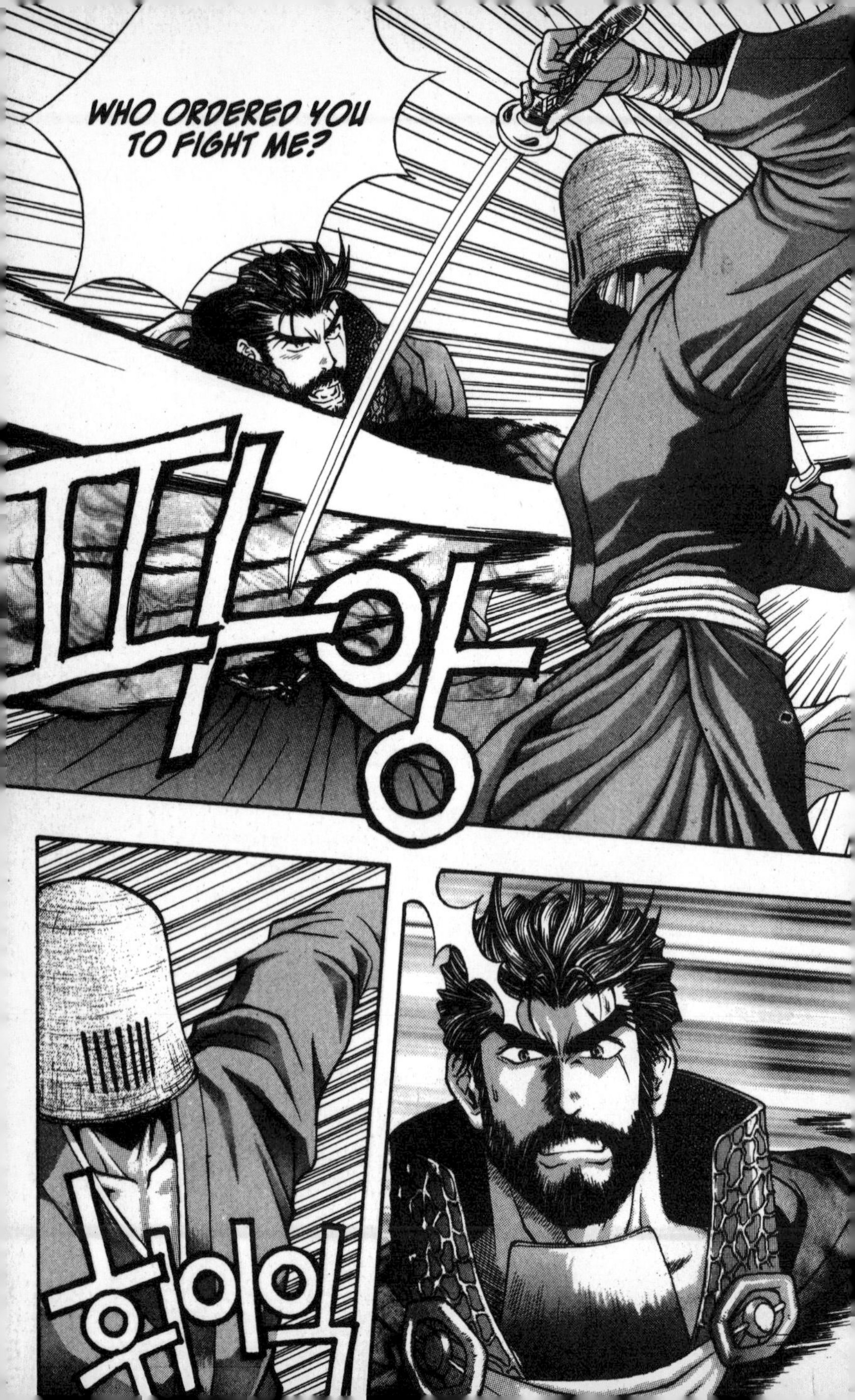
WHO ORDERED YOU TO FIGHT ME?
파앙

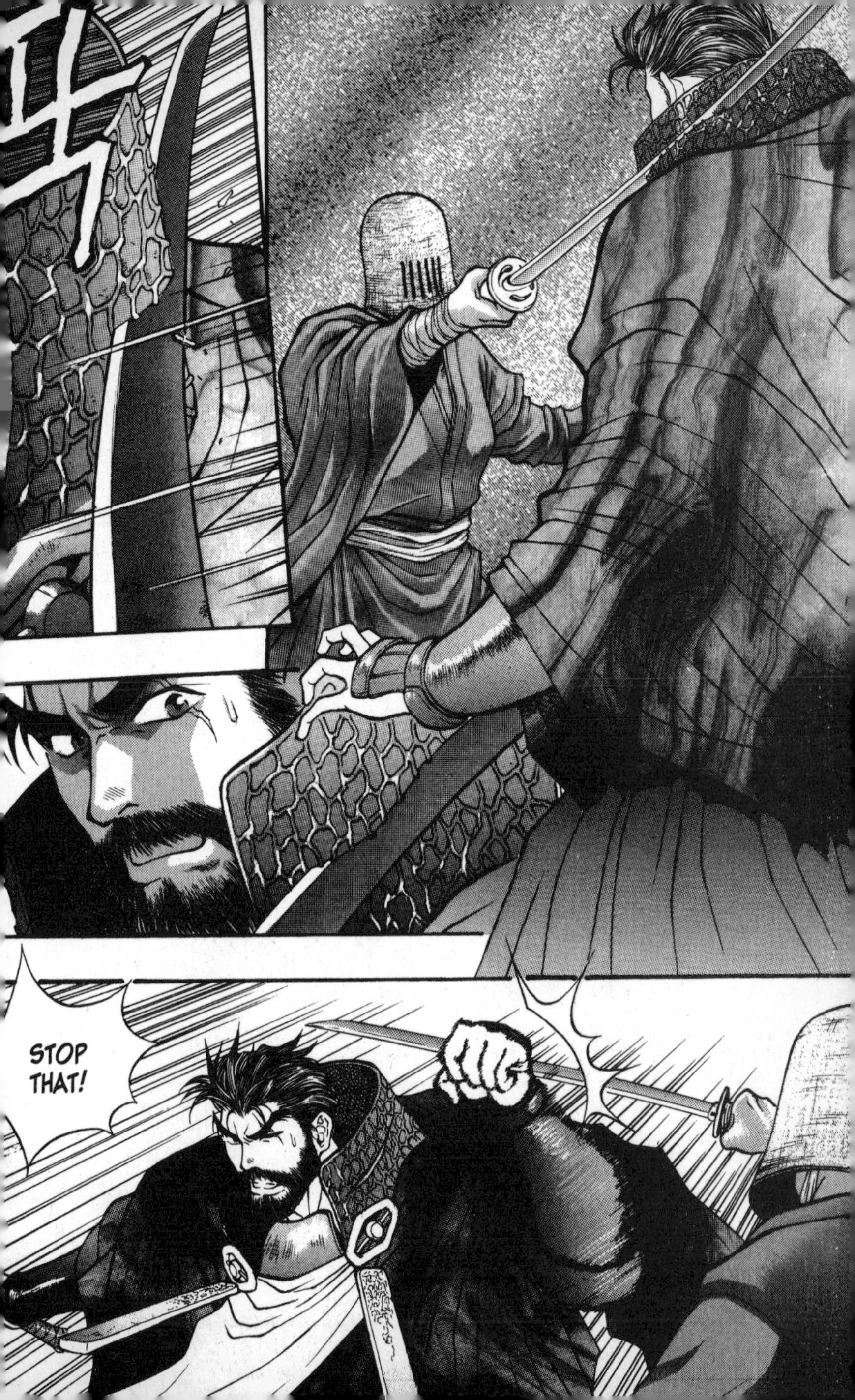
STOP THAT!

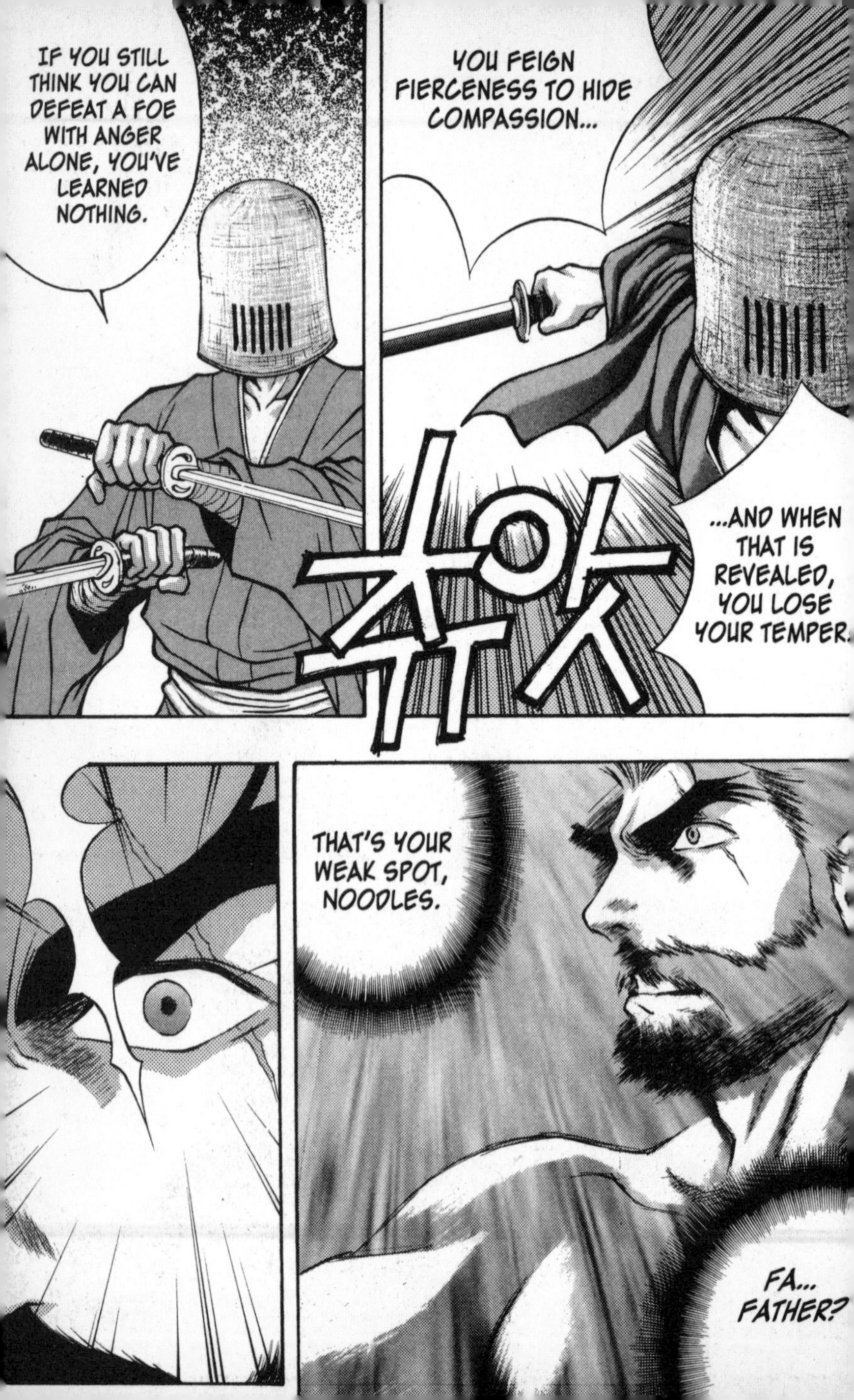
IF YOU STILL THINK YOU CAN DEFEAT A FOE WITH ANGER ALONE, YOU'VE LEARNED NOTHING.
YOU FEIGN FIERCENESS TO HIDE COMPASSION...
...AND WHEN THAT IS REVEALED, YOU LOSE YOUR TEMPER.
THAT'S YOUR WEAK SPOT, NOODLES.
FA... FATHER?

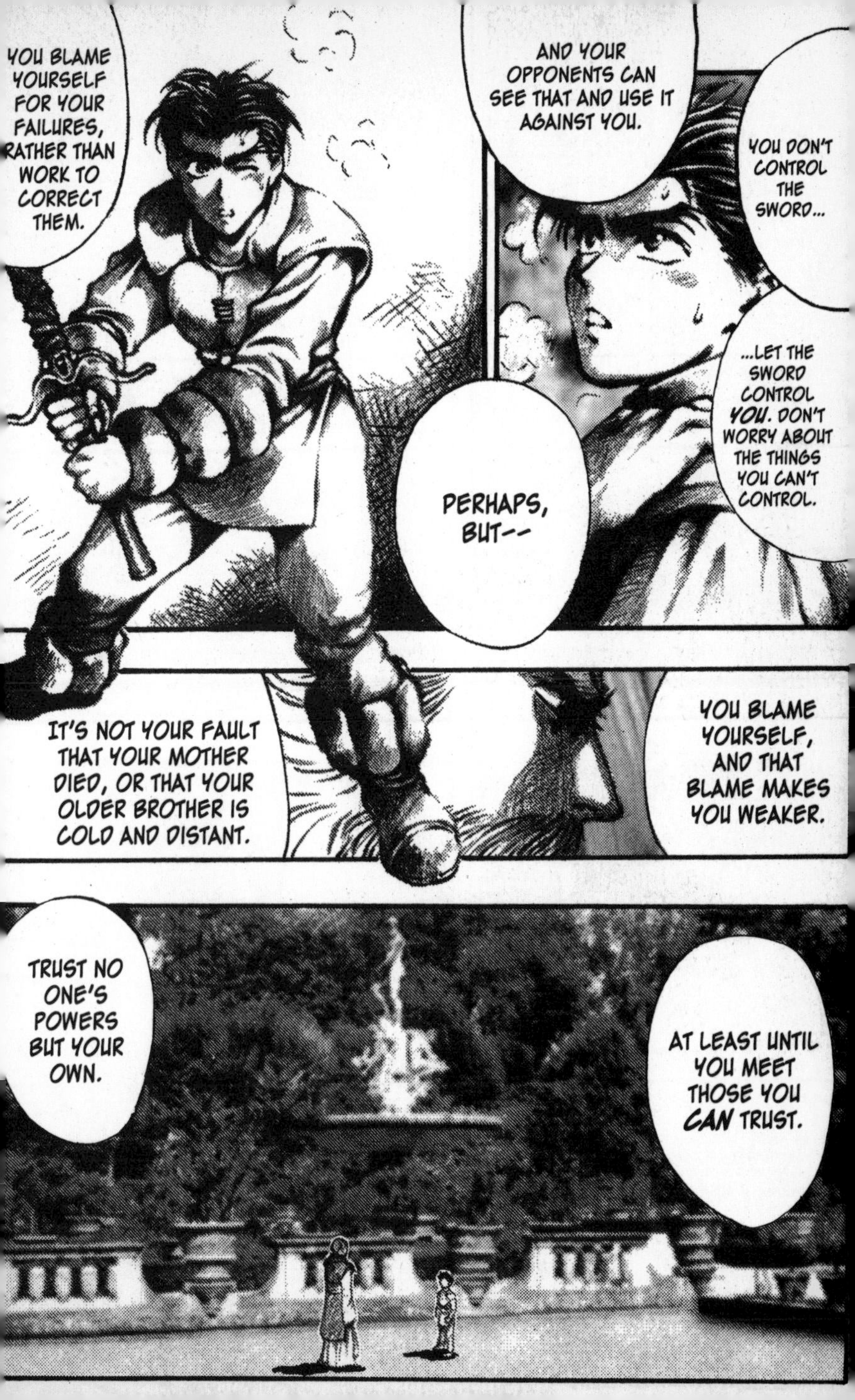

YOU BLAME YOURSELF FOR YOUR FAILURES, RATHER THAN WORK TO CORRECT THEM.
AND YOUR OPPONENTS CAN SEE THAT AND USE IT AGAINST YOU.
YOU DON'T CONTROL THE SWORD...
...LET THE SWORD CONTROL *YOU*. DON'T WORRY ABOUT THE THINGS YOU CAN'T CONTROL.
PERHAPS, BUT--
IT'S NOT YOUR FAULT THAT YOUR MOTHER DIED, OR THAT YOUR OLDER BROTHER IS COLD AND DISTANT.
YOU BLAME YOURSELF, AND THAT BLAME MAKES YOU WEAKER.
TRUST NO ONE'S POWERS BUT YOUR OWN.
AT LEAST UNTIL YOU MEET THOSE YOU *CAN* TRUST.

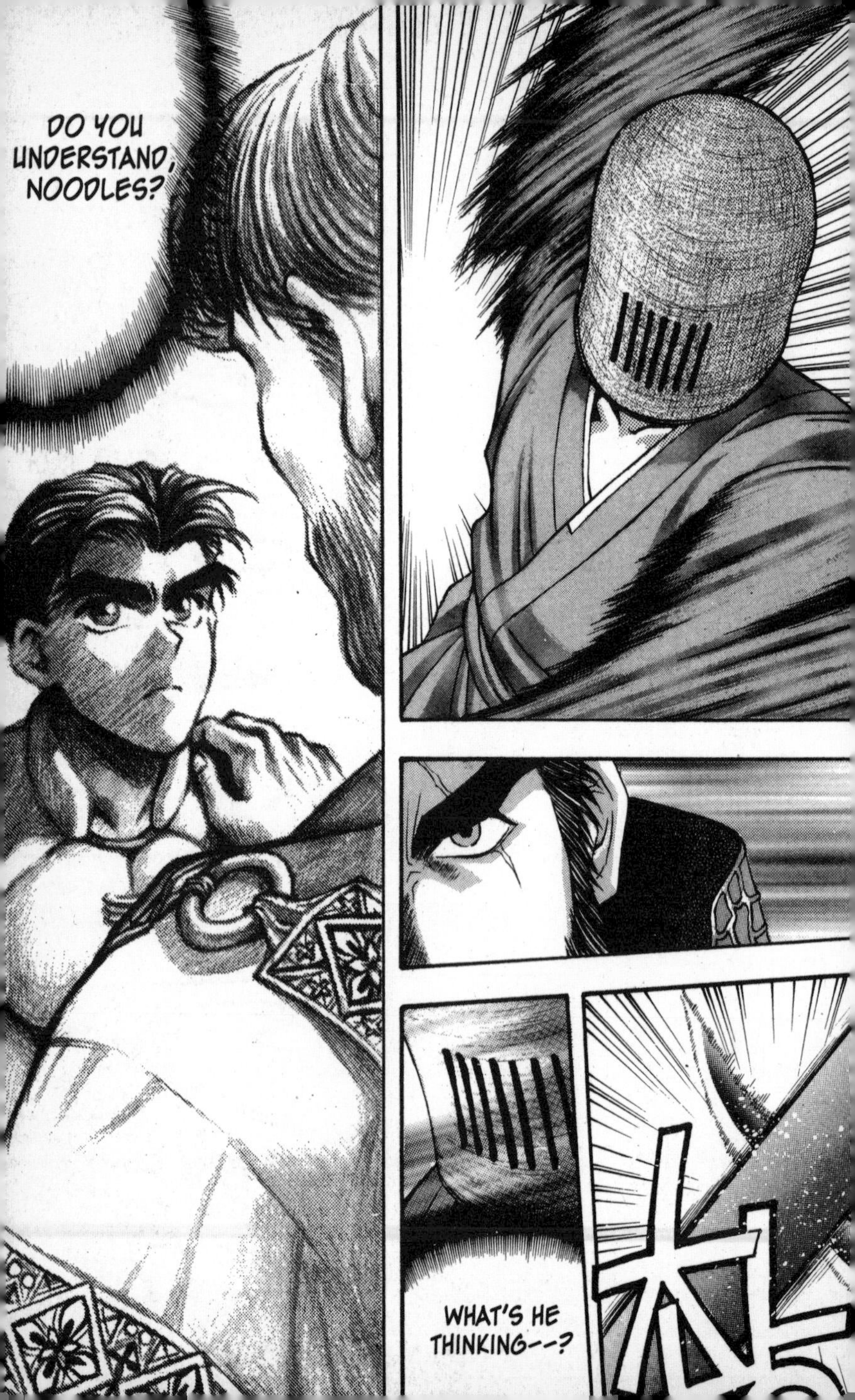
DO YOU UNDERSTAND, NOODLES?
WHAT'S HE THINKING--?

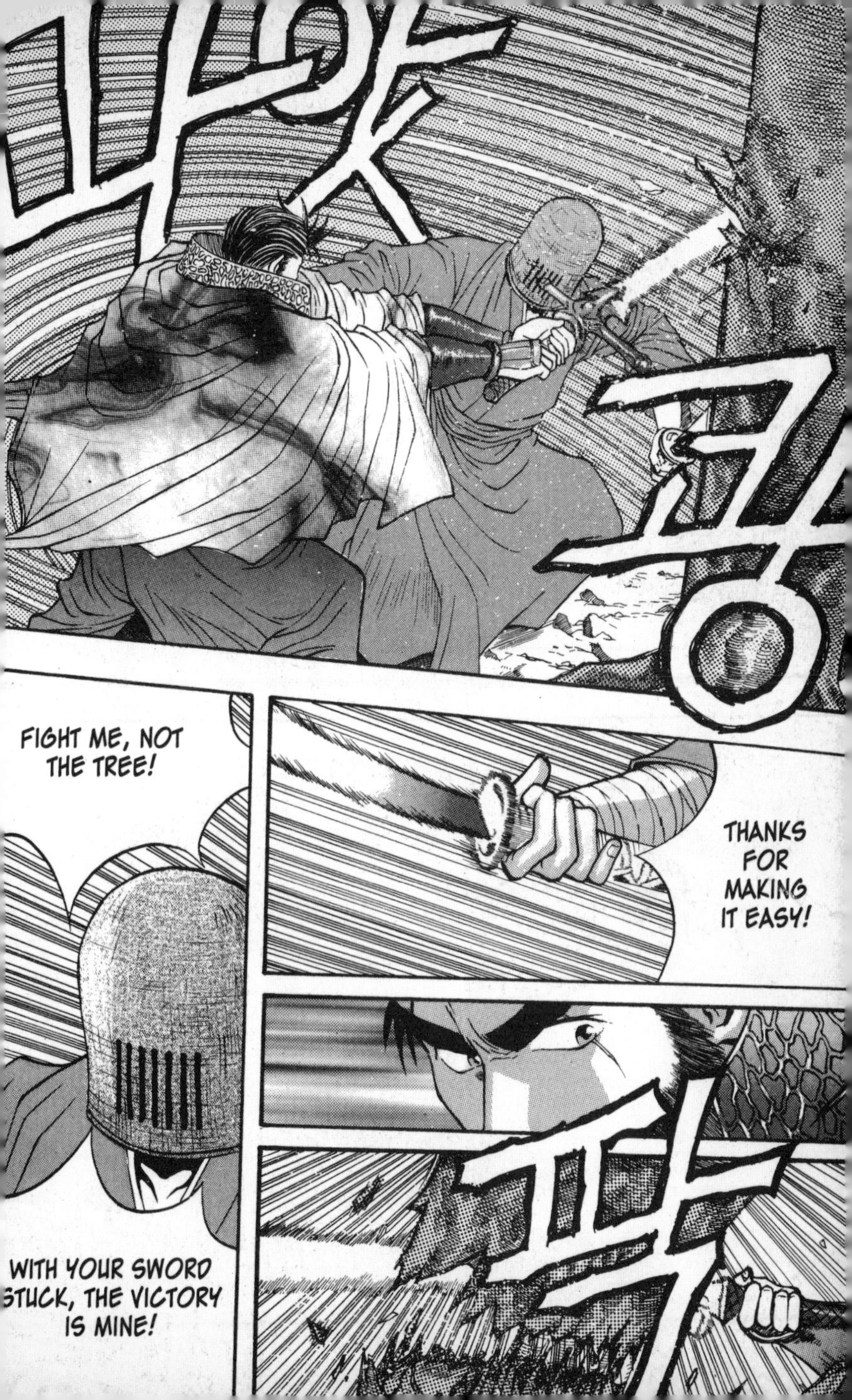
FIGHT ME, NOT THE TREE!
WITH YOUR SWORD STUCK, THE VICTORY IS MINE!
THANKS FOR MAKING IT EASY!

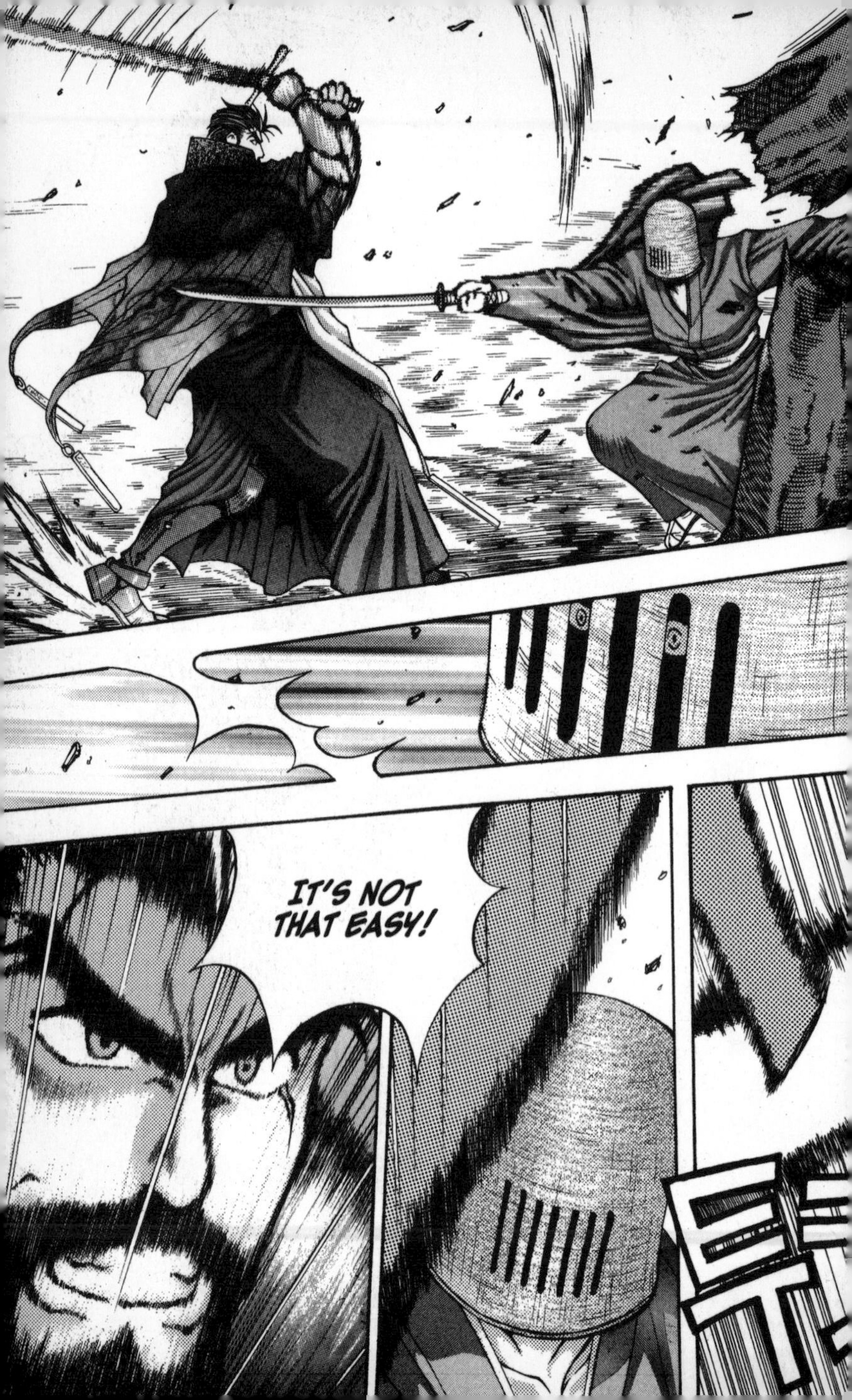
IT'S NOT THAT EASY!

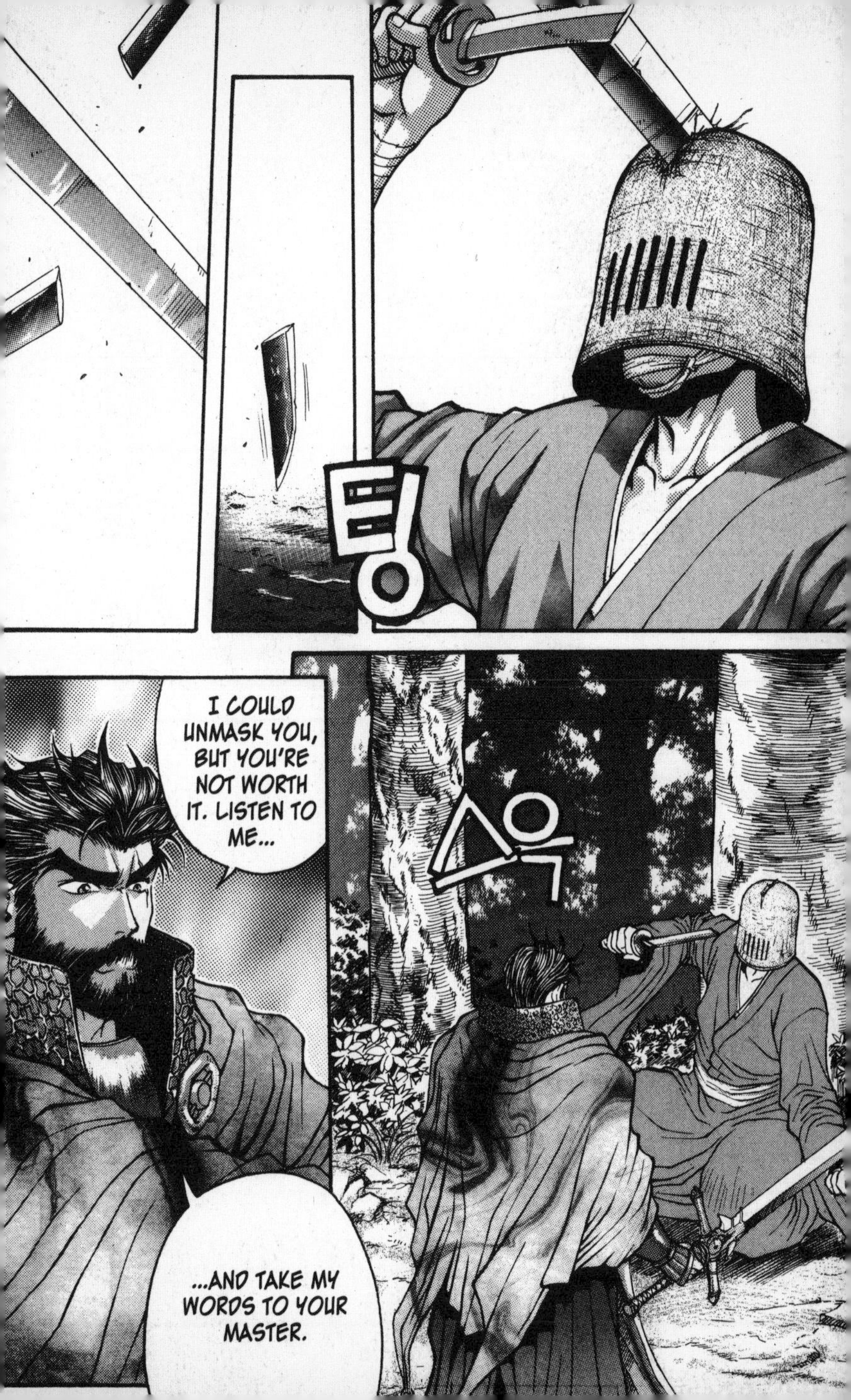
텅
I COULD UNMASK YOU, BUT YOU'RE NOT WORTH IT. LISTEN TO ME...
스윽
...AND TAKE MY WORDS TO YOUR MASTER.

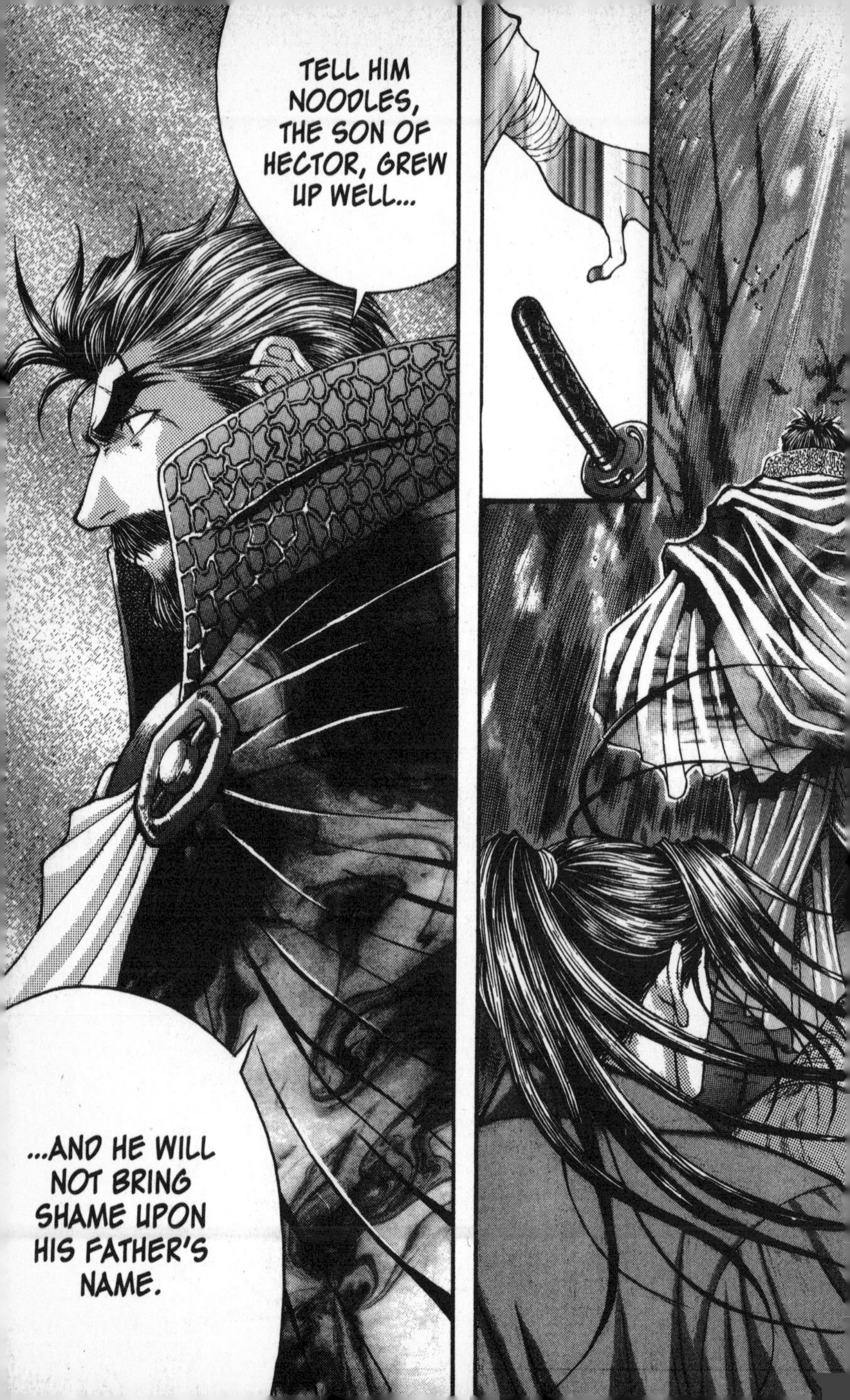
TELL HIM NOODLES, THE SON OF HECTOR, GREW UP WELL...
...AND HE WILL NOT BRING SHAME UPON HIS FATHER'S NAME.

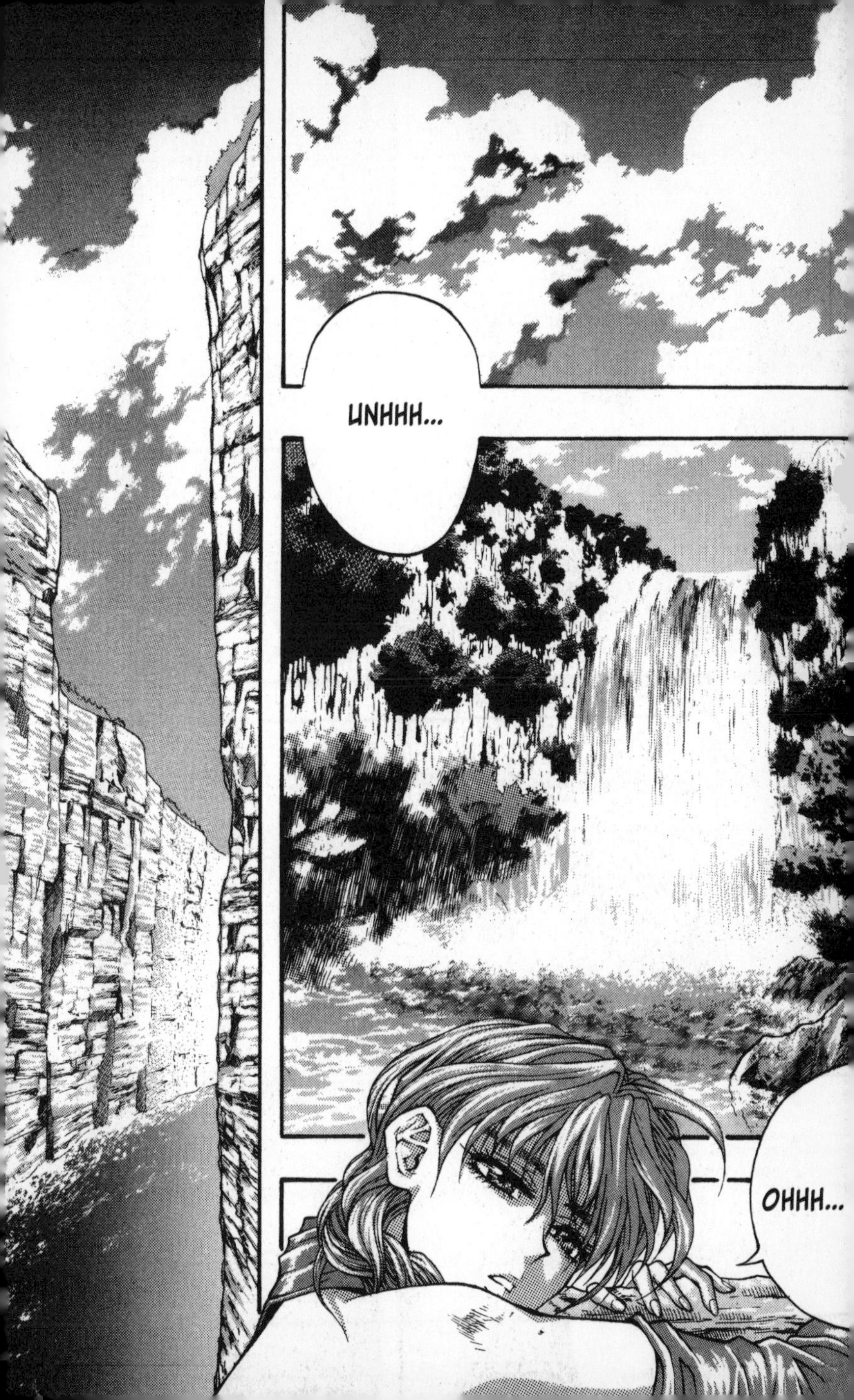
UNHHH...
OHHH...

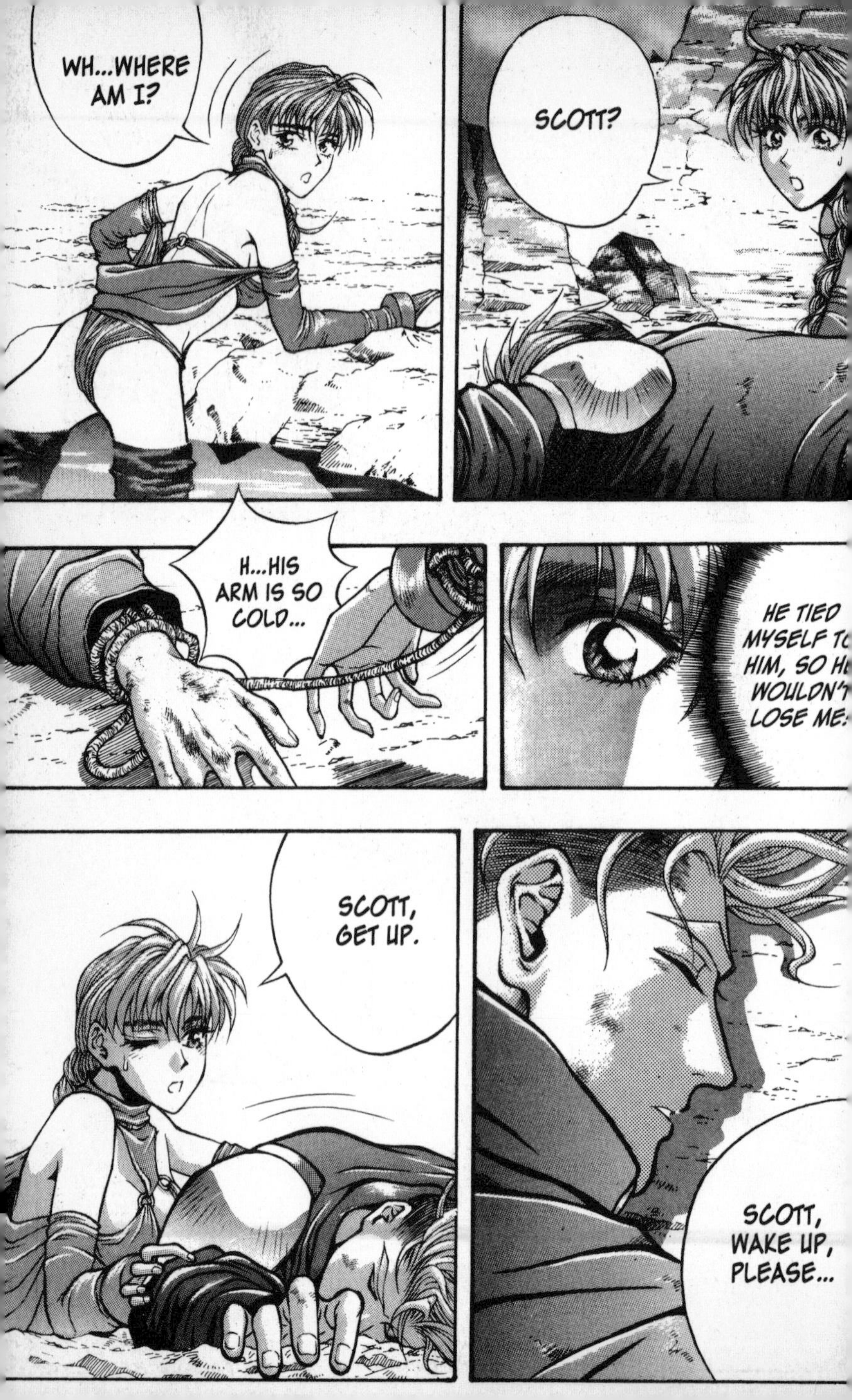
WH...WHERE AM I?
SCOTT?
H...HIS ARM IS SO COLD...
HE TIED MYSELF TO HIM, SO HE WOULDN'T LOSE ME.
SCOTT, GET UP.
SCOTT, WAKE UP, PLEASE...

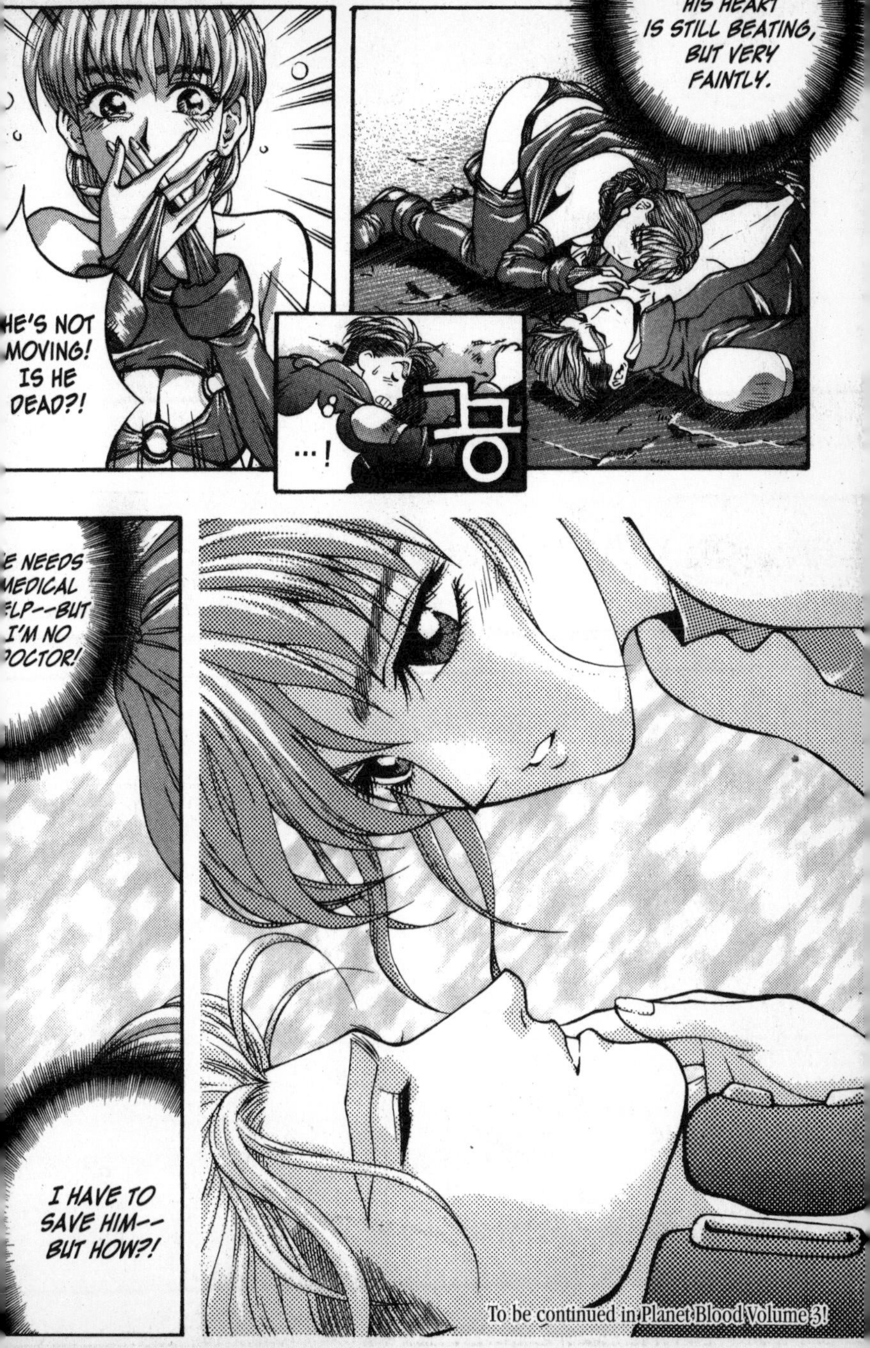
HE'S NOT MOVING! IS HE DEAD?!
HIS HEART IS STILL BEATING, BUT VERY FAINTLY.
...!
긍
E NEEDS MEDICAL ELP--BUT I'M NO OCTOR!
I HAVE TO SAVE HIM--BUT HOW?!
To be continued in Planet Blood Volume 3!

PLANET BLOOD™

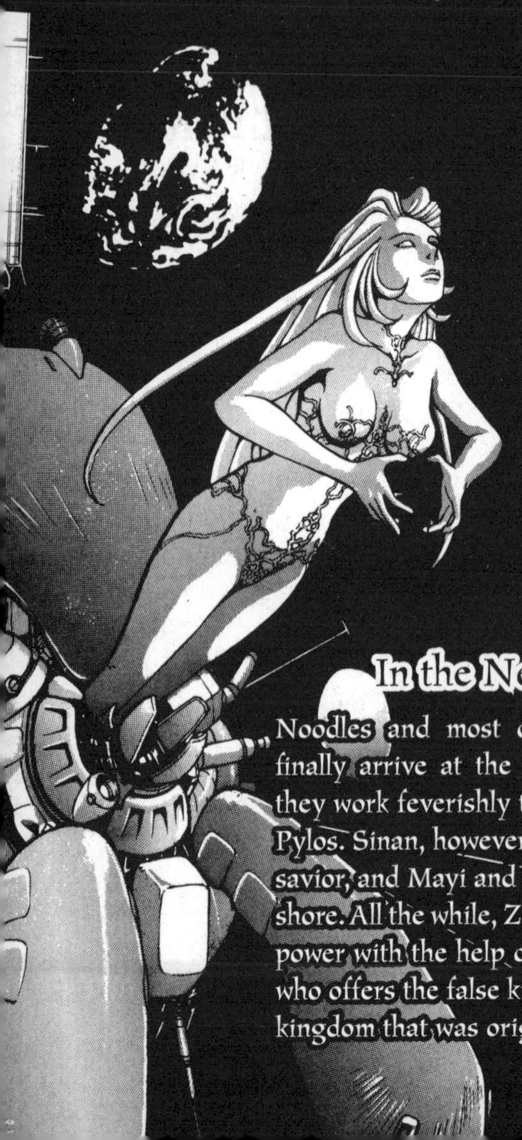

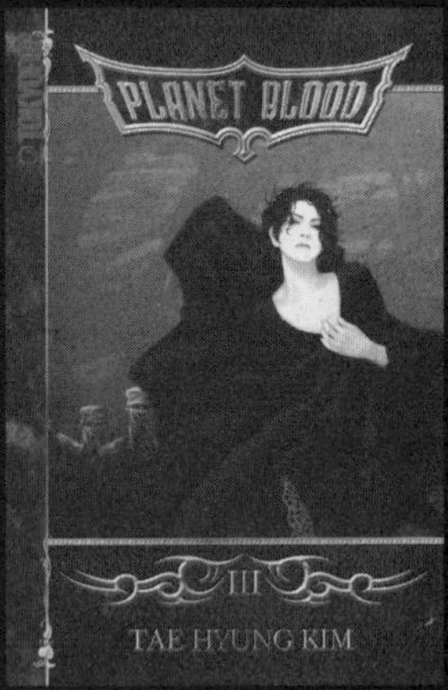
PLANET BLOOD
III
TAE HYUNG KIM

In the Next Volume...

Noodles and most of his band regroup and finally arrive at the fifth Neoptolemos, where they work feverishly to break the seal that locks Pylos. Sinan, however, is rescued by an unlikely savior, and Mayi and Scott wash up on a distant shore. All the while, Zetsos begins increasing his power with the help of the bastard son Pantera, who offers the false king the rule of Murserek, a kingdom that was originally his ally.

TOKYOPOP SHOP

VAN VON HUNTER

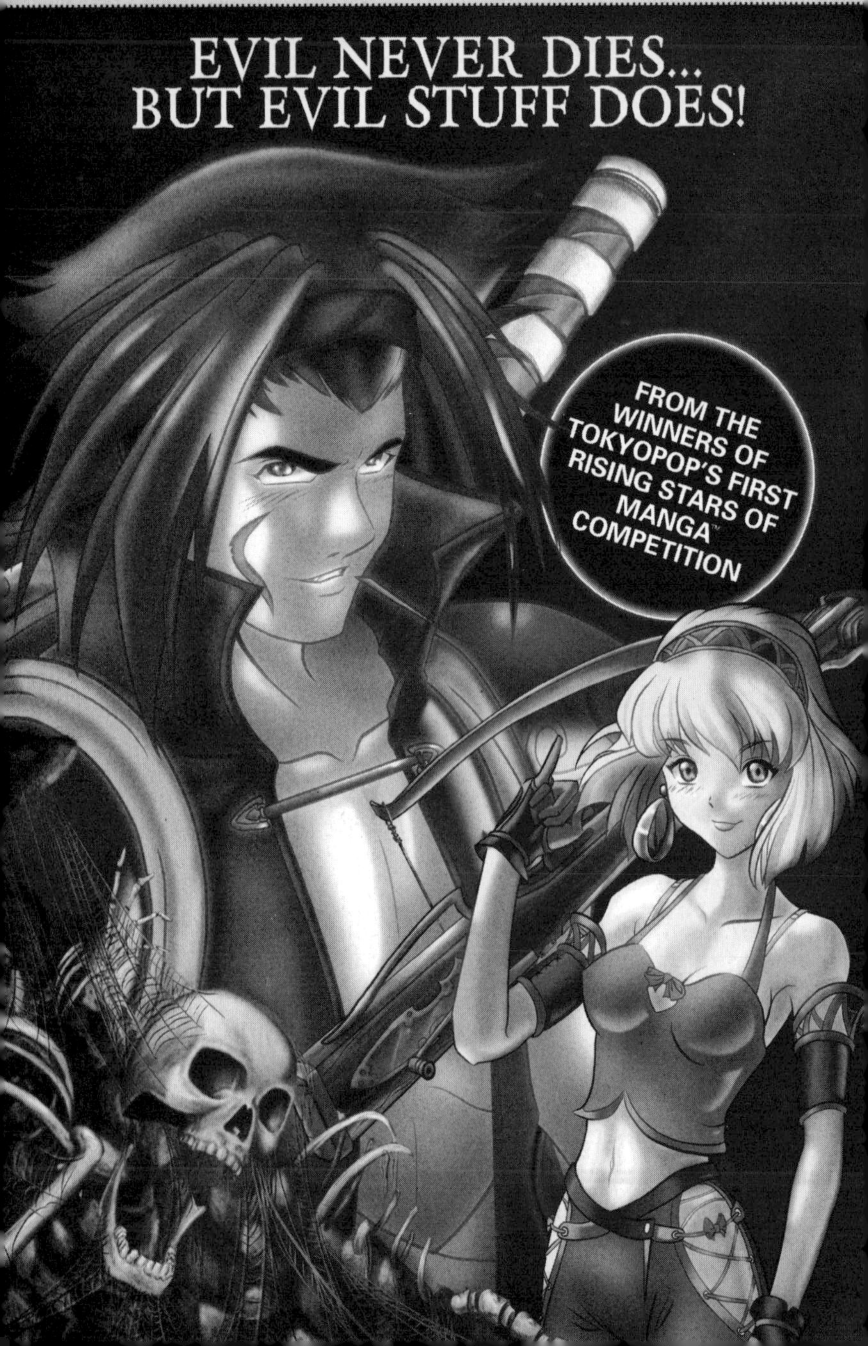
EVIL NEVER DIES...
BUT EVIL STUFF DOES!
FROM THE WINNERS OF TOKYOPOP'S FIRST RISING STARS OF MANGA™ COMPETITION